ENDORSEMENTS

"This book fills a glaring lacuna in the literature about the United Church of Christ. Rather than focusing narrowly on one of the ancestor traditions or on one chronological era, it maintains a comprehensive scope, covering the major predecessor traditions from their origins, through their union in 1957, and on to their current challenges and achievements. Unlike many texts in American church history, this volume integrates social history, institutional history, and theological history. Its primary virtue is its ability to highlight every dimension of the life of this Christian tradition, from missions, to worship, and to social commitments. Most importantly, it situates all these dynamics in a global context. This book should be essential reading for anyone who desires more familiarity with the spirit of the United Church of Christ."

Dr. Lee C. Barrett, Professor of Systematic Theology, Moravian Seminary at Lancaster

"With its diverse historical roots, the story of the United Church of Christ is complex and can be confusing. Maxfield's clear and accessible presentation sheds light on the denomination's origins, tracing the various movements and key figures that shaped its development. This book offers a detailed and informative account of how the church body's historical streams came together to form a denomination with a distinctive vision. *A Pilgrim People* is a valuable resource for anyone seeking to understand the UCC's rich history."

Scott Holl, Archivist, Eden Theological Seminary

"Chuck Maxfield's *A Pilgrim People* is a strikingly in-depth history of the United Church of Christ, from its roots in the Reformation era through its development in the context of the ecumenical movement and the myriad social challenges of the second half of the twentieth century on down to the present. As such, it is a valuable resource, not only for pastors, seminarians, and local congregations, but for scholars interested in the role of "mainline" denominations in American society."
Charles Hambrick Stowe, former academic dean and professor of Christian History at Northern Seminary in Lombard, Illinois

"Chuck Maxfield has provided a concise and accessible history of the United Church of Christ, including its antecedent denominations and groups. Pastors, seminarians, and lay members alike will appreciate this careful and readable account of the long pilgrimage toward unity of the remarkable variety of traditions that have coalesced into the UCC. Plus, he includes unique anecdotes from his own extensive research and study. I highly recommend it."
Rev. Dr. Rollin Russell, Conference Minister of the Southern Conference, Retired

"There are occasional articles or thin pamphlets that attempt to summarize the entire history of the United Church of Christ. But the only currently available wide ranging book is Charles A. Maxfield's *A Pilgrim People*. Contrary to being a long tome in complicated theological language, Maxfield offers us short precise vignettes that can help us get a quick over view of a founding, an outreach ministry, or a controversy. The index helps to track a particular stream, developments at a certain time, or notes on courageous Christian servants. For both a useful reference or an overview of our progress, it is a book worth having."
Richard H. Taylor, former Chair, Historical Council, United Church of Christ

"*A Pilgrim People* is impressive in its depth of content, including historical details that will be new to many readers. Maxfield renders our rich history into accessible sections that include complimentary perspectives from political/social/economic events and movements. Anyone interested in United Church of Christ history, theology, or polity will gain new insights and learning from the rich tapestry Maxfield weaves."

Rev. Dr. Carrie Call. Conference Minister, Penn Central Conference, United Church of Christ.

PILGRIM PEOPLE

PILGRIM PEOPLE

CHARLES A. MAXFIELD

SANTOS BOOKS
EVERY STORY SACRED

Self-published in 2005, 2008
Published by Santos Press LLC, Elizabethtown, PA 17022
Original ISBN: 097532683X
ISBN: 979-8-9955848-7-2
Cover designed by Kenzie Amrhein.

To the members and friends of the churches I have served
who showed me what it means to walk in His steps.

CONTENTS

ACKNOWLEDGMENTS

This book is possible only because many people have cooperated with me in producing it. First, I thank Christyann Ranck, my former wife, the first editor of these pages, whose tolerance of me while I focused on this project is appreciated. Second, I thank United Community Church of Cortland, New York, for a sabbatical during which I traveled to do research. Third, I thank the other historians who read my rough drafts and offered helpful feedback: Rich Christensen, John Payne, Randi Walker, Barbara Brown Zikmund, and Lowell Zuck. Fourth, I thank the archivists who willingly helped me. This includes all the staff at the Congregational Library, Boston, Evangelical and Reformed Historical Society, Lancaster, United Church of Christ Archives, Cleveland, Eden Archives, Saint Louis, and Amistad Research Center, New Orleans. I also thank the staff of the Inter-Library Loan Department at Memorial Library, State University of New York at Cortland, for their magical ability to find materials. Fifth, I thank persons on the national staff of the United Church of Christ, past and present, who have assisted me in finding information, particularly José Malayang, José Abraham de Jesús, Steven D. Johnson, Arthur G. Clyde, and Sheila Kelly.

I would like to thank Conrad Kanagy of Santos Press for making this publication possible.

Two abbreviations are used extensively throughout this book:

LTH Zikmund, Barbara Brown, ed. *The Living Theological Heritage of the United Church of Christ*. Cleveland: Pilgrim Press, 1994-2004. This is a seven volume collection of primary documents from the history of the United Church of Christ. In references, the first number refers to the volume, the second number refers to the *selection* (not the page). Selections are numbered in each volume.

NCH *The New Century Hymnal*. Cleveland: Pilgrim Press, 1995.

When I was ordained into the ministry of the United Church of Christ in 1970. I wrote in my ordination paper: "The United Church of Christ is an experiment in ecumenism. . .This union has existed in its present form for 13 years; if there is no further union in process 13 years from now, it will be a failure as a uniting church."

I believed in a "united and uniting" church moving steadily into new church unions and a fuller expression of our oneness in Christ. I fully expected most of my ministry to be carried out in a larger denomination that did not yet (in 1970) exist. For many good reasons, these new church unions did not happen: (1) A common spirit must exist in all the participants for a union to happen. Somehow it must be God's work, not ours. (2) We invested our energies in a plan of union, the Consultation for Church Union, which failed (Chapter 20, part C). (3) The UCC moved forward on reconciliation and inclusion of LGBT people (Chapter 19, part D) far ahead of other denominations, and it would have been wrong to back down. It is not a failure of the UCC that further unions did not happen. It is nevertheless a disappointment to me that the United Church of Christ still exists in 2025.

I love the United Church of Christ. I am grateful to the people of First Congregational Church, Fairhaven, Massachusetts, who guided me in my childhood and youth. I thank God for Faith UCC in State College, Pennsylvania, for its pastor Jacob Wagner, and for Lancaster Theological Seminary, where my faith grew as a reality of both heart and mind. For the Conference Ministers who were my pastors, for my colleagues in ministry, both ordained and lay, for the parishioners who taught me what it means to walk in His steps, I am deeply grateful. As pastor (and member) of dual alignment churches I have also been United Methodist, Presbyterian and American Baptist. I have learned to appreciate the gifts of these other denominations, and by comparison, to appreciate my own denomination all the more. I will always be indebted to Union Theological Seminary of Richmond, Virginia – a Presbyterian institution – for accepting me into their doctoral program, and for my two mentors, who were Christians first, and then Presbyterians and professors: James Smylie and Ken Goodpasture. I write in this book of the denomination in which I have lived my life, always aware that God has shown forth light and truth to others as well.

I wrote this book out of necessity. As Director of the Lay Ministry Program of the New York Conference UCC, I frequently taught a course on United Church of Christ History and Polity to lay ministers and to ministers of other denominations interested in the UCC. What could I use for a textbook? To get a complete view of the history of the UCC and its antecedents, one needed to read five books: Louis H. Gunnemann's *The Shaping of the United Church of Christ*; John Von Rohr's *The Shaping of American Congregationalism, 1620-1957*; David Dunn's *A History of the Evangelical and Reformed Church*; and Barbara Brown Zikmund's two volumes of *Hidden Histories of the United Church of Christ*. It would be unreasonable for me to require students to buy five books for the first half of a 20-hour course. I needed to bring together the history of the United Church of Christ into one volume.

My approach to UCC history is unusual. Instead of telling the four stories of the predecessor denominations separately, I have told one story. I have also included many stories usually omitted from the telling of our history, such as the Peace Movement, Thomas Gallaudet, and the Evangelical Synod experience in World War I. I have also chronicled my denomination's failures, as well as our accomplishments. I see history through the eyes of one who has been a local church pastor for most of my fifty-five years in ministry, and whose graduate work focused on mission history. Parish life and missions loom large in this telling of the story.

I first published this book in 2005, taking the story of the United Church of Christ up to the year 2000. I have not updated the book in the past 25 years. I believe that adoption of amendments to the Constitution and By-laws, which went into effect in 2000, represented a coming of age for the United Church of Christ. No longer hamstrung by a rigid interpretation of congregational autonomy, the denomination embraced a "covenant polity." Here and there, I have supplied more recent information to bring the text up to date.

When the United Church of Christ was formed, the synods and conferences of the two denominations were called "acting conferences" until they united. I offer to the reader this brief history of my "acting denomination," a pilgrim people, on a journey to that which is yet to be.

CHAPTER ONE

Introduction

On June 25, 1957, in Cleveland, Ohio, three hundred and forty-one representatives of the Evangelical and Reformed Church and three hundred and forty-one representatives of the Congregational and Christian Churches covenanted together, on behalf of their churches: "We do now, as the regularly constituted representatives of the Evangelical and Reformed Church and of the General Council of the Congregational Christian Churches, declare ourselves to be one body and our union consummated in this act establishing the United Church of Christ, in the name of the Father and of the Son and of the Holy Spirit. Amen."

This community of Christians, the United Church of Christ (UCC), has a story. That story stretches back to the days of the Reformation and beyond. The story unfolds from June 25, 1957, to the present and extends into the future. Who were these people? What did it mean to them to be Christian? How did they express their faith? How do they live out their faith?

Telling the story of the United Church of Christ is more complex than it looks on the surface. To define the boundaries of what we mean by "the United Church of Christ and its antecedents," I identify five ways of looking at this history – five levels that enter into defining the United Church of Christ. In this book we will use all five.

First there is the story of four churches that became two, and then one. The Congregational and Christian Churches came together in 1931 to form the Congregational Christian Churches. The Evangelical

Synod of North America and the Reformed Church in the United States merged in 1934 to form the Evangelical and Reformed Church. These two bodies united in the United Church of Christ. The traditional way of telling the UCC story is to tell the four stories, then two stories, then one story.

Second are the stories of smaller groups that are part of the UCC. These histories remained hidden as long as denominational histories followed the first level. Barbara Brown Zikmund collected some of these histories in two volumes of *Hidden Histories of the United Church of Christ*. The history of the UCC includes the Afro-Christian Convention. It also includes Hungarian Reformed, Evangelical Protestant, African Congregational and American Indian groups and others. In addition, Hawaii and Puerto Rico have their own unique histories. These formerly "hidden histories" include (a) smaller groups that united with the UCC or one of its predecessors, (b) immigrant groups whose church affiliation or beliefs in the old country caused them to associate with the UCC or one of its predecessors, and (c) native and immigrant groups to whom the UCC and its predecessors ministered in America.

Third, the formation of the United Church of Christ was, in addition to the union of churches, a union of mission boards. Some of those mission boards had an independent history before they became connected to one of the groups that joined the UCC. Three major mission boards founded by Congregationalists and Presbyterians working together, in time, became de facto Congregational boards, and later part of the United Church of Christ. These were the American Board of Commissioners for Foreign Missions (ABCFM), American Home Missionary Society (AHMS), and American Missionary Association (AMA). Their stories are also part of the story of the United Church of Christ, even though some persons in their employ may have called themselves by other denominational names.

Fourth, the story of the United Church of Christ must include an understanding of the interface of the UCC with other denominations.

One Presbyterian historian wrote of the Presbyterians and Congregationalists in New York State, "It is impossible to write separately of the histories of two denominations that were so closely related." The same could be said of Christians and Disciples of Christ in the Ohio Valley, or of the Reformed and Lutherans in Pennsylvania. We must have some knowledge of these other denominations to understand what happened in the UCC and its antecedents.

Fifth, there are some congregations of the United Church of Christ that identify with none of the above. For example, in Union Springs, New York, the Episcopal, Presbyterian, and Methodist churches united in 1994. They wanted to affiliate with only one denomination, but did not want to have "winners" and "losers" in their congregation, so they selected another denomination – the United Church of Christ. In many places, people organized a "Community Church," and after a period of time, decided to affiliate with a denomination, choosing the United Church of Christ or one of its antecedents. There are also congregations that have joined from other denominations, and congregations that have chosen to affiliate with the UCC in addition to their original denomination.

In the year 2000, the UCC was a fellowship of 5,923 congregations. The proportions of the four major branches were as follows (Greater than 100% because 122 congregations were local unions of congregations from multiple branches of the UCC):[1]

Congregational	46%
Reformed	19%
Evangelical	15%
Christian	6%

Many congregations were organized or entered the denomination after the merger process began, as follows:

Congregational Christian	6%
Evangelical and Reformed	2%
United Church of Christ	8%

These seven categories include other groups (non-ethnic) that have joined the UCC family, such as the Congregational Methodists, Evangelical Protestants, and Schwenkfelders, and congregations with clear ethnic identities, such as African American (also Cape Verdean, Haitian and Sudanese), American Indian (including Arikara, Dakota/Lakota, Hidatsa, Ho Cak, and Mandan), Armenian, Assyrian, Chinese, Asian Indian, Filipino, Finnish, German Congregational, Hawaiian, Hispanic, Japanese, Korean, Lao, Magyar, Samoan, Marshalese, Portuguese, Swedish, Taiwanese, and Welsh.

When you study the United Church of Christ, you will be struck by its diversity, and may ask, "What on earth do all these groups have in common?" I have come up with three words that describe common elements, and help to make the many stories one story. I call these the "C" word, the "P" word, and the "L" word.

"C" is for *catholic*. This word comes from the Latin and means *universal*. In the Apostles' Creed, when we say we believe in "the holy catholic Church," we affirm that the church is ONE. In spite of our many separated denominations, we see the church as one and work for its unity. In the last hundred years, we have come to use the word *ecumenical* in place of the word *catholic*. The groups that came together to form the United Church of Christ all had a *catholic* spirit. They all had a vision of the church as one and whole and larger than themselves.

"P" stands for *piety*. This word is not commonly used in the United Church of Christ today. But throughout the history of the various groups that have come together to form the United Church of Christ, it has been an important word and an important idea. Piety includes three elements: (1) inward cultivation of a relationship with God, (2) outward discipline of religious observances for nurturing that relationship, and (3) disciplines of moral and social behavior that express that relationship. Today we often use the word *spirituality*, rather than piety. Spirituality can be used as a synonym for piety only if we clearly understand that spirituality, like piety, has an outward, active, social aspect, as well as an inner dimension.

"P" can also stand for *Pietism*. This historic movement of a particular style of piety, originating in Germany in the Seventeenth Century, had a profound impact on all of the groups that eventually came into the United Church of Christ. Pietism will be explored in depth in Chapter Five.

"L" is for *liberal*. The root of liberal is *liberty*, which means to be free. At least two meanings of liberal have been pervasive throughout the UCC and its antecedents.

(1) The word *liberal,* as used in the King James Bible, most often meant *generous*, as in the phrase "a liberal gift." It implies compassion – an active concern for the needs of others. The UCC and its antecedents have expressed their liberal concern for others through missions, health and human service institutions, and social activism.

(2) The word *liberal* has often been used for freedom of thought, meaning "broad-minded." When the Pilgrims left the Netherlands in 1620 their pastor advised them, "God hath yet more truth and light to break forth from His Holy Word." Openness to new ways of thinking and doing, willingness to listen to new ideas, and tolerance of diversity have often characterized the life of the UCC and its antecedents. Groups that have formed the UCC have tended to draw the boundaries of orthodoxy broadly, rather than narrowly. They have preferred to tolerate those with whom they disagreed, rather than to exclude them.

These three words, *catholic, pious,* and *liberal,* define three themes that we will discern throughout this book, as we trace the history of the United Church of Christ and its antecedents.

******

[1] These statistics have been developed with the personal assistance of Dr. Richard Taylor, who has done extensive research in the origins of the local congregations of the UCC.

CHAPTER TWO

European Roots

The United Church of Christ looks upon itself as a continuation of the historic Christian church founded by Jesus Christ and the apostles. The heritage of the ancient and medieval church is claimed as its own. This is not an exclusive claim. Many churches, in various ways, claim to be a continuation of the historic Christian church. The United Church of Christ is one such church.

The origins of the United Church of Christ as a distinct group go back to the Protestant Reformation of the Sixteenth Century: to the Lutheran and Reformed churches on the continent of Europe, and to the Puritan movement in England.

PART A: REFORMATION ON THE CONTINENT

Martin Luther published the *Ninety-five Theses* on October 31, 1517, with no intention of creating a schism in the church. His intent was to reform the church. He protested the sale of indulgences. Church representatives proclaimed that by giving money to the church, a person could purchase an "indulgence" which could lessen someone's time in purgatory. Luther's criticism of this fund-raising strategy was theological: we are justified before God through faith in Jesus Christ, and not by anything we do.

Martin Luther (1483-1546) was born on November 10, 1483, and was burdened by a strong sense of his own sinfulness and the image of a terrifying and demanding God of punishment. He received a high-quality education in the Bible and theology, and taught at the new Wittenberg University. Finally, through his Bible studies and his own devotions, Luther discovered a loving God who established a relationship with humanity through God's gracious will, and nothing else. This new and deep conviction compelled Luther to protest the sale of indulgences in 1517.

Luther's attack on indulgences was also an attack on the authority of the Pope, who condemned Luther's teachings on June 15, 1520, and excommunicated him on January 3, 1521. At a meeting of the princes of the Holy Roman Empire, the "Diet of Worms," on April 17, 1521, Luther was challenged to renounce his writings. Luther refused, declaring, "I cannot do otherwise. Here I stand. God help me. Amen." Condemned by the Empire as well as the Church, Luther was "kidnapped" by friends on his journey home, and safely hidden in Wartburg Castle. There he translated the New Testament into German.

The Emperor of Germany, Charles V (1500-1558), also King of Spain, ruled an empire that stretched from Peru to Central Europe. Charles V wanted to take strong action against Luther, but events such as war with France or Turkey, or political intrigues in Germany or Italy postponed action against Luther. Luther's prince, Frederick III of Saxony (1486-1525), protected him. Martin Luther returned to Wittenberg in 1522, and proceeded with the reformation of the church within the borders of favorable princes. Luther published a new *Order of Public Worship* in 1523 (*LTH* 2:6), which placed greater emphasis on preaching and the singing of popular hymns. He issued a *German Mass* in 1526. In 1529 Luther published the *Small Catechism*, for the religious instruction of children (*LTH* 2:8).

When the Diet met in Speyer in 1529, the Roman Catholic majority demanded an end to reforms and restoration of the Catholic Church. The Lutheran princes on April 19, 1529, entered a formal protest, the

Protestatio, from which they received the name "Protestant." Then they organized a military alliance. The Emperor announced that the Diet of 1530 at Augsburg would resolve the theological dispute. Luther's theological assistant, Philip Melanchthon (1497-1560) prepared a statement of Lutheran beliefs and practices, the *Augsburg Confession,* and presented it to the Diet in 1530.

Luther continued to preach, write, and give leadership to the church from Wittenberg until his death, February 18, 1546. Luther stood for:

1. Justification by faith, not works.
2. The authority of Scripture superior to tradition, Popes and Councils.
3. Christ the only intermediary between humanity and God; a de-emphasis of saints, relics, and the priestly office.
4. Worship in the language of the people, with emphasis on Biblical preaching and congregational singing (*LTH* 2:7).
5. Christian vocation including every honorable occupation, not just service through the church.
6. Rejection of transubstantiation (the belief that the bread and wine in communion actually become the body and blood of Jesus Christ), but affirmation of the "real presence" of Christ in communion. Recognition of only two sacraments, Communion and Baptism.

The Lutheran Churches established in the lands of Protestant princes continued the historic Christian church in those lands, and carried forward medieval theology and piety into a new age.

Zwingli and the Reformed Tradition

All of Europe heard of Luther's protest. In other places, church reform movements began and existing movements advanced. Some reformers went further than Luther, and began what became known as *Reformed Churches.* Ulrich Zwingli directed the Reformation in

Zurich, Switzerland. Zwingli echoed much of Luther's teaching: justification by faith, the authority of the Bible, the priesthood of all believers, worship in the language of the people, etc. Zwingli was not willing to maintain features of the medieval church as Luther did, but insisted on rebuilding the church anew on a Biblical foundation. Zwingli differed from Luther in the following areas:

- Zwingli simplified worship, removed all statues and art work, walled up the organ, and simplified the Church Year.
- Zwingli advocated reform in state and society as well as in the church. For example, he successfully advocated an end to serfdom. Luther, who reacted against a Peasants' Revolt, left such matters to the princes.
- Zwingli believed Communion was a meaningful memorial of spiritual significance, but rejected Luther's understanding of the real presence.

Ulrich Zwingli (1484-1531) was born January 1, 1484, in Wildhaus, canton Saint Gall, Switzerland. In preparing for the priesthood, he received a "humanist" education. This was characterized by a return to the original sources (the Bible and early church writings) in the original languages. Humanism criticized much church practice as corrupt and superstitious. Ordained in 1506, Zwingli in 1519 began to serve the largest church in Zurich. With the cooperation of the city council he gradually reformed that church, going beyond the reforms of Luther. When the Reformed and Catholic cantons of Switzerland went to war against each other, Zwingli accompanied the Reformed army as chaplain and died in battle, October 11, 1531.

As reformation spread to other cantons of Switzerland and cities of southern Germany and the Rhine Valley, many adopted views similar to Zwingli's. Some of Zwingli's followers went even further – organizing "gathered churches," practicing "believer's baptism," and observing the Sermon on the Mount literally to the point of not fighting in war. Zwingli opposed these "Anabaptists" and encouraged the government to persecute them.

The Marburg Colloquy

Philip, ruler of Hesse (1509-1567), wanted Lutheran and Reformed churches to reconcile their differences in order to establish a military alliance against the Catholics. At his invitation, Luther, Zwingli, Melanchthon, and others met at Philip's castle in Marburg on October 1, 1529. After much debate (*LTH* 2:13), the reformers agreed to fourteen of fifteen articles of faith, but respectfully resolved to disagree on the fifteenth – the meaning of communion.

Calvin

In 1536, the French-speaking city of Geneva, Switzerland, formally became independent and Protestant. That summer a young French reformer, John Calvin, passed through town, and was invited to stay in order to establish the Reformed faith.

John Calvin (1509-1564) was born July 10, 1509, in Noyon, France, He studied at Paris and other places, receiving a humanist education in theology and law. He experienced a "sudden conversion" to Protestant Christianity, perhaps in 1533, and became a leader in the French Protestant Church. After three years of travel and writing, sometimes in France, sometimes in exile, often under assumed names, occasionally in disguise, Calvin passed through Geneva on his way to Strasbourg. In 1536 Calvin had already published his summary of the Christian faith, *Institutes of the Christian Religion*. Over the next twenty-three years he revised and republished this work until the original six chapters had grown to seventy-eight. This work became the foundational theological statement of the Reformed tradition[1] – often called "Calvinist" – on which others would build or diverge for centuries to come. Except for a brief exile, Calvin directed the Reformation in Geneva until his death, May 27, 1564.

Under Calvin's leadership Geneva became a model city of the Reformed tradition. It welcomed religious refugees from other places, who often returned to their homes to attempt to establish the Genevan system. Calvin also sent out preachers to spread Reformed religion across France and other countries of Europe. Calvinism, as developed by Calvin, included the following:

- *Church government*–Calvin identified four scriptural church officers. All were selected in some way by the people, and were ordained: (1) *pastors*–to preach and administer the sacraments; (2) *doctors (teachers)*–to instruct in sound doctrine; (3) *elders*–lay persons to have oversight of the people, and to participate with the pastors in the "consistory;" and (4) *deacons*–to minister to the poor and needy.
- *Discipline* was exercised by the consistory consistent with Matthew 18:15-17. Persons living outwardly immoral lives were confronted in order to correct their ways, excommunication being used as a last resort.
- *Worship*--Calvin used a mixture of free and written prayers. Statues and images were forbidden. Psalms were re-translated into singable meter for a cappella singing to simple "psalm tunes" that untrained voices could learn easily.
- *Communion*–Calvin tried to find a middle way between Zwingli and Luther on communion. The bread and wine were "signs" of the invisible food one received through the power of the spirit. They created unity for the believer with Christ. Calvin favored celebrating communion every Sunday, and was willing to compromise to monthly communion; however, the city council limited communion to four times a year.
- *Predestination*–Calvin believed in a loving God who had elected some to be saved. No matter what happened, nothing could alter

the will of God to save the elect. The "flip side" of this doctrine was that some were predestined to be damned. This doctrine was not an innovation; most Protestants and many Catholics believed in predestination to some degree. For Calvin the doctrine of predestination was a source of comfort and assurance; many in later generations saw in it an unjust God and a denial of human freedom.

Reformed churches practiced "presbyterian" church government, in which regional representative bodies composed of pastors and elders (presbyters) from the local churches held authority over the church.

Reformation in the Palatinate

Frederick William III (1515-1576), became Elector (ruler) of the Palatinate (*Rheinpfalz*), a Lutheran land, in 1559. Desiring peace among the theologians, he invited to the University of Heidelberg conciliatory Lutheran and Reformed theologians, including Zacharias Ursinus (1534-1583), a former student of Melanchthon, and Caspar Olevianus (1536-1587), a former student of Calvin. The Palatinate became Reformed in 1561, when the Elector directed that communion be celebrated using the Reformed service.

At the Elector's direction, Ursinus and others prepared a catechism for popular instruction, *The Heidelberg Catechism*, (*LTH* 2:21) published in 1563. The Reformed in many places throughout Europe, including the Netherlands and Hungary, soon adopted the *Heidelberg Catechism* as both an instructional tool for the young, and a declaration of faith for the church. This conciliatory catechism, emphasizing piety as well as theology, has shaped the German Reformed Church to the present day. Also in 1563, Ursinus and Olevianus produced the *Palatine Liturgy* (*LTH* 2:22). Borrowing extensively from other Reformed liturgies, this pattern for worship included the following:

- In addition to services for Sunday worship, communion, and special occasions, there was a *preparatory service* used on the Saturday before Communion.
- Churches in towns were directed to have communion at least monthly.
- A simplified church year consisted of Christmas, New Year's Day, Easter, Ascension Day and Pentecost.
- Preaching was central; communion was celebrated at a table.
- Clergy were to wear modest and respectable clothing.
- The liturgy contained written prayers, but did not exclude free prayer.

Acccording to an order of church government (*Kirchenordnung*), published in 1564, the civil ruler appointed equal numbers of clergy and laity to a "consistory." This body governed the church with a system of superintendents over district classes that met annually. When Frederick died in 1576, his son Ludwig VI (1539-1583) became Elector. He re-established Lutheranism and drove out the Reformed clergy. As a result, the faith of the *Heidelberg Catechism* spread with these refugees to several other German states. When Ludwig died, 1583, Elector John Casimer (1543-1592) re-established the Reformed faith and drove out the Lutheran clergy. Several smaller German states adopted the Reformed faith. They all used the *Heidelberg Catechism*, but each developed their own liturgy and church order, producing variety of practices among the German Reformed.

<u>Reformation in Hungary</u>

Students brought the Reformation to Hungary from Germany. The Reformation was received first by ethnically German communities, then by the Magyars (Hungarians) of the surrounding countryside. The nobles effectively determined the orientation of the church in their territory, and many favored reform. In 1526, at the Battle of Mohács, the Turks routed the Magyars. Hungary was humiliated, demoralized, pillaged, raped, and divided into three parts. In the west, the rulers of

Austria gained control, and made every effort to restore Catholicism. In the center, the Turks ruled, and, without the involvement of nobles, Protestantism became the peoples' religion. In the east, a Magyar principality, Transylvania, paid tribute to the Turks and governed their own internal affairs, and Protestantism flourished. By the end of the sixteenth century Hungary was overwhelmingly Protestant.

The first reformers in Hungary followed the teachings of Luther, but also had respect for the Reformed tradition. Other reformers moved toward Reformed theology. About 1612 the Protestants of Hungary divided, the great majority becoming Reformed, the minority Lutheran.

<u>Catholic Oppression, War and Toleration</u>

The Roman Catholic Church fought back against Protestantism with several strategies, including:

- Reform within the Catholic Church;
- More effective preaching to win back Protestants;
- Various forms of oppression in Catholic lands, including the Inquisition, which executed Protestant "heretics;"
- War.

The religious conflict culminated in the Thirty Years' War (1618-1648), during which opposing armies destroyed Germany. The Palatinate exchanged hands several times during this war. Each invasion brought with it plunder, famine and starvation, followed by disease, depopulation and wolves. During two periods of Catholic occupation, Reformed pastors were ordered to convert or depart. Reformed churches were left with no buildings, no pastors, and no services. With the Peace of Westphalia in 1648, the Reformed Church was restored to the Palatinate and Lutherans received full toleration.

In Hungary, the area ruled by Austria felt the full force of the Catholic advance. The nobles were successfully converted back to Catholicism and placed Catholic priests in the churches on their lands.

Protestant princes of Transylvania invaded Austrian Hungary four times during the Thirty Years' War, and secured treaties in which Austria agreed to allow the Reformed Churches to function. But Austria never honored those treaties. Petitions and rebellions in later years brought more promises of toleration from Austria, promises never kept.

An Austrian court from 1671 to 1681, summoned all the Protestant pastors in Hungary, and condemned them to death. Then the court showed its leniency by giving the convicted ministers the choice of becoming Catholics, resigning their ministry, or leaving the country. Of the 400 ministers, 89 refused. Imprisoned and tortured, some gave in or died. In March 1675, forty-one were forced marched to Trieste and sold as galley slaves. On February 11, 1676, a Dutch merchant purchased the thirty surviving slaves and gave them freedom. The experience of the galley slaves was the inspiration for the hymn much loved by Magyar Reformed people to this day, "Lift Thy Head, O Zion Weeping" (*LTH* 4:104).

Meanwhile, back in Austrian Hungary, the pastor-less people were forcibly converted to Catholicism. The Magyars living under Turkish rule continued in the Reformed faith. In 1682 Austria began to drive the Turks from Hungary. In spite of oppressive Austrian policies, the Reformed faith persisted in the former Turkish areas of Hungary.

By 1648 the religious map of Europe had been determined. Much of northern Germany and the Scandinavian countries were Lutheran. The Netherlands, Scotland, the Palatinate, at least half of the cantons of Switzerland, and several smaller entities in Germany were Reformed. The rest of continental Europe was under Catholic rule, while significant Reformed communities in France and Hungary were severely repressed. Only in England was the situation unresolved.

The Radical Reformation and Schwenkfeld

In addition to the Lutheran and Reformed churches, there were other expressions of the Reformation on the continent of Europe: Anabaptists, Spiritualists, and Unitarians. Kaspar Schwenkfeld (1487-1541), a Spiritualist, some of whose followers later became part of the United Church of Christ, was a German noble and early supporter of Luther. Schwenkfeld was later rejected by that reformer on doctrinal grounds. Schwenkfeld emphasized the believer's inner relationship with God. He greatly respected the sacrament of communion as an inner spiritual experience, but suspended its outward observance among his followers in 1526. Luther believed that Schwenkfeld placed too much emphasis on the divinity of Christ, to the exclusion of his humanity.

PART B: THE REFORMATION IN ENGLAND

Wyclif and the Lollards

When the Reformation message reached England, it was embraced by the remnants of an earlier reform movement, the "Lollards." Followers of John Wyclif (ca. 1325-1384), the Lollards believed:

- The Bible in the language of the people should be in the hands of the people. The Bible, not the Pope, was the highest authority in the church.
- The true church was spiritual, consisting of the elect of God. The outward visible church, filled with wealth, immorality and hypocrisy, needed to be "disendowed."
- Communion was a meaningful spiritual remembrance, but not literally flesh and blood.

The Lollards persisted as an underground movement among the poor. They emphasized preaching from the Bible and ridiculed the established church, its clergy and ceremony. Lollards were often convicted of heresy and executed in the era after Wyclif until well after Lutheran writings had reached England. Lollards and their sympathizers warmly received the writings of the continental reformers and blended into the growing Protestant movement. There the ideas and the spirit of Wyclif persisted.

Reformation by Royalty

<u>Henry VIII</u> (1491-1547), King of England from 1509 to 1547, wanted one undisputed male heir in order to avoid a dynastic war at the time of his death. When no son appeared, he appealed to the Pope for a divorce. The Pope rejected Henry's appeal for political reasons. So in 1534 Henry had Parliament pass the Act of Supremacy, by which England declared the independence of the Church of England from Rome. Under Henry's rule the Bible was translated into English and circulated freely. Protestants had limited freedom to publish their opinions. Otherwise, the church remained much as it had been.

<u>Edward VI</u> (1537-1553), King of England from 1547 to 1553, and Henry's son, was nine years old when he became king. The boy-king and those who exercised power on his behalf were Protestant. Gradually the Church of England became Protestant in worship and doctrine, and Protestants were appointed to leadership positions.

<u>Mary I</u> (1516-1558), Queen of England from 1553 to 1558, was Roman Catholic and suppressed all expressions of Protestantism. She repealed all of Edward's reforms, imprisoned the reforming bishops, and in 1554 restored the Pope's authority; England was Catholic again. On February 4, 1555, Bible translator John Rogers (ca. 1500-1555) was burned at the stake for heresy. In the succeeding years of Mary's reign almost 300 Protestants received similar treatment. Many others were imprisoned.

What was a Protestant to do in these circumstances? Many conformed outwardly, keeping their opinions to themselves. Some met in secret to worship using the *Prayer Book* adopted when Edward VI was king. Others left the country. Reformed cities on the continent welcomed these exiles, who organized English-speaking congregations. Free to govern themselves in exile, they developed along lines not allowed in England. Some abandoned the *Prayer Book* altogether, and elected Elders to discipline members in the Reformed pattern.

<u>Elizabeth and the Puritans</u>

Elizabeth I (1533-1603), Queen of England from 1558 to 1603, established the Anglican middle way, an expression of her personal piety adapted to political expediency. In 1559, with a new Act of Supremacy, Parliament again declared the Church of England independent from Rome. A new *Prayer Book* in 1559 (*LTH* 2:24) revised the second *Prayer Book* of Edward VI to be less offensive to Catholics. In 1563 a revised doctrinal statement, the *Thirty-Nine Articles*, reiterated the Protestant faith. Protestants were appointed to vacant bishoprics.

The underground church during Mary's reign returned to the established church and provided some leaders. Exiles returned. However, not all were prepared to give up the church life they had developed in exile. Desiring to purify the church of the residue of "Romanism," they became known as *Puritans*.

Puritanism became a broad movement for reform within the Church of England. We must be careful *not* to try to read into the past the denominational distinctions that came into existence at a later date. By the end of the seventeenth century, Puritanism had crystallized into several denominations: low-church Anglicans, Presbyterians, Congregationalists, Baptists, and Friends (commonly called "Quakers"). In Elizabeth's day, Puritanism was a faction *within* the Church of England, comprising many variations of opinion.

Puritans emphasized the following:

- The Bible was central to faith. Well-educated clergy were to preach the Bible in a plain way understood by all. The Bible should be available to the people in the language of the people, who should be taught to read.
- Worship should be simple and spiritual. Preachers should pray from their heart, not from a book. Set prayers, orders of worship, and responses were rejected. Only Psalms were sung, to simple Psalm-tunes. Communion was celebrated around a table, not an altar. Other vestiges of Catholicism, such as the sign of the Cross

and kneeling for communion were rejected as idolatrous or superstitious.

- The *people* were the church. Church members were expected to look for the work of the Spirit in their lives. Members elected their own leaders, who disciplined the members. Clerical vestments were rejected.
- The Christian life was to be lived by all, with moral and benevolent action and strict observance of the Sabbath (on the first day of the week).

The great majority of Puritans were *non*-separatist; they were a party within the Church of England. Disregarding the law, many Puritan clergy did not use the *Prayer Book*, and did not wear vestments. The few Puritans who were separatists rejected the Church of England as demonic, gathered their own congregations, and excommunicated members who attended the Church of England.

The first "Congregational" church was a separatist congregation gathered in London by 1567, when its Pastor, Richard Fitz, was imprisoned. Henry Barrow (ca. 1550-1593), pastor, and John Greenwood (d. 1593), layperson, leaders of a separate congregation in London were imprisoned in 1587 and hanged on April 6, 1593. Francis Johnson (1562-1618) then became pastor of this congregation and led them into exile in Amsterdam, Netherlands. The "Barrowist" movement persisted in England and in exile.

Separatist Congregationalists developed some common patterns. A congregation was a voluntary society created by a mutually agreed upon church covenant. The members governed the church at congregational meetings, elected officers, elected the ministers, received new members, and exercised discipline. Although autonomous, the local church welcomed relationships and counsel from similar congregations.

<u>The Stuarts, the Commonwealth, and Toleration</u>

A new dynasty, the Stuarts, brought to the throne of England Kings James I (1566-1625, ruled 1603-1625) and Charles I (1600-1649, ruled

1625-42). The only concession the Puritans received from the Stuarts was a new translation of the Bible, the *King James Version*, published in 1611. Stuart kings opposed Puritans and enforced high-church uniformity in the Church of England.

Non-separatist Puritans – especially clergy – found themselves in an increasingly difficult position. Separation was a serious step. The consensus of the day was: The Church is one; schism is a sin. Separation could be justified only if one could conclude that the established church was no longer a true church, but demonic, from which the true church must "come out" (*2 Corinthians* 6:17). Puritans had been fed spiritually in the Church of England, and could not declare it to be totally evil; but to them the Church felt increasingly oppressive.

Some Puritans, such as William Ames (1576-1633) and Henry Jacob (1563-1624) advocated a non-separating Congregationalism. They argued that gathered and covenanted congregations could exist in an established church. Of course it was not possible under James and Charles, but they had seen enough change in the past to believe that there could be more change in the future.

Henry Jacob returned from exile in 1616 to organize an Independent congregation in the Southwark section of London. Some called it *"semi-separatist."* As far as the law and the established church were concerned, it was separate and illegal. In their own eyes they were faithful members of the state church because they allowed their members to participate in the Church of England. Jacob's church was organized and governed as a Congregational Church. Among non-separatist Puritans, interest grew in this kind of Independent or Congregational church organization, as opposed to Presbyterianism.

The Stuart kings, besides oppressing Puritans, believed they should rule with absolute power, unchecked by Parliament. Puritans and Parliament united to oppose the King. Civil War between Parliament and King began in 1642.

Parliament called an assembly of religious authorities to meet at Westminster, beginning in 1643, to advise it on matters of religion. The

Westminster Assembly prepared a Puritan *Directory of Worship* and proposed a Presbyterian system of church government. The Assembly then prepared a statement of faith, the *Westminster Confession* (*LTH* 2:32), approved by the General Assembly of Scotland in 1647 and the English Parliament in 1648. The Assembly also prepared the *Westminster Shorter Catechism* in 1647.

The Congregational minority of five at Westminster enthusiastically supported the doctrinal statements of the Assembly, but protested against *presbyterian* church organization. In October, 1658, representatives of the Independent (Congregational) Churches of England met at the Savoy Palace in London, agreed to the *Westminster Confession* with a few minor changes, and issued a statement of Congregational Polity, the *Savoy Declaration*.

Oliver Cromwell (1599-1658), an Independent (Congregationalist), gathered a force of enthusiastic Puritans and defeated the Royalists in 1644 and 1645. In this "new model army" all strains of Puritanism were tolerated. Cromwell, as commander of the army, was the effective ruler of England, Lord Protector of the Commonwealth from 1649 to 1658. Under Cromwell, the Independents had much influence; England experienced a high degree of religious diversity and toleration for all except Roman Catholics and bishops. Cromwell's secretary, John Milton (1608-1674), also an Independent, wrote religious poetry, including *Paradise Lost* and *Paradise Regained*.

The Stuarts returned to power in 1660 with Kings Charles II (1630-1685, ruling 1660-1685) and James II (1633-1701, ruling 1685-1688). They re-established the Church of England with all its liturgies. Puritans again faced discrimination. This ended with the "silent revolution" of 1688-89, when William III (1650-1702) and Mary II (1662-1694) came to power and toleration became the law of the land.

*****

[1] The phrases "Reformed tradition" "Reformed family" and "Reformed family of churches" refer to that group of churches historically of Reformed doctrine, which includes those churches called Reformed, Presbyterian and Congregational. These terms are to be distinguished from "Reformed Church" which refers to a particular denomination.

Puritan New England

PART A: THE PILGRIMS

In 1606, in the village of Scrooby, Nottinghamshire, England, a small group of people made a covenant to be a Separatist congregation. Under the leadership of their minister, John Robinson (ca. 1575-1625) they held services in the home of Elder William Brewster (ca. 1560-1644). Harassed with fines and imprisonment, they fled to the Netherlands in 1608. They joined the "Ancient Brethren," the Separatist congregation of English exiles in Amsterdam founded by Francis Johnson. Uncomfortable with the incessant conflict in that congregation, Robinson with some of the Scrooby congregation and others from the Ancient Brethren went in 1609 to Leyden, Netherlands, where they organized another Separatist congregation.

Henry Jacob, an advocate of non-separating Congregationalism, for several years worshiped with the Leyden congregation. During this time, Robinson and his people moved away from rigid Separatism to acceptance of some participation in the Church of England.

As war clouds gathered over Europe, the Leyden Separatists negotiated with English merchants to establish a colony in North America. When the colonists-to-be left the Netherlands in July, 1620, John Robinson, who could not go with them, advised them to cooperate with any non-separating Puritans who might come to them, and invited them to be open to change, declaring, "The Lord hath more truth and light to break forth out of his Holy Word."

From the Netherlands, these "pilgrims" sailed to England, where the merchants placed on board additional passengers not necessarily motivated by religion. Arriving at Cape Cod, New England, aboard the *Mayflower* in November 1620, this mixed group founded a civil government with the *Mayflower Compact*. Patterned after their church covenant, this *Compact* gave church members and non-members equal voice in the colony's affairs. The church members, more organized and with a clear vision of the colony's purpose, always provided the leadership of the colony.

Plymouth Colony was founded in 1620 under the leadership of Separatists who were no longer rigid in their separation. Their church, the first Congregational Church in America, was in fact a branch of the church in Leyden. Their spiritual leader, William Brewster, was an Elder, not a minister. He preached and prayed and catechized the youth, but did not administer the sacraments. Services of "prophecy" were held Sunday afternoons, in which any member could comment on the application of the Scripture. Marriage was strictly a civil affair. The dead were buried with great simplicity. Sunday was the only holy day. However, when non-church members complained about having to work on Christmas Day, they were allowed to remain at home, provided they observed the day quietly.

PART B: THE PURITAN MIGRATION

Non-separating Puritans in England faced increasing restrictions, harassment, and punishment. As ceremonial conformity was pressed, it became increasingly difficult to maintain that one could be a good Puritan and stay in the Church of England. But schism was a sin. What was a Puritan to do? Puritans began to think that perhaps they could remain non-Separatists in the Church of England if they were separated by an ocean from the Archbishop and King. In America, they could put into practice their Puritan principles and still claim to be loyal members of the Church of England.

From 1630 to 1640 about 20,000 immigrants came to New England from England. This "Puritan Migration" founded the colonies and established the Congregational churches of New England. The Puritans who settled New England wanted worship to be less formal and more spiritual. They looked to the Bible for guidance in ordering church and society. The leaders of the migration were non-separating Congregationalists. Puritans of other opinions either went along with this new establishment (after all, schism was a sin), or else found themselves driven into the wilderness to found new colonies.

The Colonies

The Puritan colonies of New England each developed in its own way, some more liberal than others. In all of them, the church was organized on a Congregational pattern, but considered itself still a faithful part of the Church of England.

Massachusetts Bay Colony. Puritans dominated the New England Company which in 1628 secured a charter from the King to occupy a portion of New England. Small groups sailed in 1628 and 1629 to establish the settlement of Salem. In 1629, the church at Salem was organized on the basis of a covenant, without renouncing the Church of England. This was the first Congregational Church organized in America. The following year, eleven ships full of immigrants arrived. The immigrants founded Boston and several other towns and established the government of the Massachusetts Bay Colony in New England.

In the eyes of Governor John Winthrop (1588-1649) the new colony was "a city set on a hill." It was to be an experiment in creating a model church and society, a model that old England could observe and eventually imitate. Church and State had distinct functions, but the state nurtured the church, promoted its values, and only communicant church members could vote.

Connecticut. In 1636 Thomas Hooker (1586-1647), a pastor in Newtown (now Cambridge), Massachusetts, led much of his congregation west to the Connecticut Valley, where they founded the city of

Hartford and the Colony of Connecticut. This new Puritan colony was more liberal than the Bay, in that the franchise was not restricted to communicant church members.

New Haven. When Minister John Davenport (1597-1670) arrived in Boston, he thought the colony was not strict enough. With a following of more exact Puritans, he founded New Haven Colony in 1638. In New Haven, only church members could vote, membership standards were strict, and discipline was freely enforced. Connecticut annexed New Haven in 1662.

New England Confederation. These four Puritan colonies, Massachusetts Bay, Plymouth, Connecticut and New Haven, consulted together as the New England Confederation beginning in 1643. The meetings of this body often consisted of efforts by the Bay to establish unity by getting the smaller colonies to conform to its policies.

Other Colonies. In 1640 Thomas Mayhew (1593-1682), a resident of Massachusetts, purchased from the English merchants the right to colonize Martha's Vineyard and nearby islands. These islands were annexed to the colony of New York in 1663.

'The religious motive was less important in the establishment of a number of smaller settlements along the coast of what is now New Hampshire and Maine, although a few were havens for dissenters from Massachusetts. When the Civil War broke out in England, authorities from the Bay Colony visited each of these settlements and convinced them to side with the Puritans by recognizing the authority of the Bay.

The Polity: Cambridge Platform

When old England was adopting Presbyterianism in 1645, and some New Englanders began agitating for Presbyterianism, the Massachusetts legislature called on its churches to draw up a statement of doctrine and church government.

The Cambridge Synod, meeting from 1646 to 1648, was composed of ministers and elders from Massachusetts and representatives from the other Puritan colonies. It endorsed the new *Westminster Confession* "for the substance thereof," and commended it to the churches as "worthy of their due consideration and acceptance." The Synod expressed its respect for Presbyterians and did not believe their differences in polity were sufficient to call for schism in local congregations. The Synod published the *Cambridge Platform* (*LTH*, 3:6), which summarized the current consensus of Congregational Polity and recommended it to the churches.

- Congregational churches were created by mutual consent to a church covenant.
- Persons could be received into membership who lived outwardly moral lives and could profess their faith. Originally, a person was required to express comprehension of the basic doctrines of Christianity. Beginning in 1636, some churches in Massachusetts required persons to "declare what work of grace the Lord had wrought in them." This soon became the practice in Massachusetts and New Haven, and to some extent in Connecticut. The rigor with which this standard was applied varied greatly from congregation to congregation. The *Platform* declared, "a personal and public confession, and declaring of God's manner of working upon the soul, is both lawful, expedient and useful."
- Church officers were Pastor, Teacher, Ruling Elder, and Deacon. The first two were considered ministers, the last two laity. All officers were elected for life, and ordained. As ordination was to ministry in a local church, a minister called to another church was ordained again. Ministers ordained in the Church of England did not look upon this added ordination as in any way a rejection of the validity of their Anglican ordination. The positions of *Pastor* and *Teacher* were often combined, especially as the clergy surplus evaporated after the first generation. The position of *Ruling Elder* – a lay leader who participated in discipline – soon passed out of use. *Deacons* handled the business affairs of the church, assisted with communion, and aided the needy. Pas-

tors were ordained by laying on of hands by the minister(s) and elder of the church, sometimes by representatives elected by the congregation, and sometimes by ministers and elders of neighboring churches.

- The congregation elected officers, admitted members, and exercised discipline.
- Churches were to preserve "church-communion" with each other. Churches faced with difficult decisions or controversy could invite other churches to send ministers and representatives to a council to discuss the issue and make recommendations. These would later be called "vicinage councils," that is, councils of churches in the vicinity. The *Platform* did NOT provide for standing representative bodies. Larger Synods could be called when needed by the legislature or the churches; such synods could not exercise authority or discipline, but their decisions should be respected by the churches.

To provide for an educated ministry, the Congregational colonies founded Harvard College in 1636 and Yale in 1701. Following graduation from college, the theology student received private instruction from a minister.

<u>Puritan Piety and Worship</u>

The New England Sabbath began at sunset Saturday and ended at sunset Sunday. For twenty-four hours the struggle for survival was set aside, along with all acquisitiveness and frivolity, and the community contemplated the sacred.

Congregational churches held services every Sabbath morning and afternoon, with each service lasting approximately three hours. Every service centered on the Bible; whole chapters were read by the pastor or teacher, accompanied by enough explanation to make the meaning clear. The preacher employed his knowledge of Hebrew, Greek, Theology and History in preparing a sermon that expounded one verse of the Scripture lesson in plain language that the simplest hearer could understand. Sermons addressed the spiritual and ethical aspects of the lives of the hearers, and lasted 60 to 90 minutes. The people sang Psalms to Psalm tunes (*LTH* 3:4) in unison and without accompaniment, often "lined out" by a song leader for the benefit of those without Psalm books. The worship leader prayed for 60 to 90 minutes from his heart without written forms. In the early days a collection was taken for the benefit of the ministers and the poor, but the custom faded as the Towns assumed responsibility for both. The sacraments of communion and baptism were celebrated in public worship, never in private, and communion was usually celebrated about 6 to 12 times a year. The entire service was conducted without the aid of Prayer Books or responses or other human inventions. Even the prayer that Jesus taught his followers, commonly called the Lord's Prayer, was not recited, but was viewed as a pattern for prayer.

In addition to the congregation's two public services on the Sabbath, and a "lecture" on a weekday evening, Congregationalists also held "private exercises." These were gatherings in small groups for prayer and discussion, where lay people had the opportunity to participate and to lead. In groups composed of women, women had the opportunity to speak and to lead. In these meetings people discussed their personal sorrows and struggles and received support. Also, the family was a mini-church which read the Bible once or twice a day and offered prayers at those times and at meal times. Youth were catechized in the home.

The devout Puritan found time for personal devotions. These "secret exercises" often consisted of reading the Bible and other spiritual works, meditation, prayer, and entering in a diary one's spiritual experiences and reflections. Self-examination constituted a major element in these exercises. Before the public celebration of communion, the devout prepared in their spiritual exercises by contemplating the meaning of the sacrament.

PART C: PURITAN CONTROVERSIES

When the dissenters from old England became the establishment in New England, they soon had to deal with new dissenters. New England's leaders brought from England their assumption that a state could have only one church, and that the state should protect that church for the good of the state. They were religious zealots, convinced that they were right and that the purity of their religion should be maintained. They also acted for self-preservation. Fearful that old England might restrict their freedom or impose old England's religious conformity, New England tried to maintain the appearance of being loyal subjects of the King and members of the Church of England. New England had to maintain order and suppress heresy just like old England.

The Congregational churches of New England had only spiritual power and could do nothing in the form of punishment beyond excommunication. However, the civil power could and did require church attendance and financial support, and could fine, imprison, whip, banish, and execute persons for their religious views. The civil authority believed it was their duty to maintain orthodoxy for the good of the state.

The Puritans who settled New England were not all of one mind. Some diverged from the norm so far as to receive severe action. Others, who were orthodox in their views, still urged tolerance and criticized the state's severe actions. Through a series of controversies the New England colonies' harshness toward dissenters gradually lessened.

<u>Roger Williams</u>

Williams arrived in Boston in 1631. Offered the position of teacher at First Church, Boston, Williams refused. The people of First Church had not separated from the Church of England, and rejected Williams' appeals to repent of their non-separatism. Roger Williams was a Puritan's Puritan; motivated by the love of God, he wanted to worship God in purity of spirit and separate from all impurity of the world. Williams preached in Plymouth for a couple of years, then at Salem. In 1635 the General Court (that is, the legislature) of Massachusetts banished Williams from the colony. The authorities perceived the issues to be more political than religious, but for Williams everything was religious. The issues were:

1. Roger Williams preached against the charter of the Massachusetts Bay Colony, and called on the colony to renounce it. In the charter, King Charles, claiming to be the first Christian sovereign to discover these lands, granted them to the colony. Williams argued that the unregenerate King could not claim to be a Christian, the colony should not be founded on such a lie, and, besides, the land belonged to the Indians, not to the King.
2. Williams preached against the loyalty oath that the colony required of adult males. Williams pointed out that an oath was an act of worship. To require unregenerate persons to worship was to create hypocrites.
3. Williams called on the Salem church to separate from the other churches of the colony because the others did not separate from the Church of England. The Salem church refused.
4. Williams preached that the civil authority did not have the right to enforce the first table of the Ten Commandments (commandments 1-4), which referred to a person's relationship with God.

New England Puritans respected Roger Williams for his deep and pervasive spirituality. But Williams' Separatism led him into paths that others were unwilling to follow. In January 1636, before Williams could be sent back to England, he fled to the wilderness, where he established the colony of Providence Plantation. With other refugees from Salem, Williams organized the first Baptist Church in America in 1639. However, after a few months, Williams withdrew from that church. His drive for a pure church ultimately led him to have communion only with his wife.

<u>Anne Hutchinson</u>

In 1633 John Cotton (1584-1652) arrived in Boston, New England, and was promptly elected Teacher of the church in Boston. The following year Anne (Marbury) Hutchinson (1595-1643) arrived, one of Cotton's most ardent admirers from his former parish in Boston, Lincolnshire, England. This intelligent and devout Puritan woman held private women's meetings in her home, according to Puritan custom. At these meetings Hutchinson discussed the sermons heard in church, always praised Cotton, and found fault with the theology of all other ministers. She soon entertained a second weekly meeting that included men. Hutchinson believed the clergy – except Cotton – placed too much emphasis on works, and not enough on grace.

The colony was soon divided between the "covenant of grace" and the "covenant of works." Hutchinson's followers, under the covenant of grace, believed they could discern who was under the covenant of works and condemned them. The situation was aggravated when Hutchinson's brother-in-law, John Wheelwright (ca. 1592-1679), arrived in 1636, and at an afternoon service identified most of the colony's clergy with the antichrist. Later, Wheelwright said of the colony's civil and religious leadership, "we must kill them with the Word of the Lord," and he was convicted of sedition. The annual election for governor, May 1637, was a near riot in which the "works" candidate defeated the "grace" candidate.

The government called on the clergy to resolve the matter. This first synod of New England Congregationalists in 1637 defined the heresy of "antinomianism" without naming names. The civil authorities then applied the decision of the synod. Wheelwright was banished; then Hutchinson was brought in (*LTH* 3:3). Although supposedly on trial for "antinomianism," two other issues loomed large:

1. that as a woman she had instructed men in theology;
2. that she had shown disrespect for most of the clergy, thus creating division.

Hutchinson defended herself well through a long, belligerent interrogation, in which prejudice against her gender played a major part. But she finally made a statement that convicted herself: Hutchinson claimed direct inspiration from God. Massachusetts was a Bible Commonwealth; the Bible was the ultimate source of truth. Religious experience was highly valued, but could not be placed on the same level of authority as the Bible. Anne Hutchinson was banished; her supporters were disarmed. They purchased the island of Aquidneck, renamed it "Rhodes Island" and began a new settlement. In the Anne Hutchinson affair the Bay colony resolved a divisive theological conflict with civil actions seriously colored by sexism.

<u>Presbyterians</u>

Later leaders estimated that 20% of the Puritan Migration favored Presbyterianism. For most the differences were not sufficient to cause division. The church in Newbury, Massachusetts, was Presbyterian; Hingham had Presbyterian leanings. In the second generation, the churches in Wethersfield, Killingworth, and Woodbury, Connecticut, adopted a presbyterian system. In seventeenth-century New England, being presbyterian meant two things: (1) Church discipline and other important matters were handled by the Elders, not the congregation; (2) a "parish system" was adopted, in which anyone not a notorious sinner could receive the sacraments.

When a Presbyterian Parliament was in power in England in 1646, Dr. Robert Child of Newbury petitioned the Massachusetts Colony that either the sacraments be made available to all or dissenters be allowed to organize Presbyterian Churches. He threatened to appeal to Parliament. Child was fined, then imprisoned, and by then, there was no longer a Presbyterian Parliament to which he could appeal.

<u>Friends</u>

George Fox (1624-1691) searched for spiritual truth in civil war England, and organized the Society of Friends, commonly called "Quakers" in 1652. Fox and Friends preached a radical puritanism. Every person had an inner light – a divine spark – within them, which had more authority than the Bible. They rejected all church offices, including the educated ministry. They rejected outward sacraments. They rejected all class distinctions and all violence. Their worship consisted of sitting in silence until someone was inspired by the Inner Light to speak.

Massachusetts Bay authorities looked upon the Friends as disturbers of the social order and took strong measures against them. The first Friends to arrive in Boston, in 1656, were confined to jail until they could be sent back to England. In that and the following year, Massachusetts passed laws against the "Quakers." However, the Friends practiced non-violent confrontation; when banished, they promptly returned. In 1658, the colony made "Quakers" who returned three times from banishment eligible for the death penalty. Four Friends were executed by hanging in Boston Common by 1661. One of them, Mary (Barrett) Dyer (ca. 1610-1660), was a former member of Boston's First Church, from which she had been excommunicated with her friend Anne Hutchinson. The execution of "Quakers" was stopped by order of the King.

Not all Puritans agreed with this harsh treatment of the Friends. James Cudworth (1604-1682), one of the Assistants to the Governor in Plymouth Colony, voted against anti-Quaker laws as one of Plymouth's two representatives on the New England Confederation. Although the new laws made it illegal to entertain Friends or to attend their meetings, Cudworth invited them to meet in his home, so he could learn more about them. He concluded, "I tell you that as I am no Quaker, so I will be no Persecutor." For this he was disfranchised. The Plymouth government appointed four persons to attend Friends meetings in order to debate them. One of these four, Isaac Robinson (ca. 1610-1704), son of the Leyden pastor, became a Friend as a result of these debates.

The first Friends meeting in America was held in Sandwich, Plymouth Colony, in 1658. The Friends became more numerous in Plymouth Colony than anywhere else. Some inhabitants of that colony saw in the Friends traits that were diminishing in the Congregational Churches. In that colony, the custom of lay participation in prophesying had once been strong, and lay persons like William Brewster had often given leadership to pastor-less churches. In time, the colony elected a new governor, and the fines and whippings stopped.

<u>Baptists</u>

The Baptist Church rose out of the Congregational Church. The first English-speaking Baptist church was a secession from the separatist "Ancient Brethren" of Amsterdam. The second Baptist Church was a secession from Henry Jacob's semi-separatist Congregational Church in London. It should not be surprising that some Bible-loving advocates of regenerate churches would conclude that Baptism should occur when a person professed regeneration. In 1654, Henry Dunster (1612-1659), President of Harvard College, did not have his newborn child baptized. When pressed on the matter, he declared that he found nothing in the Bible to justify infant Baptism. All the Congregational clergy sent to him to persuade him of his error failed. He was required to resign from Harvard and retired to Scituate in Plymouth Colony, where he occasionally preached in the Congregational Church. Many others like Dunster, resisted the pressure to have their children baptized. They considered it a matter of personal conscience and did not withdraw from the Congregational Church to organize separate Baptist congregations.

John Myles (1621-1683), a Welsh Puritan who became a Baptist minister in 1645, held an important position in the Church of England under Cromwell. Fearing reprisal from the restored monarchy, he came to America, settled in Rehoboth, Plymouth Colony, in 1663, and founded a Baptist Church there. His church practiced open communion, and he was often asked to speak at the Congregational Church when their pastor was ill. However, in 1667 the Colony fined Myles for setting up a separate church. Then the Plymouth officials proposed a novel solution: if the Baptists would move, to create a Town of their own, there would be no problem. The southern portion of the Town(ship) of Rehoboth and adjoining unincorporated territory was incorporated as the Town of Swansea in 1667. The new town had one church, a Baptist Church.[1]

This "solution" tells us something about how Plymouth Colony understood the "problem." There was only one Church; schism was a sin. To have two congregations in the same small town would be schism. However, there had always been local variations in the church. If the one holy catholic church could be Reformed in Zurich, Lutheran in Wittenberg, and Anglican in England, why couldn't that same one catholic church be Congregational in Rehoboth and Baptist in Swansea? The two churches practiced intercommunion. The nature of Baptism was of less importance to Plymouth officials than preserving the unity of the church.

Baptists did not fare as well in the Bay Colony. The First Baptist Church of Boston was founded in Charlestown in 1665. Thomas Goold (d. 1675) and the other First Baptists were Congregationalists who, because they did not have their children baptized were harassed by church and civil authorities until they left. For the sin of schism, they were admonished, fined, and imprisoned, and Goold was disfranchised. For several years, the civil authorities harassed the Baptists, but popular sentiment against persecution prevented the authorities from banishing them. The Baptists moved to an island in Boston Harbor, where the authorities did not disturb them. After the colony elected a new governor, the Baptists drifted back into Boston in 1674 and were not disturbed.

Popular sentiment increasingly opposed the persecution of otherwise law-abiding citizens for religious non-conformity. Baptists in Boston and Friends in Plymouth Colony found relief in the same way: on the death or retirement of a governor, the people elected a more tolerant governor. Old England's attitudes had been changed by the Civil War. There, Congregationalists, Presbyterians, and Baptists had intercommunion, and worked together *for* toleration. New England persisted much longer in pre-civil war England's quest for religious conformity – the very quest that had caused others to drive them *from* old England. Congregationalists faced the new theological task of rethinking the unity of the church. By becoming more liberal (tolerant), old ideas of catholicity (one church in each place) were being set aside.

PART D: PURITAN MISSION

The early New England Congregationalists were *not* a mission-minded people. According to the Massachusetts Bay charter, preaching to the Indians was one of the reasons for establishing the colony, and supporters in the old country always showed an interest in the progress of this enterprise. However, the great majority of Congregational clergy ignored this responsibility. Of the few English Congregationalists who preached to the American Indians, most were lay persons. Only *two* Congregational ministers took their missionary responsibility seriously, and they devoted their lives to the cause.

Thomas Mayhew, Junior (1620-1657) began the settlement of Martha's Vineyard in 1641, soon after his father had purchased the right to settle the island. The younger Mayhew served the small settlement as pastor. Hiacoomes (1610-1690), a native of the island, came to Mayhew's services, first listening from outside, then taking a back seat. Mayhew and Hiacoomes soon became friends, Mayhew giving instruction in the Christian faith and Hiacoomes giving instruction in the local language. Soon the two of them preached to natives all over the island. Hiacoomes was received into the church in 1643 and ordained by 1649. When the younger Thomas Mayhew was lost at sea in 1657, his father, a layman, continued the work with the Indians. An American Indian Congregational Church was organized in 1659; others soon followed. By 1674, most of the island's natives identified themselves as Christian.

John Eliot (1604-1690) came to Massachusetts in 1631 and was soon elected Teacher of the Congregational Church in Roxbury. After two years of language study, he began preaching to the Indians in 1646.

John Eliot set a pattern for future missionaries by devoting much effort to linguistics. Not only did he need to speak the native language; the natives needed the same direct access to the Word of God in their own language that English people had. Eliot published a catechism in the local language in 1654. He published in an Algonkian dialect the New Testament in 1661 and the Old Testament in 1663 – the first Bible printed in America. His *Indian Primer* (1669) was used to teach the Indians to read in their own language.

Eliot believed that Indians interested in Christianity needed to live separate from the pagan influences of the Indian village, and also separate from the corruptions and prejudices of the English village. At his request, the colony granted land for the formation of villages of "praying Indians" beginning with Natick in 1651. Fourteen praying Indian towns were established in Massachusetts, plus others in Plymouth and Connecticut. In praying towns, the Indians farmed, observed the Sabbath with three-hour services, and dressed and worked much like the English in their villages. "Civilization" came with Christianity. Church membership standards were equally rigorous in both communities. The first Indian converts to Christianity as a result of Eliot's work were received in 1652; the first church at Natick was established in 1660. Daniel Takawambpait, the first Indian Congregational minister in Massachusetts, was ordained in 1681.

War broke out in 1675 between the non-Christian Indians, commonly called "wild Indians," and the English. In King Philip's War the praying Indians were looked upon as the enemy by both sides. The "wild Indians" burned their homes; the English threatened their lives. The praying Indians were placed on an island in Boston Harbor for their own safety. Hunger and disease took their toll. After the war, a much diminished praying Indian community re-established four of the Indian towns.

PART E: STEPS TOWARD INCLUSIVENESS

New England Congregationalism was a hybrid: a cross between a gathered church and a parish church. This created contradictions that could never be fully resolved. As a gathered church, they received into membership only those who could testify to a work of grace in their lives, and they restricted the sacraments to these faithful. As a parish church, they were the church for a defined geographic area – the Town – whose inhabitants were required to attend the church and support the church through their taxes.

The churches began with voluntary contributions, but they were insufficient. In 1638 the Bay Colony passed a law providing for payment of the minister through the property tax wherever voluntary contributions were insufficient. John Cotton and others protested, but only Boston was able to maintain voluntary support. Connecticut Colony adopted a similar measure in 1644. Plymouth passed a weaker measure in 1657, *permitting* the Colony to assess the tax in towns that were negligent in getting a minister. It seemed reasonable to New Englanders that those paying the bill should have a say in how it was spent. Therefore the taxpayers were invited to ratify or veto the church's selection of a minister. This early became the custom, although it was not law in Massachusetts until 1692.

By the 1650s the Congregational Churches faced another problem. The children of communicant members were baptized, making them members of the church. Now these children had grown up. Many believed in what the church taught, and lived Christian lives, but could not testify to a work of grace in their lives, therefore could not become communicant members. Now they had children and asked for them to be baptized. What should the church do? Beneath the immediate question of baptism was the more difficult question of the status of members of the parish who were intellectual believers but not experiential Christians.

This was not a problem for the Presbyterian parishes, or for the churches of Plymouth Colony, who had not required such a testimony for church membership. Neither was it a problem for many parishes, especially in Connecticut, that were lenient in their interpretation of this requirement. But most Congregationalists looked upon the requirement for communicant membership of a testimony of God's work of grace in one's personal life – an innovation of 1636 - as a fundamental feature of the Congregational system.

Several pastors favored baptizing the children of the baptized, but were reluctant to act on their own. The church in Chelmsford, Massachusetts, did go forward, baptizing 75 children of baptized members on February 1, 1657. A synod of Massachusetts churches in 1662 (*LTH* 3:7) allowed that those who were members by baptism, "understanding the Doctrine of Faith, and publicly professing their assent thereto; not scandalous in life and solemnly owning the Covenant before the Church, wherein they give up themselves and their children to the Lord, and subject themselves to the Government of Christ in the Church their children are to be baptized." (*LTH 3:21*)

These adults were still not full members – they could not receive communion or vote. Critics a century later called this a "halfway" covenant. It did create a "halfway" or second-class membership. However it was an act of inclusion, recognizing the validity of intellectual faith, and bridging the growing gap between church and community. Many congregations instituted a new ceremony in which persons gave intellectual assent to the Christian faith: "owning the covenant."

The time and manner of the adoption of this new strategy varied greatly from congregation to congregation, and resistance was strong. Several churches split over the issue. In some instances the "losers" in a church's decision migrated to form a new community. By 1692 most congregations had adopted the innovation recommended by the Synod of 1662. Many had gone further, opening their "half-way" membership to other persons in the community, not necessarily children of the communicant members. Some eliminated the testimony of a work of grace from the requirements for membership.

In 1686 the King appointed Edmund Andros (1637-1714) to govern New England directly, and the first phase of the Puritan experiment came to an end. For 66 years non-separating Congregationalism had been the established church of most of New England. In communion with the Church of England through all of its transformations, before, during and after Cromwell's Commonwealth, the church of New England maintained its piety, developed its polity, and began its missionary activity. In the tension between purity and tolerance, both state and church had been pushed in the direction of tolerance'

******

[1] The Baptist Church of Swansea later affiliated with the Christian denomination and through that avenue became part of the United Church of Christ.

Immigration, Development, and Independence

When the "silent revolution" (1688-89) brought religious toleration to England, New England's original mission – to demonstrate to England the feasibility of a Puritan establishment – became passé. No longer a "city set on a hill," New England settled down to refining its Congregational institutions. Meanwhile, England had established more colonies on the eastern seaboard of North America, where other Puritans, some Congregational and some Presbyterian, settled. All related in some way to New England Congregationalists. Yet another migration occurred in the eighteenth century: Germans came to Pennsylvania, bringing the German Reformed Church to America.

The churches participated actively in America's war for independence (1775-1783). However, political independence led to a change in the churches. The German Reformed Church issued its own declaration of independence from the church in the Netherlands. But would the Reformed Church become "American" in language? Political independence and religious freedom went together in the minds of most people, but New England Congregationalists resisted full disestablishment into the Nineteenth Century. The War of Independence, endorsed enthusiastically by the churches, produced tensions and changes they had not anticipated.

PART A: BEGINNING OF THE GERMAN REFORMED CHURCH IN AMERICA

German Settlement

The Treaty of Westphalia (1648) brought temporary relief to the Palatinate. France occupied the area 1673-80 and again in 1688. They tore up vine stalks and cut down fruit trees, burned villages and cities, and prohibited Reformed worship. Pastors were imprisoned. Reformed people were fined for not attending the Roman mass; in some places the people were driven to church, where a wafer (representing the bread of communion) was forced into their throat.

The French withdrew in 1697 and religious toleration was granted to all in the Palatinate. However the Roman Catholics retained all church property and assets. The following years saw constant conflict over property and the children of mixed marriages. In 1719 the ruler forbad use of the *Heidelberg Catechism*. Bibles, Psalm books and *Catechisms* were confiscated. Those who refused were fined or imprisoned. During the reign of Charles Philip (1661-1742), who ruled the Palatinate 1716-1742, one fourth of the population of the Palatinate emigrated. Many Reformed people went to Pennsylvania.

William Penn (1644-1718), a Friend, in 1682 founded the English colony of Pennsylvania with full religious toleration, and actively recruited immigrants from Germany. Reformed people joined Anabaptists and Lutherans in a flood of German migration to Pennsylvania, New York and Carolina. Without pastors and churches of their own, many German Reformed people became Dutch Reformed, Anglican or Presbyterian.

German Reformed people reached Pennsylvania by the 1690s. Motivated by desires for peace, religious freedom, and material security, they brought with them their Bibles, the *Heidelberg Catechism*, and Psalm Books. In a land without a religious establishment, the people had to develop new ways of being the church, relying more on the initiative of the laity. From the very beginning, Reformed and Lutheran folks built union churches (*Gemeinschaftliche Kirche*), used alternately by both congregations.

<u>Before the Coetus</u>

Samuel Guldin (1664-1745), the first German Reformed pastor in Pennsylvania, had been dismissed from his pastorate in Switzerland because of his pietism. Guldin was "born again" on August 4, 1693, between 9 and 10 a.m. Arriving in Pennsylvania in 1710, Guldin preached widely, wherever he could find listeners. Not an organizer, Guldin remained independent of any ecclesiastical organization. Beginning in 1719, he preached to a Reformed congregation in Germantown.

 John Philip Boehm (1683-1749), son of a Reformed Church minister, came to America in 1720. In Germany, as a teacher in Reformed churches, his duties included teaching school, church sexton, song leader, "reader" in the service, and preparing the bread for communion. In Pennsylvania, Boehm taught school, and read the service on Sunday. The people insisted that Boehm become their minister, although not ordained. He first served communion at Falkner's Swamp on October 15, 1725. Boehm prepared a constitution for local Reformed churches which established the local church governing board (the consistory), provided for church discipline, and accepted for doctrine the *Canons of Dort* and the *Heidelberg Catechism*. By 1736, Boehm served seven widely scattered congregations, helped by other committed lay persons.

The consistory in the Palatinate sent George Michael Weiss (1700-1762) to Pennsylvania in 1727. The newly ordained Weiss criticized John Philip Boehm for serving communion while not regularly ordained. Boehm and his congregations contacted Dutch Reformed ministers in New York, who ordained Boehm on November 23, 1729. In 1730, the poor and persecuted Reformed Church of the Palatinate asked the South Holland Synod of the Dutch Reformed Church to take oversight of the German Reformed churches in America, which they did. The Synod in the Netherlands sent ministers and financial aid to the churches in America.

Schlatter and the Coetus

The Dutch synod sent Swiss Reformed pastor Michael Schlatter (1716-1790) to Pennsylvania in 1746. The Dutch church commissioned Schlatter, "visitor extraordinary," to organize the German Reformed churches in Pennsylvania into a coetus (pronounced *seetus*). Schlatter visited the 46 scattered Reformed congregations and their pastors and teachers. On 29 September 1747, Schlatter organized four clergy and 28 elders from 19 churches into the Coetus of the German Reformed Congregation in Pennsylvania. The coetus adopted the *Canons of Dort* and the *Heidelberg Catechism* as its doctrinal standards. This representative body of pastors and elders met annually and reported to the Synod of South Holland. The coetus determined the pastoral charges – the group of churches to be served by one pastor. The assignment of pastors required the approval of both the coetus and the congregations. The coetus handled the always contentious issue of ministerial standing. Some ministers came from Europe, others were raised up locally. The coetus provided for the training of the latter, and often received ministers on "probation" for a year before ordaining or giving them full membership in the coetus. The coetus quickly brought a sense of unity and identity to the German Reformed in Pennsylvania, and provided the Synod of South Holland with a body for correspondence, to which it could assign ministers. However, many Reformed congregations remained independent.

Having known superintendents in the Palatinate, the Reformed in Pennsylvania understood Schlatter's position as "visitor extraordinary." Schlatter's commission from the Synod in the Netherlands was for six months, but he acted as if it were indefinite. The coetus split over Schlatter's leadership in 1752; Schlatter resigned, and the coetus reunited the following year.

<u>German Reformed Piety and Worship</u>

The *Palatine Liturgy* guided some Reformed pastors. Other pastors brought liturgies from other Reformed states in Germany. All exercised much freedom in worship. Worshipping with Lutherans in union churches exposed Reformed people to hymns other than the Psalms. The Lutheran pastors were almost as free as the Reformed in their worship. The *Heidelberg Catechism* was the heart of the Reformed faith. Young people memorized it, preachers preached on it, and adults remembered its teachings throughout their lives. Reformed churches provided schools where their children could learn reading, writing and the *Catechism*. The teacher, hired by the church, often served the church as Reader in the absence of a pastor.

PART B: EVOLUTION OF CONGREGATIONALISM IN NEW ENGLAND

After the Revolution of 1688-89, Britain reorganized its colonies in New England. Connecticut returned to its colonial charter. The Province of New Hampshire, separated from Massachusetts 1679-84, was restored as a royal colony. To Massachusetts Bay, which had included Maine, the new monarchs now added Plymouth Colony and Martha's Vineyard, and sent a new charter. In 1692 the Province of Massachusetts Bay became a royal colony, with a royal governor and locally elected legislature. The new Province could not place a religious restriction on the franchise. In the Eighteenth Century, Congregationalists predominated in three New England colonies, but the church increasingly evolved independent of the civil government.

<u>The Salem Tragedy</u>

On the evening of December 24, 1696, Massachusetts magistrate Samuel Sewall (1652-1730) listened to his son read the Bible: "But if ye had known what this meaneth, I will have mercy and not sacrifice, ye would not have condemned the guiltless" (Matthew 12:7). On hearing these words the elder Sewall could think of only one thing – the Salem Tragedy and the role he played in it.

In 1692 in Salem Village (modern Danvers), a group of teenage and pre-teen girls had exhibited abnormal, hysterical behavior. The community perceived them to be the victims of witchcraft, and conducted trials to prosecute those accused as responsible for the girls' affliction. In an indecorous courtroom these girls barked and screamed and claimed to see things no one else could see, that "proved" the guilt of those against whom they "cried out." Overwhelmed by this unearthly bedlam, the political and religious leadership of Massachusetts became instruments of destruction. Over a hundred were "cried out" against. On the basis of "spectral evidence" twenty lives were brought to an end.

Europeans of the Seventeenth Century took it for granted that witches existed. Tens of thousands had been executed in Europe. Popular beliefs in witchcraft had little to do with Satanism or Paganism (between which the people did not distinguish) and much to do with medieval superstition. Before 1692 New England courts had tried 58 persons for witchcraft, and executed sixteen. In many cases, when an accusation arose, the pastor met privately with accuser and accused, and charges were dropped. But in 1692 cooler heads did not prevail; the Salem courtrooms were out of control.

As a judge in those trials, Samuel Sewall *had* "condemned the guiltless." Rebecca Towne Nurse (1622-1692), devout member of the Congregational Church of Salem, searched her soul to discern what she could have done to deserve the gallows, but could find nothing. George Burroughs (1650-1692), former pastor of Salem Village, called back for trial as the chief wizard of New England, brazenly declared before he was hung, that he did not believe that such a thing as witchcraft existed. Opposition increased as the numbers cried out against grew, and the new royal governor terminated the trials.

On January 15, 1697, a Day of Repentance for what was done in Salem, Samuel Sewall stood in Old South Church as the pastor read Sewall's confession for his sins in the tragedy.

Massachusetts conducted no more witch trials. Congregationalists afterward relied more on reason and on the evidence of the visible world. More important was the conviction of Sewall and others that *mercy* (call it *compassion* or *love*) could never again take a back seat to other concerns.

A Broadening Church

New England Congregationalism became more diverse and less rigid in this period due to three influences: (1) Solomon Stoddard, (2) Brattle Street Church, and (3) the Enlightenment.

Solomon Stoddard (1643-1729), pastor at Northampton, Massachusetts for over fifty years, moved beyond the more inclusive covenants of the Synod of 1662. Beginning in 1677 he baptized all morally sincere adults, and welcomed to communion any baptized adults living without scandal. Religious experience was important, Stoddard believed, but no one could judge another's experience. He used communion as a "converting ordinance." The Northampton church experienced several "harvests" during which religious interest intensified and many persons became experiential Christians.

Boston's fourth Congregational Church, Brattle Street Church, organized itself in 1699 amidst controversy. Before the church organized, its pastor, Benjamin Colman (1673-1747), was ordained by a presbytery in England, therefore without a call from a church, and without examination by an ecclesiastical council of neighboring ministers. Brattle Street introduced innovations in both worship and polity. Brattle Street Church did not require a public testimony of religious experience for admission to membership. Instead, after a private interview with the pastor, the pastor presented the person's name to the congregation, and if no one objected, the person was received. Baptism was also offered more liberally. Church members could act as "sponsors" to a child brought by non-members for baptism. (Puritans had long rejected the Catholic custom of "godparents"). Also, all baptized persons, *including women*, were allowed to vote on the call to a pastor. Innovations in worship included listening to the scripture reading without commentary, and reciting the prayer commonly called the Lord's Prayer. In a *Manifesto*, the Brattle Street church[1] professed its adherence to the historic faith of Congregationalism, and desire for fellowship, which was eventually grudgingly granted.

Enlightenment, an intellectual movement in Europe, affected New England. Enlightenment used *Reason* to discover a God who was ethically acceptable to humans, for whom religion consisted of doing good. With Reason moderates like Samuel Willard (1640-1707) of Old South Church and Benjamin Colman of Brattle Street described a less severe God than their Puritan ancestors had known.

Saybrook

Could Congregationalism hold together in the midst of increasing diversity? Without the support of a friendly government, the *Cambridge Platform* was not enough. In 1705 a representative group of Massachusetts clergy recommended to the churches a system of standing regional bodies.

John Wise (1652-1725), pastor at Chebacco (modern Essex, Massachusetts), articulated the opposition to this proposal in a satirical tract in 1710, and the more serious *Vindication of the Government of New England Churches* in 1717. Wise praised the old congregational system for its democracy and local autonomy. He was the first to describe Congregationalism as a purely democratic system.

While Massachusetts Congregationalists rejected the proposal for standing regional bodies, Connecticut accepted a similar plan. At the Saybrook Synod in 1708 Connecticut Congregationalists approved three documents: (1) The Savoy version of the Westminster Confession (endorsed in 1680 by a Massachusetts Synod); (2) The "Heads of Agreement" of Congregational and Presbyterian Churches in London in 1691, which provided a foundation for interchange of pastors and people with Presbyterians; (3) The *Saybrook Platform* (*LTH* 3:8). This platform provided for:

- Standing "Associations" of ministers with defined boundaries and regular meetings.
- Standing "Consociations" of churches, consisting of the ministers and two lay delegated from each church, with defined boundaries and regular meetings.
- A "General Association" representative of all the regional Associations in the state, meeting once a year.
- The Consociations to take the place of vicinage councils in hearing any cases of controversy in member churches.
- The Associations to examine candidates for ministry and grant them a license to preach before they could be considered candidates for a church.
- The Associations to assist vacant churches in finding a pastor, providing them with recommendations.
- The Associations to examine any accusations of scandal or heresy against any of their ministers. The Association could then call a Consociation meeting to take disciplinary action.

After the Connecticut legislature adopted the *Saybrook Platform* in 1708, New England had two kinds of Congregationalism. Massachusetts and New Hampshire adhered to the less structured *Cambridge Platform*, while Connecticut followed the more connectional *Saybrook Platform*. The Hampshire Association, covering the Connecticut Valley portion of Massachusetts, followed the Connecticut pattern, as would Vermont. So the division was between eastern and western New England. Connecticut Congregationalism outwardly resembled Presbyterianism, which facilitated cooperation with the latter. Connecticut churches of the Reformed family took to using the words "Congregational" and "Presbyterian" as synonyms, using both to describe themselves.

PART C: ENGLISH-SPEAKING SETTLEMENT OUTSIDE NEW ENGLAND

Puritans settled in colonies outside New England throughout the Seventeenth century. As in New England, persons of Congregational and Presbyterian views cooperated in Puritan churches. Colonists from New England founded the first Puritan Churches on Long Island in 1640. By the end of the seventeenth century there were ten Puritan churches on Long Island, at least seven of which had Congregational organization. New Englanders also organized another three churches in Westchester County, New York, and at least four congregations in New Jersey.

The Presbyterian Church in Ireland sent Francis Makemie (1658-1708) to America. In 1707 he organized the first Presbytery, with churches in Maryland, Delaware and Pennsylvania. Three of the Presbytery's seven ministers were New Englanders. When the Long Island Presbytery joined in 1717, and the first Presbyterian Synod was organized, the New England presence was stronger. Eventually, almost all of the churches of New England origin in New York and New Jersey joined the Presbyterian Church. Jonathan Dickinson (1688-1747), an important leader in the Presbyterian Church, and first President of Princeton College, was born, educated and ordained in New England Congregationalism.

Most Congregationalists and Presbyterians believed that what they shared in common was much more important than their differences. Presbyterian Scotland financed much of Congregational New England's Indian Mission. Congregational New England in turn supported Makemie and practically every other significant early Presbyterian endeavor. Thanks to the actions of the Saybrook Synod, clergy and members could pass freely from one group to the other.

Puritans founded an Independent church in Charleston, South Carolina[2] about 1681, and colonists from Dorchester, Massachusetts, founded Dorchester, South Carolina in 1696. These churches formed the nucleus of a loose Association of Independent Churches in South Carolina and Georgia which was only very slowly absorbed by the Presbyterians.

PART D: THE REVOLUTION AND THE CHURCHES

Congregational preachers promoted the French and Indian War (1756-1763) as a struggle of constitutional government against despotism, Protestant freedom verses Catholic servitude. After the war, Congregationalists denounced British taxes and other restrictive measures as unconstitutional and despotic. When war broke out against England, Congregational preachers preached revolution (see *LTH* 3:11).

The German Reformed Church also supported the revolution. The Reformed and Lutheran congregations in Philadelphia in August 1775 issued a circular appealing for liberty. The British imprisoned Philadelphia Reformed pastor Casper Diedrich Weyberg (d. 1790), suspected of encouraging Hessian mercenaries to dessert. Patriots hid the Liberty Bell in Zion Reformed Church, Allentown, 1777-78.

War produced a decline in religion and morals. Pastors and people became political refugees. Church buildings were used as hospitals, barracks and stables. Regular worship became irregular at best in war zones. Young men raised with Christian morality were compelled to break the commandments: to kill and destroy. Vice became virtue. Popular interest turned away from matters of religion to war and politics. Deists like Thomas Jefferson and the irreligious Thomas Paine promulgated an ideology of independence far different from the Calvinist clergy. Following the Revolution the churches had before them the difficult task of rebuilding and of adjusting to new situations.

PART E: AMERICANIZATION AND THE REFORMED CHURCH

The American Synod

The German Reformed churches in America appreciated the help given them by the synod in the Netherlands, and respected its authority. But the relationship had problems: (1) The difference in language between German and Dutch often led to misunderstandings. (2) The churches were an ocean apart. Messages sometimes were lost. A reply might not come until a year later. (3) The coetus needed competent ordained clergy. Some of the clergy sent from Europe did not adjust to American conditions. (4) When the coetus wanted to establish a school to train ministers in America, the Synod in the Netherlands rejected the proposal as financially impractical.

The Synod in the Netherlands did not give authority to ordain to the coetus. The coetus examined candidates for ordination, reported to the synod in the Netherlands, and then waited for permission to ordain. Sometimes the Synod did not act on these requests. After waiting a year for authorization that never came, the coetus in 1772 ordained five persons.

The German Reformed coetus moved toward independence. In 1791 the coetus declared that it had the right to examine and ordain ministers without asking the synod in the Netherlands for permission. In 1792 the coetus named a committee to write a constitution, which was adopted in 1793. The German Reformed Church in the United States convened as a synod for the first time on April 27, 1793 in Lancaster. It consisted of 22 ministers, 178 congregations, 15,000 communicant members and 40,000 adherents.

The Constitution of the newly independent synod dropped the Dutch *Canons of Dort* as a doctrinal statement and used only the *Heidelberg Catechism*. Synod meetings were composed of all the clergy and one elder from each congregation. The Synod examined all candidates for ordination. Ordained ministers served for a year on probation before being seated at Synod.

The Language Question

One of the most deeply divisive controversies in the life of many congregations has been the fight over language. Many German Reformed congregations experienced this struggle in the first half of the Nineteenth Century. German Reformed people were participating fully in the civic life of the new republic. In many communities, particularly in the cities and west of the Susquehanna, German Reformed people were surrounded by English speakers, and had become bilingual. The younger generation wished to be more "American" and many left to join English-speaking denominations. But for many in the older generation, German was the language of the *Catechism*, and their prayers; worship in any other language would not be the same.

Some congregations held separate services in each language. Some congregations called a second pastor in order to have preaching in both languages. Some congregations divided peacefully, others not so peacefully. In Philadelphia, those favoring English left First Reformed in 1806. Six years later the First Church had adopted English, and the German-speakers withdrew to organize another church. Lancaster experienced a similar three-fold division much later. Other congregations hung together with considerable tension.

PART F: DISESTABLISHMENT IN NEW ENGLAND (1692-1833)

New England traveled a long and difficult journey from Toleration to Disestablishment. England's Toleration Act of 1689 was reflected in the new Massachusetts Bay charter, which in 1691 declared, "there shall be a liberty of conscience allowed in the worship of God to all Christians (except Papists)." Connecticut adopted a Toleration Act in 1708.

However, toleration did not mean disestablishment. As in England, so in New England, freedom of worship was granted to dissenters, while the government continued to support a particular church. The three Congregational colonies, Massachusetts, Connecticut and New Hampshire, continued to authorize taxation for the support of Congregational ministers.

Massachusetts Bay in 1692 adopted an Act for Settlement and Support of Ministers and Schoolmasters. Each Town, as a parish, was required to employ and support an orthodox (that is, Congregational) minister. The new charter had also placed Plymouth Colony within Massachusetts. The Baptists and Friends of several Plymouth Colony towns practiced passive resistance. Local tax assessors preferred to sit in jail rather than to assess the minister's tax. The dissenters kept provincial courts occupied with legal protests. They also corresponded with coreligionists in England, who petitioned the Crown to pressure the Province to change. Finally, in 1727-1729 Massachusetts passed a series of laws exempting Anglicans, Baptists and Friends from the minister's tax. To be exempt one had to be registered as a member of a dissenting congregation, and live within five miles of their meetinghouse. Also, the laws were only effective for a limited period of time, after which they had to be renewed. Everyone else was considered part of the Congregational parish, required to support it, and granted a vote in approving the congregation's selection of a pastor.

Connecticut had fewer dissenters. In 1729 they adopted Certificate Laws granting exemption from the ministers tax to persons who could certify that they were members of Anglican, Friends or Baptist churches.

The ideology of the American Revolution included complete religious freedom. By 1786 ten of the thirteen states had totally disestablished the church. Only Massachusetts, Connecticut and New Hampshire maintained an establishment in the form of tax support for the Congregational clergy. Disestablishment became a political issue in the new state legislatures. This last vestige of establishment was removed in Connecticut in 1818 with the adoption of a new constitution. New Hampshire abolished the ministers tax in 1819. In Massachusetts, after the Unitarian schism had placed many Trinitarian Congregationalists in the position of dissenters, the ministers tax was eliminated in 1833. Congregational leaders like Lyman Beecher had at first strongly opposed disestablishment, but afterwards came to see it as, "the best thing that ever happened to the state of Connecticut" (*LTH* 4:70).

Through the Eighteenth Century Congregational and Reformed churches developed their distinct identities, while maintaining intimate relations with Presbyterians and Lutherans, respectively. Both Congregational and Reformed embraced the American Revolution. They gradually applied its principles of liberty in the independence of the Reformed Church and disestablishment in New England. Both groups were profoundly shaped by pietism, described in the next chapter.

******

[1] The Brattle Street Church became Unitarian at the time of the Unitarian schism and later closed.

[2] Circular Congregational Church in Charleston is a member of the UCC.

CHAPTER FIVE

Pietism and the Great Awakenings

Pietism, a movement for spiritual renewal originating in late seventeenth-century Europe, directly influenced American churches in the Great Awakening of 1739-42. Although this mass movement suddenly subsided, pietism did not die out. A Second Great Awakening. lasting approximately from 1795 to 1835, brought renewal to the churches, and created institutions that gave form to the life of Protestantism in the new republic.

PART A: PIETISM IN EUROPE

Spener

Philipp Jacob Spener (1635-1705), senior pastor of the (Lutheran) Church in Frankfort, Germany, looked about him and saw a church in decay. The theologians were more interested in polemics than in piety. The clergy were more interested in advancing their professional careers than in communicating to the people. And in a land devastated by war, the people had sunk to a low level of morality. It was time for a new Reformation! Spener published his platform for reformation in *Pia Desideria* in 1675 (See *LTH* 4:39).

1. Lay people gather in small groups for Bible study and prayer.
2. Lay people engage in spiritual ministry to one another.
3. Put love into action.

4.   Avoid theological controversy.
5.   Include spiritual/intellectual formation in training ministers.

The small group for prayer and Bible study was the heart and energy source of Spener's plan. Called a *collegia piatatis*, it gave Spener's movement a name: *Pietism.* Spener's concern for a person's walk with God was not new to the Lutheran Church. Johann Arndt's (1555-1621) devotional classic *True Christianity*, and John Gerhard's (1582-1637) hymns (See *NCH* 94, 102, 226, 269, 404) had laid a foundation. Spener's movement was a revival of this spiritual dimension of Lutheranism. Pietism spread as a movement within the Lutheran Church and in other churches. Reformed people, including Puritans, had long promoted small lay-lead groups. Many responded to Spener's movement with renewed enthusiasm.

Pietists cared about feelings. They practiced acts of charity. They believed an emphasis on piety instead of polemics would build Christian unity. They believed in a devout, articulate and active laity. They practiced a strict personal moral code. Pietists could become self-righteous and judgmental. They could also be self-critical and compassionate. Pietists wrote many hymns. Reformed Pietists wrote hymns of such spiritual power that their churches began to allow hymns other than psalms in worship. The hymns of Joachim Neander (1650-1680) (*NCH* 408, 566, 2), Gerhard Tersteegen (1697-1769) (*NCH* 68, 50), and Isaac Watts (1671-1748) (*NCH* 199, 281, 379, 224, 225, 12, 27, 511, 300, 132, 25), the first two Reformed and the third an English Congregationalist, are still with us.

Zinzendorf and the Moravians

Nikolaus Ludwig von Zinzendorf (1700-1760), a pious German nobleman, allowed some religious refugees to settle on his land. These refugees, the Moravian Brethren, were the successors of a movement begun by Jan Hus (ca. 1372-1415), a Czech reformer before the Reformation who was influenced by Wyclif. Zinzendorf led the Moravians into pietism. In 1737 Daniel Ernst Jablonsky, a Reformed pastor who had been ordained a bishop for the Moravians, ordained the Lutheran layman Zinzendorf a Moravian bishop.

<u>Wesley and the Methodists</u>

John Wesley (1703-1791), an Anglican priest, was moved by an encounter with Moravians to consider pietism, and experienced a "heart strangely warmed" in 1738. John Wesley, his brother Charles Wesley (1707-1788) and George Whitefield (1714-1770) began preaching a warm evangelical faith wherever they could get a hearing. Wesley organized his *collegia piatatis*, or classes, into a network with preachers and superintendents over them. Throughout his life Wesley remained a priest of the Church of England, but his movement functioned independent of the Church, and after his death became the Methodist Church.

Wesley vehemently opposed the doctrine of pre-destination, and proclaimed a doctrine of free will: that each person has the free will to accept God's gift of salvation. The Methodist movement became a strong opponent and rival of the Reformed family of churches, even though their other beliefs were similar. Whitefield, a Calvinist, parted from the Wesleys' movement.

PART B: THE MORAVIANS AND THE REFORMED IN PENNSYLVANIA

Heinrich Antes (1701-1755), an Elder of the Reformed Church at Falkner's Swamp, in 1736 gathered a *collegia piatatis*. Antes promoted pietism among persons of many German churches and sects in Pennsylvania. In 1740 George Whitefield stayed at Antes' home, and preached to three thousand persons. In 1741 Antes hosted Zinzendorf. Encouraged by Zinzendorf, Antes invited pietists of all German denominations to a meeting on January 1, 1742, "not for the purpose of disputing, but in order to treat peaceably concerning the most important articles of faith, and to ascertain how far we might agree on most essential points for the purpose of promoting mutual love and forbearance."

Lutheran, Reformed, Moravian, Schwenkfelder, Mennonite, Brethren and Spiritualist came. Seven meetings, called "synods," were held over the next six months. Gradually the sects withdrew, leaving only Lutherans, Reformed, and Moravians. These synods organized a fellowship of pietists called "The Congregation of God in the Spirit." Within this "Congregation" several denominational *tropes*, or circles, were organized.

The Reformed trope, led by Johannes Bechtel (1690-1777), Reformed pastor at Germantown, rejected the *Heidelberg Catechism*. Bechtel wrote a new Reformed catechism agreeable to the doctrines of the Moravian Church. Zinzendorf ordained Bechtel (he had been licensed by the Reformed Church in the Palatinate) and appointed him inspector over all the German Reformed churches in Pennsylvania.

Samuel Guldin and John Philip Boehm both strongly opposed the Congregation of God in the Spirit and wrote tracts against it. Boehm, loyal to the *Heidelberg Catechism*, criticized Bechtel's catechism as lacking in theological depth and not exploring basic articles of faith. As the Congregation became increasingly dominated by Zinzendorf and the Moravians, Boehm saw the movement as an attempt by the Moravians to swallow up the Reformed and the Lutherans. Boehm criticized the aristocratic Zinzendorf's severity with those who disagreed with him.

Guldin, a pietist, attended the first synod and left disillusioned. He criticized Zinzendorf's domination of the movement and rejected what he saw as a human attempt to unite God's church. Guldin believed, "There must first be a union in Christ before there can be a union with each other. It must be a union from above, rather than a work of man."

The Congregation of God in the Spirit continued as a de facto Moravian institution. After the organization of the Reformed coetus in 1747 and the Lutheran Ministerium in 1748, the Congregation reorganized in 1748 as the Moravian Church in America. The Congregation had ordained five Reformed ministers who organized a few Moravian churches among the Reformed. Some of the Reformed people who had connected themselves to the Congregation of God in the Spirit later returned to the Reformed Church.

PART C: JONATHAN EDWARDS AND THE GREAT AWAKENING

The full impact of the Pietist movement swept through the English colonies in North America in the "Great Awakening" of 1739 to 1742. Here the key factor was not the *collegia piatatis*, already familiar to persons in the Reformed tradition, but the *revival*. The Great Awakening centered on preaching to large crowds of people, many of whom repented and made a faith commitment. The Awakening was marked by outbreaks of unusual emotional expressions. The new converts, after further counseling and instruction, were received into the existing churches. Jonathan Edwards, a Congregational pastor, was the leader of the Great Awakening in New England. The Great Awakening greatly reinvigorated New England Congregationalism, and also produced deep divisions.

Jonathan Edwards

Jonathan Edwards (1703-1758). As Lutherans look to Luther, and Methodists to Wesley, so Congregationalists and Presbyterians would for over a century look to Jonathan Edwards as the definitive articulator of Christian doctrine. Yet one of his best known biographers called Edwards' life a tragedy. He was a pastor rejected by his parish, a church leader opposed by those who thought he went too far and those who thought he didn't go far enough, and a scholar who died tragically when on the threshold of a new career. In Jonathan Edwards the old Puritan tradition, redefined in the language of the Enlightenment, embraced America's emotional version of pietism.

Jonathan Edwards graduated from Yale College in 1720. He continued to study for the ministry there, briefly served a Presbyterian Church in New York City, then tutored at Yale. In 1726 the Congregational Church in Northampton, Massachusetts, served by Edwards' aging grandfather

Solomon Stoddard, called the young Edwards to be its pastor. As sole pastor following his grandfather's death in 1729, Edwards led the Northampton church through a revival in 1734-35, and participated fully in the Great Awakening of 1740-42. Edwards' efforts to get his congregation to re-institute the testimony of religious experience as a membership requirement led to the congregation dismissing him in 1750. Edwards then became a missionary, preaching to the Indians at Stockbridge, Massachusetts, from 1751 to 1758. He was then called to be President of Princeton College, a Presbyterian school in New Jersey. Soon after his arrival there in 1758 Edwards received a vaccination for small pox, and died from the vaccination.

Edwards contributed to the life and thought of the church in at least three ways: (1) Restating the Reformed faith in ways that an age of Enlightenment could understand; (2) Laying the foundation of the future missionary movement; and (3) Promoting, analyzing and giving intellectual justification for experiential religion.

(1) <u>Restating the Reformed faith</u>: In *Freedom of the Will*, Edwards opposed the doctrine of Free Will by applying the scientific view that every "effect" has a "cause." In *The Great Christian Doctrine of Original Sin Defended*, Edwards noted that history and observation of the world provide abundant evidence of the reality of this doctrine. In such ways Edwards used the methods of the new Enlightenment science to prove old Reformed doctrines.

(2) <u>Laying the Foundation of the Missionary Movement</u>: Edwards participated in 1734 in the organization of a mission to the Indians in Stockbridge, where he later became a missionary. In *Humble Attempt* Edwards advocated regularly scheduled prayer for missions. In this and other works Edwards presented post-millennial eschatology: the belief that God is at work bringing God's reign of peace, justice and faithfulness to this world, and that God may use people to further this work. Edwards supported the work of David Brainerd (1718-1747), missionary to the Indians. Brainerd stayed in the Edwards home during his illness and death, where he was nursed by his fiancée, Edwards' daughter

Jerusha (1730-1748). Edwards edited and published Brainerd's devotional diary, *The Life of David Brainerd*. Edwards defined the greatest good as "benevolence to being in general" in his posthumously published *Nature of True Virtue*. All of these works provided the theological and devotional foundation of the missionary movement in the next century.

(3) <u>Promoting Experiential Religion</u>. Edwards described and analyzed the effects of his first revival in Northampton in *Faithful Narrative of the Surprising Work of God*. After the Great Awakening had swept through New England, its emotionalism was condemned by some and uncritically embraced by others. Edwards then published his *Treatise Concerning Religious Affections*. Edwards justified the role of emotion in religion and carefully analyzed the "affections," or emotional responses, of people in the revivals. Asking what signs were evidence of a true work of the Holy Spirit in a person's life, Edwards rejected the emotional outbursts as such evidence, and pointed rather to the practical presence of love in a person's life.

The Great Awakening

Effective preaching, calling forth emotional responses, leading to committed Christian lives, was not confined to Northampton. Dutch Reformed pastor Theodore Jacob Frelinghuysen (1691-1748) had been doing it in New Jersey. The Presbyterian Tennent family, particularly Gilbert Tennent (1703-1764) was doing it in New Jersey and Pennsylvania. A preaching tour by George Whitefield in 1739-40 coalesced these separate efforts into one movement (See *LTH* 3:9).

Whitefield's powerful preaching drew great interest and generated emotional responses. Soon many other clergy and lay people were preaching revival and creating the same emotional responses. Some cried out, fainted, or sobbed, so that sometimes the preacher could not be heard. Tens of thousands of persons joined churches, new churches were organized, and public morality improved. The churches became more representative of all classes of society, and traditional Calvinist doctrines were reinforced.

And then it was over. The fires of revival would break out here and there from time to time for the rest of the century, but the mass movement was over in a couple of years. The Awakening had been discredited by its excesses. Critics condemned the Awakening for:

1. *Itinerancy*–Preachers preached in other pastors' parishes without permission.
2. *Censoriousness*–Evangelists claimed to know who was truly converted and who was not, and condemned many ministers by name as unconverted.
3. *Lay participation*–Exhorters without Biblical or theological training preached messages not always theologically sound. To some clergy the lay exhorters were a threat to their status.
4. *Emotionalism*–Physical and emotional responses were accepted as *proof* of the genuineness of a person's conversion.

Some contemporaries declared that the principle cause for the abrupt end of the Awakening was James Davenport. Great-grandson of the founder of New Haven and pastor at Southold, Long Island, James Davenport (1716-1757), itinerated across New England in 1741 and 1742, condemning clergy as unconverted, and haranguing crowds for hours without notes or continuity of thought. Declared mentally incompetent by courts in both Massachusetts and Connecticut, Davenport ended his career as an itinerant by conducting a book burning in New London, Connecticut, in 1743. Upon returning to Southold and listening to criticism from friends, Davenport published his *Confessions and Retractions*. But the harm had been done.

Parties within Congregationalism

For the remainder of the century, four factions competed within New England Congregationalism: (1) Old Lights, (2) New Lights, (3) Old Calvinists, and (4) Strict Congregationalists.

Charles Chauncy (1705-1787), pastor of First Church, Boston, led the *Old Lights* in ridiculing revivals for their emotional excesses at the expense of "understanding and judgment." Chauncy and the Old Lights dominated the life of New England Congregationalism after the Awakening. These "broad and catholic" friends of the Enlightenment de-emphasized traditional Reformed doctrine and emphasized the reasonableness of religion.

Jonathan Edwards had trained many pastors in his home, who in turn trained other pastors, all providing leadership to the *New Lights*. Valuing both the intellect and emotions, the New Lights promoted revival, education, and missions. Most New Light clergy had long pastorates in the interior of New England, where they restored the membership requirement of a testimony to a work of grace in one's life.

New Light Eleazer Wheelock (1711-1779) founded Dartmouth College in 1770 for the education of American Indians. New Lights cooperated with New Side Presbyterians in supporting missionaries to the Indians. Samson Occam (1723-1792), was an American Indian from Connecticut educated by Wheelock and ordained by the Presbyterians.

Old Calvinists like Ezra Stiles (1727-1795) worked to bring Old Lights and New Lights together on a platform of the historic Reformed faith. They opposed both the excesses of revival and the unorthodox tendencies of the Enlightenment.

The *Strict Congregationalists*, or "Separates," advocated full separation from congregations that allowed at the Communion Table persons who were not experiential Christians. Because they refused to pay taxes to support standing order churches, Separatists were often fined or imprisoned. They supported their churches with voluntary contributions and rejected the Saybrook Platform in Connecticut (where most Separates lived) in favor of the Cambridge Platform. At one time well over a hundred Strict Congregational Churches preached a certain assurance of God's grace based on an emotional experience of rebirth. Strict Congregationalists of Connecticut met in Convention annually from 1781 to 1811. Many of these churches were mixed including both advocates of believer's baptism and advocates of infant baptism.

With the passage of time Strict Congregational ardor waned, and they became less distinguishable from the New Light churches around them. Many Strict Congregational Churches became Baptist, others reunited with churches of the standing order, or were received into the standing order consociations. Yet others moved to the northern frontier where there was no standing order church from which they were separate, and they were simply the Congregational Church.

PART D: OTTERBEIN AND THE GERMAN REFORMED CHURCH

Pietism impacted Pennsylvania's German Reformed Church from two directions. (1) Pastors and people came to Pennsylvania from Reformed Churches in Germany that had been influenced by Spener's movement. (2) In spite of the language barrier, the religious excitement of the English and Dutch speaking Awakening in America influenced German Reformed people.

Philip William Otterbein (1726-1813), ordained by the Reformed Church of Nassau, in Germany, came to America under the sponsorship of the Synod in the Netherlands in 1752. Active in the life of the German Reformed coetus, he served churches in Lancaster, Tulpehocken, and York, Pennsylvania, and Frederick and Baltimore, Maryland. The pietist sympathies Otterbein brought with him from Europe deepened in America. In his churches he consistently worked to establish church discipline and a weekly prayer meeting, and he preached a new birth (See *LTH* 4:85).

In 1767, Otterbein met Martin Boehm (1725-1812), a revival preacher forced out of the Mennonite Church. Henceforth, Otterbein and Boehm worked together promoting class meetings and revival without regard to denominational distinctions. In 1775 Otterbein met Francis Asbury (1745-1816), John Wesley's emissary to America. Otterbein and Asbury often consulted, but worked independently, each in their own language group.

Reformed pastors committed to revival held a "great meeting" at Antietam, Maryland, in 1770. The great meetings, which became annual events, resembled what would later be called "camp meetings" with people gathered from great distances to hear much preaching with enthusiasm. By 1774, under Philip William Otterbein's leadership, the meetings appointed class leaders for the *collegia piatatis* in Reformed congregations. In 1776, Otterbein and Martin Boehm began licensing (lay) preachers. The classes slowly evolved into congregations. The Antietam great meetings became the annual gathering for this fellowship.

In 1774, an independent Reformed Church in Baltimore called Otterbein to be its pastor. For the remainder of his life, Otterbein, a member of the Reformed Church, served this independent congregation. Otterbein never left the Reformed Church and continued to have many admirers – and critics – within the Reformed Church. However, he gave his energy increasingly to the development of a network of classes which, like Wesley's classes in England, eventually evolved into a new denomination.

In 1789, Otterbein, Boehm, and their associates drew up a Declaration of Faith and rules of discipline for their network of classes. In 1800, calling themselves the United Brethren in Christ,[1] they began annual conference meetings and designated Otterbein and Boehm superintendents. Revival-oriented Reformed pastors after Otterbein were not able to sustain a dual identity as he had. Several left the Reformed Church for the United Brethren in Christ; others promoted pietism from within the Reformed Church.

PART E: THE SECOND GREAT AWAKENING (1795-1835)
For approximately forty years, beginning about 1795, waves of revival swept through the United States. This Second Great Awakening,

unlike the first, established institutions that sustained revival for a long period of time. Pietism became institutionalized. Many of these institutions continued to thrive, long after revival enthusiasm faded, and are found in the United Church of Christ to this day.

<u>Revivals</u>

On Friday, August 6, 1801, people began arriving at Cane Ridge Presbyterian Church in rural Kentucky for its sacramental meeting. Presbyterians had brought this custom to America. Several ministers preached at Preparatory Services Friday and Saturday on general themes related to conversion and the Christian life. More preaching accompanied the sacrament of communion on Sunday. Sometimes a parting service took place on Monday. Congregations scheduled sacramental meetings so that they would not conflict with the neighboring churches, so that nearby ministers and people could attend.

Between 10,000 and 20,000 people came to the little log church on Cane Ridge that weekend. Between 125 and 148 wagon loads of people camped in an area the equivalent of four city blocks. Preaching took place simultaneously and spontaneously in the meeting house, a tent erected for the occasion, and at several stumps and wagons around the grounds. People fell to the ground as if struck dead, were prayed over by their friends, and eventually rose again, praising God and preaching. Preachers were Presbyterian, Methodist and Baptist, White and African American, ordained and lay. Over 800 received the sacrament, seated around tables in the meeting house, about a hundred at a time. After the parting service on Monday, many remained to sing and pray and hear preaching a couple more days.

The First Great Awakening ended a few years after it started. As a fire that has been extinguished may have a few hot coals that burst into flame much later, the First Great Awakening was followed by occasional local outbursts of revival. The fire was never completely extinguished. People like Barton W. Stone (1772-1844), the Presbyterian pastor at Cane Ridge, fanned the flames as they appeared. The sacramental meetings had become the setting for revival, growing in intensity on the frontier for a couple of years, and fanned into a raging fire at Cane Ridge; the Second Great Awakening had begun.

In New England, the New Light clergy took seriously the training of new ministers throughout the last half of the eighteenth century, and their numbers had grown. With the election of Timothy Dwight (1752-1817) to the presidency of Yale College in 1795, a promoter of revival had assumed leadership of Connecticut Congregationalism. A wave of revivals in Connecticut, 1797-1801, began the Second Great Awakening there. Revival in Connecticut was more orderly than in Kentucky. The most common physical manifestations of conversion were tears. Conversion was followed by attendance in a membership class, after which the church received the new Christian.

Revivals spread across New England, and became part of the strategy of the war against the Unitarians. As more people were won to a personal relationship with Christ, Trinitarians became more influential in society. Asahel Nettleton (1783-1844), the principle Congregational itinerant evangelist in New England, carefully avoided emotional excesses and theological controversy (see his hymns, *LTH* 3:15). Lyman Beecher (1775-1863) kept revival rooted in the church by establishing a pattern of "systematic itineration" through which settled pastors preached revival in each other's parishes.

In German Reformed churches, revivals occurred more frequently beginning in the 1820s. Those congregations surrounded by English speakers and becoming more American led the way in adopting these American religious practices. Congregational, Presbyterian and Reformed were all conscious of the growth of the Methodists, who were a revival church. Revivalists of the Reformed tradition were adopting Methodist practices – and Methodist theology – to varying degrees.

<u>Voluntary Societies</u>

The Second Great Awakening was self-perpetuating. Revivals of religion created new converts to Christianity. The new Christians joined older ones in organizing voluntary societies for benevolent and missionary purposes. One activity of some of these societies was the sponsoring of revivals. And so the cycle repeated, for about forty years. People of the Reformed family of churches who found the partisanship of American democracy repulsive, created voluntary societies as an alternative democracy. Through these societies, believers worked together to promote revivals, missions, and Sunday schools, to publish Bibles and tracts, and to work for social and moral reform. New Christians opposed dueling and slavery and supported Sabbath observance and peace through this alternative democracy. The voluntary societies democratized the church, giving lay people important responsibilities in the benevolent enterprise. Local men's and women's societies were affiliated with county and state level organizations, which later united in national benevolent institutions.

The Second Great Awakening was not just revivals; it was a network of benevolent enterprises, publishing concerns, periodicals, educational institutions and churches, held together by an army of "agents" who spoke before any available audience to promote their cause. Together they sustained the piety on which the Awakening was grounded.

Female Societies

The Second Great Awakening was predominantly a women's movement. A majority of those converted at revivals were women. In spite of limited financial means, women gave a majority of the financial support to many benevolent concerns. Women's missionary societies sent out male evangelists. Women distributed tracts, and organized to address the social problems they encountered in those visits. Through voluntary societies women established, supported and managed orphanages, and widows' homes. Voluntary societies provided women with community, an understanding of self, and fulfilment in significant activity.

In 1802 Mehetabel Simpkins (1739-1817) organized the first "Female Cent Society" in Salem, Massachusetts. This was an organization of women who pledged to give one cent per week to missions. A network of cent societies was soon established among Congregational women across Massachusetts and beyond. With their pennies, the societies provided Bibles, catechisms and hymnals for frontier settlements of northern New England and upstate New York.

PART F: REVIVAL THEOLOGY

Revivalism challenged Calvinism. The revival preacher's call to accept Jesus Christ implied that the hearer had the free will to make such a decision. Calvin's doctrines of election and predestination were obstacles to be ignored, explained away, or rejected. The theology of Nathaniel Taylor and the methods of Charles Finney created controversy in the Congregational-Presbyterian community, and eventually led theology into more liberal directions.

<u>Nathaniel Taylor (1786-1858)</u>

A frequent preacher in Connecticut revivals, Nathaniel Taylor served as pastor of the Center Church, New Haven, 1812-1822, and as the first professor of theology at the newly created Yale Divinity School, 1822-1858. Taylor did not feel compelled to defend Calvinism, but freely developed it in new directions. Contrary to the teachings of Calvin and Edwards, Taylor affirmed free will and did not defend predestination. Taylor argued not only from scripture, but often grounded his arguments on experience and reason (*LTH* 3:16).

Conservatives opposed to Taylor organized the Connecticut Pastoral Union in 1833, and the following year opened the Connecticut Pastoral Institute[2] in East Windsor, with Bennett Tyler (1783-1858) as President. The Theological Institute trained pastors in traditional Calvinist doctrine. The two factions – Taylor and Tyler – coexisted unharmoniously in Connecticut Congregationalism for decades. The "New England Theology" developed by Taylor influenced many students, including Horace Bushnell, to question orthodoxy and to move beyond.

Charles Grandison Finney

Charles Grandison Finney (1792-1875). On an October day in 1821, in a grove of trees just outside the village of Adams, New York, a young lawyer-in-training argued his case before God, and won an acquittal. Saying he had "a retainer from the Lord," Charles Grandison Finney, the young lawyer, soon preached revival across New York state in Presbyterian and Congregational churches (*LTH* 4:69). Finney was effective; he was also controversial. Many church people, including other revivalists, criticized his "New Measures," while many others imitated them.

Many revivals were characterized by "New Measures'" No official definition or list of "New Measures" existed. Asahel Nettleton, the New England revivalist, listed twenty-one new measures of Finney with which he found fault. Generally, lists of the New Measures – controversial revival methods of Finney – include the following:

1. Public prayer by women in "promiscuous" (that is, mixed male and female) assemblies. Women were generally prohibited from exercising any form of leadership over adult men in churches of the Reformed tradition. However, during a service conducted by Finney in Utica, New York, in 1826, a woman spoke. After that, women often prayed and spoke in Finney revivals. The practice remained taboo in most of the rest of the Presbyterian-Congregational community.

2. Protracted meetings–holding meetings on consecutive nights, and until very late.

3. Colloquial language in the pulpit.

4. The "anxious bench"–a special place to which persons were escorted who had been awakened to their need for conversion, but weren't converted yet. On the anxious bench, the individual became the target of prayer and preaching, and the person's conversion became the climax of the revival drama.

5. Prayer for people by name–that is, praying for people to be saved disregarding their own wishes.
6. Immediate church membership for converts.

New England revivalists Beecher and Nettleton criticized Finney's new measures. Nettleton believed that *God* converted sinners; but Finney had converted conversion into a human (Finney)-run process. Beecher arranged a meeting of eighteen ministers from New England and New York, including Finney and Nettleton, at New Lebanon, New York, beginning July 18,1827, to work out a consensus on revivals. After a week's debate, most of the New Englanders were satisfied that Finney's measures were not unsound. They reached consensus on most issues, but not on women praying in public.

Finney preached free will. He also became increasingly interested in Christian perfection – the experience of Christians after conversion that empowered them to live God's law of love. These two doctrines, like lightning rods, drew criticism to him from more conservative Presbyterians and Congregationalists. Finney often made social reform an issue in his revivals, opposing alcohol and slavery. The Chatham Street Chapel in New York City, which he served 1832-36, became a center of evangelism, urban ministry, and anti-slavery agitation. In 1836 Finney formally became a Congregationalist, and pastor of the new Broadway Tabernacle in New York City.

Charles Finney began teaching at Oberlin Seminary in Ohio in 1835, and continued as professor of theology or President to 1866. Oberlin College practiced open enrollment without regard to a person's race or gender. The influence of Finney's Oberlin College over Congregationalism in the West caused tension between eastern and western Congregationalists for many years. Finney's rough evangelistic style had mellowed, and others were more rabid abolitionists than he. But his departure from Calvinism and his interest in perfectionism caused eastern Congregationalists to question the orthodoxy of western Congregationalists.

PART G: WINEBRENNER AND THE REFORMED CHURCH

John Winebrenner (1797-1860) was elected pastor of Salem Reformed Church in Harrisburg, Pennsylvania, and two rural congregations, in 1819. Winebrenner and his consistory were soon in conflict. In 1822 the consistory submitted to synod a list of complaints against their pastor. The complaints were a mixture of petty personal vendettas (they complained he didn't visit the sick but they wouldn't tell him when someone was sick), and criticism of new measures. They complained about groaning in prayer meetings, protracted meetings lasting until 4:00 a. m., a lay preacher of another denomination filling the pulpit, and the pastor cooperating with Methodists.

There was no peace at Salem Church. A zealous young pastor, confident in his rightness, had confronted older conservative "pillars" of the church, who paid the bills and thought they should control the church. Words were said. Stands were taken. Pride wouldn't budge. The synod called on pastor and consistory to forgive and forget. The pastor was willing to make some concessions; the consistory none.

In March of 1823 more angry words were said and misunderstood. Winebrenner came to church one Sunday morning and was locked out. With about half the congregation, he walked two blocks to the banks of the Susquehanna River and held services there. The church was split. Winebrenner continued to serve the two country churches and the anti-consistory faction from Salem.

Winebrenner attended synod each year through 1825 to defend his position, then withdrew. Complaints made against Winebrenner at the 1827 synod were referred to a committee. As he did not respond to the inquiries of the committee, Synod in 1828 voted, "he ought not to be any longer considered a member of this body." In 1830 Winebrenner organized the several independent congregations that had grown out of his revivals into the Churches of God. The beliefs and practices of this new denomination parted from the Reformed Church in several areas.

An 1844 Statement of Avowed Principles of the Churches of God included:

- free will
- foot washing as a third ordinance
- believer's baptism by immersion
- "fast days, experience meetings, anxious meetings, camp meetings, and other special meetings of united and protracted effort for the edification of the church and the conversion of sinners."
- opposition to the use of intoxicating beverages, the ownership of slaves, and participation in war.

Rejected by his consistory and his synod, John Winebrenner had chosen to create a new denomination and to chart a new course.

Pietism had taken over American Protestantism with revivalism, and was institutionalized through voluntary societies. As Edwards pointed out, religion had mostly to do with emotions, and true religion expressed itself in good works. The Second Great Awakening led to the formation of a new denomination, the Christian Church, and the division of another into (trinitarian) Congregational and Unitarian (Chapter 6). Out of the institutions of trinitarian Congregationalism grew the missionary movement, which included foreign missions, (chapter 7), Sunday School, ministry to the deaf, a peace movement, advancement for women (chapter 8), home missions (chapter 9) and the anti-slavery movement (chapter 10). Yet another denomination, a union of Lutheran and Reformed, would take root in America under the leadership of German pietists with the assistance of their American counterparts (Chapter 9, Part C). The reaction against revivalism, fed by romanticism, led to new theological movements (Chapter 11). American pietism often had a catholic spirit that challenged narrow denominationalism. Pietism was always liberal in its compassion for those in need, and occasionally contributed to a liberalization of thought.

******

[1] The United Brethren in Christ united with the Evangelical Church in 1946 to form the Evangelical United Brethren, which united with the Methodist Church in 1968 to form the United Methodist Church.

[2] Name later changed to Hartford Theological Seminary.

CHAPTER SIX

Denominational Realignment

In the new environment of independence and revival, denominational alignments changed. A new denominational family, the "Christians," came into being, and New England Congregationalism experienced a schism between trinitarians and unitarians.

PART A: NO NAME BUT CHRISTIAN

In four different places, with four different sets of leaders, a new movement arose at the beginning of the Nineteenth Century. Independent of each other, and coming from different backgrounds, these four groups came to similar conclusions. Two of the groups, and part of the third, became the Christian denomination that is now part of the United Church of Christ. The fourth group, and the remainder of the third group, became the Christian Church (Disciples of Christ).

How could four groups, independent of each other, at about the same time come to similar beliefs? The answer must lie in similar circumstances. The four movements arose from a common ethos, which had been created by the American Revolution. This ethos included:

- *denominationalism as a new fact of life.* Disestablishment placed all churches on an equal footing, competing for the loyalty of the people. This competition, and their harsh words toward each other, contradicted Jesus' commandment, "love one another," and his prayer, "that they all might be one." Two factors stood out as the causes of division in the body of Christ: creeds and hierarchy (bishops and presbyteries). Therefore the abolition of both appeared to be the first step in creating Christian unity.

- *an egalitarian spirit*. After the Revolution, any pretense of privilege was taboo. Bishops and pastors were not to "lord it over" the people but to serve. Anyone could read the Bible and understand it. The Holy Spirit could empower anyone to preach. Academic degrees and ordination were unimportant.

- *revivalism*. The one over-riding question of the revival was, "Are you saved?" Other issues, such as the mode of baptism, or even the Trinity, sank into the background. Much diversity could be tolerated among Christians if the one essential unity – faith in one Lord – was affirmed.

The leaders of these four movements were:

1. James O'Kelly, who left the Methodist Church with his followers in North Carolina and Virginia.
2. Abner Jones, in New England, who came out of the Baptist Church.
3. Barton Stone, in Kentucky and the Ohio Valley, who left the Presbyterian Church.
4. Alexander Campbell, in western Pennsylvania and the Ohio Valley who left a small dissenting Presbyterian denomination.

The Christian movement that joined the United Church of Christ was composed of the followers of O'Kelly and Jones, and some of the followers of Stone.

James O'Kelly (ca. 1735-1826), probably born in Ireland, had emigrated to Virginia by 1760. James followed his wife and sons to a Methodist class meeting, was converted, and by 1775 had become a licensed preacher.

O'Kelly attended the "Christmas Conference" at Baltimore in 1784, at which time the Methodist movement reorganized itself into a denomination. The leader of the Methodist Church, Francis Asbury, called himself a bishop and exercised control of the church, appointing pastors to their charges. Dissatisfied with hierarchical organization, O'Kelly agitated through Virginia and North Carolina against having bishops. At the General Conference of the Methodist Church in 1792, O'Kelly proposed a "right of appeal" so that ministers dissatisfied with their appointment from the bishop could appeal to the Conference meeting. The proposal was defeated, and the following morning O'Kelly and thirty others left. For a year O'Kelly and his followers petitioned for reconsideration and reconciliation, but to no avail. O'Kelly and his followers then organized the Republican Methodist Church on December 25, 1793, at Manakintown, Virginia.

When the Republican Methodists met again in 1794, in Surry County, Virginia, preacher Rice Haggard (1769-1819), standing with an open New Testament in his hand, said, "Brethren, this is a sufficient rule of faith and practice, and by it we are told that the disciples were called Christians, and I move that henceforth and forever the followers of Christ be known as Christians simply."

The motion passed without dissent. Another minister moved, "to take the Bible itself as their only creed," and this also carried. These two motions defined the Christian denomination.

Abner Jones (1772-1841). The family of Abner Jones moved to the northern frontier of Vermont when Abner was a boy. His family was Calvinistic Baptist. Abner experienced conversion several times, but could not accept his church's doctrine of predestination. After working several years as a teacher and physician, Jones finally accepted his calling to preach. Jones founded the First Free Christian Church in 1801 in Lyndon, Vermont. In November, 1802, three Free-Will Baptist ministers ordained Jones, the ministers understanding that Jones was not joining their denomination.

Abner Jones traveled widely across New England and upstate New York, preaching and founding churches. Jones soon began to work with Elias Smith (1769-1846). Ordained into the Baptist ministry in Lee, New Hampshire, in 1792, Smith later questioned his church's doctrine. He resigned his position as minister in 1801 and embraced Universalism (the belief that all are saved - there is no hell). Fifteen days later he renounced Universalism and returned to the Baptist Church. Smith moved to Portsmouth, New Hampshire, returned to the ministry, and joined Jones' Christian movement. Elias Smith preached widely, but his principle ministry was religious journalism. The *Herald of Gospel Liberty*, which he began in 1808, advocated for religious liberty and created a connecting link for the many scattered Christians.

Barton Stone (1772-1844), the host pastor of the 1801 Cane Ridge revival, had been ordained in the Presbyterian Church in 1798. Ordination was a difficult step for Stone to take because he was required to affirm the *Westminster Confession*. He gave assent to the *Confession*, "as far as I see it consistent with the Word of God." That was good enough for his Kentucky presbytery.

The revival begun at Barton Stone's church at Cane Ridge continued. Besides people falling, some had "the jerks," "solemn" laughter, and other physical manifestations. "Mingled exercises," in which everyone prayed audibly at the same time, were common. The revivalists preached a doctrine of free will. To the revivalists, conversion depended more on the power of preaching and less on the inner working of the Spirit than was customary in Calvinism. Some Presbyterian elders and ministers criticized Stone and the other revivalists for these doctrinal deviations.

For two years, from 1801 through 1803, presbytery meetings in Kentucky and southern Ohio were filled with charges of heresy, acrimonious debate over revival methods, and procedural maneuvering. Both sides appealed to the Synod of Kentucky to resolve the dispute in 1803. Believing they were not being treated fairly, Stone and four other pastors came together for prayer during a recess of the Synod meeting, and resolved to withdraw from the Synod. On September 16, 1803 the five ministers organized themselves as the Springfield Presbytery.[1] The revivalists reached out to the synod for reconciliation, but to no avail. Removed from their Presbyterian Churches, the pastors of the new presbytery gathered their followers into new congregations. In one year they organized fifteen congregations in Ohio and Kentucky.

The Springfield Presbytery longed for Christian harmony, and did not wish to become a religious faction. Rice Haggard, from the O'Kelly group, visited them, and they published his tract, *The Sacred Import of the Christian Name* (*LTH* 4:2). The presbytery decided to dissolve, empowering their congregations to govern themselves, with the Bible their only creed, seeking fellowship with all Christians. On June 28, 1804, the members of Springfield Presbytery signed *The Last Will and Testament of Springfield Presbytery* (*LTH* 4:5) and became Christians simply.

Creating Christian Community

These three similar movements soon made contact and began to cooperate, although they were reluctant to create a permanent organization. Rice Haggard had provided a link between the O'Kelly and Stone groups. Christian evangelists and settlers from the South and from New England moved to the Ohio Valley and joined forces with those Christians. The *Herald of Gospel Liberty*, published by the New Englanders, carried news of all the Christian groups, and was read by Christians throughout the country.

The Christian groups soon expanded through the work of traveling evangelists. From New England the Christian movement spread to New York, New Jersey, northern Pennsylvania, and Canada. From Virginia and North Carolina Christians soon expanded southward into Georgia and Alabama, and northward to south-central Pennsylvania. The Ohio Valley group evangelized into Indiana, Tennessee and Illinois. Many Baptist congregations and a few Baptist Associations joined the Christian movement. These were "open communion Baptists," in the Ohio Valley called "Separate Baptists." They practiced believer's baptism by immersion, but received into communion persons not so baptized.

The Christians were a revival church. They often met in groves or barns, in school houses or homes, for several years before building a chapel. Their worship was simple, consisting of vigorous a capella singing, the reading of scripture, extempore prayer, and practical Biblical preaching unaided by notes. They often held three services on Sunday, as well as mid-week prayer meetings. Anyone who felt called could exhort, and women were numbered among their early preachers. The early Christians opposed a "hireling ministry" – that is, settled pastors with a stipulated salary. Elders and evangelists were ordained by several other elders. One of these evangelists recalled, "it was as natural for preachers to be traveling as it was for birds to be flying."

The early Christians resisted formal organization. However, elders often met together, and conferences of elders and lay people were held to discuss issues in the developing movement. In 1816 Elias Smith, editor of the *Herald of Gospel Liberty*, lapsed into Universalism again. After much discussion throughout the movement, Christians held a general delegated meeting in New Bedford, Massachusetts, in September, 1817. They discussed the Smith situation and the need for some kind of standards. This New Bedford meeting developed a few guidelines for church order:

- baptism to be administered only by a church's consent;
- baptized persons to seek a church relationship;
- church approval needed to ordain an elder (minister);
- elders to be church members;
- churches and ministers to be subject to discipline.

These actions marked the transition from a movement to an institution. Local conferences of churches organized throughout the denomination at this time. In 1820 delegates from the three Christian groups met together at Windham, Connecticut, and organized the United States General Christian Conference. They had no ongoing organization between their annual meetings. Local Conferences and the General Conference had no authority over local churches and pastors. General Conference often passed resolutions on many subjects, but in the view of one historian of the movement, these resolutions "fell harmless."

Christian Controversies

This new movement, thoroughly pietistic, committed to unity in Christ, and liberally rejecting the conventional standards of other denominations, soon felt the stress of theological controversy (*LTH* 4:6). Elias Smith's intermittent Universalism was only one of several issues. When Barton Stone left the Presbyterian Church, he renewed his quest for theological truth. Rejecting all creeds, and using only the Bible, he developed a theology that was rational, and consistent with revival practices. First, he rejected *predestination* in favor of free will.

Second, Stone addressed the issue of *atonement*. Most Protestants preached "substitutionary atonement." The theory was: (1) We have all sinned; (2) God requires that we be punished for our sin by death; (3) Christ died in our place. Stone could not reconcile this theory with the loving God he knew and preached. In 1805 Stone published *Atonement: The Substance of Two Letters Written to a Friend*. Stone argued that the purpose of the Cross was not to change God's attitude to us, but to change our attitude to God, to make us holy, and thus to reconcile us to God.

Third, Stone addressed the issue of the *trinity*, in 1814, in *An Address to the Christian Churches in Kentucky, Tennessee and Ohio: On Several Important Doctrines of Religion*. Stone was determined to use only the New Testament in developing his theology. The language of the creeds of the church – including the word "trinity" – he set aside as a confusing and inconsistent human invention. Stone spoke of three "distinctions" rather than three "persons" in the Godhead, and affirmed the unity of God and the divinity of Christ, but in fresh language.

Barton Stone's views won wide acceptance in the Christian movement in the west and the northeast. O'Kelly and many others clung firmly to the substitutionary atonement theory, and found other ways of expressing the trinity. However, these doctrinal differences did not inhibit their Christian fellowship. The result of Stone's theological work was to enlarge the boundaries of belief acceptable in the new Christian movement. It also caused other Protestants to distance themselves from the new movement. The doctrine of the trinity, developed in the first four centuries of Christianity, was affirmed by all other Protestants, Catholics, and Orthodox. This new Christian movement would not use the word "trinity" because it was not in the Bible. As a result, this new Christian movement, committed to the principle of Christian unity, found itself isolated from most of the rest of Christianity. Yet Stone and his followers believed everything they found in the Bible about the Father, Son, and Holy Spirit.

The mode of Baptism became an issue of dispute. The founders of the movement in New England had been Baptists, and continued the practice of believer's baptism by immersion. In the Ohio Valley, Stone was (re)baptized in 1807, and believer's baptism by immersion became the common practice. However, the churches accepted into their fellowship persons sprinkled as children, and even Friends who had not received water baptism, without requiring rebaptism. In the South, O'Kelly believed strongly in infant baptism by sprinkling. William

Guirey became the leader of the Southern Christians who advocated believer's baptism by immersion. In 1810 the Christian Church in the South split. O'Kelly and the sprinklers organized the Old North Carolina Conference; Guirey and the dunkers organized the Virginia Conference. The two groups reunited in 1854.

William Miller (1782-1849), a Baptist layman from northern New York, after two years of Bible study calculated that Christ would return and the current age end in 1843 or 1844. Joshua V. Himes (1805-1895), the Christian minister in Boston, was converted to Miller's movement in 1839, and became Miller's promoter and publicist. "Millerism" was not a new denomination, but a movement that drew supporters from most denominations. Miller was permitted to speak from many Christian pulpits, and his movement received strong support from most of the Christians in northern New England. The last predicted date for Christ's return, October 22, 1844, came and went. Following this "Great Disappointment" many Millerites fell away from religion altogether. Others found new ways to interpret events and founded Adventist churches. The Christian Church in northern New England never recovered from the Great Disappointment and much of the Christian movement there flowed into the Advent Christian Church.

All of these controversies helped to define this new Christian movement as a distinct denomination, in spite of its nondenominational intentions. The Christians were at the same time the most conservative and the most liberal of the groups that formed the United Church of Christ. They were conservative in their resistance to any change that could not be justified by Scripture. They were liberal in their tolerance of diversity of doctrine, which they described as the freedom of conscience of the individual in interpreting the Scriptures.

Christians and Disciples

In addition to the movements begun by O'Kelly, Smith and Stone, a fourth similar movement began, led by Thomas and Alexander Campbell.Thomas Campbell (1763-1854), Scotch-Irish minister in a dissident

Presbyterian group, came to America in 1807. He soon became pastor of a congregation of the Associate Synod of North America. Censured by his denomination for allowing persons not of that denomination to receive communion, he withdrew, and in 1809 published *Declaration and Address* (*LTH* 4:18) and organized the Christian Association of Washington.[2] That same year his son, Alexander Campbell (1788-1866) arrived in America, and soon took over leadership of the Association.

The Campbells led a "Restoration" movement. Rejecting the accumulated human creeds and traditions of the centuries, they worked to restore the church to the New Testament model. This rejection of human traditions, they believed, was the way to achieve Christian unity. They soon adopted believer's baptism by immersion and weekly communion. This restoration movement in 1813 consisted of one congregation, which in that year affiliated with the Baptists. Campbell's restoration movement spread down the Ohio Valley as a faction within the Baptist church. However there were tensions. Baptist churches at that time subscribed to the Philadelphia Confession of Faith, but the restorationists rejected all creeds.

In 1830 a Baptist association in Eastern Ohio that was dominated by restorationists voted to cut its ties with the Baptists by dissolving the Association. Other congregations withdrew from their Associations, and the restorationists became a distinct movement of independent congregations, calling themselves Disciples of Christ.

Disciples and Christians soon discovered each other in Kentucky and Ohio, and found they had much in common. Their common quest for Christian unity drove them to question why any distinction between the two groups should exist. For two years Campbell and Stone discussed the prospects for union and the issues that appeared to divide them, through editorials in the religious newspapers they published. Barton Stone entered into dialogue with Disciples pastor John "Raccoon" Smith, which led to a series of public meetings in Lexington and Georgetown, Kentucky, well attended by Christians and Disciples in the region. In a public meeting Raccoon Smith declared, "God has but one people on earth. . . . Let us all come to the Bible, and to the Bible alone, as the only book in the world that can give us all the Light we need." Barton Stone replied, "I am willing to give him now and here my hand." The two communities celebrated their unity in Christ with communion on Sunday, January 1, 1832, at Hill Street Christian Church in Lexington.

It is difficult to speak of two groups of autonomous congregations as uniting. There were no votes of representative bodies, and no written agreement to sign. Two groups of Christians simply recognized each other as kin and chose to walk together. Disciple Raccoon Smith and Christian John Rogers were appointed to visit the churches, and to encourage them to walk together, like the churches of Lexington. Christian Barton Stone and Disciple John T. Johnson promoted the union through the printed word.

Any union involves give and take. Stone adopted the Disciple custom of weekly communion with no difficulty. With regard to theological speculation on the trinity and other subjects, Stone pledged to only use the language of the Bible in the pulpit. He wrote, "Let us cease to speculate on the doctrine of Christ, and learn his simplicity. Let us confine ourselves to the language of the Bible as much as possible. Speculations are unprofitable and injurious to growth of vital piety, and stand in the way of Christian union."

Stone acquiesced to the Disciple practice of only offering communion to persons who had received baptism by immersion. Actually Stone's statements on this subject are contradictory. He insisted that he personally continued to offer communion to all, while he defended the exclusive Disciple position. However Stone insisted on use of the Christian name. Most of the Christians of the Ohio Valley chose to join Barton Stone in this walk together with the Disciples. However some dissented.

David Purviance (1766-1847) and Matthew Gardner led the opposition to this union. Purviance had been ruling elder at Cane Ridge, and was the only person ordained by the Springfield Presbytery during its brief existence. He served on the state legislature in Kentucky. After moving to Ohio in 1807 he was both pastor and legislator there. Purviance and other continuing Christians were unwilling to surrender their open communion or their tolerance of broader theological diversity (see *LTH* 4:20). A minority of the Ohio Valley Christians continued in the fellowship of the United States General Christian Conference.

PART B: THE UNITARIAN SCHISM

In the late Eighteenth and early Nineteenth Centuries the Congregational churches of New England were moving doctrinally in two opposite directions. On the one hand, New Light pastors trained new pastors in the doctrines of Edwards. These Edwardsians provided the interior of New England with evangelical leadership that embraced the *Westminster Catechism* and promoted revivals. On the other hand, pastors in the affluent and cosmopolitan maritime cities preached a gentler philosophy. They believed that people were essentially good and capable of doing the right thing. They elevated Reason over Revelation, which had to be explained in accord with Reason. Skepticism toward the supernatural led some to disregard the divinity of Christ, which led to a disregard of the doctrines of atonement and trinity. They ridiculed revivals and emotional religion. For them, Religion was Morality, and was always reasonable.

As the divide deepened, occasional conflicts occurred over the calling of a pastor or a congregation's adoption of a creed. Conflict often occurred between church and parish – the taxpayers of the parish often desiring a less demanding faith than the communicant members of the church.

Jedidiah Morse (1761-1826) was eager to provide the spark and fan the flames of conflict in defense of the trinitarian faith. Born in Woodstock, Connecticut, to a devout Congregational family, Morse attended Yale College, where he was converted in a revival in 1781, and graduated in 1783. Morse then remained in New Haven, where he studied theology and taught in a girls' school. He then was ordained in 1786, served as pastor of a Congregational Church in Midway, Georgia, for a year, then assisted in a Presbyterian Church in New York City. Called to the Congregational Church in Charlestown, Massachusetts, in 1789, he served there until 1819. Jedidiah Morse had a highly combative personality, "the sort of man who could never stand in friendly opposition to anyone,"[3] and he tended to see conspiracies in the designs of those he opposed. His zeal and vision shaped the beginning of the organized opposition to the Unitarians. But his contentiousness ended up alienating even his friends, and other more temperate personalities assumed leadership of the movement he began.

Once settled in the Boston area, Morse supported revivals and opposed every trend away from orthodox theology. When vacancies occurred in the positions of professor of divinity at Harvard College in 1803 and president of the college in 1804, Morse urged the appointment of orthodox candidates. After many delays and much debate, Henry Ware (1764-1845), whom Morse considered a unitarian, was elected professor of divinity in 1805.

The Trinitarian Strategy

Following the Unitarian appointments at Harvard in 1805, Jedidiah Morse immediately took action to organize evangelical Congregationalists. He first worked to unify the New Light and Old Calvinist factions of Congregationalism against the common enemy. Then he led that coalition in a fourfold strategy:

1. Establish a periodical to shape the opinion of the supporters of the orthodox faith.
2. Create a new educational institution to prepare a new army of clergy with orthodox doctrine and evangelical piety.
3. Unify the Congregationalists of Massachusetts in a statewide organization to defend orthodoxy.

4. Start new trinitarian churches in Boston, to contest with the older non-trinitarian churches for the loyalty of the masses of the growing metropolis.

<u>A religious journal</u> – In June, 1805, one month after Henry Ware's installation at Harvard, Morse began a monthly publication, the *Panoplist*. Taking its name from *Ephesians* 6:11, "put on the whole armor (panoplia) of God," the *Panoplist* gave a call to arms to the faithful to spiritual combat against the enemies of the faith. In three months it achieved a circulation of 2,000, more than any other religious periodical in America at the time. With articles on doctrine, practical piety, biography, and events in church life, Morse and his associates informed the trinitarians.

<u>A school to train ministers</u> –After a couple of years of coalition building, fundraising, and promotion in the *Panoplist*, Andover Theological Seminary opened on September 28, 1808. This was a new kind of educational institution (*LTH* 3:13). Previously candidates for ministry completed college, then studied with a pastor or college professor before ordination. Andover offered college graduates a three year program with a growing faculty.

<u>Connectionalism</u> – A General Association of Massachusetts had been organized in 1803, consisting of representatives of the district clergy associations. However, for several years only three to five of the twenty-four associations attended – all in the west. Promoted by the *Panoplist*, the General Association slowly grew to ten associations in 1810 and more thereafter. The General Association had no authority over churches or clergy. By affirming the doctrine of the *Westminster Catechism*, it presented itself as a defender of the historic faith. Some Congregationalists feared any church organization to be a threat to local autonomy. Nathanael Emmons (1745-1840), New Light pastor who had educated eighty-seven other pastors, had declared, "Associationism leads to Consociationism, Consociationism leads to Presbyterianism, Presbyterianism leads to Episcopacy, Episcopacy leads to Roman

Catholicism, and Roman Catholicism is an ultimate fact." The Mendon Association, to which Emmons belonged, was the last to join the General Association, after Emmons' death in 1841. Many of the *Panoplist* leaders did want consociations, and had no problem being Presbyterian when outside New England. They encouraged the General Association in 1814 to study the proposal of 1705 for consociations (rejected in Massachusetts, but adopted in Connecticut as the *Saybrook Platform*), and promoted it in the *Panoplist*. After two years of study the plan was dropped. The Congregationalists of Massachusetts were not prepared to go that far.

New churches in Boston – Of nine Congregational churches in Boston, only Old South Church was clearly trinitarian. The *Panoplist* leaders organized new congregations in Boston, preaching the evangelical faith, and attracting the many immigrants to the city from the more orthodox rural areas. The first new congregation, Park Street Church,[4] was organized February 27, 1809. By 1842 twelve more trinitarian congregations had been organized in Boston.

The War of Ideas

Jedidiah Morse's son, Samuel F. B. Morse (1791-1872), (he would later invent the telegraph and Morse Code), an art student in England in 1815, noticed a book in a bookstore, *Life of Theophilus Lindsey*, by Thomas Belsham. The book included letters to British Unitarians from Boston area clergy, in which they claimed that most of the city's clergy held unitarian views. They further acknowledged the clergy were unwilling to fully disclose these beliefs to their parishioners. Samuel sent a copy of the book to his father, who promptly published the relevant sections, titled *American Unitarianism*, in April, 1815. The *Panoplist* reprinted much of the material in a review, and highlighted the pattern of deception that showed contempt for the people.

One of Boston's clergy who felt offended, William Ellery Channing (1780-1842), wrote a tract criticizing the publication and review. Samuel Worcester (1770-1821), one of the *Panoplist* group and pastor of Tabernacle Church, Salem, replied with another tract. By December 1815 Channing and Worcester had each published three tracts. The trinitarians considered these tracts to be the definitive statements of the controversy. The Unitarians were forced to acknowledge their true views. Worcester clearly articulated the orthodox doctrines of the trinity, atonement, and the divinity of Christ. He argued that these doctrines were central to the Christian faith, and that the failure of preachers to proclaim them was sufficient cause for the orthodox to separate and to organize new churches.

The Worcester Family. Noah Worcester, of Hollis, New Hampshire, had sixteen children by two wives. Four of his sons became ministers. When the churches of New England divided into two camps, trinitarian and unitarian, two of those preacher-sons found themselves on each side of the division. Sons Noah and Thomas became unitarian while Samuel and Leonard remained trinitarian.

Noah Worcester (1758-1837), the son, was ordained in 1787 at Thornton, New Hampshire. In 1810, with the assistance of his brother Thomas, he wrote *Bible News, or Sacred Truths Relating to the Living God, his only Son and Holy Spirit*. This work was embraced by the unitarians as placing him clearly in their camp. Noah had seen combat in the Revolution at the Battle of Bunker Hill. In later years he came to oppose all war on Biblical and moral grounds, and wrote in 1814 *A Solemn Review of the Custom of War*. He organized the Massachusetts Peace Society the following year.

Samuel Worcester (1770-1821) was ordained at Fitchburg, Massachusetts, in 1797. An orthodox Calvinist, Samuel was driven from that church by Universalists in 1802. He served Tabernacle Church of Salem, Massachusetts, 1803-21. His writings in support of the trinity and other orthodox doctrines were hailed as cogent witnesses to the trinitarian cause. When Andover students expressed their desire to be sent out as foreign missionaries, Samuel supported their cause in the state General Association. He was named the first corresponding secretary of the American Board of Commissioners for Foreign Missions (ABCFM). In that capacity he established many precedents that shaped the missionary movement long after his death.

Samuel Austin Worcester (1798-1859), son of Leonard Worcester, was ordained in 1825 and appointed by the ABCFM to be a missionary to the Cherokee. His work included translating religious material into the Cherokee language, and establishing a press and newspaper in Cherokee. When he refused to recognize the sovereignty of Georgia over Cherokee land he was convicted and place in the Georgia penitentiary. His appeal, in *Worcester v. Georgia* in 1832 was won in the Supreme Court but never recognized by the state of Georgia. Worcester later worked with the Cherokee in Indian Territory.

Channing made the clearest defense of the Unitarian position in an 1819 ordination sermon, *Unitarian Christianity*. This resulted in numerous other tracts and rebuttals. This war of words was conducted in a better spirit than most such wars. Both sides refrained from name-calling, ridicule, and the distortion of the other's positions. The trinitarians believed they were preserving their "catholicity" in the sense of their doctrinal unity with Christians in all times and places. The campaign was ultimately an act of piety – of devotion to their Lord Jesus Christ.

The Battle in the Courts

The decade of 1810-1820 saw a series of battles in local parishes, fought out in church councils and the courts of the Commonwealth of Massachusetts. These cases set precedents that determined events in scores of other churches in the succeeding decades. Prominent Senators, cabinet members and state officials presented the cases of the contending parties in church councils; the cases were widely reported and discussed.

The *Cambridge Platform* had provided that a church with problems could call on representatives from neighboring churches to come to a meeting – called an Ecclesiastical Council – to hear the case and give advice. If the two parties could agree on the issue and whom to invite, a mutual council was called. If they could not agree, either or each party could call their own *ex parte* council. By the nineteenth century these councils had ceased to have a geographical base, each party inviting those clergy and churches that would favor its cause. Also, by the nineteenth century, state law had recognized the right of the parish to call a council.

Conflict in Sandwich led to *Burr v. Sandwich* (1812), in which the state Supreme Court ruled that the Parish could determine which was the real First Church and entitled to the support of the Parish. In *Baker v. Fales* (1820), dealing with conflict in Dedham, the court ruled that the Parish was the legal trustee of all assets and property of the church, and these assets belonged to whatever group the Parish declared to be the church (See *LTH* 3:14).

The battle in the courts of church and state was conducted with more animosity, pettiness, and cruelty than the battle of the tracts. The system of mutual and *ex parte* councils had proven ineffective, causing the *Panoplist* group to call more desperately for a system of standing geographic consociations. In battles between Parish and Church, the parish was usually anti-trinitarian and the church, orthodox. The courts – dominated by Unitarians – took a legal position that gave all the power to the Parish. As a result, trinitarians were repeatedly driven from their meetinghouses and forced to start afresh, free of the Town's financial support. Each case increased the antagonism and deepened the divide between the two parties.

Division of the Churches

Slowly but steadily, the plague of schism spread from Town to Town across eastern New England. Over one-third of the Congregational churches of Massachusetts divided. By 1840 the General Association of Massachusetts counted 126 "exiled churches" – orthodox churches having to start over from scratch. They had no share of the property, furnishings or invested funds of their former parishes. Many of the most affluent and influential persons had been left behind, but in the cases of the exiled churches alone, 75% of the membership came out. New England Congregationalism was "born again" in the Unitarian schism, with a new beginning founded on faith in Christ rather than on tradition and memory. Thousands of trinitarian Congregationalists had to find new ways to fund their churches, and a new way to function independent of the Town government.

The Unitarian schism was social and political as well as theological. The affluent, highly educated, urban Unitarian leadership often appeared condescending toward the less affluent trinitarians with more emotional religion. Trinitarians criticized the Unitarian monopoly of the leading offices of the state government.

The trinitarians won the "religious war" by portraying themselves as the true inheritors of New England's ancient religion, and by portraying their opponents as innovators. Trinitarian institutions produced another movement that gave more energy, cohesion, and strength to their cause than all the other institutions: the missionary movement.

******

[1] Named for Springfield, Ohio.

[2] Named for Washington County, Pennsylvania.

[3] Conrad Wright, *The Unitarian Controversy* (Boston: Skinner House Books, 1994), 61.

[4] Now affiliated with the Conservative Congregational Christian Conference (CCCC).

CHAPTER SEVEN

Mission to the World

Protestantism enveloped the earth in missionary work in the Nineteenth Century. Many new Christians, the fruit of this work, would later emigrate to the United States and join the United Church of Christ.

Jonathan Edwards laid the theological foundation of the missionary movement. His student and friend, Samuel Hopkins (1721-1803), pastor for many years in Newport, Rhode Island, further developed Edwards' ideas. The missionary movement was founded on the following ideas:

- <u>Christocentric</u>–Missionaries and their supporters were devoted to Christ, determined to proclaim Christ with power and to imitate Christ in self-sacrifice for others.
- <u>Post-millennial eschatology</u>–The millennium, that golden age of peace and well-being when, "the earth shall be full of the knowledge of the Lord as the waters cover the sea," (*Isaiah* 11:9b) will come gradually. God will use human beings to create that golden age, step by step.
- <u>Disinterested benevolence</u>–Jonathan Edwards defined the greatest good as "benevolence toward being in general." Samuel Hopkins refined this idea and called it "disinterested benevolence." Benevolence is to will that which is good. It is disinterested when there is no payback. As the Good Samaritan helped a stranger

out of compassion, not expecting to receive anything in return, the Nineteenth Century Protestant was called to will the good of others, never asking: What's in it for me?

- <u>The evangelical imperative</u>–The risen Christ had commanded his disciples: "Go ye therefore, and teach all nations, baptizing them in the name of the Father, and of the Son, and of the Holy Ghost; teaching them to observe all things whatsoever I have commanded you" (*Matthew* 28:19-20). The missionaries obeyed the clear command of Christ and went.

The missionary movement was a broad movement of benevolence – "doing good" in every possible way. The greatest good that one could do for another was to proclaim Jesus Christ, and thus open to a person the way to eternal life. The aim of the missionary movement was to be God's instrument in transforming this world into the realm of God.

PART A: THE SOCIETIES

Three early missionary societies contribute to the story of the United Church of Christ. The London Missionary Society (LMS) brought the gospel to Samoa, from where immigrants would later come to join the UCC in the United States. The American Board of Commissioners for Foreign Missions (ABCFM), created by Congregationalists, enlisted the support of Congregationalists, Presbyterians, Dutch and German Reformed in sending missionaries around the world. Missions included Hawaii, the Armenians of Western Asia, and several American Indian groups. The Basel Evangelical Missionary Society, from Switzerland, sent missionaries to Germans in America, where they organized the Evangelical Synod. Basel also sent missionaries to Germans in Russia, where their piety shaped a movement that later came to America.

<u>London Missionary Society</u>

On September 21, 1795, Protestants of various persuasions came together in London, England, to organize a society, later called the London Missionary Society, to send out missionaries. This event brought two signs of the coming realm of God together in one event: the world-wide spread of Christianity and Christian unity. In 1796 the LMS adopted its *fundamental principle*: "As a union of Christians of various denominations in carrying on this great work is a most desirable object, so, to prevent, if possible, any cause of future dissension, it is declared to be a *fundamental principle of The Missionary Society* that its design is not to send Presbyterianism, Independency, Episcopacy, or any other form of Church Order and Government (about which there may be differences of opinion among serious persons), but the glorious Gospel of the blessed God, to the heathen; and that it shall be left (as it ought to be left) to the minds of the persons whom God may call into the fellowship of His Son from among them to assume for themselves such form of Church Government as to them shall appear most agreeable to the Word of God."

This event inspired others in Europe and America to organize missionary societies in the same catholic spirit. By 1818 the other major British denominations had each organized a denominational missionary society, leaving the LMS a Congregational body.[1]

American Board of Commissioners for Foreign Missions

Samuel John Mills (1783-1818) grew up in Torringford, Connecticut, where his father was pastor of the Congregational Church. In 1800, after receiving counsel from his mother, he experienced a sense of "the glorious sovereignty of God." The next time he saw his father, young Mills said, "that he could not conceive of any course of life in which to pass the rest of his days, that would prove so pleasant, as to go and communicate the Gospel salvation to the poor heathen."

Young Mills entered Williams College in the Fall of 1806 and shared his thoughts on a missionary life with a few friends. On September 7, 1808, five students formed a secret society, whose object was "to effect, in the person of its members, a mission or missions to the heathen." They called themselves "The Brethren." Mills went to Andover Seminary in 1810, where the Brethren reorganized, and soon recruited more members. In spite of his earlier intention, Mills did no go out as a foreign missionary.

The Massachusetts and Connecticut missionary societies sent Mills and a colleague on an exploratory trip west in 1812-13, to investigate the spiritual condition and needs of the new settlements. He went on a second trip, 1814-15. Mills' reports of these trips, emphasizing the need for Bibles in the West, led to the founding of the American Bible Society (ABS) in 1816.

Mills took up the cause of colonization – the settlement of freed slaves in colonies in Africa. He was present on January 1, 1818, when the American Colonization Society was organized. Commissioned to explore the coast of Africa for possible sites for a colony, Mills arrived there on March 12, 1818. However he became ill, and died at sea on June 17, 1818.

Students at Andover Seminary, intent on going out as foreign missionaries, consulted with their professors and some local clergy, challenging them to support a mission. Together they laid the matter before the General Association of Massachusetts. On June 29, 1810, the General Association established an "American Board of Commissioners for Foreign Missions" (ABCFM), and appointed a board of five persons from Massachusetts and four from Connecticut, with the understanding that the General Association of Connecticut could name the Connecticut representatives in the future. The ABCFM held its first meeting on September 5, 1810, elected Samuel Worcester corresponding secretary, and began collecting funds. The first missionaries were ordained at Salem on February 6, 1812 (see *LTH* 5:1). Within a month three couples and two single men sailed from America as missionaries to British India.[2]

The act of incorporation for the ABCFM, which passed the Massachusetts legislature on June 20, 1812, changed the Board into a self-perpetuating body, with membership determined by the Board itself, and not by the General Associations of Massachusetts and Connecticut.

When the Board met in 1812, it added several Presbyterians to its membership. The ABCFM claimed to be undenominational, but received most of its support from Congregational and Presbyterian churches and on a smaller scale from Dutch and German Reformed Churches.

The German Reformed Church supported missions through the American Board beginning in 1838. This church had its own missionary society for raising funds and directed its support to one missionary couple of German Reformed origin, Benjamin (1807-77) and Eliza C. (Abbott) Schneider (1809-56). However the German Reformed churches never raised sufficient funds to support this couple, and in 1865 withdrew from the ABCFM.

The American Board was closely related to the anti-Unitarian movement of eastern New England. That movement had created Andover Seminary and the *Panoplist*, and advanced the General Association of Massachusetts. The first missionaries were educated at Andover, and the General Association created the ABCFM. The *Panoplist* promoted missions, and in 1821 was sold to the ABCFM, becoming the *Missionary Herald*. Samuel Worcester, first corresponding secretary of the Board, wrote tracts that presented the trinitarian case; Jeremiah Evarts (1781-1831), second corresponding secretary (1821-31), edited the *Panoplist*. The missionary movement, an outgrowth of the piety promoted by the *Panoplist* group, inspired and united its trinitarian supporters.

Basel Mission and Its Offspring

In May, 1815, a young man of Basel, Switzerland, inspired by a missionary sermon during his church's monthly *missionsstunden* (prayer meeting for missions), volunteered to be a missionary. This person's offering of self led to the founding of the Basel Foreign Mission Society on September 25, 1815 (See *LTH* 4:40).

Pietists in Basel had organized the *Christentumsgesellschaft* (Christendom Society) in 1780, which coordinated a network of pietist fellowships scattered across southwest Germany and neighboring Switzerland, that prayed, studied the Bible, and promoted acts of

Christian love. These groups, mostly Lutheran in Germany, and Reformed in Switzerland, remained in their *Landeskirchen* (state churches). The *Christentumsgesellschaft* organized the Basel Mission, which immediately founded a school to train missionaries. These missionaries were sent out by other missionary societies, including 109 under the Anglican Church Missionary Society. In 1822 the Basel Mission began sending out its own missionaries.[3]

The Basel mission did not promote one denominational confession, declaring in 1821, "only the word of God, clearly and generally understood as contained in the Holy Scripture . . . shall be spread among non-Christian peoples." In 1842 the Director at that time further explained, "It has been . . . ever the belief of the Mission of Basel, that the subdivision of the one Evangelical church into different forms of confession is an aspect of the human limitedness, . . . that none of these possess alone and absolutely the truth, but that they complement each other."

The Basel Mission identified with the unionist spirit of the Prussian Union Church and other *Landeskirchen* created across Germany from 1817 on, that united Lutheran and Reformed.

Basel Mission intended to send missionaries only to non-Christian peoples. However, after repeated requests from Germans in non-German lands, the society did respond. By 1829 Basel graduates were serving in German colonies in Russia, and in 1833 Basel sent its first missionary to Germans in America.

The Basel Mission drew support from a network of local and regional auxiliary societies across Europe. In time, some of these auxiliaries organized as separate but cooperating missionary societies. These included the Rhenish Missionary Society (1828, sometimes called Barmen Mission),[4] and the North German Missionary Society (1836, sometimes called Bremen Mission).[5] When missionaries sent by the Barmen Mission to the American Indians asked to work with the Germans in America, the Barmen Society in 1837 reorganized an auxiliary society in Langenberg, as The Evangelical Society for the Protestant

Germans in North America, commonly called the Langenberger Union.

<u>Other American Societies</u>

The ABCFM, the first national voluntary society in America, was soon followed by others, often with the involvement of the same leaders. Mills' explorations led to the founding of the American Bible Society (1816) (ABS).

The *Panoplist* group organized other societies in New England which evolved to become national societies. They founded a tract society in 1814, which through mergers with other groups became the American Tract Society (ATS) in 1825. In New England in 1816 they founded an organization to receive funds to provide scholarships for persons studying for the ministry. In 1826 this became the American Education Society (AES).[6] The ABCFM cooperated closely with these groups. The ABS and ATS supported the printing of Bibles and tracts in the ABCFM mission fields. The AES promoted the missionary vocation. Societies for Sunday Schools, Peace, Home Missions, and anti-slavery developed in similar ways, and will be discussed in later chapters of this book.

PART B: THE MISSIONS

LMS, ABCFM and Basel Mission have contributed to the life of the United Church of Christ through several missions.

<u>Cherokee and Choctaw</u>

Cyrus Kingsbury (1786-1870), of the ABCFM, established large mission stations among the Cherokee in 1817, and the Choctaw in 1818. Under the leadership of mission-educated Cherokee of mixed ancestry, the Cherokee nation developed along the lines of what persons of European ancestry called civilization. Some Cherokee became successful farmers, merchants and traders. The Cherokee developed a form of government, a body of laws, and eventually (1828) a constitution. The Cherokee nation had its own legislature, judiciary, taxes and treasury. In

1828 the Cherokee nation had a printing press and a bilingual newspaper.

The federal government wanted to remove the Indians of the Southeast to lands west of the Mississippi River. The ABCFM missionaries were prohibited from attending a treaty council in 1830 at which the Choctaw gave up their lands. The Choctaw were removed in the winter of 1831-32.

Because it had a mission to the Cherokee, the American Board was drawn into politics, at first very reluctantly, then vigorously. A Cherokee delegation to Washington asked Samuel Worcester to advise them on treaty negotiations in 1819. Jeremiah Evarts made several trips to Washington on behalf of the Cherokee. In the winter of 1829-30 Evarts wrote articles for major newspapers, held public meetings in major cities, and organized petition campaigns to urge Congress to honor its treaties with the Indians. This first major effort in which American citizens were mobilized nationally by a religious organization for a specific political cause ended in failure. The Indian Removal Bill passed Congress in May, 1830.

Jeremiah Evarts (1781-1831), lawyer, journalist and activist, was the second corresponding secretary of the ABCFM. Raised in northern Vermont, Evarts found a deep relationship with God when he was attending Yale College. He closely associated himself with the trinitarian branch of Congregationalism in their religious "war" with the Unitarians. In 1810 he became editor of the *Panoplist*, which later was turned over to the ABCFM and became the *Missionary Herald*. He served the ABCFM as treasurer beginning in 1812, and corresponding secretary from 1821 until his death. In his struggle against Indian removal, he organized petition drives, mass meetings, letter-to-editor writing, and he visited Washington to directly appeal to members of the government. He lamented, "how tame and timid, and how vacillating and inconstant - how yielding and compromising - nine-tenths of even

Meanwhile, the state of Georgia passed laws declaring all Cherokee laws null and void, and requiring Whites in Indian territory to swear a loyalty oath to the state. Several missionaries refused and were arrested (*LTH* 5:35). Missionaries Samuel A. Worcester (1798-1859) and Elizur Butler (1798-1857) were convicted on September 16, 1831, and sentenced to four years' hard labor in the Georgia penitentiary. ABCFM lawyers appealed the case to the Supreme Court, where Chief Justice John Marshall declared in *Worcester v. Georgia* on 2 March 1832, that Georgia laws over the Cherokee were null and void and ordered the immediate release of the missionaries.

The state of Georgia refused to recognize the Supreme Court decision and President Andrew Jackson would not enforce it. Jackson's re-election in November, 1832, guaranteed that the Cherokee would receive no relief. Perceiving that nothing more could be achieved by their protest, Worcester and Butler requested and received pardons and release in January 1833.

Then followed several years of disorder and conflict. In January of 1833 white settlers began arriving, claiming the land of the Cherokee – and the missions. Believing removal was inevitable, several Cherokee leaders took it upon themselves to negotiate an unauthorized and illegal treaty with the federal government. They thought they should make the best deal they could with the government, which they did; but they had no legal right to do so, and were branded by others as traitors.

In the summer of 1838 the Cherokee were rounded up and placed in detention camps. In the Fall and Winter of 1838-39, 12,000 Cherokee followed the "trail of tears" to their new homeland. Two ABCFM missionaries, Elizur Butler and David Butrick, accompanied the Cherokee on the journey. It was a journey of sorrow, sickness and death. Butler estimated that 2,000 died on the journey, although official records indicated that less than 500 died.

<u>Hawaii</u>

The mission to Hawaii began in 1819 with white missionaries assisted by Hawaiians who had received education from the ABCFM in New England (*LTH* 5:21). When the first missionaries arrived at Hawaii they learned that the king had recently died, and the new king had abolished the old religion. The missionaries and their supporters were convinced that God had prepared the way, and was blessing their enterprise. However, having gotten rid of one religion, the Hawaiians were not sure they wanted another. The missionaries preached, gave the Hawaiian language written form, published books in Hawaiian, taught school in Hawaiian, advised the political leaders, and looked for ways to develop the economy.

A revival from 1837 to 1839 brought most of the Hawaiian people either into membership or into sympathy with the church. Hawaii confronted the American Board with a problem in 1848: success. What do missionaries do when the people to whom they were sent become overwhelmingly Christian? The Board began a process, lasting from 1848 to 1863, of "devolution," gradually diminishing support. The churches organized the self-governing Hawaiian Evangelical Association in 1863. The Board and the Hawaiian government encouraged the missionaries and their children to remain and become Hawaiian citizens. Ordained missionaries accepted calls to churches, the unordained turned to secular jobs. The churches of Hawaii established the Hawaiian Missionary Society, and began sending out missionaries to Micronesia in 1852.[7]

<u>Western Asia</u>

The mission of the ABCFM to western Asia was different from its other missions. Instead of evangelizing to gather a church, missionaries encouraged reformation in existing churches. They believed reformed Eastern churches could evangelize western Asia. Begun in 1819, by 1834 the Board's Western Asian missions included Syria (Beirut), Greece, Turkey and Persia.

ABCFM missionaries arrived in Constantinople in 1831, and soon found many Armenians eager for reformation. At first the Armenian patriarch supported the Protestant missionaries and reformers. But the sultan, the ruler of Turkey, could appoint and remove patriarchs at will. Within the Armenian Church periods of tolerance of the reformers and periods of persecution alternated frequently. Reform-minded Armenians organized a secret society for the promotion of piety, the *Parebashdoutian Miapanautune* in 1836. On January 25, 1846, the Patriarch officially excommunicated Vertanes Eznak Gregorian, a priest who was leading the evangelical reform, and all who supported him. On July 1, 1846, the reformers organized the Armenian Evangelical Church. The ABCFM supported this new church, and it grew rapidly.

<u>Germans in Russia</u>

As the Russian Empire expanded it looked for loyal colonists to settle newly conquered territory. In 1763, Empress Catherine II issued a manifesto, inviting European colonists to settle in the Volga River Valley. She offered them full religious freedom, exemption from military service, virtual self-government, land and other benefits. Many Germans came and settled. Later rulers issued similar decrees and waves of German immigrants came 1804-09, and then again 1816-37, to what is now the southern Ukraine and Moldova.

The German colonists were mostly Lutherans, also many Catholics and some of the Reformed faith. In the German colonies the pastor appeared about once a month or less. On other Sundays the local school teacher read a sermon. The school teacher, a layman, had received some religious training at the teachers' college, and often became the spiritual leader of the community.

The Russian government established a "General Consistory" in 1819 to govern the Lutheran churches. In 1820, the few Reformed churches were incorporated into this "General Consistory of Evangelical Churches in Russia." Pietism, called *stundism* because of its devotional hours (*stunden*), was strong in the German colonies of Russia, but opposed by the General Consistory. However, missionaries trained by Basel continued to come to Russia, nurturing lay leadership and promoting stundism.

Samoa

Thirty London Missionary Society missionaries arrived in Tahiti on March 5, 1797. Most of the missionaries deserted, three were massacred, and two went native, until by 1801 only five were left. LMS efforts to establish a large mission station, teaching the arts of civilization, had failed. Henry Nott (1774-1844), who in England had been a bricklayer, was left the leader of the leaner mission that concentrated on language study, scripture translation, preaching and friendship. As Tahiti passed through a series of civil wars, the consistently non-violent and non-partisan missionary, showing respect and compassion to all, began to draw the interest of the Tahitians. Between 1812 and 1815 most of the Tahitians became worshipers of the Christian God.

Missionary John Williams (1796-1839) arrived in Tahiti in 1817 when the Christian faith was spreading to nearby islands. The energetic and restless Williams later wrote, "for my part, I cannot content myself within the narrow limits of a single reef." He traveled widely across the Pacific, depositing native evangelists on any island that would receive them. When Williams was on Rarotonga, in the Cook Islands, with no way to leave, he built a boat, the *Messenger of Peace,* with materials available, and set sail.

The *Messenger of Peace* arrived at Samoa in 1830, and on August 21, eight native teachers landed on Savai'i. In spite of ongoing warfare, the teachers discovered a desire among the Samoans for a new *loti* (religion). English missionaries arrived in 1835 and churches were soon organized on Savai'i (1837), Upolu (1838), and Tutuila (1839).

In November 1839, Williams and twelve Samoan teachers set sail to the west. After Samoan teachers were deposited at Rotuma (north of Fiji), and Tanna (in Vanuatu), they reached Erromango (in Vanuatu), where Williams and another English missionary were killed by natives on November 20, and eaten. Samoan missionaries would later share the Christian message at Vanuatu, the Loyalty Islands (belonging to New Caledonia), Niue, and New Guinea.

Christianity grew on Samoa despite ten intertribal wars between 1830 and 1873. The missionaries occasionally mediated conflict, and Samoan Christians showed kindness in victory. The Samoans left behind old customs and traditions with the old religion. They created a parliament, and promulgated a code of laws, with the advice of the missionaries, who also aided in developing commerce.The translation of the Bible into Samoan, begun by missionary George Pratt in 1835, was completed in 1855, then published in 1860. In 1844 the mission founded Malua Institute, which conducted a four year program to train native teachers and preachers. At first the Institute only enrolled married men, the wives and children also receiving instruction.

Dakota

Thomas S. Williamson (1800-79) went to the Dakota people of Minnesota in 1835 as a missionary of the American Board. He accepted the invitation of Joseph Renville (1779-1846), a mixed-ancestry trader, and began a mission at Renville's trading post at Lac-qui-Parle. Renville and his family were the mission's first converts and charter members of the mission's Presbyterian Church. Renville wrote several hymns, including "Wakantanka Taku Nitawa," (*NCH* 3, 341) and held his own evening religious meetings with the Indians. Also, Renville the fur trader had a small fighting force at his trading post, that provided protection for the missionaries from the opponents of Christianity. The mission made slow progress; in 1856, after twenty years' work, the mission churches counted only 43 members.

The Dakota confined to reservations in Minnesota rebelled in the summer of 1862. In six weeks, over 400 white settlers were killed, and several organized battles fought. Christian Indians spoke against war in council, but were not fully trusted by the leaders. Homesteads of Christian Indians were destroyed along with those of whites. In the Indian camp, Presbyterian Elder Paul Mazakutemane with the assistance of John B. Renville (son of the trader), managed to gain control of many white captives being held in the camp, established a camp of those friendly to the whites, and separated from the hostile camp. After defeat at the Battle of Wood Lake, September 23, the hostiles fled to the west. On September 27, the friendly camp and the military met and the hostages were released.

In the Fall and Winter of 1862 the white community of Minnesota was swept by a racist frenzy and a lust for revenge. The leaders of the war were on the prairie or in Canada, but the military had in custody the 1200 Indians from the friendly camp. A military commission "tried" the captives with complete disregard for law, and condemned three hundred and three to be hung. The government placed the convicted in a prison in Mankato. The rest of the Dakota in Minnesota, mostly women and children, were interned in a camp at Fort Snelling. President Lincoln intervened, had a commission review the trial record case by case, and only thirty-eight sentences were sustained. On 26 December 1862, "the remaining thirty-eight condemned mounted the scaffold chanting their death song, reluctantly allowed the white caps to be adjusted over their heads, and then attempted to grasp each other's hands in a final gesture of solidarity. The trap was sprung." The tradition maintained by Dakota people today is that they sang the Christian hymn, "Wakantanka Taku Nitawa."

The prisoners, feeling that their old religion had failed them, now inquired about Christianity. One of the elders of the Presbyterian Church, Robert Hopkins Caske, was in the Mankato prison. As his fellow prisoners turned to him to learn about the Christian God, he became their spiritual leader, and led services twice a day. Thomas Williamson reported on his visit to the prison on February 3, 1863: "I wrote in their own language a confession of faith and covenant. After appropriate religious exercises we read and explained the confession and told them that we were ready to baptize such as heartily adopted it. We baptized on that day two hundred and seventy-four."

John P. Williamson (1835-1917), son of Thomas, ministered to the Dakota interned at Fort Snelling, mostly women and children. Here also the people were eager to learn the new religion. Over a hundred and forty were baptized that winter at the internment camp.

In the spring of 1863 the prisoners at Mankato were moved to Davenport, Iowa; those at Fort Snelling were moved to a new camp on the Missouri River in Dakota Territory. The congregation in the prison was organized into classes, each class corresponding to a Dakota band. Each class had one or more *hunkayapi* (Elders), who were ordained by the church. In the predominantly female community at the reservation on the Missouri River, John Williamson appointed deaconesses, to take charge of women's prayer meetings. The children also had meetings, conducted by themselves.

In 1866 the eastern Dakota were given a Reservation in Northeast Nebraska, and the communities in Davenport and on the Missouri were transported to this new home. The two churches were united to form Pilgrim Church at Santee Agency.

PART C: MISSION THEORY

When the American Board of Commissioners for Foreign Missions began its Indian missions in 1817 it echoed the policies of previous missions, working to make Indians, "English in their language, civilized in their manners, and Christian in their religion." New policies regarding the conduct of missions evolved gradually out of experience in the mission field. At the suggestion of a council of Choctaw chiefs in 1823, the Board abolished large mission stations and dispersed the missionaries.

Following the invention of a Cherokee alphabet, and the insistence by the Cherokee that their kinsman David Brown (co. 1790-1829) translate the Bible from the original Greek into Cherokee, the Board resolved to make greater use of the Indian languages.

Rufus Anderson (1796-1880) became an assistant to Evarts in 1823, and one of three "co-equal" secretaries in 1832, he being responsible for foreign correspondence. Calling himself "senior secretary" from 1835 until his retirement in 1866, Anderson became one of the leading missionary theorists and administrators of the century. He focused on the one "great object" of missions (evangelism), devolution, and the development of churches that were self-governing, self-supporting, and self-propagating.

When Rufus Anderson and his associates assumed leadership of the American Board, they immediately began to institute new policies (See *LTH* 5:16). David Greene (1797-1866), secretary for Indian missions, introduced the new thinking in Instructions he gave to two missionaries to the Anishinaabe (Ojibwa), on June 10, 1832. The mission would have "no, large secular establishments, agricultural or mechanical. . . . The great object of your mission, the object never to be for a moment lost sight of, is to preach the gospel of Christ directly to old and young, with the intention and earnest desire of being made the instruments of their speedy conversion."

While earlier Indian missions had been shaped by a three-fold mission--to evangelize, civilize, and anglicize--now there was only one "great object," the proclamation of the Gospel. The missionaries were also instructed to learn the Anishinaabe language and to study the Indian religions. After learning the language they were to give it a written form, and to translate elementary books and Scripture tracts.

In addition to this focus on the one "great object" of evangelization, Rufus Anderson advanced a second new policy: "devolution." In 1841, Anderson advocated the raising up of a native ministry as soon as possible:"...the elders, or pastors, whom the apostles ordained over the churches they gathered...were generally, if not always, *natives of the country*. In this way the gospel soon became indigenous to the soil, and the gospel institutions acquired, through the grace of God, a self-supporting, self-propagating energy." This principle of developing independent churches that would be self-governing, self-supporting, and self-propagating became a central principle of mission policy under Anderson's leadership.

In the 1846 annual report, the secretaries described another aspect of devolution, cautioning their supporters not to expect the native Christians to be just like them: "It hardly seems liberal or wise to bring every opinion and practice and institution of other communities to the standard of our own, and severely condemn whatever does not accord with it. . . . It surely is possible that what seems to us so wrong, others, in a different state of society, and with different training, and with other facts before them, may honestly think to be the best arrangement practicable."

While native Christians were given abundant advice, they were ultimately responsible for determining how to live out their faith in their society. Anderson's new policies encountered resistance from many missionaries and misunderstanding from supporters, but he persisted.

******

[1] The London Missionary Society began missions to Tahiti (1797), India (1798), South Africa (1799), China (1807), Guyana (1809), Madagascar (1818), Samoa (1830), and Jamaica (1834).

[2] In addition to its mission to west India, the Board soon added missions to Sri Lanka (Ceylon, 1815), the Cherokee (1817), the Choctaw (1818), Hawaii (1819) and Western Asia (1819). The ABCFM acquired several more Indian missions through the absorption of other societies in 1826 and 1827. The American Board also started new missions in China (1830), among the Anishinaabe (1831), to Thailand (1831), to the Pawnee (1834), Dakota (1834), in Liberia (1834), to South India (1834), to the Indians of Oregon Territory (1835), and among the Zulu in South Africa (1835).

[3] Basel established missions in Ghana (1828) and India (1834).

[4] The Barmen Mission established several missions in Indonesia and a mission in South Africa.

[5]The Bremen Mission, sent missionaries to the Ewe of Ghana and Togo (1836), and to Germans in America.

[6] The AES through merger became the American College and Education Society and still later became part of the Congregational Board of Home Missions.

[7] Teams of native evangelists and American missionaries reached out to Kusaie (1852), Ponape (1852), Ebon (1857), Kiribati (1857), and Truck (1879).

CHAPTER EIGHT

Mission's Multiple Fruit

The first eight missionaries sent out by the ABCFM encountered many difficulties. Before they arrived in India the United States had declared war on Britain, the ruler of India. Also on the journey, three of the eight converted to the Baptist faith and withdrew from the ABCFM, sending one of their number back to gather support from Baptists in America. One of the eight, Harriet (Atwood) Newell, died after they were denied access to India. Her journal, which described a life committed to Christ, was widely published, along with a sermon by Leonard Woods given on the occasion of her death. That publication generated a flood of support for missions. Many applied the missionary spirit to their lives at home.

Samuel Nott, Jr. (1787-1869), another one of the first eight ABCFM missionaries, who returned from India in poor health, in 1823 wrote the first book of children's sermons, in the preface of which he wrote, "a real desire that the gospel should be preached to *every creature*, will show itself at home." For Nineteenth Century American Protestants the missionary was the ideal Christian. Not everyone could be a foreign missionary, but each person could discover a mission at home. Every Christian could take part in the advancement of the realm of God.

This chapter describes several facets of this diffused missionary spirit. First are three organized movements for the advancement of God's realm, (1) Sunday Schools, (2) a school for the deaf, and (3) Peace. Then follows a description of the expanding role of women in the life of the church, a movement closely related but not completely dependent on the missionary movement.

PART A: THE SUNDAY SCHOOL

Robert Raikes (1736-1811), of Gloucester, England, was concerned about children working in factories who had no opportunity to go to school. In 1780 he hired four women to teach poor children on Sundays. Thus the modern Sunday School movement began: teaching literacy using the Bible. The movement came to America and quickly became popular in all denominations.

When the Nineteenth Century began, New England Towns had public schools, and Reformed Churches in Pennsylvania had parochial schools. Both public and parochial schools taught religion along with reading, writing and arithmetic. In both, expenses could exclude the very poor. The function of the first Sunday Schools, in England, Pennsylvania and New England, was to provide education to the children of the poor, similar to what was provided in public and parochial schools.

Lay Christians organized and conducted the first Sunday Schools. Although leaders might be from a particular congregation, and they might use that church's building, the school was independent and in no way under the control of the church. The first Sunday School located in a Congregational Church opened in Bath, New Hampshire, in 1805. First Reformed Church, Philadelphia, Pennsylvania, in 1806 was the home of the first Sunday School in a Reformed Church. The first Sunday School in a Christian Church opened in Kittery, Maine, in 1826.

In Massachusetts Joanna Prince and Hannah Hill opened the first Sunday School in 1810 in Beverly. Prince taught a school in her mother's home on weekdays, and conducted the Sabbath School to reach children unable to attend during the week. Each Sunday the class met in her school room before morning worship and again after the afternoon services. Although Prince and Hill were both members of Joseph Emerson's Congregational Church, the school was non-denominational. Like the weekday school the Sabbath School taught literacy using religious literature.

Some ministers opposed Sunday Schools at first for several reasons:

- Clergy saw the lay led Sunday Schools as a threat to their authority.
- The teachers were not trained.
- Many teachers were women.
- The schools were either too sectarian (a Christian criticism) or too non-sectarian (a Reformed criticism).
- It was an inappropriate activity for the Sabbath.
- Those ragged children would make a mess of the church building.
- Sunday Schools are not mentioned in the Bible (a Christian criticism).

In spite of the objections, the movement spread rapidly. As public education became more widespread and more secular, the Sunday School assumed the distinct function of religious education, and included all children, not just the poor. The first Sunday Schools used catechisms to teach reading and religion. After the first quarter of the Nineteenth Century, the Bible replaced the catechism. Books of Bible Questions were published, and students memorized large portions of scripture.

The American Sunday School Union (ASSU), organized in 1824, began promoting a one year cycle of scriptures in 1825 and became a major publisher of children's religious literature. Sunday School libraries provided reading material for children and their families throughout most of the Nineteenth Century, before communities established public libraries.

In Massachusetts, Congregationalists, Baptists, Episcopalians and Methodists united in organizing the Massachusetts Sabbath School Union (MSSU) in 1825. Their purpose was to promote Sabbath schools, and to provide inexpensive books. Two denominations soon withdrew, leaving the Congregationalists and Baptists, and the MSSU began publishing children's religious literature. In 1832 Baptists and Congregationalists dissolved the union; Congregationalists reorganized as the Massachusetts Sabbath School Society (MSSS). Congregationalists wanted to have at least one publishing concern in the country that was exclusively Congregational.

Under the direction of Asa Bullard (1804-88) from 1834-74, the MSSS sent missionaries to organize Congregational Sabbath Schools throughout the country. Congregational Sabbath School unions in other states became auxiliary to the MSSS. The MSSS revived interest in the *Westminster Catechism*, publishing 350,000 copies from 1835 to 1850.

The Reformed Church Synod organized the Sunday School Union of the Reformed Church in the United States in 1835, auxiliary to the ASSU. The synod appointed an agent of the union and named a publishing committee. In 1840 the Reformed Church published a Sunday School hymnal.

Denominational Sunday School unions encouraged Sunday Schools to affiliate with their congregations in order to have a more unified ministry. This transition was well under way in Congregational churches by 1850. However in the Reformed Church the numerous union Sunday Schools in union churches made a denominational connection difficult.

In the first half of the Nineteenth Century the Sunday School became the principle educational tool of the church. This organized expression of pietism, conducted to a large extent by women, lifted up the importance of children, and unleashed new creativity in the production of religious literature for children.

PART B: GALLAUDET AND THE DEAF

Alice Cogswell (1805-1830) had spotted fever as a child, and as a result was deaf. Her father, Dr. Mason F. Cogswell, a physician in Hartford, Connecticut, wanted to help her. He read about projects in France and England that enabled the deaf to communicate with signs, and wondered if he would have to send Alice overseas to receive this instruction, or if an institution could be created in America.

At the instigation of Alice's father, the General Association of Connecticut in 1811 requested the clergy to do a census of the deaf. Their report the next year indicated 74 such persons, enough to justify an institution for them in Connecticut. Funds were collected to establish an institution. But who would go to Europe to learn the new form of communication and bring it back to Connecticut?

The Cogswell's neighbor had a son, Thomas H. Gallaudet (1787-1851), a student at Andover Seminary. Gallaudet took an interest in Alice, and communicated some words to her using gestures. In April, 1815, Dr. Cogswell gathered friends to form an association that would found an institution for the deaf in America. All except Gallaudet were convinced that the person to go to Europe and head the institution was Thomas Gallaudet.

Thomas Gallaudet (1787-1851). Following his graduation from Yale College in 1805, Thomas Gallaudet studied law, then tutored at Yale, then briefly went into business before entering Andover Seminary. Only after entrance into seminary did Gallaudet make a profession of religion and join a Congregational Church in Hartford. Licensed to preach and graduated from Andover in 1814, Gallaudet was reluctant to accept a call from a church because of poor health. Gallaudet founded the Connecticut Asylum for the Education of Deaf and Dumb Persons in 1817. In 1821 he married one of his students, Sophia Fowler (1798-1877), and they raised a family of hearing children that all conversed interchangeably with sounds or signs. In 1830 Gallaudet resigned his position at the asylum to devote himself to writing children's religious books. He wrote nine volumes of scripture biographies,

The Child's Book of the Soul, and several others widely used in Sunday Schools. The American Tract Society sold over 600,000 copies of Gallaudet's books, and the ABCFM translated them into at least nine other languages for use in mission schools. In 1835 the secret Look Upward Press Onward Society (LUPOS) hired Thomas Gallaudet to investigate the spiritual needs of German settlers in the West. As the agent of LUPOS, he was instrumental in bringing missionaries from Basel to the Mississippi Valley. Thomas Gallaudet also promoted public education, organized the first teachers' convention in 1830, and prepared textbooks. He served as chaplain of a prison in Hartford, 1837-45, and chaplain of the Retreat for the Insane at Hartford from 1838 to his death in 1851. In the life of Congregational minister Thomas Gallaudet, the missionary spirit of the time found expression in love for children and for those on the margins of society.

Gallaudet reluctantly accepted the call of his neighbor's association and went to Europe in 1815. Receiving a cold reception from philanthropists in England and Scotland, he found it necessary to go to France and to accept the help of a Roman Catholic. Abbé Sicard, director of the Royal School for Deaf-Mutes in Paris cooperated fully with Gallaudet who in three months had mastered Sicard's sign language. One of Sicard's assistants, a deaf-mute, Laurent Clerc, came to America with Gallaudet for three years to assist in the work.

The Connecticut Asylum for the Education of Deaf and Dumb Persons opened on April 20, 1817, supported by voluntary contributions and subsidized by the state. In his opening discourse Gallaudet claimed the asylum to be a sign of God's coming realm, partially fulfilling the scripture.

> Then the eyes of the blind shall be opened,
> and the ears of the deaf shall be unstopped.
> Then shall the lame man leap as an hart,
> and the tongues of the dumb sing. (*Isaiah* 35:5-6a)

Delegations from other cities came to Hartford to observe, in order to establish similar asylums elsewhere.

PART C: PEACE

In 1819 Jesse Appleton (1772-1819), President of Bowdoin College, was dying. When William Ladd, a prosperous farmer, visited him, Appleton spoke with joy of all the new benevolent societies of the day, and of their work. He was especially enthusiastic about the Peace Societies. Ladd recalled, "This was almost the first time I ever heard of them. The idea passed over my mind as the day-dream of benevolence; and so everyone views the subject, who does not examine it."

Ladd might have forgotten about this conversation had he not soon after read Noah Worcester's *Solemn Review of the Custom of War*. This short book, Ladd said, "riveted my attention in such a manner as to make it the principal object of my life to promote the cause of peace on earth and good-will to man." The Nineteenth Century's principal apostle of peace had received his call.

William Ladd (1778-1841), son of a merchant from Portsmouth, New Hampshire, had little interest in his studies at Harvard. In 1797 he left college to serve as a seaman on one of his father's ships. By his third voyage he was captain. When his father died in 1806 Ladd returned to Portsmouth to manage the business. When the War of 1812 put an end to peaceful commerce, Ladd retired to a farm in Minot, Maine. There he made a profession of faith and joined the Congregational Church. Following his encounter with the dying Appleton and his reading of Worcester's *Solemn Review*, Ladd devoted the rest of his life to writing and speaking on behalf of peace. In 1828 he brought together the Massachusetts, New York, and other Peace societies into the American Peace Society (APS). It was an uneasy alliance of the strict non-resisters of New York and the broad peace advocates of Massachusetts. Ladd, the general agent of the APS, promoted its broad educational efforts. In 1837 Ladd's Congregational Association in Maine granted him a license to preach "for the purpose of facilitating his labors in the cause of peace."

The peace movement never attained the popularity of other movements of benevolence. But it was an integral part of the network of benevolent societies engaging the interest and support of the same people. Peace was clearly at the center of the millennial vision that motivated the whole missionary/benevolent enterprise.

and they shall beat their swords into plowshares,
and their spears into pruning hooks:
nation shall not lift up sword against nation
neither shall they learn war anymore. (*Isaiah* 2:4b-c)

Christians disagreed on how God would use them to achieve this vision, but some felt compelled to action. Many more endorsed the dream if not the actions of the more militant advocates of peace. The organized peace movement in America began with David Dodge in New York and Noah Worcester in Massachusetts. William Ladd brought these two movements together and shaped a national movement.

David Low Dodge (1774-1852), organized the New York Peace Society in 1815. Dodge believed that the Gospel prohibited all war, revenge and fighting.   In conscience he could neither vote nor hold office in a government that used any form of coercion. Noah Worcester (1758-1837) settled at Thornton, New Hampshire, where his pastor, Experience Estabrook (1755-99) introduced him to pacifism. Estabrook opposed all war as immoral. In 1814 Worcester published his *Solemn Review*. He linked the peace movement to other benevolent enterprises moving toward the millennium. He advocated a Congress of Nations to standardize international law, and a World Court to settle disputes. In 1815 he organized the Massachusetts Peace Society. Although Worcester personally opposed all violence, his Peace Society was broad based, to include all who strove for peace.

Ladd, like Worcester, was personally committed to non-violence, but promoted a broad based peace society educating for peace and a Congress of Nations.

In the midst of a "religious war" between Unitarians and Trinitarians, a handful of peace advocates from both sides of the schism met together in harmony. Unitarian Noah Worcester was the inspiration behind the Peace Society that met at trinitarian Old South Church in Boston. The object of the society was to educate people on the evil of war until the thought became odious in the minds of people, and to promote alternatives to war.

Congregational minister Henry Clarke Wright (1797-1870) became an agent for the APS in 1836. Wright took an increasingly strong non-resistance position at odds with Ladd's vision of the Society. Wright and the abolitionist William Lloyd Garrison called a convention in September, 1838, which established the New England Non-Resistance Society. Members of this new society pledged, "All human governments *at present existing*, are based on the principles of violence and retaliation. Therefore I cannot approve or maintain any of them." True non-resisters did not serve in the military, vote, hold office, serve on juries, or sue in court.

Two peace societies with two very different philosophies competed for several years. The Non-Resistance Society called on people to personally commit to non-resistance. The Peace Society educated the populace on peace and advocated international alternatives to violence. Wright was the Non-Resistance Society's only agent, and when he left for Europe in 1843 the organization began to fall apart.

Congregational minister George C. Bekwith (1800-70), general secretary of the APS after Ladd's death, increased efforts to include people who were non-resisters in the Society, and promoted a Congress of Nations, World Court, and arbitration.

Although the numbers of peace activists were few, they influenced other movements of benevolence. The Foreign Missionary societies, although never identifying with the Peace Societies, saw themselves as heralds of peace. Gordon Hall (1784-1826), of the first company of ABCFM missionaries, claimed to be a non-resister. In 1813, before he had the opportunity to preach to a native, he had convinced three British officers in India to resign their commissions. The Massachusetts Sabbath School Society published a children's book, *The Little Soldier: A Plea for Peace* in 1837. Written anonymously by Sarah Tuttle, this book described the horrors of war and presented all of the arguments of the APS.

Agents of the Peace Society encouraged representative church bodies to pass resolutions in favor of peace. The Christian denomination in 1854 declared, "There is nothing presented in international war that is in accordance with either the letter or the Spirit of the gospel, and we cannot but regard it as a direct denigration of both . . . War alone never settles a difficulty between two nations; nor determines which of the two nations is in the right "

Pietists were not the only persons who dreamed of peace. Inspired by the millennial vision, they organized with others, developing strategies to make the dream a reality.

PART D: WOMEN IN MISSION AND THE CHURCH
Female Missionaries

Sybil Moseley (1792-1848) wanted to be a missionary. In 1818 it was not enough for a woman to believe this was God's call; she also had to receive the "providential call" of a marriage proposal from a man preparing to be a missionary. In December, 1818, she received such a proposal. This presented Sybil with a dilemma. On the one hand this appeared to be the answer to her prayers; on the other hand she felt no affection whatsoever for this man. She sought counsel from a pastor who advised her that if the Lord wanted her to become a missionary, the Lord "would make a way for her heart to go as well as her feet." Sybil said "no."

Sybil taught school in Canandaigua, New York, and continued to pray for an opportunity to be a missionary. On 28 September 1819 she attended the ordination of the first missionaries going to Hawaii, at Goshen, Connecticut. Driving up to the parsonage the night before, Sybil had difficulty understanding the directions to her lodgings. A kind man, Hiram Bingham, took her there. Hiram was one of the missionaries for Hawaii. He made inquiries of a half dozen people who knew her, then asked Secretary Samuel Worcester to set up a private interview. Hiram and Sybil were married October 11, (Thomas Gallaudet preached the sermon) and They embarked on October 23.

Sybil's story demonstrated both the opportunities and limitations women faced at that time. The missionary movement opened to women opportunities unlike any they had before; but a woman was still dependent on a man for the opportunity. There was no shortage of women ready to respond to the "providential call." Such a marriage proposal was a call to consecration in God's service, a call to usefulness, and a call to adventure.

The missionary wife had an overwhelming task. Besides presiding over a model home carefully scrutinized by the natives, she also had the responsibility of teaching and evangelizing the female half of the population. Missionary women were sometimes forced by circumstance to carry out tasks of spiritual leadership they were not allowed to do back home.

Missionary wives pleaded with the Board to send out single female missionaries to help them with home and children so they could do more missionary work. A few single women were allowed to serve as teachers in Indian missions.

Betsy Stockton (ca. 1798-1865) was the first single woman to be sent overseas by the ABCFM, and also the first African American. Assigned to assist a missionary family, she taught school in Hawaii for several years before returning home. Her school in Hawaii was the first school for the children of commoners. After her return to America Betsy Stockton taught briefly in a

Methodist mission school to American Indians in Canada, and in 1828 became director of a school for colored children ages 2 to 5 in Philadelphia.

Female Education

The supporters of missions, male and female, believed in female education. Previously, affluent women had received "ornamental" education – dancing, drawing, perhaps a little French – to make them attractive to suitors. Now Protestant educators advocated a regimen comparable to men's. Education for both women and men should promote healthy bodies, inquiring minds, and devout souls. Women, as well as men, should cultivate their intellectual powers, to prepare themselves to be useful in the world.

Joseph (1777-1833) and Rebecca (Hassletine) Emerson opened a seminary for women in Byfield, Massachusetts in 1816. This school moved when Congregational minister Emerson received a new call to a church, to Saugus, Massachusetts, in 1821, and to Wethersfield, Connecticut, in 1824. One of Emerson's students, Mary Lyon (1797-1849) established Mount Holyoke Female Seminary in 1837. Mount Holyoke used the same textbooks as men's colleges, and courses were demanding. The school gave its graduates competence and confidence. Every advance that women have made in the professions has been made possible because female education in either women's colleges or co-educational colleges, prepared women to do the job.

Women Praying and Preaching

Nancy Gove Cram (1776-1816) was a Free Will Baptist from Weare, New Hampshire. After her husband ran off with another woman, Nancy went west. After preaching through an interpreter to the Oneida Indians, she went to Charleston, New York in 1812. At the close of a funeral sermon by a Baptist minister, Cram knelt and prayed in public. Afterwards, people who had been deeply moved by her prayer asked her to hold meetings and preach. Cram's preaching resulted in revival. Feeling unqualified as a lay person to serve communion or to organize a church, she found male ministers of the Christian denomination who organized her converts into a congregation. After four years of preaching, Cram returned to New Hampshire, and soon died.

Abigail Hoag Roberts (1791-1841) was raised in upstate New York, the seventh of nine children. Her family of origin was active in the Religious Society of Friends, where it was not uncommon for women to speak in mixed assemblies. In 1809 she married Nathan Roberts, who consistently supported her religious work. Converted by Nancy Cram, Abigail immediately began speaking at her revival meetings, and continued after Cram's death to evangelize across New York and New Jersey. Her work resulted in the organization of at least fifteen Christian congregations. After 1827 her base of operations was the Milford, New Jersey, Christian Church. She retired from active evangelistic work in 1838 because of ill health. Never formally ordained, she was remembered by some as "acting pastor" of the Milford church.

Churches of the Christian denomination did not ordain women in the first half of the Nineteenth Century. Christians made a distinction between proclaiming the Word, which women had been doing since the *Acts of the Apostles*, and exercising the authority of the office of pastor, which they believed was forbidden to women (*LTH* 4:8-11). However, women played a significant role in the life of the laity-affirming Christian denomination.

Antoinette Brown Blackwell (1825-1921). At the age of nine, Antoinette Brown professed faith and was received into membership in the Henrietta, New York, Congregational Church. She participated actively in church life and pursued her education, never sharing with others her secret dream of entering the ministry. Following graduation from Oberlin College in 1847, she was allowed to study theology there, but at graduation was not given a degree because of her sex.

Following completion of her studies, Brown traveled across the northern United States speaking for Women's Rights and other reform movements. The Congregational Church in South Butler, New York, called her to be its pastor. She began her ministry in this small rural parish in the Spring of 1853. Without the support of the Congregational clergy or churches, the South Butler Church ordained Antoinette Brown to the Christian ministry on September 15, 1853 (*LTH* 4:77-79), the first woman to be ordained into the ministry in America

Antoinette Brown battled for women's rights and her own right to speak and preach throughout her life. Two weeks prior to her ordination, Brown attended a World Temperance Convention in New York City as a delegate from her congregation. She was not allowed to speak. Newspaper reports of this intelligent, modest young woman being hooted down by clergy, helped make it easier for other women to speak at public gatherings in the future. Brown became a celebrity with many invitations to lecture.

Antoinette Brown enjoyed the parish ministry. However she began to question some of the church's Calvinistic doctrine, including the doctrine of eternal punishment in Hell of all not predestined for heaven, including children. On her request, Antoinette Brown was dismissed from the ministry of the South Butler Church on July 20, 1854. For the remainder of her life, Antoinette Brown Blackwell, now a Unitarian, did social work in New York City, wrote on social and philosophical subjects, and spoke for women's rights. Antoinette Brown Blackwell, first woman ordained in America, was the lonely pioneer. It would be over a decade before another woman would be ordained in America.

CHAPTER NINE

Conquering the Valley and Beyond

	Old School Presbyterian	New School Presbyterian	Saybrook Platform Congregational	Cambridge Platform Congregational
Doctrine	Westminster Confession defines church's doctrine	Westminster Confession expresses church's faith	Savoy Version of Westminster Confession expresses church's faith	Westminster Catechism expresses church's faith
Polity	standing Presbyteries, etc., govern church	standing Presbyteries, etc., for consultation, also have authority	standing Associations for consultation, also have limited authority	vicinage counsels for consultation only
Local Church Highest Authority	session of ordained elders and pastor	session of ordained elders and pastor*	congregation	congregation
Lay Representation at Regional Bodies	ordained elders	ordained elders*	delegates elected by congregation	delegates elected by congregation
Heresy Trials	frequent; may appeal to Synod and General Assembly	seldom; may appeal to Synod and General Assembly	seldom; may appeal to Association	seldom; may call vicinage counsel (non-binding)
Ethnicity	predominantly Scotch-Irish	predominantly New Englanders	New Englanders	New Englanders
Missionary Societies	denominational	interdenominational	interdenominational	interdenominational
First Qualification of Clergy	Doctrine	Piety	Piety	Piety
Slavery	for, against, or neutral	against or neutral	against or neutral	against or neutral

FOUR BRANCHES OF THE ENGLISH-SPEAKING REFORMED TRADITION IN NORTH AMERICA, 1800-1850

The challenge to Christianize and civilize "The Valley" – the valley of the Mississippi River that stretched from the Appalachians to the Rocky Mountains – excited church leaders. All denominations expended funds and exerted effort to establish churches and civil society in "The Valley." In 1846 and 1848 with the annexation of territories beyond The Valley – Oregon Territory and the Mexican Cession – churches extended their work.

Only 110,000 people lived in the states and territories west of the Appalachians in 1790, about 3% of the total population of the United States. Eighty years later almost twenty-one million lived there; 54% of the nation's population. Territories west of the Mississippi River became part of the United States in 1803 with the Louisiana Purchase, but counted less than 400,000 people in 1830, or 3% of the nation. By 1870 almost seven million people, almost 18% of the nation, lived west of the Mississippi.

Congregational, Reformed and Evangelical Churches organized in the west in a variety of ways:

1. Colonies from the East or from Europe migrated as a unit to a new location in the West, bringing the church with them.
2. In the new settlements people worshiped together and requested their denomination or missionary society back East or in Europe to send a minister to organize them into a church.
3. Denominations and missionary societies sent preachers to the new settlements to preach wherever they could gather listeners, and to organize churches wherever they found sufficient interest.
4. Occasionally an ordained minister settled in the West, farmed, and gathered a congregation.
5. Organized churches with pastors reached out to establish new "preaching points" in their vicinity. Some grew into churches.
6. In later years the Sunday School missionary became the pioneer, helping new communities organize Sunday Schools. The home missionary followed to establish a church.

Most denominational strategies centered on funding the home missionary (#3 above). However all of these patterns contributed to the churches' conquest of The Valley and beyond.

PART A: CONGREGATIONAL/PRESBYTERIAN EXPANSION

Plans of Union and Accommodation

In 1801 the Presbyterian General Assembly and the General Association of Connecticut entered into a Plan of Union to avoid competition in the frontier settlements. The Plan provided guidelines for when minister and congregation were of different denominations, and also provided for mixed congregations (*LTH* 4:71).

The request of the Congregational Middle Association of New York to the Presbyterian Albany Synod to establish a more intimate relationship, resulted in the Accommodation Plan of 1808. Under this plan Congregational churches joined presbyteries while retaining their name, their form of internal government, and representation at presbytery by delegates (rather than by ordained elders). The Middle Association then joined the Synod with the same standing as a presbytery.

To better understand this history, it is helpful to think in terms of four branches of the English-speaking Reformed tradition in America. New England Congregationalism functioned under two distinct forms of church government, the Cambridge Platform, in Massachusetts, and the Saybrook Platform in Connecticut. The Presbyterian Church divided into the New Side and the Old Side from 1741 to 1758. United at the beginning of the Nineteenth Century, Presbyterian tension between Old School and New School intensified until the church divided in 1837, and remained divided until 1869. In both schisms, New Englanders of Congregational background were the major element in the New Side/School.

Saybrook Platform Congregationalists and New School Presbyterians both favored interdenominational missionary societies like the ABCFM, were more concerned about a pastor's piety than doctrine, and accepted anti-slavery agitation as an expression of Christian faith. New School Presbyterians approached doctrinal statements and regional bodies more casually than Old Schoolers. They seldom called for heresy trials. Saybrook Platform Congregationalists and New School

Presbyterians believed in the millennium, which was coming soon, where there would be no separate denomination. They mixed easily and saw themselves as one people with two names. As a result of the Plan of Union and Accommodation Plan: (1) Congregational home missionaries founded hundreds of Presbyterian churches; (2) New England Congregationalists entered the Presbyterian Church; (3) the development of distinctly Congregational regional bodies west of New England was postponed; and (4) about half the membership of the Presbyterian Church came from a Congregational background.

<u>Missionary Society of Connecticut</u>

The Missionary Society of Connecticut (MSC) described the missionary labors of Seth Williston in central New York in 1800: "From the first of March to the middle of December, he spent 36 weeks in the service of the society; during which time he preached almost every day, and attended conference as opportunity presented. He visited from house to house; catechized and instructed children in public and private; attended funerals, and visited the sick. He formed one church . . . admitted 17 persons into churches already formed . . . administered the Lord's Supper 6 times; and baptized 3 adults and 52 children."[1]

Seth Williston (1770-1851) was licensed by the North Association of Hartford in 1794, and sent to the "Chenango country" (the counties of Broome, Delaware, Chenango, Cortland, Tompkins, Tioga and southern Cayuga, New York) by the General Association in 1796. Williston could not offer the sacraments or organize churches, so he requested ordination. On June 7, 1797, the North Association of Hartford made Williston Congregationalism's first ordained evangelist, and first person ordained without a call to a church. Williston traveled constantly, talked religion with everyone he met, and stayed in the homes of any who showed him hospitality (although he had difficulty sleeping in some beds, "being disturbed by creatures much smaller than myself"). He was always on the lookout for spiritually alive persons with whom to organize a church.

The adventures of Seth Williston were repeated by over a thousand other home missionaries, Congregational, Reformed, Evangelical and Christian, who followed the frontier west.

The General Association of Connecticut began sending missionaries to the "new settlements" of northern New England and upstate New York in 1780. At first the Association recruited experienced settled pastors to itinerate (travel) through the new settlements for four month periods. The Association paid their travel expenses and pulpit supply in their absence; their congregation continued to pay their salary. However these short term tours did not have lasting effects. The General Association settled on a new plan: to send licensed ministers to the new settlements full-time to preach and gather churches. A licensed minister was a person who had completed studies for the ministry and had been approved by an Association to preach in churches, with the understanding that he was an acceptable candidate for ordination.

Inspired by the formation of the London Missionary Society in 1795, the General Association of Connecticut organized the Missionary Society of Connecticut in 1798 for the purpose of sending missionaries to the new settlements. Most were newly ordained evangelists like Seth Williston.

Missionaries from newly organized missionary societies in Massachusetts joined missionaries of the MSC, and organized churches on the Plan of Union. By 1816 at least 200 Congregational churches had been gathered in New York. The Congregational associations of New York were absorbed into the Presbyterian Church through the Accommodation Plan.

Connecticut's claim to a strip of land "from ocean to ocean" based on a royal charter was settled by allowing Connecticut to reserve for its use the land in a region called "New Connecticut" or the "Western Reserve" in northeast Ohio.[2]

The MSC sent Joseph Badger (1757-1846) to New Connecticut in 1800, where he organized Congregational churches. Badger enjoyed cooperation with Presbyterian ministers and people coming from Pennsylvania. Congregational churches of the Western Reserve gathered in 1814 to organize an Association, but one Presbyterian minister, Thomas Barr, pleaded that this action would exclude him. Instead, the churches organized the Presbytery of Grand River. All clergy belonged to presbytery, while the congregations in their local affairs functioned as Congregational churches. Proclaiming a common faith, Congregationalists and Presbyterians worked in harmony in the Presbyterian Synod, organizing churches that internally resembled New England Congregational churches. Other MSC missionaries traveled as far as Missouri, organizing Presbyterian churches.

American Home Missionary Society

In 1825 several Andover students began to advocate for a national home mission society. They envisioned a society with, "no sectional interests, – no local prejudices, – no party animosities, – no sectarian views." They also advocated a new system. This new society would settle educated clergy in each community and subsidize local pastors' salaries until the local church could assume full responsibility.

These student appeals led to the formation of the American Home Missionary Society (AHMS) in 1826. The predominantly Presbyterian United Domestic Missionary Society (UDMS), joined immediately and in effect became the AHMS. Most of the New England societies affiliated in 1828. The MSC became auxiliary in 1832. As a matter of policy, the AHMS organized Presbyterian churches, believing this to be the most effective basis for unified work.

Theron Baldwin (1801-70), a student at Yale Divinity School, talked to his fellow students about going to the frontier as a group, serving churches, and together founding a seminary. In 1829 seven students signed a solemn pledge with this intent. This Illinois Association met regularly at Yale, sharing their prayers and their preparations for this venture. Eventually this "Yale band" included eleven home missionaries in the service of the AHMS, who settled in Illinois beginning in 1829, and founded Illinois College in Jacksonville. Through the remainder of the Nineteenth Century, several other "bands" of seminary students, who had studied together, settled in proximity to each other, to develop church and civilization on the newly opened frontier.

<u>Collapse of the Plan of Union</u>

For a decade, each annual meeting of the Presbyterian General Assembly experienced intensified polarization. In the eyes of the Old School, the Plan of Union was corrupt. Local churches that belonged to presbyteries were not organized in a Presbyterian way. Lay persons who were not ordained elders sat, spoke, and voted at presbytery, synod and general assembly. They blamed the AHMS and believed that missionary societies should be under the direct control of the church. In 1837 with an Old School majority, the General Assembly excinded (ejected) three synods in upstate New York and the Western Reserve Synod in Ohio, called on other synods to correct alleged abuses, revoked the Plan of Union, and directed the AHMS to stay out of its presbyteries. After a year of chaos, the excinded synods, with churches from other synods, reorganized as the (new school) Presbyterian Church. New School Presbyterians continued to work with Congregationalists, the Plan of Union, and the AHMS.

Meanwhile Congregational discontent with the Plan of Union had been growing. It was an unequal union. Congregational churches belonging to presbyteries faced steady pressure to conform to the Presbyterian pattern. As the conflict within the Presbyterian Church intensified, some Congregational churches decided to leave presbyteries and organize associations. For a few congregations the reluctance of the Presbyterian Church to take a stand against slavery was a reason to withdraw.

In 1846, at the invitation of the General Association of Michigan, midwestern Congregationalists met in Michigan City, Indiana, and called for more support for Congregational churches in the West and an end to the Plan of Union. In 1852 the first national gathering of Congregationalists, the Albany Convention, unanimously renounced the Plan of Union (*LTH* 4:71). As one delegate explained it, "they have milked our Congregational cow but they have made nothing but Presbyterian butter and cheese." The Convention also established a fund for the erection of church buildings in the West. Congregationalists continued to work with the AHMS for church planting, but became more insistent that Congregational churches be established. New School Presbyterian support for the AHMS declined, and in 1861 the New School withdrew from the AHMS, leaving it a Congregational agency.

<u>Congregational Home Missions</u>

After the Albany Convention, Congregationalism grew in the West from three sources: (1) Congregational churches withdrawing from presbyteries; (2) independent Congregational churches that had never joined presbyteries; and (3) new churches organized by the AHMS. Regional associations and state organizations were established. Wherever Congregationalists established statewide organizations, the churches gained strength and the fellowship grew.

<u>Welsh Congregationalists</u>

Welsh Protestants migrated to America throughout the Nineteenth Century, to the coal regions of Pennsylvania and farming areas of Ohio, New York, Illinois, Wisconsin, Iowa and other states. In 1900 over 267,000 persons who were either born in Wales or their children were living in the United States.

The Puritan movement of the Seventeenth Century and the Evangelical movement of the Eighteenth Century deeply effected Wales. Three Protestant denominations developed: Union of Welsh Independents (Congregational), Calvinistic Methodists (Presbyterian), and Baptists.

Welsh communities in America organized union churches on a Congregational pattern. When their numbers became sufficient, Baptists and Presbyterians organized separate churches, leaving the original church Congregational. Smaller communities maintained union churches which organized with the Congregationalists. By 1872 the

Welsh had organized 154 Congregational churches in the United States.

Welsh Protestants brought with them a love of music, a repertoire of Welsh hymns, and the ability to sing congregational hymns in four part harmony. They brought strong Sunday Schools, for both children and adults, and a high level of Biblical literacy. Most Welsh pastors were self educated and bi-vocational, thoroughly examined by representatives of the churches before ordination. Preachers, choirs and members from the Welsh churches in an area gathered annually for several days of preaching and music, called a *gymanva*.

Welsh immigrants arrived at Philadelphia on the *Maria* in 1795 and settled in Ebensburg, Pennsylvania, where they organized a Congregational Church in 1796. Some of this group continued west, reaching Cincinnati, Ohio. Another early colony developed around Utica, New York (1801). Welsh Congregationalists organized their own Associations, or *gymanvas* in several states. Welsh churches both received and gave aid to the AHMS, and participated in state Congregational bodies.

PART B: REFORMED CHURCH EXPANSION

German Reformed people from Pennsylvania migrated south along the eastern slope of the Appalachians to Virginia and North Carolina, and westward across the mountains into the Valley of the Mississippi. Larger numbers of Reformed people migrated directly from Germany and Switzerland to The Valley. The Pennsylvania Germans and the new Germans shared the *Heidelberg Catechism* and the German language, but little else. In America for a century, the Pennsylvania Germans had begun a process of accommodation:

- To become bilingual and increasingly English-speaking.
- To separation of church and state, and the consequences of that policy for church financing.
- To revivals, in some cases with "new measures."
- To voluntary societies, including Sunday Schools.

The new German immigrants knew none of this. The Reformed Church in the United States, by including both communities, became more diverse.

Ohio Synod

German Reformed pastors followed settlers from Pennsylvania into Ohio. Jacob Christman (ca. 1745-1810), ordained at the request of six North Carolina congregations in 1798, began preaching on the Western Reserve, on January 29, 1804, at Springboro. He organized a congregation and celebrated communion there on May 29, 1804. In 1809 he moved to Ohio where he died the following year. Other pastors soon followed.

In 1820 the five Reformed pastors and fifty congregations in Ohio organized the Ohio Classis. Pastors in Ohio Classis began privately educating persons for ministry. The annual journey across the mountains to attend synod for examination and ordination was a hardship for pastors and elders. However synod would not delegate to Ohio Classis the authority to ordain.

In 1824 the Ohio Classis reorganized as a synod. This was understood to be a geographic separation only. The earlier synod, now called the Eastern Synod, and the new Ohio Synod, held the same faith and communicated and cooperated with each other.

In 1842 the two synods agreed to each send two delegates to the other synod to promote cooperation. The Ohio Synod established a Board of Mission in 1845, which depended on its eastern counterpart for financial support. The Ohio Synod continued to plant new churches in Ohio and in 1840 followed German migrants into Indiana.

Eastern Synod

The German Reformed Synod in 1812 asked all congregations to take a missionary collection, and proposed sending licensed seminary graduates on missionary tours of two to three months. The following year Synod resolved that *all* licensed graduates go on a missionary tour before taking a charge.

George Leidy (1793-1879) offered himself to the synod to do missionary work in 1819. As a result, the synod elected a Missionary Committee which examined, ordained and commissioned Leidy to be missionary to Virginia, North Carolina, South Carolina and Tennessee. Leidy quickly visited thirty congregations, but found that southern heat destroyed his health. He served struggling charges in northern Virginia, western Maryland and western Pennsylvania for the rest of his ministry.

The German Reformed Synod made several attempts at organizing its Home Mission work. However it could not agree on how the work should be done. In 1821 several members of the Synod participated with Presbyterians and Dutch Reformed in organizing the United Domestic Missionary Society, which later became the AHMS. In 1826 the Eastern Synod, hoping to stimulate interest among the laity, created a Missionary Society, a voluntary association with dues of one dollar. In 1832 the Synod reversed itself, electing its own Board of Missions, directly accountable to Synod. In 1834 the Synod's Board of Missions established an auxiliary relationship with the American Home Missionary Society (AHMS). By 1837 the AHMS was supporting thirteen Reformed ministers. However that year the cooperation ended. The classes kept their funds, supporting neither the AHMS nor the Synod Board of Missions.

The 1847 Synod reorganized its missions, appointing Samuel Miller (1815-73) its first Missionary Superintendent. Miller toured the West that year on behalf of both Eastern and Ohio Synods. Slowly the Board received support, and by 1857 seventeen missionaries in the Midwest were receiving aid from the Board.

<u>The Reformed Church's Southern Frontier</u>

German Reformed settlers in the Shenandoah Valley of Virginia and western North Carolina had throughout the Eighteenth Century received only an occasional missionary tour from members of the coetus in Pennsylvania.

Johannes Braun (a.k.a. John Brown; 1771-1850), born in Oldenburg, came to America in 1797 and affiliated with Otterbein's congregation in Baltimore. Braun studied with Reformed pastors, was licensed in 1800, ordained in 1803, then served Reformed Churches scattered over six counties in the Shenandoah Valley. For thirty-five years he was the only settled Reformed pastor in Virginia.

North Carolina Reformed churches survived for a while with only occasional pastors. The North Carolina classis organized in 1831 with sixteen congregations and five ministers.

Western Expansion

Three colonies of Reformed settlers from Europe established strong Reformed centers in the Midwest. Reformed people from Ladbergen, Westphalia, came to America in 1830, settled at New Knoxville, Ohio, and organized a church in 1838. People from the Swiss canton of Glarus began to settle in New Glarus, Wisconsin, in 1845. A company of immigrants from the German principality of Lippe came to America on the *Agnes von Bremen* in 1847, and settled in the Town of Herman, Sheboygan County, Wisconsin. They joined the Reformed Church in the United States in 1854, and developed a theological school called Mission House.

From these scattered colonies and other settlements of Reformed people from Pennsylvania, Germany and Switzerland, the Reformed Church expanded across the Midwest. German Reformed home missions struggled, not always successfully, to keep up with the migration of its people (See *LTH* 4:99).

PART C: THE EVANGELICAL UNIONISTS

The Evangelical Church of the Union

On September 27, 1817, King Friedrich Wilhelm III (1770-1840; ruled 1797-1840) of Prussia called on the Lutheran and Reformed to unite in a common communion service on the 300th anniversary of the Reformation, October 31, 1817 (*LTH* 4:36), thus forming one united church. This movement of church union quickly spread to other principalities until about half the Protestants of Germany were affiliated with union *Landeskirchen*. The King acted out of a desire to establish order after the chaos of the Napoleonic Wars. In the face of the ferment of ideas in that period, and the challenge of rationalism, the differences between Lutheran and Reformed appeared trivial.

Most people embraced with joy the actions of the monarchs. According to one observer of the unifying communion service, "After the close of the service, members of the till now separated churches embraced each other with brotherly affection, and walked hand in hand towards their dwellings. Especially did the married of different confessions, who in the greatest numbers presented themselves at the table of the Lord, testify their joy and gratitude to God, that they in future could solemnize this feast of love with their partners and children."

Basel and related missionary societies greeted with joy this affirmation of the catholic principle on which they were founded.

<u>A Missionary Strategy for America</u>

Following the Napoleonic Wars, Germans began coming to America in increasing numbers. The early immigrants were poor peasants, fleeing from famine and depression. Following the defeat of revolutions in 1830 and 1848, large numbers of educated Germans with rationalist views came to America looking for political freedom. But most immigrants were farmers of modest means. Some Germans settled in cities, but most moved west, seeking farmland. The area around Saint Louis soon became the largest of several centers of German settlement. Religious Germans appealed to Basel and the other societies for pastors.

Frederick A. Rauch (1806-41), who was affiliated with the unionist Evangelical Church in Germany before he came to America, taught at the German Reformed seminary. He advocated a new strategy in missions to Germans in America. Others believed that the Pennsylvania German churches should work with the new immigrants. Rauch argued in a series of articles in the AHMS's *Home Missionary* in 1835-36 that German missionary societies should be invited to send missionaries to organize unionist churches among the Germans in the west. He reasoned that

- The German spoken by Pennsylvanians was inferior to the German spoken by the new immigrants.
- Pennsylvania's Lutheran and Reformed churches did not have enough pastors to care for themselves.
- The new immigrants preferred united churches, and old divisions should not be reintroduced.

Initial Outreach of the Missionary Societies

The Basel Mission and its offspring were primarily interested in missions to non-Christians. Appeals for pastors from the German diaspora were met only after the needs of other fields were met. Missionaries to America were often persons who were not as well qualified as others who went to foreign fields. The societies also expected the churches in America to support the missionaries once they arrived. However, the missionaries were expected to continue to correspond with Basel, to cooperate with other missionaries sent from Basel, and to consult with the Basel Mission on important questions.

Friedrich Schmid (1807-83), of Basel Mission, arrived in Ann Arbor, Michigan, on August 20, 1833. He soon organized and gave pastoral leadership to Zion Church in Ann Arbor, and frequently visited Protestant German communities across Michigan.

Basel soon sent more missionaries to America in response to requests from Germans in the Saint Louis area. Two missionaries who arrived in 1834 settled with German communities in Ohio. The following year Basel sent Johann Jakob Riess (1811-55), who finally reached Centerville, Illinois, in the Saint Louis area.

Barmen mission sent Philipp Jakob Heyer (b. 1807) to Borneo in 1834. Heyer became ill, and when it became evident that he was unfit for tropical service, the Board sent him to America. His first assignment was to go to the American Indians of Oregon, and secondly, if that was not practical, to the Germans in America. Heyer reached Missouri in 1836 and accepted a call to a German church. The following year Barmen Mission sent Louis Eduard Nollau for the Indian mission. The Barmen Board finally gave up on American Indian missions, and allowed Nollau to remain in Missouri.

Louis Eduard Nollau (1810-69) experienced a religious conversion and entered the Rhenish Mission Institute in Barmen, Germany. In 1837 he was sent by the Barmen Mission to America, to work with the Indians of Oregon Territory. However on the way he stopped in Missouri and ministered to the German immigrants there. He gathered the verein of pastors in his home, helped to found the seminary, a hospital and an orphans' home.

In December, 1835, the Basel directors received a letter from some Connecticut Congregationalists, requesting missionaries to the Germans of the west. The New Englanders represented a secret society called "Looking Upward, Pressing Onward Society" (LUPOS). Concerned about Catholic efforts to evangelize the west, LUPOS requested Protestant German missionaries to evangelize Catholic Germans in the Mississippi Valley. LUPOS offered to fund the missionaries.

Basel sent Georg W. Wall (1811-67) and Joseph A. Rieger (1811-69), who arrived in New York City May 31, 1836. After consulting with their sponsors in Hartford, (See *LTH* 4:38) Wall and Rieger went west. The financial panic of 1837 sunk LUPOS, which gave no more financial support. Wall became pastor in Saint Louis, Rieger in Alton, Illinois.

In America there were no *Landeskirchen* for the missionaries to join, only a complex pattern of competing Lutheran synods. A few joined Lutheran synods, but most preferred to operate in a unionist spirit.

<u>Irenic Pietism</u>

The theological divisions and ecclesial unions of Germany shaped the development of German churches in America in the Nineteenth Century. German religious thought consisted of three competing factions.

1. *Pietists* persisted in their prayer meetings, family prayers and missionary societies, emphasizing the inner relationship with God.
2. *Rationalists* rejected the divine origin of the Bible, the divinity of Christ, the possibility of revelation, and miracles. They ridiculed all religion as superstition.
3. *Confessionalists* clung to the Reformation confessions, emphasizing right doctrine, rejecting church union and avoiding contact with other communions.

Within each group were varying degrees of belief:

1. Separatist pietists judged and condemned the lack of piety in others, while more irenic pietists respected and sought to cooperate with all.
2. Some rationalists scoffed at all talk of God and religion. Others continued to believe in God and to value the church, but through the use of reason selectively questioned certain doctrines and practices. These moderate rationalists often called their churches "Protestant."
3. Old Lutherans restricted communion to their own synod. Other Lutherans, just as firmly attached to the Reformation confessions, recognized a broader fellowship.

In America the boundary between the irenic pietists and Protestants was not firm. They participated in each other's ordinations, and local congregations often changed their affiliation.

The Kirchenverein Des Westen

Louis Nollau of Gravois Settlement, and George Wall of Saint Louis, invited other United Evangelical pastors to meet at Nollau's parsonage on 14 October 1840. The reason was, "the need of fellowship and fraternal cooperation." The meeting was also a defensive action, to keep from being swallowed up by the eastern Lutherans and the "Ultra Lutherans" who became the Missouri Synod.

Nollau and Wall were joined by three other pastors; two more were unable to attend but later signed the minutes. Of the seven, two were sent by Barmen Mission, three by Basel, one by the Ohio Synod of the Reformed Church, and the last was a farmer, called by a church, who returned to Germany, passed his examinations, was ordained, then came back to his church in Missouri.

The ministers who met in Nollau's parsonage in 1840 agreed to organize *Der Deutsche Evangelische Kirchenverein des Westens*. They called it a *verein*, rather than a synod, because *verein*, translated "union" "association" or "conference" implied local church autonomy and a smaller scale organization than a synod. The verein was to be composed of pastors and churches. However throughout its history few churches joined and it was principally a pastors' association. The verein examined candidates for ministry and accepted candidates and ministers arriving from Europe on probation for a year before ordaining or receiving them. The 1840 meeting also named a committee to prepare a catechism and another committee to prepare a book of worship. The verein affirmed the confessional statements of "our Evangelical mother church in Germany" (*LTH* 4:45) although there was no formal connection. The verein was formally constituted at its next meeting, May 3, 1841.

The rationalist press viciously attacked the new verein (*LTH* 4:46). The result was a libel suit, the removal of one pastor from office, and the division of another church. The Lutheran Synod of the West also criticized the verein as one more sect in a land with too many denominations. But the AHMS, which only supported ministers with standing in an evangelical denomination, was grateful that the verein now provided that authorization. The new verein struggled for several years with a handful of pastors, carefully examining its new arrivals from Germany. The AHMS from 1841 to 1861 subsidized twenty-one verein pastors and sent boxes of clothes.

Verein pastors generally served a church, and preached at numerous other locations, many of which developed into churches. Verein pastors promoted biblical knowledge, and cultivated a personal relationship with God. A few pastors, generally those subsidized by the AHMS, reported revivals and counted conversions, but most verein pastors made no such claims.

Many congregations held prayer meetings (*stunden*) at which any person could speak and pray. The churches of the verein observed the church year, and Lent was a season of intense spirituality – sometimes with daily services – calling for repentance and conversion.

Membership requirements varied greatly. In Germany persons at age fourteen who could recite the catechism were confirmed. German congregations in America that leaned toward rationalism received anyone who paid dues. But the AHMS insisted that it would only aid churches that required "evidence of a new heart, of having been born again by the spirit of God," for membership. The verein defended the rite of Confirmation but added to the confirmation process a personal interview of candidates for membership concerning their spiritual life.

Louis Nollau wrote the *Evangelical Catechism*, published in 1847. Andreas Irion (1823-70) revised it in 1862 by simplifying language to facilitate memorization (*LTH* 4:53). Although intended for instruction, the Catechism came to be viewed as a doctrinal statement.

Worship in the verein followed different German liturgies, greatly simplified by frontier circumstances. Further deliberation led to the *Evangelische Agende* (Book of Worship) published by the verein in 1857. Although the verein maintained the right of free prayer, it was unpopular because of its abuse by rationalists. Singing was complicated by the variety of hymn books brought from Germany until the verein published the *Evangelische Gesangbuch* (Hymnal) in 1861 (See *LTH* 4:56).

Three documents, the *Evangelical Catechism, Evangelical Book of Worship*, and *Evangelical Hymnal* created denominational identity and unified churches of the verein.

Every congregation with sufficient resources conducted a parochial school. Many churches also established Sunday Schools, which covered the same material as the day schools, and were viewed as a mission activity of the church.

The Kirchenverein grew rapidly. By 1865 the verein had 122 pastors in nine states. But the great majority of churches served by Kirchenverein pastors never joined the verein. More congregations requested pastors than the verein could provide. However, the verein believed it had a missionary responsibility to reach out to unchurched communities with the gospel.

In 1854 the verein appointed its first *reiseprediger* (itinerant preacher), Theodore H. Dresel. Provided by the verein with a horse and saddle bags, Dresel traveled from his base in Burlington, Iowa, across Iowa, Illinois and Wisconsin. The verein gave instructions to its second reiseprediger, Karl Hoffmeister (1819-97), in 1855, to not intrude on other denominations, and to avoid all appearance of proselytism. Hoffmeister also traveled throughout Iowa. The reisprediger was dropped in 1857 for lack of funds.

The United Evangelical Synod

The Kirchenverein was not the only group of German unionists in America. The German United Evangelical Synod of North America organized in Cincinnati, Ohio, in 1844. In 1854 the Synod organized two districts, centered around Buffalo and Chicago.

C. F. Soldan organized the Buffalo section of the United Evangelical Synod, founded Trinity Evangelical Church in Rochester, New York, in 1842, and became pastor of Saint Paul's Church, Buffalo, in 1845.

Karl Siebenpfeiffer (1832-82) became the next leader of the Buffalo area unionists. Born in Wachenheim, Bavarian Rheinpfalz, he graduated from Heidelberg in 1856. As there was an abundance of pastors in Germany, he came to America, served several churches in the Buffalo area, and went to Trinity Church, Rochester, in 1862. Siebenpfeiffer emerged as the leader of a group of ten pastors who in 1858 withdrew from the United Evangelical Synod and organized what later became the German United Evangelical Synod of the East. This Buffalo group included two pastors from Cleveland, Ohio, and one from Evansville, Indiana. They withdrew from the United Evangelical Synod because they were offended by the domineering personalities of two Synod officers, Josef Fischer and Josef Hartman.

The first German church in Chicago, Saint Pauls, organized in 1843. Although most of the congregation was unionist, their first pastor was Old Lutheran. The Missouri Synod Lutheran Church was organized at St. Paul's on April 26, 1847. The congregation refused to join that synod, and fired the Old Lutheran pastor. Josef Fischer served the church from 1848 to 1851. Then Joseph Hartman (1824-86) had a long pastorate, 1851 to 1885.

Born in Bornheim, Rheinpfalz, September 18, 1824, Hartman was educated at Bonn and Utrecht, and came to America in 1849. After two years of ministry in New York State, Hartman went to Chicago. He immediately joined Fischer as a leader of the United Evangelical Synod.

In May, 1859, twelve pastors met at Saint Paul's church, withdrew from what was left of the United Evangelical Synod, and organized the German United Evangelical Synod of the Northwest, with Hartman as President and Fischer Vice-President. They withdrew because they believed rationalism was too strong in the United Evangelical Synod, which soon disappeared.

These two synods, centered in Buffalo and Chicago. both had warm relations with the Kirchenverein, and made use of their worship book, song book, and catechism.

<u>Evangelical Protestants</u>

Many of the independent unionist churches identified with the rationalist Evangelical Protestant movement. The Evangelical Protestants affirmed the *Augsburg Confession* and *Heidelberg Catechism* as "norms for its faith," but were less dogmatic than other churches. This group embraced new theological currents from Germany, and was more affirming of amusements and Sabbath recreation than other churches.

Evangelical Protestants in America identified with the unionist churches in Germany, but predated them. A Lutheran-Reformed union church in Pittsburgh, organized in 1782, reorganized in 1812 as one united congregation.[3] This first German Evangelical Protestant Church in America organized several other congregations in the Pittsburgh area. Holy Ghost Church in Saint Louis (1836) also had fellowship with this group. In 1862 August Kroell (1806-74) and Gustav William Eisenlohr (1811-81), Evangelical Protestant pastors in Cincinnati, organized the Protestant Union of Free Christian Congregations of North America. Because each congregation fiercely guarded its independence, this Protestant Union never grew.

<u>Reflection on Chapters 5 through 9</u>

Pietism, a particular movement of piety, grew through two Great Awakenings, created a new denominational family, divided another, and gave birth to the missionary movement. The missionary movement called on the pious to put into action the prayer *thy kingdom come*. The missionary-minded Christian prayed and gave money for that kingdom. The mission could be the proclamation of the gospel on the other side of the earth, founding churches on the frontier, printing tracts, Bibles or religious newspapers, education of ministers, women, the deaf, or the children of one's own neighborhood, or the advancement of world peace. Catholicity was another characteristic of the coming kingdom embraced by the missionary societies and churches. In the face of the multiplicity of denominations, the formation of the Christian Connection, the Congregational-Presbyterian Plan of Union, the Lutheran-

Reformed union churches, and the Kirchenverein were all attempts to affirm unity in Christ. Pietism expressed a liberal concern for the spiritual and material well being of all persons of any color or gender. Where piety was rated more highly than orthodoxy, greater variety of doctrine was accepted. One other mission, most controversial of all, remains to be examined: the movement to abolish the institution of slavery.

******

[1] "Conference" could be any church meeting, and frequently meant a meeting to examine candidates for membership in a congregation. When attending funerals he usually preached.

[2] The Western Reserve included the modern counties of Ashtabula, Lake, Geauga, Portage, Cuyahoga, Lorain, Medina, Erie, Huron, most of Summit and Mahoning and parts of Ashland and Ottawa.

[3] Now called Smithfield UCC, Pittsburgh, Pennsylvania.

CHAPTER TEN

Slavery and Freedom

PART A: AFRICAN AMERICANS AND SLAVERY BEFORE THE ABOLITIONIST MOVEMENT

<u>Lemuel Haynes and Phillis Wheatley</u>

Lemuel Haynes (1753-1833) He never knew his father, knew only that he was Black. His mother, who was White, refused to recognize him. At the age of five months he was bound as an indentured servant until the age of twenty-one. Lemuel Haynes served David Rose of Granville, Massachusetts. His master taught him religion, and his mistress treated him as one of the family; Haynes attended public school. When the church at Granville, without a pastor, asked Haynes to lead a service and read a sermon, he read his own sermon.

After serving in the Revolution, Haynes taught school in Wintonbury, Connecticut (now Bloomfield). Haynes was licensed to preach in 1780 and for five years preached in Granville. In 1783 he married Elizabeth Babbit, a white school teacher and member of the congregation. The Litchfield Association in Connecticut ordained Haynes in 1785. He served congregations in Torrington, Connecticut, West Parish of Rutland (1788-1818) and Manchester, Vermont, and Granville, New York. Haynes was a New Light Congregationalist whose writings expressed that group's theological concerns. Only rarely did he write about slavery (*LTH* 5:31).

Phillis Wheatley (ca. 1753-84) No one knew the age of the little African girl sold on a Boston dock in 1761. As she was losing her baby teeth, they guessed she was seven or eight. John and Susannah Wheatley bought her, and they called her Phillis Wheatley. The Wheatleys treated Phillis like one of the family, not like their other slaves. She had a room in the main house, and ate at table with the family except when they had guests. Within sixteen months of her arrival Phillis understood English and was reading the Bible. While a teenager, Phillis wrote a poem, "On the Death of the Reverend George Whitefield," which became popular in America and England among Whitefield's admirers. That same year, 1770, Phillis was received into membership at Old South Church, Boston. In 1772 the Wheatleys gave Phillis her freedom, and she went to England, where she published *Poems on Various Subjects, Religious and Moral*. Back in Boston she married in 1778 John Peters, a free Negro from Newport, Rhode Island. Phillis Wheatley Peters wrote a few more poems, including *Liberty and Peace*. She worked in a boarding house, where she died in 1784.

Lemuel Haynes and Phillis Wheatley had much in common. As Black people in a White world, both won acceptance by achievements valued by that White world; both also experienced discrimination. Both treasured the heart-felt religious faith of the Great Awakening. That faith was the focus of their life's work. Neither wrote principally on issues of race and slavery. But when they did address these subjects, their views were clear: Both Haynes and Wheatley were convinced that the ideals of the Declaration of Independence would soon lead to freedom and equality for all. Both had the good fortune of having masters who respected them as children of God. Haynes and Wheatley demonstrated that persons of African ancestry were not inferior in intellect or piety to white New Englanders, by the standards of the latter.

<u>Slavery and the Slave Trade</u>

In North America slavery became equated with race. Slave traders from Newport, Rhode Island, and other northern seaports transported over half a million Africans to Britain's North American colonies, and more to the West Indies. Most of those transported to the southern colonies worked as field hands; of the smaller number transported to the north, most worked as domestic servants. Most African Americans were not as fortunate as Lemuel Haynes and Phillis Wheatley. Most never had the opportunity to learn to read, or to use their intellects for anything other than hoeing tobacco or picking cotton. Racial prejudice justified slavery, and slavery reinforced racial prejudice. Fear of rebellion made slave owners more severe. Marriage and family were not legally recognized for the enslaved in some states, and male masters could rape female enslaved servants with impunity. By 1790 24% of the United States population was of African origin: 694,000 enslaved and 63,000 free.

<u>Early Opponents</u>

Most white Americans accepted slavery as a feature of society that had always existed. A few raised their voices in opposition. Samuel Sewall was asked to give legal advice to Adam, an enslaved person promised freedom who had not received it. Sewall turned to his Bible, concluded that slavery was contrary to the Word of God, and in 1700 wrote *The Selling of Joseph* (*LTH* 5:30). Samuel Hopkins, the disciple of Jonathan Edwards, served the Congregational Church in Newport, Rhode Island – the capital of the slave trade – from 1770 to 1803. He condemned slavery in *Dialogue Concerning the Slavery of the Africans* in 1776, and organized an anti-slavery society in 1789. The Methodist Church, when it organized in 1784 prohibited its members from owning enslaved persons. James O'Kelly condemned slavery in *Essay on Negro Slavery* in 1789, and continued his opposition to the institution after he left the Methodist Church. Barton Stone favored the excommunication of slave holders in 1800, and declared in the deed of emancipation of his enslaved in January, 1801, "that involuntary unconditional slavery is *inconsistent* with the principles of Christianity." He and his wife moved from Kentucky to Illinois in 1834 as it was the only legal way to free the enslaved persons she had inherited. Virginia Reformed pastor Johannes Braun spoke against slavery in 1812 (*LTH* 5:32).

<u>Post-Revolutionary Movement of Abolition</u>

The ideals of the Revolution led to action against slavery in the United States. Beginning in 1780 the states from Pennsylvania north abolished slavery. In some states this was a gradual process taking several decades. The Northwest Ordinance of 1787 prohibited slavery from the western areas north of the Ohio River. In 1808 Congress abolished the slave trade. Anti-slavery societies promoted abolition in every state of the union. The abolition of slavery in the North did not guarantee full civil rights to Americans of African descent.

PART B: THE AMERICAN ANTI-SLAVERY MOVEMENT

The first national Negro Convention, held August 1830 in Philadelphia, condemned the activity of the American Colonization Society. They saw in its activity a program to get rid of Blacks by sending them to Africa. The convention insisted that colonization was not a solution to the problem of slavery; African Americans needed to be granted freedom and full civil rights as Americans. This strong position led some White Americans to re-examine their support of colonization and to become more committed to abolition. The successful abolition of slavery in Jamaica in 1833 convinced more benevolent Americans that immediate emancipation could work in America. From 1830 to 1863 anti-slavery sentiment grew in the northern United States, while pro-slavery sentiment in the South hardened.

Arthur and Lewis Tappan

Arthur and Lewis Tappan Arthur Tappan (1786-1865) of Northampton, Massachusetts, went to New York City in 1815, prospered in a dry goods business, and joined the Presbyterian Church. Lewis Tappan (1788-1873), Arthur's brother, went to Boston in 1803, where he was apprenticed to an importer. Lewis became a member of Ellery Channing's church and was briefly editor of a Unitarian periodical. He urged the formation of a Unitarian denomination, and when the American Unitarian Association organized in 1825 he was its first treasurer. Tappan's Unitarian beliefs were challenged first by the earnest piety of a handyman who prayed to Jesus for mercy, and second by his admiration of the benevolent and missionary enterprises that trinitarian faith generated. After seeking counsel from Lyman Beecher, Lewis Tappan left Unitarianism in 1827, and also left Boston to join his brother in New York. Arthur and Lewis Tappan participated actively in the formation of national benevolent societies. (They were active in organizing the ABS, AES, ASSU, ATS and AHMS.). Arthur never gave a speech or wrote an article, but he held office in many societies and gave them crucial financial support. Tappan money made possible the founding in 1833 of Oneida Institute, an inter-racial school to train ministers in Whitesboro, New York, and in 1835 Oberlin College. The Tappans established and funded "Free Presbyterian" (no pew rents) churches in New York and convinced Charles G. Finney to serve one of them. With Finney the Tappans joined Broadway Tabernacle, a Congregational Church, in 1836, and continued in Congregational churches the rest of their lives. Arthur and Lewis Tappan became unconditionally and emphatically committed to the cause of racial equality. When William Lloyd Garrison (1805-79), an abolitionist editor, was convicted of libel and placed in a Baltimore jail in 1830, Arthur Tappan paid his fine. Arthur Tappan was the first president of the New York Anti-Slavery Society, and was also elected president at the organization of the American Anti-Slavery Society in Philadelphia in December, 1833. The Tappans began publishing an abolitionist journal, *The Emancipator* in 1836.

Amistad

In June, 1839, the schooner *Teçora* arrived at Havana, Cuba, with a shipload of Africans to be auctioned as slaves. After the sale, the new owners placed 53 Africans on the schooner *Amistad* for transport to eastern Cuba. En route to their new home, the Africans led by Singbe (a.k.a. Cinque; ca. 1817-79) rebelled, took control of the ship, and commanded one of their captors to sail them back to Africa. The new ship's captain sailed east during the day and west at night, gradually zig-zagging up the coast until sighting Long Island on August 26. The U.S. Navy took possession of the Africans and placed them in jail in New Haven, Connecticut.

Abolitionists Lewis Tappan, Simeon S. Jocelyn (1799-1879) and Joshua Leavitt (1794-1873) organized the Amistad Committee on September 3 (*LTH* 5:33). They appealed for funds and secured legal counsel for the prisoners. The Amistad case ultimately found its way to the Supreme Court, where former president John Quincy Adams argued for the Africans. On March 9, 1841, the Court freed the Amistad captives. The Amistad Committee housed, fed, and taught the Africans, and raised funds with the intention of returning them to Africa with a missionary and a teacher. The Amistad Committee invited the American Board of Commissioners for Foreign Missions (ABCFM) to conduct this mission provided they did so on anti-slavery principles (not receiving donations from slave holders). The ABCFM refused.

Talcott Street Congregational Church[1] in Hartford, Connecticut, and its pastor, James W. C. Pennington (1809-70), invited other African American Christians to a convention on August 18, 1841 at which they organized the Union Missionary Society (UMS). This was an anti-slavery missionary society committed to sending African American missionaries to Africa. The UMS began collecting funds for a mission to accompany the Amistad passengers to Africa. They recruited a teacher, but could not gather sufficient funds.

On November 21, 1841, Americans said farewell in a worship service to the Amistad Africans and to five missionaries, two of African ancestry commissioned by the UMS and three of European ancestry commissioned by the Amistad Committee. In 1842 the Amistad Committee joined the UMS, and Lewis Tappan became corresponding secretary of this inter-racial missionary society. The Amistad incident, which stretched across two years, received much publicity and generated increased support for the abolitionist movement. White Americans saw the humanity of the Africans, the inhumanity of slavery, and the common love of freedom.

<u>Radical and Christian Abolitionists</u>
The American Anti-Slavery Society divided at its 1840 annual meeting. William Lloyd Garrison, spokesperson of radical abolitionism, had an exacting personality and was critical of all who were not in full agreement with him. His espousal of the cause of Non-Resistance led him to criticize the designs of other abolitionists to organize an anti-slavery political party. The division at the annual meeting was occasioned ostensibly over the appointment of women to the executive committee.[2] However the underlying causes were Garrison's personality, his Non-Resistance, his opposition to use of the political process, and his criticism of organized religion. Garrison had managed to offend practically every other abolitionist leader, to alienate potential allies, and to energize the opposition.

Lewis Tappan led the "Christian abolitionists" while Garrison led the "Radical abolitionists." The Christian abolitionists organized the American and Foreign Anti-Slavery Society. This however was not their main vehicle of action. Christian abolitionists worked primarily through a political party – the Liberty Party – and a missionary society – the American Missionary Association. Tappan's *Emancipator* became the most widely read abolitionist journal, with a circulation at least seven times that of Garrison's *Liberator*.

Battle in the Voluntary Societies and the Churches

Amos A. Phelps (1804-47), corresponding secretary of the American and Foreign Anti-Slavery Society, attended major ecclesiastical meetings to press the cause of abolition. The abolitionists secured resolutions and petitions from associations and presbyteries that put abolition on the agenda of national bodies.

The American Home Missionary Society at first resisted discussion of the subject of slavery. Beginning in 1847 it criticized slavery and maintained a diminishing number of missionaries in slave states. After repeated petitions, the Society declared in 1853 that it did not commission slave holders as missionaries. In December, 1856, the AHMS Executive Committee resolved that it would not grant aid to churches containing slave holding members, except in unusual circumstances. The AHMS then sent a letter to all of its missionaries inquiring if their churches contained slave holders. The German Evangelical pastors in Missouri who received this inquiry replied that their churches abhorred slavery and they were free to speak against it (*LTH* 4:51). Only one Kirchenverein congregation had slave holders – three men who each owned one slave. This was considered a scandal, but they were not disciplined.

The Christian Quadrennial Convention in 1854 in Cincinnati adopted a resolution condemning slavery and urging southern members to release their enslaved persons. Southern delegates walked out. Southern Christians organized in 1856 as the General Convention of the Christian Church, South, with William B. Wellons (1821-77) as President.

The American Board of Commissioners for Foreign Missions avoided discussion of slavery for as long as it could. The 1845 annual meeting joined in a full discussion of the subject. Some Cherokee and Choctaw owned slaves and were members of churches founded by ABCFM missionaries. Phelps and other abolitionists argued that slave holders should be excommunicated, and the Board should not in any way support churches that included slave holders. Rufus Anderson considered any discussion of slavery a distraction from the Board's one grand object of world evangelization. He viewed the abolitionist proposal to be a step backward from the process of devolution--of recognizing the right of mission churches to govern themselves rather than imposing the values of mission supporters.

Edward Beecher (1803-91) and his brother-in-law Calvin Stowe (1802-86) introduced a new theological concept into the debate. The sin of slavery they argued was an *organic sin*. The *system* of slavery was sinful. Excommunicating *individuals* would be counter-productive; the system had to be changed. The Beecher family and Leonard Bacon (1802-81) represented a third branch of the movement against slavery. Just as firmly opposed to slavery as Garrison's *Radical abolitionists* and the Tappans' *Christian abolitionists*, these *anti-slavery people* attacked the system rather than the person. Anti-slavery views became popular across a broad spectrum of society and were adopted by the Republican Party and Abraham Lincoln.

The Beecher Family

In the Beecher family we see a gradual evolution from revivalism to liberalism. *Lyman Beecher* (1775-1863), son of a blacksmith, grew up in Connecticut, graduated from Yale, and was ordained in 1799. From 1810 to 1826 he was pastor of the First Congregational Church of Litchfield, Connecticut. Lyman was an energetic promoter of revivals and supported the benevolent and reformist movements of his day. From 1832 to 1852 he served as President of Lane Seminary in Cincinnati, Ohio. The senior Beecher supported colonization (sending Blacks back to Africa). A large majority of the students at Lane supported abolition, and withdrew as a group in 1834. He belonged to the Presbyterian Church when in Ohio, and was tried for heresy in 1834 for support of revivalistic "new measures" but acquitted. Lyman Beecher married twice, and had thirteen children, eleven of whom survived to adulthood. They included:

Catherine Esther Beecher (1800-78) promoted female education and established schools wherever she lived. She advocated teaching as an occupation for women, promoted the idea of kindergarten, and invented the academic discipline of home economics.

Edward Beecher (1803-91) grew up never feeling alienated from God or rebelling from God. He had a religious experience of God's grace in his youth, and many more experiences throughout life. After briefly pastoring Park Street Church in Boston, 1826-30, he served as President of Illinois College, 1830-44. When his friend, Elijah P. Lovejoy, was murdered by a pro-slavery mob, Edward wrote *Narrative of the Riots at Alton* (1838). This placed him in the anti-slavery category, although never a hard line abolitionist. He came East to pastor another church in Boston, raise funds for western colleges, and edit the *Congregationalist*. He returned to Illinois in 1855 to serve the Congregational Church in Galesburg and to lecture at Chicago Theological Seminary (CTS). In 1871 Edward moved to Brooklyn, New York. Without savings for retirement, he depended on his prosperous brother, Henry Ward Beecher. The intellectual of the Beecher family, Edward understood the relationship between God and humanity in organic – or even cosmic – terms, rather than in individualistic terms. His lectures at CTS on "The Christian Organization of Society" examined social structures from a faith perspective.

Harriet Elizabeth (Beecher) Stowe (1811-96) is best known as the author of *Uncle Tom's Cabin*. She wrote many other books and articles, at least one of which reflected the idea of organic sin before her brother and husband presented the doctrine in 1845.

Henry Ward Beecher (1813-87) served Plymouth Congregational Church of Brooklyn, New York, 1847-87. Ward Beecher became one of the most popular preachers in America. An advocate for women's suffrage and the abolition of slavery, Ward Beecher condemned the "barbarism" of the Calvinistic view of atonement, and embraced the concept of evolution. He was not an original thinker, but used his magnetic personality to popularize liberal ideas. Described as "an adulterer, a liar and a hypocrite," when one of his extra-marital affairs was exposed, Ward Beecher and his supporters used threats, bribery and other forms of manipulation to suppress the story. Congregational Councils were ineffective in dealing with such a popular figure.

Charles Beecher (1815-1900) was a pastor in Indiana, New Jersey and Massachusetts. During reconstruction he served as Superintendent of Public Instruction for Florida.

Isabella (Beecher) Hooker (1822-1907) became active in the movement for women's suffrage.

Thomas Kinnicut Beecher (1824-1900) was pastor in Elmira, New York. His church became an early "institutional church" - that is, a church building used actively throughout the week for community activities.

James Chaplin Beecher (1828-86) was a ship's officer in the East India Trade for five years, then engaged in coastal trade. He then attended seminary, was ordained in 1856, and went as a missionary to China. During the Civil War he enlisted in the Union Army and eventually recruited and led an African American regiment. After the war he returned to the ministry.

<u>American Missionary Association</u>

On October, 1845, the month after the ABCFM had rejected the abolitionist appeals, Amos Phelps attended the Liberty Party convention. He called a private meeting of delegates concerned about missions. As a result a Convention on the Subject of Missions was held in Syracuse, New York, February 18-19, 1846. The Syracuse meeting recommended establishment of an anti-slavery missionary society. A second convention, at Albany, New York, September 2-3, organized the American Missionary Association (AMA). The UMS joined the AMA, providing the foundation on which the new Association was built. Lewis Tappan, elected Treasurer, was the effective leader of the AMA until after the Civil War.

The AMA conducted a variety of missions before the Civil War, including:

1. The Kaw-Mendi mission in Africa, begun by missionaries who went with the Amistad Africans under the UMS.

2. A mission to freed slaves in Jamaica, begun in 1837 by an independent committee, adopted by the AMA in 1847.

3. Support of missionaries in Hawaii and Thailand who withdrew from the ABCFM because of its lack of a strong anti-slavery position.

4. Missions among the Anishinaabe, begun in 1843 and conducted by Oberlin graduates in Ohio, adopted by the AMA in 1848.

5. Missions to African Americans in New York City, and refugees in Canada, begun by the UMS.

6. Home Mission support of white abolitionist congregations.

The AMA continued to agitate against slavery through the pulpit and the press.

Fugitive Slave Law

The Fugitive Slave Law of 1850 permitted slave catchers to pursue runaway slaves into free states, and mandated severe penalties for citizens who did not cooperate with them. As a result, Northerners witnessed and were offended by the oppression of the enslaved, and anti-slavery sentiment grew. Isabella Beecher, wife of Edward, witnessed the scandal of slave chasing in Boston, and wrote to her sister-in-law, Harriet Beecher Stowe, urging her to use her writing ability to "make this whole nation feel what an accursed thing slavery is." While attending a communion service at the Congregational Church in Brunswick, Maine, Harriet had a vision of the climactic scene around which she wrote her book. *Uncle Tom's Cabin* appeared first in serial form in the *National Era* then as a book in 1852.

In *Uncle Tom's Cabin*, Stowe described the horrors of slavery and expressed the doctrine of organic sin that her husband and brother had articulated in 1845. A diverse parade of characters, black and white, good and evil, marched through the pages of *Uncle Tom's Cabin*. Everyone was in some way tarnished by association with the sin of slavery. Harriet Beecher Stowe expected that her sympathetic treatment of some slave holders would receive positive responses in the South, and condemnation from radical abolitionists. But the opposite resulted. Her portrayal of the degradation of slavery in human terms aroused anti-slavery feeling in the North.

Kansas

The Kansas-Nebraska Act passed Congress in May, 1854. The territories on the Great Plains were to determine for themselves whether they would be slave or free. The result was a competition between free and slave advocates to settle the territory and to deter their opponents. Numerous acts of terrorism and several pitched battles followed. Congregationalists were among the company of free-state settlers. The AHMS and AMA sent the first and second home missionaries to Kansas in 1854. Other colonies of free-state people came, including a Connecticut Colony that left New Haven in the spring of 1856, provided with twenty-five rifles for which Henry Ward Beecher had raised the funds (called "Beecher's Bibles").

Civil War

For more than a quarter of a century, the sentiment against slavery among northern Christians had been growing. Abolitionists looked to the Civil War as a war of liberation for the enslaved. All northern churches urged support of the war. Even the Reformed Church, which had never publicly discussed slavery, and where the common sentiment disapproved of both slavery and radical abolitionism, called for prayers for the union.

PART C: RECONSTRUCTION

Fortress Monroe

On May 23, 1861, three slaves fled to Union-occupied territory in eastern Virginia. General Benjamin F. Butler (1819-93) had no authority to free the enslaved, but he had no intention of returning them. So he declared them "contraband": property that could not be returned because they could be employed in the Southern war effort. Soon a flood of refugees fled to the Union Army's Fortress Monroe in Hampton, Virginia. Lewis Tappan wrote to Butler, and received permission to send a missionary to the contrabands at Fortress Monroe. Lewis C. Lockwood (1815-1904) arrived September 3, 1861. He found the Black Baptist church of Hampton, with limited resources, had already begun relief efforts. Lockwood supported and extended their efforts. He had expected to preach and hand out clothing, but he found the local Black community had started a school. He reported, "It was suggested by the children themselves." The contrabands, prohibited by law from learning to read, eagerly wanted the power and opportunity that came with literacy. Lockwood supported Mary S. (Kelsey) Peake (1823-62), a free mulatto, who established a school at Fortress Monroe on September 17. Lockwood distributed more than a hundred barrels of clothing by December, and preached in cooperation with local Black exhorters. Responding to the desires of the African American community he placed education at the center of the AMA work in the South.

Schools

The AMA sent teachers, a significant minority of whom were African American, to establish schools for the "contrabands" – after emancipation the "freedmen" – of the South. Close behind the Union Army, a predominantly female army of "school ma'ams" settled upon the South; the AMA entered a massive literacy campaign for southern Blacks. In ten years, 1861-71, the AMA commissioned 3,470 missionaries and teachers for the South, who taught 164,723 pupils in 343 day schools and 156,376 in night and Sunday schools.

Other societies soon organized to send teachers and material relief south. By 1865 about eighty such societies were at work. In 1866 many of these groups federated in the American Freedmen's Union Commission (AFUC). The AMA and the AFUC competed for financial support from the general public and the government.

The federal government established the Freedmen's Bureau in 1865 within the War Department. Under the direction of General Oliver

Otis Howard (1830-1909), a Congregationalist, the Freedmen's Bureau virtually governed the South until 1872. Howard worked closely with AMA corresponding secretary George Whipple (1805-1876) in developing education in the South. Theoretical lines of separation between church and state were blurred into non-existence, as Howard and Whipple worked hand in hand, acquiring land, building schools, hiring and transporting teachers, and appointing superintendents in this massive educational crusade. Congregational minister Lyman Abbott, secretary of the AFUC, protested to Howard against "the appropriation of public funds for the support of religious institutions." The AFUC, a secular institution, instructed its teachers to not teach religion. The AMA, receiving most of its leadership and support from Congregationalists, had by 1869 received official endorsement from twelve denominations, and supported missionaries and teachers of more. The AMA was therefore not connected with one specific denomination, but its teachers saw themselves as Christian missionaries and used religious materials in their schools.

The AFUC federation soon fell apart, as western evangelical Christians objected to the non-evangelical leadership of New England Unitarians. The Cincinnati, Cleveland and Chicago sections withdrew from the AFUC and affiliated with the AMA, and in 1869 the AFUC dissolved. At least eight other denominations established departments to work with the Freedmen. Combined, they had fewer teachers and less financial support than the AMA. While the AMA was leading in the reconstruction of the South, the AMA was being reconstructed. In four years, 1861 to 1865, contributions to the AMA multiplied by a factor of six to over a quarter of a million dollars (not counting barrels of relief or the direct aid of the Freedmen's Bureau). To finance the southern educational effort, the AMA terminated as soon as possible its work in Jamaica, Thailand, Hawaii, Canada, and among abolitionist congregations. Responding to a clear need, the AMA rapidly redefined itself and reallocated its resources. AMA participation in common schools fell sharply after 1871 as the schools became part of the newly established state public school systems.

Higher Education

The American Missionary Association decided to prepare African Americans to teach in common schools as quickly as possible by upgrading a few schools to be normal (teacher training) schools and colleges. The AMA sent Francis L. Cardozo (1837-1903) back to his home city of Charleston, South Carolina, to found a teacher training institute, Avery Institute, in 1865. The AMA founded a "colored high school" in Nashville which received a charter the following year as Fisk University. Hampton Institute, in Hampton, Virginia, was established in 1868 on the site of Mary Peake's school. Other schools soon followed.[3] Members of Washington's First Congregational Church founded Howard University in 1857; the AMA subsidized its Theological Department. The support of higher education required a longer term commitment to the AMA than the common schools. By 1871 over a thousand graduates of AMA High and Normal schools were teaching school in the South.

Jubilee Singers

In 1871, Fisk University ran out of funds. George Leonard White (1838-95), school treasurer and volunteer choral director, had a desperate idea. He proposed to tour the North with a chorus of their best singers to raise fund for the school. The principal handed him the school's meager funds, White borrowed from his personal belongings, and the troupe departed on October 6, 1871. The chorus encountered discrimination in transportation, accommodations and dining, but they were often received in the homes of former abolitionists. As they gained popularity, their experiences publicized discrimination in the North. White rehearsed the chorus, but Samuella "Ella" Sheppard, a Fisk student, directed and accompanied the group on stage. At first their concerts consisted of the popular songs of the day with an occasional opera aria. They sang no comedy or minstrelsy. At White's insistence the chorus sang one or two religious songs of the enslaved. White had attended Black churches in Nashville and admired their music. However he did not use these 'plantation melodies' in his music classes. He knew that the students did not enjoy singing songs that reminded them of conditions that they wanted to forget. Occasionally though, a few of these students would come to his home in the barracks. On these moments, 'with windows closed and shades drawn,' they sang for him the sorrowful songs of their sojourn in slavery."

Performed reverently, not as a caricature, the deep feeling and spiritual power of these songs deeply affected their White audiences. The chorus changed its program and sang mostly spiritual songs. Observing the tears in the eyes of their White audiences, the singers came to value their own spiritual and musical heritage. White named the chorus, the "Fisk Jubilee Singers." They performed for small audiences in Ohio, barely paying their expenses. After their first paid concert, in Chillicothe, Ohio, the chorus, moved by news of the Chicago fire, directed that night's proceeds to the sufferers in Chicago.

The chorus sang for the National Council of Congregational Churches at its first meeting, in Oberlin on November 16. The pastors and delegates spread the news of these singers and their penetrating songs. Money wasn't sent back to Tennessee until they sang at Henry Ward Beecher's church in Brooklyn, New York, December 22. Then they prospered. From 1871 to 1878 several troupes of Jubilee Singers sang across the North, England and Europe, raising $20,000 for Fisk. They had introduced the world to the *spiritual*.

African American Congregational Churches

After the Great Awakening, African Americans were occasionally admitted into the communion of northern Congregational churches. In the South, Christian, Reformed and Congregational churches all had "slave galleries" permitting slaves to attend worship seated in a separate area. Slaves and free Blacks who showed evidence of piety were received into the communion of these churches. In 1820 African American Congregationalists in New Haven, Connecticut, organized Dixwell Avenue Congregational Church. Others soon followed.

The AMA did not organize Black churches in the South right away, because:

1. Their resources were committed to education
2. Although most AMA support came from Congregationalists, money and workers came from over a dozen denominations, and the Association did not want to take actions that might alienate these supporters.
3. Any sectarian activity could jeopardize the assistance of the Freedmen's Bureau.
2. In the opinion of AMA leaders, existing Black churches in the South did not use discipline to enforce ethical standards. They did not want to organize churches until they had gathered a group willing to practice ethical discipline.

In Charleston, South Carolina, African Americans who left the slave galleries at Circular Church organized Plymouth Congregational Church in 1867. A few other African American Congregational churches organized. In November 1869 the AMA held a consultation at Chattanooga, Tennessee, of the churches in the South related to it, to chart a strategy for church extension. The consultation recommended the formation of regional associations and adopted a "church beside the school" policy. Churches developed as companions of the AMA schools; the two institutions supported each other. Associations soon organized across the South that were predominantly African American, with a few White churches. All were in principle open to persons of any color.

Afro-Christian Churches

Slaves often gathered to worship outside of the purview of their owners in "hush harbors," secluded informal structures, often built of tree branches. African-American exhorters led the worship. Traditional African spirituality influenced the worship, "preaching and singing looked back to African chants; the shouting was closely akin to African dance. The feeling aspect of religion dominated." Providence Christian Church, composed of free and enslaved Black Christians, was dedicated in 1854 (now located in Chesapeake, Virginia). Following the Civil War, the Southern Christian Convention appointed William Wellons and two other elders to assist African American Christians in organizing churches and ordaining pastors. The North Carolina Colored Christian Conference organized in 1866. The Black Christian Conferences were self-governing, having fraternal relations with their White counterparts. Worship was free and emotional. Pastors received their appointments for the year at Conference meeting, as Methodists did. In 1892 several colored Christian Conferences came together to create the Afro-Christian Convention.

<u>Summary</u>

The sin of slavery had finally been abolished. The long struggle of African Americans and a small minority of Whites had borne fruit. But enormous inequalities remained. The churches made the radical changes for which the times called. The AMA, a missionary society created by the abolitionist movement, transformed itself into an education society. Leaders of the Christian denomination in the South, in spite of poverty and defeat, reached out to their neighbors and established parallel self-governing African American Christian conferences. Christian abolitionists and anti-slavery people, motivated by pietism, stood up for justice, and saw part of the millennial vision come to pass. The Christian and Congregational communities now included growing numbers of persons of color. But full inclusion into the church had not yet come. Racism was far from dead.

******

[1] Now Faith Congregational UCC.

[2] It is difficult today to understand why this action caused the division. Those who withdrew were Finneyites, in whose revivals women first spoke, and the Tappans had championed women's right to vote in the Free Presbyterian Churches.

[3] Colleges still related to the UCC as a result of AMA work in the South are: Fisk University, Nashville, Tn (1866); Talladega College, Talladega, Al (1867); Dillard University, New Orleans, La (formerly Straight University, 1869); Tougaloo College, Tougaloo, Ms (1869); LeMoyne-Owen College, Memphis, Tn (formerly LeMoyne College, 1872); Huston Tillotson College, Austin, Tx (formerly Tillitson Normal and Collegiate School, 1876).

CHAPTER ELEVEN

Romanticism

A new spirit swept through Western Civilization in the Nineteenth Century, called *romanticism*. This movement had a variety of expressions, some contradictory, in music, art, literature and philosophy as well as religion. The following characterized religious romanticism:

1. Romanticism emphasized *feeling*. It reacted against the Enlightenment, for which *thinking* was everything. Romanticism did not reject *thinking*, but insisted that *feeling*, in particular religious feeling, was real and needed to be considered in one's *thinking*. Intuitive thinking was also valued.

2. Romanticism valued beauty--in music, art, architecture, in the spoken word and in the drama of liturgy.

3. Romanticism affirmed continuity with the past. In a day when many were vehemently anti-Catholic, Protestant romanticists affirmed continuity with positive values of the medieval Roman and ancient Greek Church.

4. Romanticists held an *organic* view of the church. It was not a voluntary society of individuals, but an organism created by Christ and the apostles. Membership in the church placed a person in spiritual unity with Christians of all places and times. As an organism the church, and its doctrine, were not static, but evolving through time.

5. Romanticists looked upon a person's relationship with God as a lifelong process of development, not one sudden ecstatic experience (although experiences were valued). It was a relationship lived out in the community of the church, not as an isolated individual.

6. Romanticists believed in the *supernatural*, which could never be fully comprehended by human reason. However the supernatural and natural worlds were not antagonistic, but organically related. They were comfortable with *mystery*–with the finitude of human knowledge. They saw *value* and *beauty* in many different doctrines and practices.

Friedrich Schleiermacher (1768-1834), who became the principal theologian of the new Evangelical Union Church of Germany, established romanticism as a significant factor in German Protestantism. In America, Romanticism produced the Mercersburg movement in the German Reformed Church, where theological controversy was followed by a war over liturgy. Congregational pastor and theologian Horace Bushnell introduced romanticist concepts into that community. Romanticism influenced church architecture, music and liturgy in all branches of American Protestantism.

PART A: THE MERCERSBURG MOVEMENT
John Williamson Nevin

A Presbyterian candidate for the pulpit of the Reformed Church in Mercersburg, Pennsylvania, preached impressive sermons Sunday morning and evening in the Fall of 1842. At the close of the evening service he brought out the "anxious bench," and invited those wishing prayers to come forward. The small Reformed church had not experienced such excitement and confusion before. Sitting in the chancel that evening was John Williamson Nevin (1803-86), professor at the Reformed seminary in Mercersburg. He was invited at the end of this service to address the congregation. Nevin criticized the Bench, and contrasted true and false revival. In the days that followed, congregants and students debated, and Nevin gave a series of lectures to elaborate his position. He published them in 1843 as *The Anxious Bench* (*LTH* 5:11). A conflict that would agitate the Reformed Church for over three decades had begun.

John Williamson Nevin (1803-86), from south-central Pennsylvania, was raised on the *Westminster Catechism* and the Bible in a devout Scotch-Irish Presbyterian family and church. As a student at Union College, Schenectady, New York, after attending meetings conducted by "anti-New Measures" Congregational revivalist Asahel Nettleton, Nevin professed faith and joined the Presbyterian church. After attending Princeton Seminary, Nevin taught at Western Seminary, in Pittsburgh, from 1829 to 1840. In 1840 the Reformed Church elected him professor at their seminary in Mercersburg, and he transferred his affiliation to the Reformed Church.

In *The Anxious Bench,* Nevin condemned "new measures" as superficial and individualistic. The church as a *community* has a relationship with God, Nevin argued. It is not simply a collection of individuals, each with their own individual relationship with God. He contrasted the system of the *Bench* with the system of the *Catechism*. Healthy evangelism could take place through the life of the church, where persons nurtured by the catechism, family worship, Biblical preaching, pastoral visitation, and church discipline, came into relationship with God. On August 8, 1844, Nevin preached at the first triennial convention of the Eastern and Ohio Synods of the German Reformed Church and the Synod of the Dutch Reformed Church. In his sermon, *Catholic Unity*, Nevin spoke of the believers' spiritual unity with Christ that bound them to one another, and the duty to work for unity.

Philip Schaff

In July 1843, two representatives of the Eastern Synod of the German Reformed Church went to Europe to recruit a German professor to join John Nevin on the faculty of the seminary at Mercersburg. In July they interviewed and recommended Philip Schaff (1819-93).

Philip Schaff (1819-93) was born in the first week of January, 1819, in Chur, canton Graubünden, Switzerland. His mother, married to a man who was not Philip's father, was fined for adultery and ordered out of the city. His father, fined for wanton behavior, died within a year. The local pastor saw that this orphan got a good education. When young Philip got into trouble and was expelled, the pastor recommended him to a school in Kornthal, Würtemberg. This homesick fifteen-year-old boy went into the woods, about three a.m. one morning, to cry and to pray. There "he began to realize for the first time what it is to have peace with God." Attending the University of Tübingen for two years, and Halle and Berlin his third year, Schaff encountered the whole spectrum of German intellectual thought. From Ferdinand Christian Baur he gained a dialectic view of history. From Isaac Dorner he saw how the highest scientific culture could be combined in simplicity and humility with Christian faith. From Johann A. W. Neander he acquired an organic understanding of history. From the Prussian Union Church he gained a spirit of "evangelical catholicity."

The Synod in America confirmed the invitation to Schaff in October, 1843. He was ordained at Elberfeld, April 12, 1844, and arrived in America just in time to hear Nevin's sermon on *Catholic Unity*. Baptized Reformed, confirmed Lutheran and ordained in the Evangelical Union Church, Schaff's respect for the Reformed tradition was genuine, but his spirit of evangelical catholicity was much broader. Schaff was received into the German Reformed Church in the U. S. on the basis of his assent to the *Heidelberg Catechism*. Philip Schaff's inaugural address at Reading, Pennsylvania, on October 25, 1844, stirred up controversy. Delivered in German, *The Principle of Protestantism* (*LTH* 3:26) affirmed the continuity of Protestantism with medieval Catholicism, criticized the individualism and subjectivity of contemporary American Protestantism, and looked forward to a day when Protestants and Catholics would be reconciled.

Schaff had arrived in a state with deep-seated hatred between Protestants and Catholics, where anti-Catholic riots had recently taken place. Joseph F. Berg (1812-71), pastor of First Reformed in Philadelphia, and publisher of an anti-Roman Catholic periodical, criticized Schaff's "romanizing" address. Berg's Philadelphia classis resolved to condemn *The Principle of Protestantism* and what the classis perceived to be its heresies. The Synod of 1845 thoroughly examined the Philadelphia classis charges in a virtual heresy trial, and after four days of debate, overwhelmingly vindicated and affirmed Schaff.

<u>Mercersburg Theology</u>

Nevin and Schaff worked together effectively to define and promote their "Mercersburg Theology" and to train in it ministers for the Reformed Church (see LTH 4:88,90). In 1846, Nevin published *Mystical Presence*, in which he advocated for Calvin's view of the sacrament over Zwingli's. Nevin affirmed that the sacrament is not just commemorative or figurative. but has objective force. He also affirmed the "spiritual real presence" of Christ was received through faith by the receiver of communion. That same year Schaff presented his understanding of the organic development of the church in *What Is Church History?* Also in 1846 seminary classes were canceled on Good Friday and worship services held – the beginning of greater acknowledgment of the Church Year.

Nevin and Schaff continued writing against individualistic religion and for a corporate and developmental understanding of the church (see *LTH* 3:27,28). In 1849 Nevin began publishing the *Mercersburg Review*, which he edited for three years. Nevin resigned from the seminary in 1851, but continued active in the church and its college. Schaff continued training ministers at Mercersburg until 1863. He accepted a position at Union Theological Seminary in New York in 1870, and transferred his membership to the Presbyterian Church. Former students of Nevin and Schaff succeeded them on the faculty of the seminary for several decades (See *LTH* 4:98). The most significant in promoting Mercersburg Theology was poet and theologian Henry Harbaugh (1817-67), previously pastor in Lancaster and Lebanon, who taught from 1863 to 1867 (See *LTH* 4:96).

Reformed Church in the South On Its Own

The seminary provided Reformed churches with a steadily increasing supply of pastors sympathetic to Mercersburg theology. Opposition led to schism in one area. The North Carolina Classis withdrew from the German Reformed Church in 1853, "until we are satisfied that said synod has not held or defended the heresies of Mercersburg" (*LTH* 3:29). The North Carolina Classis approached the Dutch Reformed Church in 1855, concerning affiliation. The proposal became a debate over slavery because three pastors in the North Carolina classis owned slaves. The Dutch Reformed Church said no. In 1857 the Presbyterian Synod of North Carolina proposed union. In this case, as the German Reformed churches would have to replace the *Heidelberg Catechism* with the Westminster standards, and would be scattered into several presbyteries, the classis said no.

The German Reformed Church continued to propose reconciliation with the classis. In 1867 the North Carolina Classis returned to the German Reformed Church.

Liturgical Controversy

Ever since German Reformed churches began using the English language, they had been requesting Synod to provide an English language liturgy. Most favored a translation of the *Palatine Liturgy* with modifications. A committee appointed to the task did not act until Philip Schaff became chairperson in 1852. This committee in 1857 presented Synod with a *Provisional Liturgy* to be used experimentally in the churches. The *Provisional Liturgy* went much further than originally intended and was shaped by the following principles:

1. Continuity with the church in all times and places was expressed through the use of materials from the ancient, medieval and Reformation churches, and several denominations.
2. Congregational participation increased through use of responses and the Creed.
3. Worship, as the sacrifice of the people, focused on the "altar." The words of worship were to be expressions of praise addressed to God rather than calls to conversion addressed to the people.
4. The Church Year was used extensively, with a lectionary, and collects for each Sunday.
5. God was to be worshiped in beauty, in the words of individual prayers as well as in the drama of the liturgy.

Approved for provisional use, the liturgy received sharp criticism for the following reasons (See *LTH* 4:93):

1. The service was too liturgical and left insufficient room for free prayer.
2. The theology behind the liturgy assumed a high view of the ministry and the effectiveness of the sacraments. The use of the word "altar" for "table" implied a doctrinal change.
3. The questions used in the Confirmation service differed from those mandated by the church's constitution.

Eastern Synod appointed a committee to make changes in the *Provisional Liturgy* in response to the criticisms. In 1866 this *Revised Liturgy* was approved for use in the churches. Substantially the same as the *Provisional Liturgy* (See *LTH* 3:32-33), the *Revised Liturgy* did make changes to satisfy the constitutional question. Very few congregations adopted the *Revised Liturgy* in its entirety. However pastors increasingly used material from it in their leadership of worship. Reformed people, many of whom worshiped on alternate Sundays with a Lutheran service in Union Churches, witnessed a similar struggle over liturgy in that denomination. Gradually people of the two denominations became accustomed to a more liturgical service.

<u>Opposition</u>

In February, 1867, opponents of the *Revised Liturgy*, calling themselves "Old Reformed," developed a strategy: (1) call a general conference of opponents of the *Revised Liturgy*; (2) found a college and teach theology, providing an alternative to the denomination's college and seminary; and (3) start a monthly journal. The well-attended convention at Myerstown, Pennsylvania, September 24-25, 1867 (*LTH* 4:94), gave the Old Reformed the opportunity to consult and to formulate their position. The *Reformed Church Monthly* began publishing in 1868 (for Old Reformed views see *LTH* 4:89,91,92,95). A committee named by the convention purchased property in Collegeville, Pennsylvania, and in 1870 opened Ursinus College. In 1871 the Old Reformed organized the Ursinus Union to aid new Old Reformed congregations and students for the ministry.

John H. A. Bomberger (1817-90), who had served on the liturgical committee, joined the opposition in 1861 and soon became its leader, serving as president and professor of theology at Ursinus and editor of the *Monthly*. The conflict over liturgy became bitter and personal, as Eastern Synod in 1868 publicly humiliated Bomberger, accusing him of slander and ordering him to retract statements. The Mercersburg group made efforts to censure Bomberger for teaching theology without the authorization of synod. They also tried to overrule the actions of congregations in supporting Ursinus College instead of the church's college and seminary. However at the General Synod of 1872 the Old Reformed had a majority and these actions were prevented. In spite of the depth of bitterness in this theological war, at no point did the leaders of either side seriously contemplate schism.

<u>Peace Commission</u>

Weary of a quarter century of conflict, General Synod in 1878 created a Peace Commission, which developed a consensus theological statement and presented it to General Synod in 1881 (*LTH* 3:34; See Chapter 12, Part B, Peace Commission Report). General Synod accepted their report and reappointed them a Liturgical Commission. This commission presented a *Directory of Worship* to General Synod in 1884. The *Directory* was a compromise, containing much of the *Revised Liturgy*, without theologically objectionable passages, and without using the word "altar." Referred to the classes, it received sufficient approval to be authorized for use in the churches in 1887. Now the Reformed Church had three liturgies acceptable for use: the *Revised Liturgy* of 1866, the *Directory* of 1884, and less liturgical worship favored by the Old Reformed.

PART B: HORACE BUSHNELL

"The Kingdom of Heaven as a Grain of Mustard Seed," an article in the *New Englander* in the Fall of 1844, contrasted the Biblical concept of growth with the revival concept of conquest. This article criticized missionary and benevolent institutions ("bustle cannot save the world") and called for the cultivation of inner piety as the only sure source of Biblical (slow, steady) growth. The Hartford Central Association asked the author to speak further on the subject, which he did in 1846. This association of Congregational ministers voted unanimously to have the talks published. In 1847 the Massachusetts Sabbath School Society (MSSS) published an expansion of the article, *Discourses on Christian Nurture* (*LTH* 3:17; 5:11). The author, Horace Bushnell, was plunged into controversy that would surround the rest of his ministry.

Horace Bushnell (1802-76) Raised on a farm in New Preston, Connecticut, Horace Bushnell attended Yale College and Divinity School, and served North Congregational Church in Hartford from 1833 to his retirement in 1858. Like the Mercersburg theologians, Bushnell had been influenced by

European romanticism, in particular by Samuel Taylor Coleridge's *Aids to Reflection*, and translations of works of Schleiermacher.

In *Christian Nurture* Bushnell argued that a person could be raised from birth to be a Christian, and never need be "converted." Bushnell's thesis ran against the whole revival system of the churches. Critics questioned his belief in the doctrine of original sin and the need for new birth. After the storm of criticism arose, the MSSS ceased distribution and returned the copyright to Bushnell. Bushnell plunged into even greater controversy with his 1849 publication *God in Christ*. Bushnell rejected the "substitutionary atonement" theory in favor of "moral influence" – the beautiful love of God demonstrated in the Cross can move a person to faith. Perhaps most significant of Bushnell's writings was a long preface to *God in Christ*, titled "A Dissertation on Language." Bushnell saw words as symbols which could only approximate the reality they represented. All language was therefore limited; no creed was final.

In 1849 charges of heresy were brought against Bushnell. According to the Saybrook Platform, only after the Ministers' Association arraigned a minister could he be tried for heresy by the consociation. The Hartford Central Association, after thorough examination, voted in support of Bushnell, 17-3. Conservatives in Fairfield West Association complained to the General Association of Connecticut. The General Association refused to act on their complaints. Fairfield West ministers continued to agitate for four years. In 1852 North Church withdrew from its Consociation and became independent, thus removing Bushnell from any possible action against him.

Bushnell, like the Mercersburg theologians, understood the church as an organism, and conversion as a process nurtured in community. Unlike the Mercersburg theologians, he did not become involved in liturgical issues. Bushnell laid the foundation for the development of Liberal Theology.

PART C: THE AESTHETIC IN RELIGION

Romanticism's appreciation of beauty reached local congregations in the Nineteenth Century. Clapboards and bricks were replaced by stone; the straight lines of colonial meetinghouses by gothic arches. Clear glass windows were replaced by stained glass; the light of the knowledge of God by the cloud of the mystery of God. A cross and candles appeared on many communion tables, which in some cases became an altar. The song leader was replaced by the organ. These changes occurred not all at once, but slowly and unevenly. The Evangelical Synod brought to America the tastes of Nineteenth Century German Protestantism. They used liturgies from the beginning; pastors preached from a lectionary; the Church Year gave structure to life; organs were purchased as soon as they could be afforded.

Mercersburg theologians also prepared hymnals with hymns of every age of the church's history, and material usable with the Church Year. The Reformed Church published *Hymns of the Reformed Church* in 1874. Philip Schaff in 1859 published *Deutsches Gesangbuch*, which was the basis of the Kirchenverein's *Evangelische Gesangbuch*. Henry Harbaugh prepared a songbook for children, and wrote, "Jesus I Live to Thee" (*LTH* 4:97).

Congregational churches slowly adopted innovations. Old South Church in Boston acquired an organ in 1820, First Church of Hartford in 1822. By century's end they were commonplace. Congregational Churches appointed a Committee on the Improvement of Worship in 1886, which reported in 1889. About one-third of the nation's Congregational churches responded to a survey sent out by this committee, and reported the following innovations:

Innovation	% of churches
Have choir	85%
Read Psalm responsively	73%

Receive Offering as a religious exercise	67%
Open worship with Doxology	65%
Say Lord's Prayer in unison	38%
Follow Responsive Reading with Gloria Patri	26%
Frequently use chants	13%
Recite Apostles' Creed	4%
Pastor uses written prayers	4%

The report observed that the use of unison prayer in Sunday Schools had pioneered the way for the churches. The report encouraged these innovations as ways of increasing congregational participation in worship. Concerning the Church Year, the survey found the churches observing the following:

Holy Day	% of churches
Christmas	88%
Easter	100%
Good Friday	21%
Palm Sunday	10%

Children's Day (97%) and Thanksgiving (85%), not part of the liturgical Church Year, were high days in Congregational Churches.

Affirmation of the aesthetic in religion, living in continuity with the church of the past, viewing spiritual growth as an ongoing process, and stillness before the mystery of God, were all characteristics of romanticism. The influence of romanticism was steadily growing in the groups that would become part of the United Church of Christ.

CHAPTER TWELVE

Liberal Protestantism

Between the close of the Civil War (1865) and the close of World War I (1918) United States society was transformed:

1. Business organized itself into corporations which accumulated wealth and power and employed large masses of laborers. Class distinctions sharpened as a new aristocracy of wealth developed.
2. The United States evolved from an agricultural nation to an urban one, with one third of its people in cities.
3. The telegraph and railroad improved communications and transportation, reducing isolation.
4. Increasing immigration led to a nation over 30% foreign born. Native born Protestant Americans often perceived the foreign born, especially Roman Catholics and Socialists, to be a threat to American democracy.

In addition to these social changes, new intellectual currents flowed into the United States:

1. Charles Lyell (1797-1875) published *Principles of Geology* in 1830. This explanation of fossils and the features of the earth's crust proposed a vast time frame that could not be reconciled with a literal interpretation of the chronology of *Genesis*.

2. New proposals for social organization – socialism, communism and anarchism – conceived of a millennium with social justice, but without God.

3. Biblical scholars in Germany analyzed the Bible as a work of literature and reached conclusions that some believers perceived to be threats to their faith.

4. Charles Darwin (1809-82) in *Origin of Species* (1859) proposed a theory of evolution through natural selection attributing creation to an internal natural process rather than to a force external to nature.

All of these social changes and intellectual currents challenged traditional Protestant faith. Persons in the four denominations that later became the United Church of Christ responded to these changes in three ways. (1) Some embraced change, rethinking their theology; (2) some reacted to change and embraced other-worldly theologies that condemned this world; (3) some continued with the same old theology, oblivious to the change all around them. This chapter explores (a) the new theology, (b) efforts by the denominations to reach theological consensus, (c) changes in piety, (d) confrontations to the new theology by traditional believers, and (e) the fundamentalist reaction.

PART A: A NEW THEOLOGY FOR A NEW DAY

Preparers of the Way

Several persons prepared the way for the new theology. Revivalists Charles Finney and Nathaniel Taylor abandoned the harsher aspects of Calvinism. Mercersburg theologians left individualism in favor of a corporate, or "organic" understanding of the church, the faith, and society. Horace Bushnell identified words as approximate symbols, thus requiring greater tolerance of different viewpoints. Other transitional figures into liberal theology were Austin Craig and the Beecher brothers, Edward and Henry Ward.

Austin Craig (1824-81), the principal theologian of the Christian denomination, grew up in New Jersey, and attended Lafayette College in Easton, Pennsylvania. He served churches in Feltville, New Jersey, Blooming Grove, New York, and New Bedford, Massachusetts. He served Antioch College as President, and taught at Meadville Seminary. From 1869 until his death he directed the affairs of the Christian Biblical Institute, the Christian denomination's school for training pastors. Craig wrote frequently in Christian denomination periodicals (See *LTH* 5:29). He opposed the use of any creed, insisting that "faith" not "opinion" was the basis of Christian fellowship. Craig actively promoted cooperation with Unitarians in higher education. Although the Bible was his life, he encouraged his students to study it critically, as a book that contained human invention as well as God's Word. According to Craig, the words in the Bible were not God's word, but symbols that can create in our minds ideas that only approximate God's Word. Like Bushnell, he believed that children could grow up Christian without a conversion experience. Like the Mercersburg theologians, Craig denounced anti-Roman Catholic prejudice. Craig's life was devoted to keeping his denomination open to persons of faith of *all* opinions.

Progressive Orthodoxy

The theology that developed in response to the changing world, sometimes called the "New Theology" or "Progressive Orthodoxy," found many expressions, but often included the following beliefs:

- The Calvinist extension of predestination to children – that some who died as children or infants were destined to Heaven, others to Hell – was rejected. Liberals believed that persons dying in childhood had the opportunity to be saved.
- Liberals emphasized God's immanence and de-emphasized transcendence. Christianity was described as a "natural religion" in that it could be derived from observation of nature without special revelation.

- The supernatural was de-emphasized. Miracles of the Bible were explained rationally or rejected.
- The theory of evolution blended with belief in God's immanence and the post-millennial eschatology of an earlier era to produce an overpowering confidence in *progress* moving humanity into the realm of God.
- Christian doctrine had to be made consistent with modern science.
- Religion, to be relevant, had to be practical, which meant ethical. The teachings of Jesus were given more importance than his death and resurrection.

On September 5, 1857, two years before he published his theory of evolution, Charles Darwin wrote to Harvard botany professor Asa Gray (1810-88) and for the first time outlined his theory of the evolution of species through natural selection. Gray confirmed Darwin's theories with his own observations, and encouraged Darwin to publish. A Congregationalist who described himself as orthodox and a believer in the Nicene Creed, Gray took the lead in advocating Darwinism in America. From Gray's perspective the theory of evolution and the Christian faith were in perfect harmony.

Andover Seminary, founded for the defense of trinitarian orthodoxy, became a major proponent of liberal theology. First it added German Bible study and theology to its curriculum. In 1863 Egbert C. Smyth (1829-1904) (The "y" in Smyth is pronounced like the "I" in light). joined the faculty, soon followed by other liberals. In 1884 they began publishing the *Andover Review*, expressing their liberal views, which they called "Progressive Orthodoxy."

Lyman Abbott (1835-1922), who succeeded Henry Ward Beecher as pastor of Plymouth Congregational Church, 1887-99, became a famous advocate of liberal theology. Abbott was most influential as a journalist, editing the journal Ward Beecher founded, *Christian Union* (name changed to *Outlook* in 1893) from 1876 to 1922, and publishing numerous books. Abbott rejected doctrines of the resurrection of the body and a literal second coming of Christ. He could not reconcile the "fires of Hell" with his understanding of a merciful God, and believed that all who did not accept Christ before death would have opportunity after death. He applied the principle of evolution to the Bible, seeing it as evolving from inferior to superior content. He saw humanity evolving, becoming more God-like, and he praised the inevitable progress of history.

Social Gospel

The social gospel addressed the gospel to society as a whole, as well as to individuals. It stood for social justice, especially in upholding the claims of the industrial laboring class and the poor. The social gospel was grounded in the conviction that the Church must move beyond charity, to advocacy for a more just ordering of society.

The idea of the social gospel was not completely new. Jeremiah Evarts had taken a stand for social justice when he opposed Cherokee Removal. The missionary movement criticized social evils in non-Christian societies. The abolitionist movement worked for a more just ordering of society by advocating the abolition of slavery. Edward Beecher had defined slavery as an "organic sin" that required a collective–not individualistic–solution. Beecher declared in 1865, "Now that God has smitten slavery unto death, He has opened the way for the redemption and sanctification of our whole social system." Washington Gladden was more specific when he declared in 1876, "Now that slavery is out of the way, the questions that concern the welfare of our free laborers are coming forward."

The great social cause of this period was Temperance – an organized effort to prohibit the manufacture and sale of alcoholic beverages. Some advocated for women's suffrage. Many linked these two issues: when men drank abusively, women and children suffered; women's suffrage would bring Prohibition.

German Evangelical educator Daniel Irion (1855-1935) explained the commandment "you shall not kill," in 1897, "Where people are oppressed by hard labor, poor wages, high interest, unsanitary or dangerous living or working conditions, their lives *are embittered* and may be *shortened* by the worry, overexertion or disease or accident thus brought on; those responsible for the oppression thus become *murderers.*"

Some pietists, like Irion, responded to the social gospel, but not to liberal theology; some liberal theologians were too captive to their class background to identify with workers. However in most cases the two movements overlapped. The social gospel held in common with liberal theology: (1) a systemic ("organic"), as opposed to individualistic, understanding of social problems and their solution; (2) a concern to develop theology in response to the contemporary world; (3) an emphasis on the humanity of Jesus, and his compassion; and (4) a religion of action rather than words.

Washington Gladden (1836-1918) became the principal proponent of the social gospel in the Congregational Church. He was a liberal in theology, rejecting Calvin's predestination, original sin, and eternal punishment, and embracing evolution and Biblical criticism. He applied the gospel to issues of labor and management when he spoke to the national meeting of Congregational Churches on "Christian Socialism" in 1889, and "The Church and the Social Crisis" (*LTH* 5:50) in 1907. Gladden favored a mixed economy with elements of capitalism and socialism, and constantly advocated for the rights of labor. He became a leader in the Congregational denomination, serving as Moderator of the national church, 1904-07. Gladden was raised by his uncle in Owego, New York. He joined the Congregational Church in 1853, after a preacher told him he didn't need a special spiritual experience to join. He was ordained in 1860, and pastored Congregational Churches in Brooklyn, New York (1860-66), and North Adams, Massachusetts (1866-71), edited the New York *Independent* (1871-74), pastored North Church, Springfield, Massachusetts (1875-82), then moved to Columbus, Ohio, where he served the First Congregational Church (1882-1914). Gladden served on the City Council, 1900-02, and promoted public ownership of utilities.

At the request of the American Home Missionary Society (AHMS), Josiah Strong (1847-1916) wrote *Our Country* (*LTH* 5:57) in 1885, to promote home missions. An instant success, it sold 175,000 copies by 1916. In *Our Country*, Strong described the perils of Romanism and immigration, and claimed a special mission for the Anglo-Saxons to the world. He went on to condemn the "aristocracy of wealth" in the face of poor working conditions for the masses. Strong pointed to the city as the church's new mission frontier. Elected General Secretary of the Evangelical Alliance in 1886, Strong revived that voluntary society for Protestant cooperation. He organized a series of conferences bringing together social gospel advocates of many denominations. Strong awakened the church to the challenge of the city and began the process of interdenominational organization to face that challenge.

Others promoted the social gospel in the groups that became the United Church of Christ. Graham Taylor (1851-1938), ordained into the ministry of the Dutch Reformed Church in 1873, became a Congregationalist in 1880. He was called in 1892 by Chicago Theological Seminary to become the first professor of Christian Sociology in an American seminary, and taught until 1924. In 1894 Taylor and his family and four students moved into a dilapidated house in a Chicago slum, and founded Chicago Commons, a settlement house where students received first-hand experience in ministry to and with the poor. A similar project, Andover House, had been established in 1892 in the South End of Boston, where Andover students ministered under the direction of Robert A. Woods.

German Evangelicals identified with the work of Germany's *Innere-Mission*. As a result they became aware of Religious Socialism (the European equivalent of the Social Gospel) from the work of Adolf Stöcker. While admiring Stöcker's concern for the poor, Evangelical Synod leaders never imitated his anti-semitism. The Caroline Mission, a city mission founded in Saint Louis in 1913, was patterned after Stöcker's work in Berlin. That same year Julius Horstman (1869-1954) introduced the Evangelical Synod to the social gospel, presenting a paper to the General Conference meeting, "The Gospel of the Kingdom and Its Task in the Twentieth Century."

Articles on the social gospel began appearing in German Reformed periodicals in the 1890s (See *LTH* 5:37). Theodore F. Herman (1872-1948), born in Güttingen, Germany, educated in both Germany and the United States, became the strongest advocate of the social gospel in the Reformed Church. He served as professor of Theology at Lancaster Seminary beginning in 1910, and as President of the school, 1939-47.

PART B: THE CHURCHES EXPRESS THEIR FAITH

In a time of transition and theological ferment, where does the church stand? Each of the four groups that would compose the United Church of Christ, felt a need to define their faith in some way in this period. None of these statements were considered tests of faith – but testimonials to faith. They were produced to achieve a consensus – to find common ground – where the advocates of new ideas and the defenders of the old could stand together.

Cardinal Principles of the Christian Church

Southern Christians walked out of their national meeting in 1854, over the slavery issue, and organized themselves as the General Convention of the Christian Church, South, in 1856. At their next meeting, after the Civil War in 1866, they adopted Principles of the Church, commonly called the "Cardinal Principles," probably written by

William Wellons, president of the Convention. Christians rejected all creeds, but used the "Cardinal Principles" to explain their denominational distinctiveness. As originally adopted, they were:

1. The Lord Jesus Christ is the only head of the Church.
2. The name Christian to the exclusion of all party or sectarian names.
3. The Holy Bible, or the Scriptures of the Old and New Testaments, our only creed or Confession of Faith.
4. Christian character, or vital piety, the only test of fellowship and church membership.
5. The right of private judgment and liberty of conscience the privilege and duty of all.

Christians in other parts of the nation quickly began using these Principles. As the Christians were not a creedal church, there has never been an official wording or order of these principles, and often a sixth is added, as at the time of the reunion of the church (See *LTH* 4:21,33).

Evangelical Catechism and Commentary

The *Evangelical Catechism*, written in 1847 and revised in 1867, was endorsed by the Evangelical Synod for religious instruction, and shaped the faith of that church. The *Catechism* provided common ground for Lutheran and Reformed by emphasizing piety over doctrine. Daniel Irion produced a commentary on the Catechism in 1897, translated into English by Julius Horstman and published in 1916 as volume two of *Evangelical Fundamentals* (*LTH* 4:54). A later revision of the *Catechism* in 1929 contained modest changes that revealed the influence of the social gospel and liberal theology (See *LTH* 4:67).

Congregational Confessions

When Congregationalists gathered in 1865 in Boston, their agenda called for the preparation of a statement of faith. Debate centered around the word "Calvinist" to describe the Congregational faith. While the overwhelming majority considered themselves Calvinists, a significant minority objected to the use of a party name in the document. The word "Calvinist" was dropped. They adopted the *Burial Hill Declaration* (*LTH* 4:82) a brief summary of faith contained in a strong affirmation of catholicity, which made reference to the *Westminster Confession* and its Savoy Version.

When Congregationalists organized a National Council in 1871, they adopted a Constitution which made brief reference to "the great doctrines of the Christian faith, commonly called evangelical," and adopted a declaration on the Unity of the Church (*LTH* 6:2).

From the time of its adoption the *Burial Hill Declaration* received criticism, centered around (1) its endorsement of the *Westminster Confession*, (2) its traditional theological language, and (3) its style – being difficult to use as a local church covenant. The National Council in 1880 created a commission to develop a new creed. Sensitive to the concern for local autonomy, the creed was to be received (not "adopted") by the National Council in 1883 and forwarded to the churches for their use as they saw fit.

The *Commission Creed of 1883* (*LTH* 4:83) was a consensus statement. Neither liberals nor conservatives got everything they wanted, but 22 of the 25 commissioners found enough in the Creed to give their assent. The Creed called the Scriptures "the authoritative standard" of the church, omitting the word "infallible" used in the constitution of 1871. It affirmed both natural and supernatural revelation. It affirmed both God's sovereignty and human freedom. It declared, "that Jesus Christ came to establish . . . the Kingdom of God, the reign of truth and love, righteousness and peace." Although mentioning "final judgment" and "everlasting punishment," the document did not use the word "Hell." In other respects the document expressed traditional evangelical Calvinist doctrine.

Thirty years later the National Council of 1913, in adopting a new Constitution, included a new statement of faith, which firmly endorsed the social gospel. Commonly called the *Kansas City Creed* (*LTH* 4:84), this faith statement was short enough to be used as a creed in worship.

Peace Commission Report

The Reformed Church's Peace Commission Report of 1881 was not a Creed. It was a series of ten theological statements, adopted by the General Synod, in an attempt to bring about reconciliation between two warring factions in the church. It was a consensus statement in which neither side got all they wanted, but that both sides could accept. The Report endorsed Old Reformed beliefs that the sacrament is only effective when accompanied by faith of the believer, and that ministers "are not lords of faith but servants." It endorsed the Mercersburg idea of one church both visible and invisible. The Peace Commission Report provided theological boundaries within which the church could move forward in relative peace.

Each of the four denominations, in its own way, created doctrinal statements that contributed to a sense of denominational identity in this period of denominational formation. For Congregationalists and Reformed, consensus statements were needed to define common ground on which traditional believers and new theologies could stand. Mercersburg Theology in the Reformed Church, and Liberal Theology in Congregationalism, could be tolerated by pietists whose faith was shaped by an earlier era.

PART C: CHANGING PIETY
Changing Practices

Changes in society led to changes in piety. When an industrialist required seven days of labor from his workers, the Sabbath was destroyed. Church discipline, an effective form of social control in a small community, lost effectiveness in large cities. The proximity of large immigrant populations, with different attitudes toward Sabbath observance and alcohol consumption, made American Protestant ways more difficult to maintain. While some resisted change, others embraced it. In 1878 Lyman Abbott affirmed the positive values of amusements in an article, "All Things Are Yours." In 1890 when a member of Lyman Abbott's Plymouth Church was convicted of forgery and sentenced to prison, the congregation voted to retain him on the church rolls, declaring a sinner needed the church, was loved by Christ, and should not be excommunicated.

While traditional patterns of piety were declining, other disciplines of nurturing the spiritual life and practicing the Christian life were on the rise.

- Liturgy and the Church Year were sources of spiritual nourishment for German Evangelicals. The Mercersburg movement gave the German Reformed a catholic liturgical spirituality.
- The spiritual formation of children and youth received more attention. Catechism, Sunday School, and Parochial School continued to nurture the faith. Catechisms united all ages in a common expression of the faith in the Evangelical and Reformed communities, although the use declined among Congregationalists. A new movement, Christian Endeavor, promoted Christian community and commitment among youth and young adults. In 1871 the Christian denomination established a camp meeting on Cape Cod, Massachusetts, later called Craigville. Gradually the camp meeting evolved into youth camping.
- Stewardship – the regular and proportionate giving of one's wealth to the church, became in this period a common spiritual discipline and a legitimate act of worship.
- Devotional literature, Bible studies for the laity, poetry, and hymns, continued to be produced in abundance. In 1877, after attending a Church Council that refused to install a minister who would not preach damnation, Washington Gladden attended a prayer meeting, then wrote "The Great Companion," better known today as the hymn, "O Master Let Me Walk With Thee" (*LTH* 5:52).

<u>What Would Jesus Do?</u>

Charles M. Sheldon (1857-1946), pastor of Central Congregational Church, Topeka, Kansas, sparked interest in his Sunday evening services by writing religious novels, and reading them in installments, creating in his hearers an interest in returning for the next episode. On October 4, 1896, he began reading *In His Steps*. It began with a man approaching a parsonage and asking for work. At Sunday worship the unemployed man returned, and asked the congregation what it meant to walk "in His steps" (*LTH* 5:51). The pastor then challenged the congregation to ask before every important decision, "What would Jesus do?" The remainder of the novel traced several persons as they shaped their lives by that question.

The Advance, a Congregational periodical, published *In His Steps* in serial form, then in 1897 as a book, and by 1900 had sold over 600,000 copies. By then other publishers had discovered a defect in the copyright, and scores of unauthorized editions flowed from publishers around the world. In 1930 Sheldon estimated that over twenty million copies had been sold, not counting translations in over twenty languages. *In His Steps* continues to be published, and read, and to shape the piety of millions.

PART D: LIBERAL PROTESTANTISM IS CHALLENGED

The new ideas of liberal theology threatened long cherished beliefs of many Christians. In the 1880s a series of incidents occurred, in which the guardians of tradition challenged the innovators.

<u>Karl Otto</u>

Karl Emil Otto (1837-1916), educated in critical Bible study at the University of Halle, was sent to America in 1865 by the Berlin Missionary Society to work in the Wisconsin Synod Lutheran Church. Finding that synod had become anti-unionist, he transferred to the Evangelical Synod in 1868. Otto became a professor at the German Evangelical seminary in 1870, and served as Inspector (President) from 1873 to 1879. Admired by his students, Otto combined a reverence for Scripture with the methods of literary criticism. He insisted on explaining the Bible on its own merits, not through the lens of nineteen centuries of interpretation (See *LTH* 4:59).

In the opinion of some Evangelical pastors, because Otto did not find church doctrine in the Bible, he was unbiblical. The seminary board, petitioned to examine his teaching, reviewed all his lecture notes and writings and concluded in April, 1880, "the doubts raised about Professor Otto's teaching have no basis in fact."

Otto published a series of articles, from May to August, 1880, which reignited the controversy. He did not find a fully developed doctrine of original sin in *Genesis 3*. The Synod's General Conference meeting in September, 1880, demanded Otto promise in the future to maintain true doctrine. Otto denied the charges, affirmed the authority of Scripture, and claimed the freedom of interpretation. The Conference affirmed the demand that he alter his teaching, 47-9. Otto felt obligated to resign from the seminary and the Synod.

After a brief exile, Otto returned to the Synod. From 1890 to 1904 he taught at the Synod's college in Elmhurst, Illinois. In ten years at the seminary and fourteen years at the college, Otto educated a new generation of Evangelical pastors to value free inquiry and Biblical research as enhancers of faith rather than destroyers of faith.

<u>The Andover Controversies</u>

Robert Hume (1847-1929), born in Byculla, India, to American Board of Commissioners for Foreign Missions (ABCFM) missionary parents, came to America at the age of seven, following his father's death. He graduated from Andover Seminary in 1873, and returned to India the following year. Hume founded a theological seminary at Ahmednagar in 1878, and was its director until 1926.

Hume heard native converts to Christianity express their concern for the eternal state of their non-Christian parents and grandparents. Was there no hope for them? Hume found hope for them in a teaching of Progressive Orthodoxy of the Andover faculty: "future probation."

Future probation was the belief that persons who died without the opportunity to accept Christ, would have that opportunity after death. The idea was not new. Philip Schaff and Edward Beecher both believed in it, but kept the controversial doctrine to themselves. However, to some of the conservative promoters of missions, this doctrine gave the heathen an escape from the fires of Hell that would reduce the rate of conversions. In 1886, when Hume came to America on leave and his ideas became known, future probation became the central issue in a struggle to prevent the spread of Progressive Orthodoxy. The ABCFM postponed Hume's return to India. ABCFM Home Secretary Edmund K. Alden (one of the three commissioners on the Commission Creed of 1883 who voted against the Creed) began questioning candidates for missionary service on this matter, which he considered critical.

At the ABCFM meeting of 1886 in Des Moines, Iowa, a major debate took place, over a motion to approve the Board's new practice of examining missionary candidates with regard to doctrine. The Board had in the past consistently claimed that it did not judge a candidate's theological qualifications, but accepted as sufficient the decision of an association, presbytery or classis to ordain. Liberals at Des Moines argued that as future probation was not excluded from the *Westminster Confession* and the Creed of 1883, it was one of those matters over which reasonable people should be free to disagree (See *LTH* 5:25). However, the ABCFM, a self-perpetuating corporation, sustained the actions of its leaders.

Questions of polity became intertwined with theology and mission policy. The Andover controversy brought out the undemocratic nature and independence of the self-perpetuating ABCFM Board. The two motives of denominational unity and theological freedom combined to bring about constitutional change in 1893, creating closer ties between the churches and the Board, and limiting terms of office. Alden resigned that year, the Board recruited new leadership, and the theological controversy came to an end.

Meanwhile, another battle in the controversy was taking place at Andover. In 1882 the seminary trustees had called Newman Smyth (1843-1925), brother of Egbert Smyth, to the faculty. The Board of Visitors, a committee committed to preserving orthodoxy at Andover, vetoed the decision of the Trustees. Newman Smyth then became pastor of Central Congregational Church, New Haven.

In 1886 the Board of Visitors adjudged that the teaching of professor Egbert C. Smyth was contrary to the Andover Creed, and he was removed from office. Smyth challenged the legality of the action in state courts, and in 1891 the Massachusetts Supreme Court found the Board of Visitors action to be legally flawed. The following year the Board chose to not seek further action; Smyth continued to teach.

<u>George Gilbert</u>

George H. Gilbert (1854-1930) received Congregational ordination and became New Testament professor at Chicago Theological Seminary in 1886. Gilbert seemed to imply that Jesus' death was not necessary for salvation. At issue were Biblical criticism and liberal theology. On reviewing the proofs of Gilbert's newest book, the Seminary Board was not confident of his orthodoxy; Gilbert resigned in 1900. Opinion gradually changed, and in 1905 no one questioned the calling of a liberal to the faculty. In all of these controversies – Otto, Graham and Andover – the liberals had a sincere Christocentric faith that appealed to the students. Those opposed to change won the first victories, but new views ultimately prevailed.

PART E: FUNDAMENTALISM

In times of great social change, while some embrace change as progress, others condemn change as evil. Yet these reactive views are also a change from what went before. What became known as Fundamentalism held to Pre-Millennial eschatology which saw the world as evil and to be destroyed, rather than as God's world, to be transformed.

The Post-millennial eschatology of Jonathan Edwards undergirded all of the missionary and benevolent efforts of the first half of the Nineteenth Century. Liberals did not talk about eschatology, but their belief in progress had similar implications. Many who could be called moderate or traditional, especially those active in the missionary movement, continued to hold post-millennial views. However pre-millennialism was growing in popularity. While some Fundamentalists separated themselves from all who did not believe as they did, others had a more catholic spirit and cooperated across lines of denomination and theology. Fundamentalists preached substitutionary atonement, the inerrancy of the Bible, pre-millennial eschatology, the divinity of Christ, miracles, and Hell.

Dwight Moody (1837-99), the most effective lay evangelist of the last half of the Nineteenth Century, started out a Congregationalist, but soon became independent. He promoted interchurch cooperation in his evangelistic campaigns and received strong support from Congregationalists. He developed a complex of private schools and conferences around his home Congregational church in East Northfield, Massachusetts. Moody's views were pre-millennial, but he had a catholic approach to evangelism, cooperating with all evangelical Christians.

Cyrus Scofield (1843-1921), born in Michigan and raised in Tennessee, served in the Confederate Army in the Civil War. Afterward he studied law, and was elected to the Kansas state legislature. President Grant appointed him a federal attorney. His work was affected by his drinking and he left that position to practice law in Saint Louis. In 1879 he accepted Christ as his Savior, gave up drinking, and joined Pilgrim Congregational Church. After studying theology for eighteen months Scofield was commissioned by the AHMS to go to Dallas, Texas, where he was ordained pastor of First Congregational Church in 1883. In 1886 the AHMS appointed him part-time superintendent of the Society's work in Texas and Louisiana, while continuing at First Church.

While at Dallas, Scofield founded an independent faith mission, Central American Mission, in 1890. In 1896 he proposed the founding of a Bible college which grew into Dallas Theological Seminary. Scofield became a popular speaker and teacher of pre-millennialism, and developed Bible Correspondence Courses.

From 1902 to 1909 Scofield devoted himself to preparing his reference Bible. Published in 1909, the *Scofield Reference Bible* contained chain references to document pre-millennialism. It is still in print and popular among Fundamentalists everywhere. The review of the work in the *Congregationalist* (August 28, 1909), claimed, "Bible students who prefer . . . the interpretations of fifty years ago to anything of more recent date, will thoroughly enjoy *The Scofield Reference Bible*."

Cyrus Scofield's *Reference Bible* became the Bible of Fundamentalism. Scofield and the Congregational denomination were drifting apart. In 1902 Scofield's First Congregational Church of Dallas split, the dissenters organizing Central Congregational Church. In 1908 First Congregational withdrew from its Association when the association ordained a liberal. In 1910 Scofield transferred his ministerial standing to the southern Presbyterian Church. Scofield explained that after several years of working on the *Reference Bible*, "I lifted my face from my work and found that the denomination, in whose fellowship I have found great and true men of God, had resolutely moved to positions to which I could not follow. . . My memory holds too many instances of kind things said and done by my Congregationalist brothers to leave any room for anything but gratitude and esteem; but...the designation 'Congregationalist' would not now describe me. It stands for certain liberties which I do not allow myself, and for a certain attitude toward the Bible and historic Christianity which is not my attitude."

CHAPTER THIRTEEN

Denominational Formation

The development of more "business-like" denominational organization paralleled the rise of big business. In the period between the Civil War and the First World War, the five groups that would form the United Church of Christ (including the Afro-Christian Convention) developed national organizational structures. Along with a unified national body came the organization of church related agencies and bureaucracy. The German Reformed Church created a General Synod in 1863. The German Evangelical *Kirchenverein* became a synod in 1866, the same year in which the Christian denomination reorganized. Congregationalists created a National Council in 1871. The African American conferences of the Christian Church created the Afro-Christian Convention in 1892. Each of these events marked the acknowledgment of a denominational identity. Recognizing, sometimes reluctantly, that they were denominations, these groups often intensified their quest for Christian unity. The establishment of business-like organization and the quest for unity, complemented each other in the story of denominational formation in this period. Meanwhile, women slowly gained a greater role in the organizational lives of the denominations.

PART A: NATIONAL ORGANIZATION
Reformed General Synod

The German Reformed Church chose to celebrate the three hundredth anniversary of the *Heidelberg Catechism*, by uniting its two synods, Eastern and Ohio, under a General Synod, which convened for the first time on November 18, 1863. The new General Synod organized its work under four boards – a fifth was added later: (1) Sunday School, (2) Foreign Mission, (3) Home Mission. (4) Orphans Home, and (5) Ministerial Relief. In 1896 several publications were placed under the jurisdiction of the Sunday School Board and it became the Sunday School and Publications Board. It built a seven-story building at 1505 Race Street, Philadelphia, which became denominational headquarters. Responsible for pensions for ministers and their widows, the board of Ministerial Relief was an Eastern Synod project until turned over to General Synod in 1905. The work of the Reformed Church for four decades presented a puzzling pattern of projects conducted by classes, synods, and General Synod, without any apparent design. Most of the General Synod boards at first did nothing; only with the passage of time, as trust developed, and the boards received full-time leadership, did these "paper boards" evolve into effective coordinators of denominational program.

General Synod met every three years. In 1869 they dropped the word "German" from the title, becoming the Reformed Church in the United States. General Synod appointed a Temperance Commission in 1911 and a Commission on Social Service in 1917.

Christian Connection

In 1866 the Christian general convention reorganized, taking the name American Christian Convention, and organizing its work into five departments: (1) missions, (2) education, (3) publishing, (4) Sabbath School, and (5) treasury. Each department was directed by a Secretary, and the five secretaries constituted the Executive Board of the Convention. In 1890 Christians rejoiced in the reunion of Southern Christians with the national Convention (*LTH* 4:33). In 1894 a Department of Christian Endeavor was added for youth work. The Convention devoted much of its energy to the development of educational institutions and the publishing concern. The Christian Publishing Association purchased property in Dayton, Ohio, in 1872, giving the Christian denomination a headquarters. A movement steadfastly opposed to denominationalism had accepted the necessity of denominational organization in order to do its work.

Evangelical Synod

In 1866 the *Kirchenverein* reorganized as the German Evangelical Synod of the West. The name change recognized that the loose pastoral association had evolved into a strong church body. With the name change came two organizational changes. First, the General Conference meeting became a delegated meeting with limited representation from each of several districts. Second, the office of President became a full-time position with indefinite tenure.

The Evangelical Synod debated the merits of the position of President for several decades. The President could veto any district decision, and had to approve every ordination. Some complained about having a "bishop." However, the persons who held the office did not exercise power arbitrarily. The position was made part-time, to be filled by a local church pastor, 1880-89, and again 1898-1909. In 1872 the term of office was limited to the interval between General Conference meetings, which lengthened from two to three, then four years (See *LTH* 4:58).

In 1872 the German Evangelical Synods of the Northwest and the East united with the German Evangelical Synod of the West, which in 1877 changed its name to the German Evangelical Synod of North America. With the addition of the Chicago-based and Buffalo-based synods, the Evangelical Synod became national in scope. In 1872 the three synods brought to the union the following:

Synod	Pastors	Congregations
West	194	219
Northwest	56	82
East	33	36
Total	283	337

The Synod gradually accumulated denominational boards, and by 1890 had the following: (1) Seminary, (2) Publishing House, (3) Home Missions, (4) Foreign Missions, (5) Christian Education, (6) Benevolent Institutions, (7) Church Building Fund, (8) Budget and Finance. Later a Pensions and Relief Board was added. The synod also had a "supreme judiciary," to act on complaints against officers or on constitutional questions, but it was seldom used. The Publishing House, located at 1718 Chouteau Avenue, Saint Louis, became the denomination's headquarters.

National Council of Congregational Churches

When Congregationalists from across the United States met in Albany to revoke the Plan of Union in 1852, they adjourned with no provision for any future national meeting. One interstate Congregational body that met regularly was the "triennial convention" of pastors and delegates from seven mid-western states (Michigan, Indiana, Wisconsin, Illinois, Minnesota, Iowa, Missouri) to oversee the work of the Congregational seminary in Chicago. The third triennial convention, in 1864, called for another national meeting to address the needs of the West and South. This 1865 meeting in Boston adopted the *Burial Hill Declaration*, encouraged the support of specific voluntary societies which it identified as Congregational, and adjourned without making provision for another meeting. Resolutions and correspondence among state organizations resulted in a national meeting at Oberlin, Ohio, November

15, 1871. The meeting adopted a constitution for a National Council of Congregational Churches.

The National Council had no authority over local congregations, existed for consultation only, and established no bureaucracy to carry on its work between triennial meetings. The provisional committee, appointed to make arrangements for the next meeting, became by default the voice of the Council between sessions, a role recognized in 1913 when it became the Executive Committee. The Moderator had no official responsibilities beyond the actual meeting of the Council. However, beginning in 1901, Moderators traveled and spoke widely as unofficial spokespersons of the denomination. The Secretary had the responsibility between meetings of collecting and reporting statistics. In 1913 this position was changed to full-time General Secretary, responsible for coordinating the work of the denomination.

Congregational organization was unique. Other denominations created a national organization first, and then created Board, Departments, and Commissions to carry out its work. Congregationalists, by contrast, had established several strong voluntary societies to carry out their work, long before the formation of the National Council. The National Council frequently discussed the relationship of the Council to the Societies, the Societies to each other, and the Societies to the churches. However, the Council had no power to impose its will on the autonomous Societies. The National Council recognized the following Societies:

- American Board of Commissioners for Foreign Missions (ABCFM)
- American Home Missionary Society (AHMS) (name changed to Congregational Home Missionary Society (CHMS) in 1893)
- American Missionary Association (AMA)
- American College and Education Society was a merger in 1874 of the American Education Society (AES) and the Society for the Promotion of Collegiate and Theological Education in the West

(1843). This agency provided scholarships for theological education and subsidized colleges and seminaries.
- Congregational Sunday School and Publishing Society, a merger in 1868 of the Massachusetts Sabbath School Society (MSSS) and the Doctrinal Tract and Book Society (1829).
- American Congregational Union (later called the Congregational Church Building Society), founded in 1853 to gather funds for the erection of church buildings.
- American Congregational Association, founded in 1853, built a mission house at 14 Beacon Street, Boston, to house any interested Congregational agencies and a library.
- Congregational Board of Ministerial Relief, established in 1907 to provide pensions and other benefits to clergy.

The National Council proposed a reorganization in 1874 – that the ABCFM transfer all its work with American Indians to the AMA, and the AMA transfer its foreign work to the ABCFM. This would clarify their fields of service as foreign (ABCFM) and domestic (AMA). After further negotiations and discussion the change was effected in 1883.

After the Andover controversy, agitation increased to make the Societies in some way accountable to the churches. The ABCFM and CHMS responded to the pressure by receiving some representatives of the churches into membership. After thorough consultation with the societies, the National Council adopted a new constitution at Kansas City in 1913. Besides strengthening the Executive Committee and creating the office of General Secretary, the new constitution created a Commission on Mission to coordinate the work of the various societies and their fund raising. The new constitution also made delegates to the National Council delegates to all of the societies (each society also had other delegates), assuring accountability to the churches.

Afro-Christian Convention

Although with a membership with limited financial resources, the Afro-Christian Convention managed to support itself. It met biennially and by 1900 had a publishing house, divisions of Christian Education, women's auxiliaries, local and foreign missions.

Synods, Districts and Conferences

Each denomination developed its own pattern of intermediate organizations for fellowship, inspiration, counsel and action, between the local church and the national church. Generally these groups consisted of clergy and lay delegates from the churches. The Reformed Church required lay delegates to be ordained Elders. Evangelical districts tended to be clergy dominated because many congregations served by Evangelical pastors did not join the Synod. Among some ethnic groups, such as the Welsh and the Dakota, district meetings were attended by a large proportion of the church membership, and were inspirational occasions.

These intermediate units often had responsibility for ordaining ministers and for home mission work within their borders. Some sponsored educational and benevolent enterprises. Among Evangelicals, the Reformed, Christians and Afro-Christians in the South, an intermediate organization could appoint pastors to their charge. However, as a practical matter, placement took place only with the consent of the pastor and charge.

The Evangelical Synod organized itself into districts, which by 1924 had multiplied to nineteen, and generally followed state lines. Each district had a District President, who was also pastor of a church, and who often saw his role in the district as pastoral.

In 1914 the Reformed Church in the United States was organized in 61 classes, grouped together in eight synods. The original Eastern and Ohio Synods were subdivided to create new synods, and new German-speaking synods were created for congregations of recent German immigrants.

By 1900 Christians had gathered over 160 local Conferences for fellowship and inspiration. Christians organized three multi-state regional bodies, the New England Christian Convention (1845), Southern Christian Convention (1847), and Afro Christian Convention (1892). These regional conventions published journals, established educational and benevolent institutions, and conducted home and foreign missions. In the mid-Atlantic and mid-west regions state conferences undertook similar objectives.

Tracing the development of Congregational intermediate bodies is confusing because Congregationalists in different regions gave different definitions to the same terms. Congregationalists in Maine organized what they called a "Conference" in 1826, with lay and clergy delegates from district conferences (consociations). Ohio adopted this Conference plan when it organized in 1852. The "Conference" system predominated in Congregationalism by the end of the century. In 1907 the National Council urged a standardization of terms: district consociations to be called Associations; state consociations to be called Conferences. The National Council also encouraged the Associations to take direct responsibility for ordinations, and to phase out vicinage councils.

In each state Congregationalists established voluntary societies which met at the same time as the state Conference. The most important of these was a Home Missionary Society, auxiliary to the AHMS. The state Home Missionary Society organized congregations and subsidized pastors salaries. The AHMS appointed a superintendent to supervise the home missionary work in the state. The superintendent became the pastor to subsidized pastors and churches and the effective head of Congregational work in the state. Other state voluntary societies were auxiliary to national societies and had staff, which was on occasion assigned to more than one state. It was not unusual for a superintendent of Sunday School work, superintendent of women's work, and an agent of the ABCFM who promoted stewardship, to work with the Home Mission superintendent as the "staff" of the state conference. In the first half of the twentieth century the CHMS promoted the development of Conference staffs, selected by the Conferences, and supported by Conference funds. Conferences retained some mission giving instead of sending it all to the societies, and worked for the goal of self-support. Christian conferences also had parallel voluntary societies, and the Reformed Board of Home Missions occasionally appointed superintendents for the work of a synod.

<u>Educational Institutions</u>

Congregationalists approached the founding of educational and benevolent institutions in a different way from the Reformed, Evangelical, Christian and Afro-Christian. Congregationalists saw themselves as participating in the building of a new "empire for Christ." As each new territory was organized, and then received into statehood, Congregationalists worked to establish the institutions of Christian civilization. Motivated by their faith, Congregationalists founded academies and colleges to provide leaders for this new empire. General Associations received contributions from churches to establish colleges. There was often no effort to ensure a church connection with such schools. Some became part of state college systems, others became independent private colleges. Some had a "historical connection" with Congregationalism that became irrelevant with the second generation of administrators. In only a few instances, where denominational identity and denominational needs were strong, did any formal connection persist.

This loose relationship to educational institutions contrasted sharply to the strong organizational ties that Reformed, Evangelicals, Christians and Afro-Christians had with their schools and benevolent institutions. For these groups the educational institutions were essential to the welfare of the church, to provide pastors, parochial school teachers, deaconesses and a well educated lay leadership. The schools were of, by, and for the denominations.

The Reformed Church seminary, which had been located at Carlisle, York and Mercersburg, moved in 1871 to Lancaster, Pennsylvania. The faculty were considered officers of the church, elected by synod. To prepare students for theological education, the seminary began a "classical department," which became Marshall College in 1836, and in 1850 was moved to Lancaster, united with another school, and became Franklin and Marshall College.

The Christian denomination struggled for years to establish schools for theological training. Some Christians and Unitarians had founded Meadville Theological School in Meadville, Pennsylvania in 1843. Christians were teachers and students, but the school had no formal connection with the denomination. The Christian denomination founded Antioch College at Yellow Springs, Ohio, in 1853, open to all without regard to race or gender. The college developed serious financial trouble, was bailed out by the Unitarian Church in 1858, and turned over to a Board of Trustees where the Unitarians held a majority.

The *Kirchenverein* established a school to train pastors at Marthasville, Missouri, in 1850. Patterned after Basel and the other mission schools of Europe, Marthasville had strict discipline with an interest in both the spiritual and intellectual development of the students (*LTH* 4:43). The school was moved to Wellston in 1883, near the "Eden" stop of the train, from which the school acquired the name Eden Seminary. In 1924 Eden Seminary relocated to Webster Groves, Missouri.

The Evangelical Synod had two other educational needs: (1) to prepare students for seminary, and (2) to train teachers for parochial schools. The Synod founded a "proseminary," patterned after the *proseminar* of Germany, to prepare students for theological education with a liberal arts curriculum. It soon absorbed a teachers' seminary. As part of the merger agreement of 1871 with the Synod of the Northwest, the proseminary/teacher's seminary moved to Elmhurst, Illinois, and developed into Elmhurst College.

The Ohio Synod of the Reformed Church founded Heidelberg College and Seminary at Tiffin, Ohio, in 1850. In 1907 the theological departments of Ursinus and Heidelberg united as Central Theological Seminary, which located in Dayton, Ohio, in 1908. In 1934 Central was merged into Eden Seminary. The North Carolina Classis of the Reformed Church founded Catawba College in 1851 which received financial support from the whole church after 1923.

After the rejection of the Plan of Union, Congregationalists in the Midwest were eager to establish a Congregational seminary to promote Congregationalism across the region. To make the school accountable to the churches, they organized the "triennial convention," a meeting of clergy and lay delegates from Congregational Churches in a seven state region to do the official business of the seminary. The first triennial convention met, and Chicago Theological Seminary opened for classes, in 1858.

The German Reformed colony from Lippe that settled in Town Herman, Wisconsin, founded Mission House in 1860 to train German-speaking pastors. A project of Sheboygan Classis, Mission House came under the jurisdiction of the Synod of the Northwest in 1867, and received support from the other German synods as they were organized. Like Eden, Mission House was patterned after the mission schools of Europe. The proseminary courses evolved into a college, which in 1957 took the name Lakeland College.

The Christian Bible Institute, established by the Christian denomination in 1869, offered courses for persons going into the ministry and also encouraged persons already in ministry, who had not received formal education, to come for a year. Austin Craig directed the institute from its inception until his death in 1881. Originally located in the Town of Starkey, on the western shore of Seneca Lake in New York, in 1872 it relocated to Stanfordville, Dutchess County, New York.

The North Carolina Conference of the Afro-Christian denomination began offering classes at Franklinton, North Carolina, in 1871. In 1880 it was founded as the Franklinton Literary and Theological Institute and supported by all of the conferences of the Afro-Christian Convention. It provided training for pastors in the Afro-Christian Convention.[1]

<u>Religious Journalism</u>

Religious periodicals kept people connected and promoted a free exchange of ideas. Religious journals have come in a variety of forms and styles. There have been quarterlies, monthlies, biweeklies and weeklies. They have been owned and operated by individuals, corporations, and church bodies. Papers have often changed hands, merged, and changed editorial position.

General denominational magazines, sometimes called "parish papers," addressed to pastors and lay people of a denomination, circulated information and discussed issues. Elias Smith, Christian, began *The Christian's Magazine, Reviewer and Religious Intelligencer* in Portsmouth, New Hampshire in 1805, and renamed it *Herald of Gospel Liberty* in 1808 (*LTH* 4:14-16). It became the official paper of the Christian denomination in 1862. The Afro-Christian Convention published *The Missionary Herald and Christian Star.* Congregationalists founded the *Boston Recorder* in 1816. The *Congregationalist* presented itself as a more progressive alternative in 1849. The *Advance*, a Chicago based Congregational paper, was established in 1867. The German Reformed Church's paper, the *Messenger*, began publication in 1829. The Ohio Synod published *Christian World* beginning in 1854. The Evangelical Synod began publishing an English language paper in 1902. First called *Messenger of Peace* (*LTH* 4:52), in 1913 it became *Evangelical Herald.* These papers were merged when their denominations merged, and in 1958 became the *United Church Herald.* From 1972-83 it became a joint venture with the Presbyterians called *A. D.* After the demise of *A. D., United Church News* began publishing in 1985.

Missionary Societies published periodicals to promote their work, the best known of which was the ABCFM's monthly *Missionary Herald.* Seminaries published quarterly scholarly journals for their alumni and scholars, beginning with the Reformed Church's *Mercersburg Review* in 1848. *Prism*, published from 1985 to 2011, contained scholarly articles. Papers in German, Dakota and Magyar addressed those constituencies. To these could be added papers promoting the views of a particular party within a church, and papers addressed to particular constituencies, such as youth, and Sunday School teachers. Through myriad mergers and name changes, the denominations have used journalism to connect with their constituencies.

PART B: REACHING OUT FOR CHRISTIAN UNITY

A yearning for a fuller expression of Christian unity grew alongside the development of denominational organization. In 1865 and 1871 Congregationalists felt compelled to explain that the creation of a denomination was not a rejection of catholicity. All four groups found inspiration in their denominational unity to seek greater unity.

Lutheran-Reformed

Lutheran and Reformed came to America from Germany on the same ships, settled in the same rural neighborhoods in Pennsylvania, built churches together, established common parochial schools, and married each other. From the beginning, Lutheran and Reformed congregations shared buildings, each congregation with its own pastor leading worship on alternate Sundays. As population increased many congregations each established their own building, but new union churches continued to be built in rural areas, as follows,

Years	new union congs. organized
1800-1850	67
1850-1900	53
1900-1910	3

No new union churches were organized after 1910. Through consolidation, separation, and closure, the 273 union churches reported in

1914 were reduced to 236 in 1953. Union churches often maintained common Sunday Schools and cemeteries. The two denominations were seasoned by the same German pietism, influenced by the same American revivalism, and struggled alike over the issue of language. Lutheran and Reformed denominations endorsed the same German language magazines and hymnals for use in union churches.

Lutheran and Reformed joined together in founding Franklin College in Lancaster in 1787. When both denominations desired a theological seminary, in 1818, they created a joint committee to add a seminary department to Franklin College. However the discussions collapsed in 1820, and each denomination created their own seminary.

In 1822 the Lutheran Ministerium of Pennsylvania resolved unanimously to appoint a committee to study the possibility of a general Lutheran-Reformed union. The following year the Reformed classis in Ohio passed a similar resolution. In 1828 two Pennsylvania classes petitioned Synod in favor of union. In 1832 the Ohio Reformed Synod again proposed union. In 1836 the Lutheran delegates to the Eastern Reformed Synod again proposed either union or federation, and the synod responded warmly.

Nothing came of all these resolutions and warm feelings. No plan was developed, no decisive action taken. The opportune time passed away. Each denomination diverted its attention to union with other geographic synods of its own denomination. A confessional movement in Lutheranism, parallel to the Reformed Mercersburg Movement, emphasized the doctrinal differences. Each denomination produced their own hymnals. The Reformed Church bought out the Lutheran interest in Franklin College. In 1872 the Lutheran Church rejected pulpit and altar fellowship with non-Lutherans.

German Reformed and Dutch Reformed

The Dutch Reformed of New York and the German Reformed of Pennsylvania both related to the Reformed Church in the Netherlands in the colonial period. They had a common doctrinal base and organization. When the Dutch Reformed established an independent synod in 1792 they retained the *Heidelberg Catechism, Belgic Confession,* and *Canons of Dort* as their doctrinal standards. The German Reformed, organizing a synod the following year, retained only the *Heidelberg Catechism*

The two Reformed synods sent delegates to each other's meetings from 1813 to 1853, and transferred ministerial standing when requested. When the Dutch Reformed proposed a joint seminary, the German Reformed rejected the idea in favor of working with the Lutherans. In 1844 the Dutch Reformed Synod and the two German Reformed Synods (Eastern and Ohio) held the first Triennial Convention, for consultation and cooperation. Only two conventions were held. The Dutch Reformed withdrew, and by 1855 had cut off all correspondence with the German Reformed Church because they considered the Mercersburg theology heretical.

From 1870 to 1872 the two Reformed Churches again discussed union. But it was not consummated because of the different doctrinal standards.

The two Reformed churches entered discussions again in 1887, and proposed a federal union with common boards and separate synods (See *LTH* 6:43.45). The proposal received the approval of the German Reformed classes by 1890. However, a vocal minority in the Dutch Reformed Church, fearing schism from some of their conservative western churches, prevented the adoption of the plan.

Free Will Baptists, Christians, and Congregationalists

Since Free Will Baptists had ordained Abner Jones to be the first Christian minister, the two groups had frequent cooperation and conversations. The obstacle to union was Free Will Baptist insistence on believer's baptism by immersion.

In 1885 Christian and Free Will Baptist ministers of New England and New York developed a basis of union. Endorsed by several regional bodies of both denominations in 1886 and by the American Christian

Convention, it was rejected by the Free Will Baptists who feared insufficient doctrinal harmony.

In that same year, 1886, the National Council of Congregational Churches received an invitation from Free Will Baptists to enter into discussions. Although acknowledging much similarity, the next National Council, in 1889, noted that the discussions had not born fruit.

Christians and Christian Union

James F. Given (1825-67) left the Methodist ministry and organized the Christian Union at Columbus, Ohio, in 1864. This new denomination was a coalition of mostly ex-Methodists who opposed the Methodist Church's abolitionism and support of the Union in the Civil War. Christian Union adopted an organization that closely resembled the Christian denomination. Christian Union's "Seven Cardinal Principles," which included the Christian Church's principles, added, "no politics in the pulpit." A cluster of Christian congregations in Missouri, far removed from their roots in North Carolina, affiliated with the Christian Union.

In 1873 Christians and Christian Union in Iowa united in one state conference, but after several years they each went their own way. In 1886 Christian Union presented a proposal for union to the Christian denomination (See *LTH* 6:24). The Christians agreed, and the two denominations cooperated, but no actual union took place.

Congregational and Episcopal

Episcopal appeals for Christian unity were carefully studied by Congregationalists, who remembered that the first Congregationalists "were not willing separatists," but continued to think of themselves as part of the Church of England. Congregationalists studied and discussed the Chicago-Lambeth Quadrilateral (*LTH* 6:5) – what Anglicans considered the four essentials any union must have – first proposed in 1886. The National Council concluded in 1895 that Episcopal insistence on re-ordination of other ministers by bishops in apostolic succession made further discussion impractical (See *LTH* 6:6).

Congregationalists and Episcopalians continued discussions to 1923 (See *LTH* 6:7-10) to see if pastors of one denomination could serve members of the other in communities where the other did not have a congregation. The Congregational side agreed to re-ordination by an Episcopal bishop of the Congregational ministers involved. However the Episcopal Church was unwilling to ordain under those conditions.

<u>Congregational Methodists</u>

On May 8, 1852, several local preachers and other lay persons of the Methodist Episcopal Church, South, met in Monroe County, Georgia, and organized a new denomination, the Congregational Methodist Church. Congregational Methodists were Methodists who opposed what they considered the undemocratic, clergy-dominated organization of the Methodist Episcopal Church, South. This new denomination, centered in Georgia and eastern Alabama, spread across the South before the Civil War.

In 1887 AHMS superintendent for Florida and Georgia Sullivan Gale discovered the Congregational Methodists and concluded they could live harmoniously in the Congregational denomination. That year the Georgia Conference of Congregational Methodists united with the much smaller organization of white Congregationalists in Georgia. Over the next several years Gale recruited several other Congregational Methodist Conferences into the Congregational Church. About one third of the Congregational Methodists joined the Congregationalists.

The Congregational Methodists gave the Congregationalists an instant white constituency in the South – and controversy over segregation (See Chapter 14, Part C, Color Line Debate). Many of these predominantly small rural churches died out, others have fallen away from the denomination, some returned to the continuing Congregational Methodist denomination.

<u>Congregational and Christian</u>

At the instigation of the New Jersey Christian Association, the Christian Convention in 1894 initiated discussions with the Congregational Church. In 1897 representatives of the two groups met and developed what became known as the Craigville Proposal (*LTH* 6:18; see also *LTH* 6:36). It was a proposal for mutual recognition that would not disturb existing institutions. In 1898 the proposal was rejected by the Christian Convention due to opposition from Southern and Western parts of the church. Some Christians opposed union with any group bearing any name other than Christian.

<u>Congregational, Methodist Protestant, United Brethren, and Christian</u>

Congregationalists began discussions in 1898 with Methodist Protestants – a Methodist group that did not have bishops. United Brethren in Christ and Christians joined the discussions in 1903 (See *LTH* 6:3). Because the other three groups insisted on creeds, the Christians dropped out. In 1907 an "Act of Union" (*LTH* 6:4) was presented to the churches. Congregationalists in 1910 asked the other groups to reconsider the Congregational concern to guarantee autonomy to local congregations, which they were unwilling to do, and the proposal died.

<u>Reformed and Presbyterian</u>

The German Reformed Church and the Presbyterian Church shared the Reformed faith and presbyterian polity; proposals for union arose consistently. The Reformed Church in the Netherlands corresponded with the German Reformed, Dutch Reformed and Presbyterian churches in America in the period 1741-53, to see if the two Reformed churches could be included in the Presbyterian Church. John Philip Boehm absolutely rejected the proposal. (1) He did not understand English. (2) He was unwilling to give up the *Heidelberg Catechism*. (3) Neither would he give up the Reformed liturgy for special occasions.

In 1823 the German Reformed Church and the Presbyterian Church agreed to correspond and to send delegates to each other's meetings. After 1838 the Reformed corresponded with both Old School and New School Presbyterians. The Old School closed correspondence in 1854 out of dissatisfaction with Mercersburg theology.

The Reformed Church continued correspondence with the New School and after 1869 with the reunited Assembly.

From 1903 to 1906 the two denominations discussed union, and in 1911 presented to the churches a Plan of Union. The Reformed classes rejected what to them looked like absorption, and the project was dropped (*LTH* 6:47).

Local Cooperation and Federation

Small communities that could not support several denominational congregations searched for new forms of cooperation. The denominations in Maine began in 1890 a pattern of closing all but one congregation in small communities, each denomination getting their share. Beginning about 1895 major denominations – including Congregationalists and Christians – began forming Federated Churches. In these churches separate denominational organizations, each with their own membership rolls and benevolences, shared ministerial leadership. By 1920 about 300 Federated Churches had been formed across the country. These churches of necessity allowed right of private judgment and tolerance of doctrinal diversity.

Interchurch cooperation had been promoted by Josiah Strong for the social gospel, and by Dwight Moody for evangelism. State and city councils of churches arose, beginning with the Interdenominational Commission of Maine (1894) and the Greater New York Federation of Churches and Christian Workers (1895). The movement for a national federation began in 1900. Congregationalist Elias B. Sanford (1843-1932) gathered representatives of denominations in 1905, to create a constitution for a Federal Council of Churches of Christ in America (FCC) (*LTH* 6:51) (Now the National Council of Churches of Christ). By 1908 thirty-two denominations had ratified the constitution and the Council began to function. Social Gospel advocates provided the core of the FCC, but its activities included evangelism and education.

Elias Benjamin Sanford (1843-1932) was the driving force behind the formation of the Federal Council of Churches. A native of Connecticut, Sanford entered the Methodist ministry in 1865. In 1867 he transferred to the Congregational ministry and pastored churches in Connecticut. He edited religious journals from 1873 to 1882, then returned to the parish. Sanford became secretary of the Open and Institutional Church League in 1895. This organization was committed to social service and inter-church cooperation. He became general secretary in 1905 of a new organization, the National Federation of Churches and Christian Workers. From this point Sanford worked for the formation of the Federal Council of Churches. It came into being in 1908 with Sanford as corresponding secretary. He retired in 1913.

PART C: WOMEN IN THE CHURCHES

A movement for equality of voice and office for women in the church paralleled the movement for women's suffrage in civil society. Women organized and carried out missionary work, while a handful of women entered the ministry.

Formation of Women's Mission Boards

Local women's groups in Congregational churches had been supporting missions since the American Board of Commissioners for Foreign Missions (ABCFM) was founded. In 1834 David Abeel, a Dutch Reformed missionary of the ABCFM, proposed that women organize societies to support women in mission to women. The churches of England responded to his proposal. In America, Dutch Reformed philanthropist Sarah Doremus planned the organization of a women's board, but ABCFM secretary Rufus Anderson discouraged her. The project was dropped until after Anderson's retirement.

In 1868 Sarah Bowker organized the Woman's Board of Missions, a network of local women's organizations to promote missions, and to send out women missionaries under the direction of the ABCFM, to minister to women. A Woman's Board of Missions of the Interior, in Chicago (1869), Woman's Board of Missions for the Pacific Islands, in Honolulu (1871) and Woman's Board of Missions for the Pacific, in California (1873) completed the network. This movement created a woman's organization in almost every congregation, affiliated with state and national organizations. They provided the ABCFM with over 20% of its receipts and a steady supply of single female missionaries. In 1920, of 73 persons commissioned as missionaries by the ABCFM, 56 were women.

Elvira S. Yockey established a similar movement in the Reformed Church in the United Sates. She organized the Woman's Missionary Society of the First Reformed Church, Xenia, Ohio, in 1877. Similar societies sprang up in other congregations. In 1887 the denomination organized the Woman's Missionary Society of the General Synod, with Elvira Yockey as President (*LTH* 4:103, see also *LTH* 5:8).

The Christian Church organized the Woman's Board of Foreign Missions in 1886, and a Woman's Board for Home Missions in 1890.

The National Evangelical Union of Women organized in 1921, but Evangelical Synod women actively supported benevolent institutions before then.

Elimination of Women's Mission Boards

In the first three decades of the Twentieth Century, denominational leaders promoted more efficient denominational administration and unified fund raising. They came to look upon denominational women's missionary societies, parallel to the (men's) denominational boards, as inefficient. In the Congregational community advocates of efficiency called for the consolidation of the women's boards with the ABCFM. With some misgivings, the women's boards united with the ABCFM in 1927, the women being assured that at least one-third of the ABCFM corporate membership and Prudential Committee would be female. As a result of this integration of mission work, women no longer held key leadership positions, and financial support declined.

The congregation's Women's Missionary Society became a Women's Fellowship with a less focused definition of purpose. The women's missionary organizations of the other denominations that made up the UCC lost their distinctive missionary function in the first round of church mergers.

Lay Officers

Henry Dexter reported in *A Handbook of Congregationalism* in 1880 that Congregational churches in the old days restricted the voting privilege at congregational meetings to adult male members. "Modern notions have led many of them to adopt a different policy. It is, however, believed that a majority still hold to the earlier practice."

Hugo Kamphausen, of the Evangelical Synod, writing in 1924 recalled that "say 25 years ago–many good old German men vigorously opposed the new trend," of woman's suffrage in congregational meetings. He identified this trend with the Americanization process, often accompanying the adoption of English in worship. He observed, "thus far we have not heard of women serving on church councils nor have they served as delegates to church conferences," but there was no constitutional provision against it, and in time it would come.

For the Reformed Church the election of women to consistories was a more complex matter. Elders and Deacons were ordained, and only Elders could represent the congregation at classis and synod; a change in church constitution was required.

The *Reformed Church Messenger* in 1922 asked its readers to respond to the question, "Should women be eligible for office in the church and for membership in our Church judicatories?" To the surprise of the editors, every essay received in response to this inquiry was in the affirmative.

The 1923 General Synod received an overture from Eastern Synod calling for a constitutional amendment granting to women, "the same rights, privileges and prerogatives of representation of holding office in congregations, Classes, District Synods and General Synod, which now belong to men." After thorough discussion throughout the church, the General Synod in 1929 adopted an amendment giving women "the same constitutional rights as men." The amendment was referred to the classes for their action. As this amendment fell two classes short of the two-thirds needed for adoption, it was rewritten to exclude the ordained ministry and resubmitting to the classes. General Synod in 1934 received a report of approval of the rewritten amendment by the classes. Women received the right to serve on consistories and denominational boards at the Synod meeting at which the Reformed Church united with Evangelical Synod and began the process of going out of existence.

In the Evangelical Synod women had served on Church Councils and District and General Conferences by then. The constitution of the Evangelical and Reformed Church made no distinction between men and women, clearly implying and interpreted to mean that women could serve in any position.

Gradually women assumed new roles in the life of the congregation, but the key lay leadership roles continued to be filled almost exclusively by men.

Ordained Women

Mary A. Bevier of Colorado wrote in the *Home Missionary* in 1902 of her experience four years before: "Few of the people where I lived went to church, and there was no church within eighteen miles. Children were growing up to know nothing about God, and how were they ever to believe the Gospel that they never heard? This seemed to be my call to preach." Typical of the handful of ordained women of her day, Bevier felt called by necessity, and served in a remote location for a salary most men would not consider. One woman, Antoinette Brown, had been ordained in 1853. However, her ordination did not have the sanction of her Association, and she remained in the Congregational ministry for only ten months. The next woman to be ordained was in the Christian Connection, Melissa Garrett (1834-1924), at Ebenezer Church, Clark County, Ohio, March 7, 1867. When the Deer Creek

Conference of the Christian Church met the following September they voted:

Resolved:–That while we do not approve of the ordination of women to the Eldership of the church, as a general rule, yet as sister Melissa Timmons has been set forward to that position at the request of the church of which she is now a member, therefore,

Resolved:--That we send her credential letters of an ordained minister of good standing in this Conference.

Melissa (Garrett) (Timmons) Terrell pastored in Christian churches in Ohio, Iowa and Missouri.

By 1871 the Eastern Virginia Christian Conference had licensed Talitha Briggs, a woman of color, to preach to "the colored." When the Virginia Christian Colored Conference organized 11 December 1873, with six churches and eight ministers, Briggs was on the list of ministers. Cassandra Faulk, another woman of color, had been licensed to preach in the North Carolina and Eastern Virginia Colored Conference by 1884, as she was already preaching in two congregations.

The Congregational Yearbook first mentioned a woman licensed minister in 1883, and ordained women in 1889. Emma Newman (1838-1922) appears to be the first woman licensed by a Congregational Association, at Dial, Kansas, in 1883. She had been serving churches since 1873 but was never ordained. Mary Moreland, of McLean, Illinois, and Annis B. Ford Eastman of Tompkins County, New York, were ordained in 1889. The National Council of Congregational Churches first took note of ordained women in 1919, when it appointed a commission to study the situation. The commission reported in 1921 that 1.2% of Congregational clergy were women. These 67 women were employed as follows:

Pastors of Churches	18
Joint Pastorate	14
Religious Education or Church Assistant	14
Not Indicated	21

All the women pastors of churches were serving very small congregations. Virtually all of the joint pastorates were clergy couples. Most of the "not indicated" group were married, several to pastors. The Commission concluded there was no need for the National Council to make any ruling on the ordination of women other than gratefully acknowledging their existence. "We can neither challenge the validity of their ordination nor deny the fact of their evident usefulness."

In 1930 the Congregational denomination reported 131 women ministers, 2.2% of the total, and the Christian denomination reported 55 ordained women, 4.6% of the total. Women made little progress in the ministry in the middle third of the Twentieth Century; in 1970 only 2.5% of the ordained ministers of the United Church of Christ were women.

Beatrice Weaver (Later Beatrice Weaver McConnell) graduated from Lancaster Seminary and was ordained a minister of the Evangelical and Reformed Church in 1948, a first on both counts, without controversy.

******

[1] Other schools founded by Congregationalists include Olivet College, Olivet, Mi (1844), Pacific University, Forest Grove, Or (1848), Yankton College, Yankton, SD (1862) , Doane College, Crete, Ne (1872), Drury College, Springfield, Mo (1873), Northland College, Ashland, Wi (1892), Bangor Seminary in Bangor, Me, in 1816, for men of limited means, and Pacific School of Theology, Berkeley, Ca, initiated in 1869. The Southern Christian Convention established Elon College

in 1889. The Defiance College, Defiance, Oh, affiliated with the Christian Church in 1903.

CHAPTER FOURTEEN

Mission to America

The period roughly from 1870 to 1920, a time of liberal trends in theology (Chapter 12) and denominational development (Chapter 13), was also a time of missionary expansion. Chapters 14 and 15 describe the mission to America of the denominations that would become the United Church of Christ. Chapter 16 places them in their global context of world missions and the concern for peace.

The newly organized denominations vigorously undertook their mission to America, which had several aspects. The term *Home Missions* was used in Nineteenth Century America for church extension – starting new churches on the frontier and subsidizing their pastors' salaries (see chapter 9). In the latter part of the century the home mission boards also reached out to the waves of new immigrants coming to America (Chapter 15), and to the cities. The term *Inner Mission* as used in Germany described a wide variety of missions of humanitarian and spiritual service in the homeland, supported by voluntary contributions. As church extension under a state church was conducted with state funds, that particular activity was not included in *Inner Mission*. In this chapter, the term *Inner Mission* refers to institutions of humanitarian service established by the church in its home country. *Christian Education*, both for those in the church and as a mission to others, developed in new directions. With the abolition of slavery, abolitionists turned their attention to the condition of the *African Americans* and the *American Indian*.

This chapter explores four dimensions of the mission to America of the newly organized denominations, (a) Inner Mission, (b) Educational ministries, (c) African American ministry, and (d) American Indian missions.

PART A: INNER MISSION

On September 22, 1848, Johann Hinrich Wichern (1808-81) called on the Protestant churches of Germany, assembled together at *Kirchentag* (a massive church conference) in Wittenberg, to address the increasingly urbanized, industrialized and dechristianized German nation with an intensive *Innere-mission*. Wichern defined the Innere-Mission as: "The *collective* and not *isolated* labor of love which springs forth from faith in Christ, and which seeks to bring about the internal and external renewal of the *masses within Christendom* who have fallen under the dominion of those evils which result directly and indirectly from sin, and who are not reached, as far as their spiritual renewal they ought to be, by the established official organs of the Church." The church responded to Wichern's appeal and established the Inner Mission of the German Evangelical Church at Berlin, January 4, 1849.

Wichern, educated for the ministry, never received a call to a church. On October 31, 1833, with his mother and sister, Wichern moved into a small house to provide a home for delinquent and neglected boys–*Das Rauhe Haus*. This mission multiplied and Wichern trained men to serve as housefathers in other homes across Germany. Earlier, Amalie Sieveking (1794-1859) had in 1832 organized a women's society for the care of the sick.

Theodor Fliedner (1800-64) was pastor of a small Protestant congregation in Kaiserswerth, on the Rhine. In 1833 a discharged female convict, Minna, came to Fliedner's house and received shelter. Others followed and Fliedner established a "Magdalene home" for these women. Fliedner had a vision of greater labors of love. He believed the ancient order of "deaconess" should be revived, through which unmarried women could be trained in arts of service to others. In 1836 he established the Deaconess Mother House. Deaconesses were soon directing hospitals, orphanages, and sanatoria for the insane in Kaiserswerth and around the world.

The concept of *Innere-Mission* – institutions of caring conducted by the church – came to America with German immigrants. Louis Nollau and Saint Peter's Evangelical Church in Saint Louis founded a hospital in 1856, which became Good Samaritan Altenheim (Old People's Home). After a cholera epidemic in 1858 left many orphans, Nollau founded the German Protestant Orphans' Home (Evangelical Children's Home). Evangelicals in Louisville had organized a Protestant Children's Home in 1851.

The Civil War created an army of orphans. German Reformed pastor Emanuel Boehringer (1823-64) of Philadelphia gathered orphans from the streets into his home. The General Synod established a Board for Orphans Home in 1863 (See *LTH* 5:47). Boehringer's growing institution moved to Womelsdorf in 1867, becoming Bethany Children's Home. The Reformed Church also founded Saint Paul's Children's Home at Butler, later Greensburg, Pennsylvania. Saint Paul's Evangelical Church of Chicago founded Uhlich Children's Home in 1868. Evangelicals organized homes for children and the aged in Buffalo, New York (1875), and Detroit, Michigan (1879). The German Synods of the Reformed Church organized Fort Wayne Children's Home (1883).

Evangelical pastors in Saint Louis urged the establishment of an order of deaconesses in their denomination, and in 1889 organized the Evangelical Deaconess Society of Saint Louis. This Society was not composed of deaconesses but of persons who wished to see the order established. Its Board of Directors consisted of four clergy, four laymen and four women. Inclusion of women as voting directors was a breakthrough for the Evangelical Synod. The Society acquired property for a home and hospital. On August 18, 1889 Katherine (LaPorte) Haack (1840-1919), a pastor's widow, and her adopted daughter, Lydia

Daries (1869-1948), were set apart as the first Deaconess sisters of the Evangelical Synod in North America (See *LTH* 4:49). Originally working as visiting nurses, they brought those needing more care into their home, which became Evangelical Deaconess Hospital (*LTH* 5:48). The deaconesses wore distinctive garb, similar to the European deaconesses. The deaconess movement spread rapidly across the Evangelical Synod, and institutions multiplied. They established hospitals in Evansville (1892), Chicago (1906), Faribault, Minnesota (1909), Milwaukee (1910), Cleveland (1914), Marshalltown, Iowa (1914), and Detroit (1917). Deaconesses also established an institution for the developmentally disabled at Marthasville, Missouri (1893), homes for the aged at Bensenville, Illinois (1894) and Dorseyville, Pennsylvania (1928), and a children's home at Hoyleton, Illinois (1895). Deaconesses also engaged in parish work (*LTH* 4:50).

The Reformed Church established a deaconess training school and home for the aged at Allentown, Pennsylvania in 1903 (See *LTH* 4:102). Also the North Carolina classis founded Nazareth Children's Home (1906) and Potomac Synod founded Hoffman Home for Children (1910). The Southern Convention of the Christian Church established a Children's Home in Elon, North Carolina, in 1904.

Evangelical pastors in Saint Louis, with the help of seminary students and deaconesses, founded Caroline Mission, for ministry with the city's poor, in 1913. Another such mission, Back Bay Mission, in Biloxi, Mississippi, was founded by the Evangelical Synod in 1923.

The Reformed Church and the Evangelical Synod both established ministries to the newly arrived immigrants. The Harbor Mission consisted of a German Reformed pastor who greeted immigrants as they arrived in New York, and assisted them in any way possible. The Evangelical Synod had a similar mission at the port of Baltimore, which as immigration subsided in the twentieth century ministered to seamen of other nations.

All denominations found ways to express compassion for those in need. For the Evangelical Synod, "Inner Mission" became the central expression of mission, and shaped denominational identity. The order of deaconesses opened to women new avenues for service as well as responsibility in administering significant institutions.

PART B: MINISTRY TO CHILDREN AND YOUTH

The educational ministry of the church evolved through changing ideas of childhood, education, and theology.

Parochial Schools

In the Evangelical Synod in the late Nineteenth Century between 40% and 50% of the congregations conducted parochial schools–all that could afford it. The training of parochial school teachers continued to be a priority of Elmhurst College. In 1883 Synod congregations employed 110 full time teachers. However, as public education became more widespread, the children spoke more English, and World War I compelled the Synod to seek fuller integration into American society, the parochial schools closed. Elmhurst discontinued the training of parochial school teachers in 1916.

Sunday School

The Sunday School had become an almost universal institution in American Protestantism by the late Nineteenth Century. Trends in Church education cut across denominational lines, and effected the groups that became the United Church of Christ in similar ways at about the same time. From about 1885 to 1910 advances in knowledge regarding child development, education, and psychology suggested new approaches for Sunday Schools. Increasing numbers of persons, mostly women, received education in these areas in preparation for careers in church education, and advocated change. The Religious Education community promoted three changes:

1. Graded Lessons–Bible lessons should be prepared appropriate to each age group, and designed to build on each other through the years.
2. Use of extra-Biblical material--Educators urged instruction in church history, worship, the Christian life, and doctrine, in addition to the Bible.
3. Replacement of content-centered lessons with child-centered lessons.

A conference in 1906 advocated graded lessons. Denominations began publishing them in 1909. By 1915, two-thirds of the Congregational Sunday Schools responding to a survey were using graded lessons. A broadening of content soon followed. The Sunday School, an institution created by and fostering the piety of the Nineteenth Century, was being carried in new directions by progressive education grounded in liberal theology.

Religious educators organized the Religious Education Association in 1903, to work for change. Some early full-time educators were deaconesses. Florence Fensham opened the Congregational Training School for Women in Chicago in 1909, after a short-lived Deaconess training program folded. Elon College began offering a course for religious educators in 1918. Evangelical Synod established the Oakwood Institute in Cincinnati in 1923 to train religious educators and other lay workers.

Denominations developed summer conferences to train the volunteer teachers. Evangelical Leadership Training Schools (ELTS), summer schools for religious educators, began at Elmhurst in 1914 and were soon duplicated in other locations across the country. About 1914 the Christian Church also organized summer schools for lay people. The Reformed Church began summer leadership training conferences in 1925.

<u>Ministry to Youth</u>

Francis E. Clark (1851-1927), pastor at Williston Congregational Church, Portland, Maine, faced a dilemma. Young people professed their faith and joined the church, but did not fit into the organizational life of the adult church. On February 2, 1881, Clark organized the first Society of Christian Endeavor. This organization run by the youth with a weekly prayer meeting prepared young converts for responsible adult membership.

Christian Endeavor spread rapidly from church to church, crossing denominational and international borders. Clark presided over the creation of an international organization, United Societies of Christian Endeavor, in 1885.

Christian Endeavor was a response to a new social reality: Youth. Education extended a person's time of dependence beyond puberty; teens found themselves in a limbo between childhood and adulthood. Christian Endeavor created a church experience relevant to this new community.

The Evangelical Synod, isolated by language from the mainstream of American Protestantism, created its own *Jugendbund* in 1902, after 1913 called the Evangelical League. The Reformed Church had authorized the Heidelberg League for its youth in 1896, however most local youth groups were affiliated with Christian Endeavor. In 1922 Clark wrote that only the Methodists had separated themselves from Christian Endeavor. In 1936 the Christian Youth Council of North America met and Congregational Christian delegates organized a National Council of the Pilgrim Fellowship. The Evangelical and Reformed Youth Fellowship organized at about the same time.

Youth camping grew in importance. Regional bodies and denominations acquired campgrounds. Christians developed summer programs for youth about 1914 at Craigville, in Massachusetts. Eastern Synod of the Reformed Church founded Camp Mensch Mill in 1928. The Evangelical Synod conducted youth camping at Dunkirk in western New York. Heavily used by youth camps, lay schools, meetings and work camps, these campgrounds fostered significant Christian fellowship, and an awareness of church larger than the local congregation.

PART C: AFRICAN AMERICANS IN THE SOUTH AFTER RECONSTRUCTION

In 1877 Federal troops withdrew from the South; white Americans forgot about the freedmen. Racist attitudes steadily increased in this period, given intellectual support from "social Darwinism." This was a perversion of evolutionary theory which proclaimed that some races and ethnic groups were meant to dominate others and should carry out the law of nature, "the survival of the fittest," by oppressing others. This doctrine was given an altruistic facade, "the white man's burden," to justify imperialistic expansion and domination of others. Even humanitarian and benevolent enterprises of liberal Christians in this period were often founded on a premise of inequality.

African Americans were the targets of terrorism – arson, rape, beatings and lynchings. The rights they received during Reconstruction were slowly eroded. Two Supreme Court decisions, *Plessy v. Ferguson* (1896) and *Williams v. Mississippi* (1898) intensified the oppression. The first justified segregation; the second permitted state election laws which for all practical purposes disfranchised African Americans. In the years that followed, southern society was totally segregated and terrorism intensified.

Two graduates of American Missionary Association (AMA) schools rose to leadership in the African American community. Booker T. Washington (1856-1915), a graduate of Hampton and principal of Tuskegee, urged Blacks to work for economic self-reliance. W. E. Burghardt DuBois (1868-1963), a graduate of Fisk and professor of Sociology at Atlanta University (1897-1910, 1934-44), urged Blacks to demand legal and political rights.

Throughout this period the AMA stood firmly for both economic advancement and legal rights, supported schools and churches, and spoke out against injustice. However, in spite of its efforts, the AMA could not even hold back the tide of segregation in its own denomination.

Schools

Throughout this period of terror the AMA schools continued to graduate a steady stream of African American leaders to teach in schools, preach in churches, and otherwise give leadership to the African American community.

The AMA, which through Reconstruction had a strong record of using persons of both colors to teach, soon came under criticism for not giving African Americans teaching positions in colleges. In 1877 the AMA resolved to "make haste slowly" in this area. It was very slow; in 1895 only 4% of the faculty of AMA colleges were African American.

Churches

The AMA, which had been transformed by the needs of Reconstruction from an anti-slavery society to an education society, went through another transformation as Reconstruction ended. The Freedman's Bureau had closed; most of the common (elementary) schools had been turned over to the states; other denominations had established their own missions to the freedmen; the AMA now had closer ties and official support from the developing Congregational denomination. The Congregational constituency urged the AMA to do more church work.

The AMA appointed Joseph Edwin Roy (1827-1908), a white minister, to be Field Secretary in 1878. Roy moved to Atlanta – the first AMA secretary to live in the South – and focused on founding churches. In seven years (1878-85) AMA church work in the South grew from 4,212 members in 64 congregations to 7,512 members in 113 congregations, and new Congregational associations were founded.

After this spurt of growth, Black Congregationalism grew slowly. The congregations depended financially on the AMA, which assigned pastors to churches. Gradually the theological departments of the AMA colleges provided Black Congregational pastors.

In 1914 AMA churches in the South numbered 165. Because of the poor rural economy, many African Americans migrated north. The AMA began sending pastors north to organize the migrants into congregations in northern cities.

The Afro-Christian Convention continued to grow. Reorganized in 1914, the Convention advanced under the leadership of Smith A. Howell, president for the next twenty years. The Afro Christian Convention in 1916 counted seven conferences with 153 congregations. With limited support from northern white Christian churches, the Convention struggled to maintain an educational institution at Franklinton, North Carolina (See *LTH* 6:28), for the education of pastors and teachers, from 1878 to 1930.

Smith Allen Howell (1860-1938) was born into slavery in Nansemond County, Virginia in 1860. He was converted at age 15, completed studies at Franklinton Christian College, licensed to preach in 1879 and ordained in 1885. He served churches in eastern Virginia, at the same time also teaching school. He became president of the Afro Christian Convention in 1914 while continuing as pastor of Wesley Grove Christian Church of Newport News. Howell went to South America in 1909 to supervise the establishment of Christian mission work in Guyana. He also served as President of Franklinton Christian College.

Color Line Debate--Part 1

Piedmont Congregational Church organized in Atlanta, Georgia, in 1882, and received support from the American Home Missionary Society (AHMS). The AMA protested. The establishment of an all-white congregation supported by one missionary society in a city that already had a predominantly Black congregation of the same denomination (First Congregational Church), supported by another society, appeared to be establishing a color line. Both societies were on record opposed to segregated churches.

Representatives of the two societies met in Springfield, Massachusetts, in December, 1883. They agreed to the following principles:

1. Neither society would give aid to any congregation that would refuse to receive an applicant for membership based solely on color.
2. Churches receiving aid from either society were expected to fellowship with other churches in the geographic association in which they were located.
3. The societies agreed to consult with each other before supporting churches in communities where the other was at work.

Piedmont Congregational Church and the AHMS agreed that any "colored person suitably qualified" would be received into membership. In spite of the agreed upon principles, a de facto color line was slipping into the Congregational community.

<u>Color Line Debate–Part 2</u>

Central (formerly Piedmont) Congregational Church of Atlanta, and three other white congregations, united with Congregational Methodists in 1888 to create the United Congregational Conference of Georgia. The formation of this all white Conference in the same geographic area as the predominantly Black Georgia Association, renewed the color line debate. The AMA protested. The Georgia Association presented several proposals for uniting the two bodies, but did not receive a reply.

Two Georgia delegations went to the meeting of the National Council of Congregational Churches in 1889, asking to be seated. The Council seated the Association delegates, and received the Conference representatives as "honorary delegates." In 1890 the Georgia Association (Black) became an Association of the (White) General Congregational Convention of Georgia.

Congregational Methodists in Alabama organized a General Congregational Convention of Alabama in 1892 without consulting the existing (predominantly Black) Alabama Association. Proposals from the Association for union were rejected by the Convention. The National Council in 1898 and 1901 refused to seat either delegation and called on them to unite.

The white churches in Georgia withdrew from the General Convention in 1903, leaving it a Black group, and united with the all White Florida Conference, to become the General Congregational Association of Florida and the Southeast. In 1904 the National Council seated the separate Black and White delegations from Georgia and Alabama. Segregation had won. By 1915 Congregational organization throughout the South was segregated. The CHMS supported White churches; the AMA supported Black churches.

PART D: AMERICAN INDIAN MISSIONS

"The North American Indian . . . possessed not only a superb physique but a remarkable mind. But the Indian no longer exists as a natural and free man. Those remnants which now dwell upon the reservations present only a sort of tableau–a fictitious copy of the past." With these words Charles "Ohiyesa" Eastman, a member of the Lakota nation, expressed the nostalgia and despair of American Indians. When he wrote his memoir in 1902, *Indian Boyhood*, the noun "Indian" was often preceded by the adjective "vanishing." When confined to Reservations, the old Indian way of life vanished. As religious beliefs were intimately intertwined with all of life, the old Indian religion, forced underground, appeared to be vanishing on the Reservation. Indian land vanished from the map as Reservations were reduced in size, and Reservation land was opened to American homesteaders. By 1901 the American Indian population of the United States and Alaska had fallen below 270,000. Some Americans wanted to erase the reservations entirely from the map and absorb the Indians into American culture. But the American Indian did not vanish.

When Charles "Ohiyesa" Eastman wrote those words in 1902 in the preface to his *Indian Boyhood*, the noun "Indian" was often preceded by the adjective "vanishing." When confined to Reservations, the old Indian way of life vanished. As religious beliefs were intimately intertwined with all of life, the old Indian religion, forced underground, appeared to be vanishing on the Reservation. Indian land vanished from the map as Reservations were reduced in size, and Reservation land was opened to American homesteaders. By 1901 the American Indian population of the United States and Alaska had fallen below 270,000. Some Americans wanted to erase the reservations entirely from the map and absorb the Indians into American culture. But the Indians did not vanish.

A Conference of "Friends of the Indian" met at Lake Mohonk, New York, every year from 1883 to 1916. These Eastern liberals used their considerable influence to bring into effect government policies which they believed to be beneficial to the American Indian. Lyman Abbott, who became a leader of the "Friends of the Indian," never set foot on a reservation and had little personal contact with Indians. He based his belief about what was best for the Indian on his experience with freedmen during Reconstruction. African Americans strove for equal rights before the law as Americans, for education, for land, and for integration. Abbott transferred this agenda to the American Indian. The "Friends of the Indian" opposed Indian sovereignty, urged the government to disregard its treaties with the Indians, and to grant land "in severalty" (individual ownership). Through their influence the Dawes Act was passed in 1887, which divided Indian lands in severalty with the remaining land opened to homesteaders. Abbott, who had opposed the close collaboration of the AMA and the Freedmen's Bureau as a violation of the separation of church and state, also opposed governmental support of church run schools on reservations. In 1894 Congress adopted a plan to gradually phase in government schools and phase out aid to religious schools.

What was the consequence of the efforts of the "Friends of the Indian" on the Reservations? The Dawes Act led to moral decline and further exploitation of the Indians, and is considered today to have been a disaster. Religious schools run by the Congregationalists had not pressed acculturation as aggressively as government schools, which increased the severity of the war on Indian language and culture.

American Indians had different concerns from African Americans. Indians wanted *sovereignty*, not *integration*, the survival of Indian *nations*, not *individual* advancement within an American nation. They had good intentions, but the "Friends of the Indian" did as much harm to the Indians as their enemies.

Dakota Mission

The Isanti[1] Dakota had passed through crisis, 1862-66, and had adopted the Christian religion. In 1866 the Dakota Mission was on the threshold of a new era, with two tasks: (1) to train the Isanti in their new religion, developing self-supporting and self-governing churches, and (2) to reach out to the Wiciyena and Titonwan divisions of the Dakota/Lakota nation, using native pastors as quickly as they could be prepared. The Dakota Mission was also experiencing a transition in leadership, as children of the pioneer missionaries replaced their parents.

Then the mission divided. Following the reunion of old-school and new-school Presbyterians in 1869, ABCFM missionaries were allowed to transfer to the Presbyterian Board of Foreign Missions. The Dakota Mission was the last mission to have its status resolved, in 1871, and the only one to split.

The schism created in 1871 was totally irrelevant to the Dakota people, and the missionary families intended to continue to work together, disregarding their different denominational affiliations. As a result, the missions and churches developed a network of institutions through which they worked as if they were one.

1. <u>Ptaye Owoglake</u> On June 21-24,1872, the missionaries called together a "mission meeting" of all the missionaries, "native helpers," and a representative from each congregation, of both denominations, to discuss common concerns. Through this representative group, meeting annually, they hoped to continue to work in unity. This "official" meeting had thirty-six persons in attendance. However over 600 people showed up for preaching, worship, discussion, fellowship, and the reception of new members. The Ptaya Owoglake, as it developed, resembled the pre-Reservation Lakota encampments for religious ceremonies, now given a Christian content. The representative organization contemplated by the missionaries gave way to Lakota direct democracy, through which Presbyterians and Congregationalists functioned as one.

2. <u>Santee Normal Training School</u>, founded in 1870, trained Indian pastors and teachers, and later functioned as a boarding school for children and youth.

3. <u>Iapi Oaye</u>, a monthly Dakota-language paper started in 1871, bound together Dakota Christians of both denominations with reports from native missionaries and discussion of issues.

4. <u>Wotanin Wašte</u>, the native missionary society, founded at Ptaya Owoglake in 1875, received funds from Dakota congregations to support native missionaries. The two denominations worked together in Wotanin Wašte until 1894.

5. <u>Language work</u>–The translation and publication of the Bible, hymnal, dictionary, grammar and reading books in Dakota continued to be supported jointly by the two denominations. Most significant in the life of the churches was the hymnal, *Dakota Odowan*. Many of the hymns were translations of popular gospel songs of the day. A few were original Dakota hymns written by

Joseph Renville and others, to native tunes which were "translated" into European notation.

Dakota Presbytery had been reorganized in 1868 as an ethnic and linguistic, rather than geographic, presbytery. Dakota Association was organized in 1888. However, missions and churches continued to function as one to such an extent that many members did not realize the difference. Denominational leaders "back East" never understood this unique relationship, and applied consistent pressure on Presbytery and Association to conform to denominational norms. Through the Twentieth Century they succeeded in slowly eroding the solidarity that had once existed between the two groups. By 1896 the Dakota Association counted twelve congregations on four reservations.

New President Ulysses S. Grant decided in 1869 to "clean up" the corrupt Indian agency by assigning reservations to missions. The mission or church "nominated" the agent for a given reservation, and the President then appointed the agent, who was accountable to both government and church. While other missionary societies gathered like wolves around a carcass to get a good share of assignments, the ABCFM remained aloof, and only held a relationship to one reservation for one year.[2] With Grant's Peace Policy came exclusion. Wotanin Wašte missionaries were excluded or discriminated against at Roman Catholic and Episcopal Reservations. Presbytery and missionaries protested loudly against this "outrage" against religious liberty, and slowly gained limited access.

The Dakota Mission was transferred from the ABCFM to the AMA in 1883. The AMA placed greater stress on education and was more willing to cooperate with the government. With government funding the AMA supported a large missionary teaching force. In 1886 the government ordered all schools conducted by missionary organizations to conduct all instruction in English. The missionaries protested, dropped some programs, and complied. In 1888 a government inspector visiting Santee School objected to the use of Dakota in devotional exercises. In

1892 the AMA and other mission boards resolved to no longer accept government support for their schools. After severe cutbacks in personnel and programs the AMA resumed its educational ministry.

Fort Berthold

The Hidatsa, Mandan and Arikara were farming Indian nations that lived along the Missouri River. Gradually migrating upstream, these once large nations were reduced in smallpox epidemics of 1781 and 1837 to small remnants. The survivors of the Hidatsa settled at Like-a-Fishook Village in 1845, were soon joined by the Mandan remnant, and in 1862 were joined by the surviving Arikara. They always maintained friendly relations with the United States government, which recognized them as the Three Affiliated Tribes of Fort Berthold.

The ABCFM sent Charles Lemon Hall (1847-1940) to Fort Berthold in 1876. He had been ordained by the Dakota churches, Congregational and Presbyterian, with leaders of both groups, White and Indian, participating. Children sent to Santee School in 1881 were converted, and returned home to share their new faith with their families. Otter and Miriam, daughters of Poor Wolf, and Ernest Hopkins, were among the first of these new Christians.

The Dawes Act scattered the people of the Three Tribes, making new congregations necessary. Native pastors were licensed in 1916, one of whom, Edward Goodbird, was ordained in 1925.

The Ho Cak[3]

The Ho Cak, formerly called "Winnebago" by English and French speakers, used to live in farming settlements across much of Wisconsin. As non-Indians pressed into their territory, the Ho Cak surrendered land in a series of treaties from 1829 to 1837. The Ho Cak then became a pilgrim people, located by the Federal government on Turkey River in northeast Iowa (1840), Long Prairie, Minnesota (1847), Blue Earth, Minnesota (1855), Crow Creek, South Dakota (1863), and Thurston County, Nebraska (1865). Throughout this period, some Ho Cak people drifted back home to Wisconsin, and were forcibly removed when discovered by authorities. Forced removals ceased in 1874, and the Ho Cak were allowed to homestead in Wisconsin.

One Sunday, Professor Henry W. Kurtz (1823-89), of Mission House, was caught in a snow storm on his way home from a preaching assignment. An Indian found him, fallen asleep, and took him to safety. After that incident, Kurtz urged the Reformed churches to do something for the Indians. In 1878 Sheboygan Classis sent Jacob Hauser, a returned missionary from India, to the Ho Cak near Black River Falls, Wisconsin. The community received him, and he started a school. Jacob Stucki (1857-1930) replaced Hauser in 1884. The first baptisms of Ho Cak people of Black River Falls occurred on January 2, 1898–David Decorah (1876-1945), John and Martha Stacy, and King of Thunder. Decorah was later licensed as assistant pastor, and John Stacy was an active evangelist until 1945.

The "Winnebago Mission" was transferred from the Sheboygan Classis to the Board of Missions of the German Synods in 1917. That same year the Stuckis began a boarding school in their home. The Woman's Missionary Society of the Reformed Church established the Winnebago Indian School in Neillsville in 1921. The Winnebago Indian Mission Church (now called Ho Cak Church) was organized in 1922. Mitchell Whiterabbit (1917-86), of the Ho Cak nation, ordained in 1945, served the "Winnebago Mission" Church 1947-69.

<u>Reflection</u>

It is difficult to write about this period (1870-1920), when even the liberals were racists. Certainly there were racists before this time. But people like Jeremiah Evarts and Lewis Tappan spoke and acted courageously, inspired by a Biblical doctrine of human worth. But this period (1870-1920) was the heyday of "Jim Crow." The United States took up the "white man's burden" of Imperialism. "Social Darwinism" and "survival of the fittest" were commonly held ideas. That the church was captured by the spirit of the times, rather than by the gospel, is seen in the misguided efforts of the "Friends of the Indian," the "make haste slowly" policy of the AMA, and the segregation of Congregationalism.

Certainly the church had significant accomplishments in this time:

- The rise of Inner Mission and the Deaconess movement.
- The beginning of Youth Ministry.
- The ordination of a few women.
- Outreach to new immigrant groups (Chapter 15) and advances in global mission (Chapter 16) (Excepting the embrace of American imperialism in Hawaii).
- The spirituality expressed in *In His Steps* and *O Master Let Me Walk with Thee.*

However, the church's vision was blurred. It failed to stand firmly *against* the norms of the society in which it found itself, but blended those norms with its own.

******

[1] The Dakota/Lakota nation can be divided into three divisions, the Isanti in the east, the Wiciyena to their west, and the Titonwan further west. These divisions represent three dialects, "D" "N" and "L" speakers respectively. The name for the nation, Dakota, Nakota or Lakota, is affected by the dialect change, but refers to the entire nation, whichever dialect is used.

[2] Sisseton Reservation, 1871. The AMA then supervised Sisseton, and also Fort Berthold and four other reservations.

[3] This Indian nation calls itself "Ho Chunk." The congregation spells its name "Ho Cak." The meaning and pronunciation are the same. "Ho Chunk" is an English phonetic spelling of the name spelled "Ho Cak" in the orthography of the written language.

CHAPTER FIFTEEN

The New Americas

Thirty-seven million immigrants arrived in the United States between 1840 and 1920. For the Evangelical Synod and the Reformed Church, ministering to the new German immigrants, many of whom already identified with their denominations, resembled the "home-mission" work of Congregationalists with English-speakers. However other immigrants came, who had some resemblance by doctrine, polity or piety, with Congregationalists or the Reformed. Some of these immigrant groups, each with their distinctive heritage from the "old country," responded to these American denominations and became part of their life as a group.[1]

PART A: GERMANS FROM RUSSIA

<u>The Brotherhood in Russia</u>

Wilhelm Staerkel, born in Russia, converted in revival, and educated at Basel, became pastor of the Reformed Church in Norka, in the Volga region. In 1871 he organized the scattered pietist prayer groups among Germans in Russia into the *Brüderschaff* (Brotherhood). The local brotherhoods were organized into conferences which met annually, not for business, but for worship. Johannes Albert organized the Brotherhood in the Ukraine.

The organization of the Brotherhood accomplished two ends. First, it promoted experiential religion. Second, it established boundaries, keeping the movement in the church and avoiding excesses. In Russian revivals persons were moved to tears and repentance, but the emotional excesses of American revivals were avoided. Singing occupied about half the time of a prayer meeting.

Immigration

The German colonies lost the privileges they were originally granted by the Russian government. In 1866 the German colonies lost control of their schools. In 1871 German men were made subject to the military draft. In 1890 Russian teachers were placed in German schools. By decree in 1897 the language of instruction became Russian. Many Germans decided it was time to move again.

In 1872 the first group of immigrants traveled from Odessa, in south Russia (now the Ukraine) to southern Dakota Territory. More followed until war ended immigration in 1914. By 1900 over 300,000 Germans from Russia and their children lived in the United States, the largest numbers in North Dakota, Kansas, South Dakota, Nebraska and Colorado. Others went to Canada, Argentina and Brazil.

German Russians in the German Reformed Church

The Reformed Church in the United States made contact with the German Russians in 1875. Jakob Orth (1837-83) had been converted in a revival, graduated from a teachers' seminary, taught school in Worms, south Russia, was active in the Brotherhood, and settled in Sutton, Nebraska, in 1873. He was ordained by the Reformed Church after an intensive course of a few weeks at Mission House. The Brotherhood was active in most German Russian Reformed churches in America. German Russians constituted most of the Reformed Churches in the Dakotas and Nebraska, and many of the churches in the neighboring states and provinces.

Many of these German Russian Reformed people were reluctant to surrender any authority to the Synod or General Synod, remembering the difficulties they had with the predominantly Lutheran consistory in Russia. Unwilling to accept financial aid from the Synod, they had difficulty keeping pastors. About 5% of the German Russians in America affiliated with the Reformed Church.

German Congregationalists

In addition to supporting Kirchenverein pastors, the American Home Missionary Society (AHMS) also supported German pastors who organized German Congregational churches. Many of these pastors came from the Pilgrim Mission of Saint Chrischona (*Die Pilgermission zu St. Chrischona*). Founded in 1840 in Basel by the same people who founded Basel Mission, Saint Chrischona Mission placed greater emphasis on evangelism. The AHMS found these missionaries more compatible with the AHMS requirement of regenerate membership in churches.

The AHMS organized the first German Congregational Church in Dubuque, Iowa, in 1847. This small movement among Germans from Germany grew using revivals. In 1862 they organized the German Association of Iowa. In 1875, after almost thirty years of labor, German Congregationalists could count only 23 congregations and 841 members, half in Iowa.

Emmanuel Jose (1840-87), of Odessa, was educated in a teachers' seminary, active in the Brotherhood, and emigrated to Sutton, Nebraska in 1874. He joined the German Congregational Church, was licensed to preach in 1875 and ordained in 1876. Jose soon organized several congregations in Dakota Territory. German Congregationalism spread rapidly among German Russians *through* the Brotherhood. The Congregational emphasis on regenerate membership appealed to the Brotherhood. They also valued autonomy in the Congregational Church. It was not the autonomy of the local congregation, but the autonomy of the German Associations within the denomination that they admired.

The local congregations, like the local brotherhoods in Russia, were closely related. The Association grouped the congregations into pastoral charges. The Apostles Creed was the standard of doctrine. The rite of Confirmation, usually following an intensive short-term period of instruction, was preserved, but was not equated with church membership. German Congregationalism flourished among Germans from Russia, who soon overwhelmed the German Congregational movement. They willingly accepted aid from the AHMS. About 30% of the Germans from Russia affiliated with the German Congregational Church (See *LTH* 6:17).

German Congregationalists organized the General Conference of the German Congregational Churches (*Die Allgemeine Evangelische Kirchenversammlung der Deutschen Kongregationalisten*) in 1883. German Congregationalists organized state associations, each was nominally affiliated with the Congregational State Conference, but in practice was an integral part of the German General Conference.

The CHMS appointed a general superintendent for German work, nominated by the General Conference, who directed the work of the General Conference. Moritz Ernst Eversz (1842-1922) superintended the General Conference through its period of greatest growth, 1888-1920.

The German General Conference wanted a German-language theological institution in America to prepare pastoral leadership for its churches. Chicago Theological Seminary (CTS) established a German Department for that purpose in 1882. In 1902 it became the German Institute, under the control of the General Conference. The German Conference conducted a proseminary to prepare students for the CTS program. The proseminary was moved several times, eventually closing in 1932. The German Institute, after a couple of moves, in 1932 became the Yankton School of Theology.

German Congregationalists connected with each other through a parish paper, *Der Kirchenbote*, established in 1882. This expanded into a publishing concern. In addition to *Der Kirchenbote*, the press published a hymnal (beginning in 1899), a Manual for German Congregational Churches (1902, 1922), a Catechism (1904, translated 1928), and Sunday School materials (beginning 1906). Most congregations adopted the Manual (*Handbuch*) as the basis of their local church government. The Catechism, solidly Biblical, incorporated the essential doctrines of the Lutheran and Heidelberg Catechisms. The General Conference by 1936 numbered 215 congregations with over 23,000 members.

PART B: THE CHINESE IN AMERICA

Chinese emigration to America began with the California gold rush of 1848. About 95% of the immigrants were men, who intended to earn money and return to China. First Congregational Church of Oakland, California, began a Sunday School for the Chinese in 1868. In 1870 three men from that school were baptized and received into membership in the church.

The American Missionary Association (AMA) resourced Congregational work with the Chinese in America, in cooperation with a California Chinese Mission, founded in 1876. Jee Gam was the leading evangelist. William C. Pond (1830-1925), pastor of a Congregational Church in San Francisco, began to superintend this AMA work in 1874. The AMA work with the Chinese took three forms:

1. Schools–The AMA began Sunday Schools and night schools to teach English to Chinese immigrants.
2. Churches–At first Chinese converts were encouraged to join the English-speaking Congregational churches. The Chinese were marginal in these churches and encountered prejudice. Pond then advocated the development of "branch churches" – Chinese fellowships related to White churches. A few became self-supporting congregations.
3. Advocacy–Chinese faced prejudice and discriminatory laws in America. The Oriental Exclusion Act of 1882 terminated Chi-

nese immigration; Chinese communities in America dwindled. The AMA in its publications and its meetings condemned exclusion and called for its repeal.

Chinese Congregationalists in California organized the Chinese Congregational Missionary Society, which in 1887 sent Chui Get to Canton (Guangzhou), China, to minister with Chinese who had encountered Christianity in America.

William C. Pond (1830-1925) grew up in Bangor, Maine, the son of Enoch Pond, President of Bangor Seminary. William went to California in 1853 under the sponsorship of the American Home Missionary Society. After being a pioneer pastor in San Francisco and the gold fields, he in 1874 began serving a congregation that welcomed Chinese men, Bethany Congregational Church in San Francisco. In that year, the American Missionary Association (AMA) appointed him superintendent of mission work among the Chinese in California. In addition to his congregation and this mission, he had a third job: fundraising for the new Pacific School of Religion. Later, the AMA asked him to also superintend work with the Japanese.

PART C: CONGREGATIONALISTS AND MISSION COVENANT

A vigorous pietist movement persisted within the Lutheran state Church of Sweden, rooted in German pietism and invigorated by early nineteenth-century contact with British Methodism. Carl Olaf Rosenius (1816-68) was succeeded by Paul Peter Waldenström (1838-1917) as leader of the movement. Known as "Mission Friends," these pietists met in small groups, listened to lay preachers, and continued to participate in the Lutheran Church. Waldenström organized the Mission Friends as the Swedish Mission Covenant in 1878, still a movement within the state church.

From 1851 to 1930 over a million Swedes came to America. A state without a state church presented a new situation to Swedish Pietists. Mission Friends was organized within the Augustana Lutheran Church, which was organized in 1860. Mission Friends also gathered where there was no Lutheran Church; some organized independent congregations. George Wiberg, a Mission Friend, organized a Swedish Congregational Church in Worcester, Massachusetts, in 1880. He encouraged others to so affiliate, and was sent by the AHMS to Minnesota. Wiberg inspired Marcus W. Montgomery (1840-94), AHMS superintendent for Minnesota, to promote Swedish work by the AHMS, and in 1884 Montgomery was appointed superintendent for Swedish work. That same year he traveled to Norway and Sweden and met with Waldenström and other leaders. Wiberg, Montgomery, and Waldenström were all convinced that American Congregationalists were the equivalent of Swedish Mission Friends, and that the latter should affiliate with the former.

Some Mission Friends in America organized the Evangelical Free Church in 1884. Others organized the Evangelical Covenant Church in 1885. At that 1885 meeting Congregational representatives offered to create a Swedish Department at Chicago Theological Seminary (CTS), to train their pastors. The Evangelical Covenant accepted the offer. The Swedish Department of CTS opened in 1885, became an "Institute" with partial control from Swedish Congregational churches in1903, and closed in 1916. The Department's first professor, Fridolf Risberg (1848-1921), nominated by Waldenström, later became a Congregationalist and encouraged the Mission Friends to affiliate.

The National Council of Congregational Churches in 1889 proposed that the Evangelical Covenant Church affiliate with the National Council as an autonomous ethnic conference. Representatives of the two groups met in Chicago, February 5-6, 1890, to discuss the proposal. The Swedish group rejected the proposal, considering the Congregationalists too "worldly."

The Mission Friends were divided into several groups: Evangelical Covenant, Evangelical Free, Congregational, independent, and Augustana Lutheran. A theological divide soon cut across these organizational divisions. Fundamentalism, expressed in pre-millennial eschatology, opposition to church organization, and condemnation of amusements, appealed to many. The majority saw Fundamentalism as an extra-biblical doctrinal standard and opposed its official adoption, but it was unofficially pervasive. By 1906, 106 Mission Friend congregations were Congregational. In succeeding years most of these congregations joined the Evangelical Covenant.

Congregationalists and Mission Friends were not as similar as some leaders believed. Congregationalists, influenced by liberal theology, were moving away from regenerate membership. Mission Friends were increasingly influenced by Fundamentalism. Many leaders were not far apart, and were moved by a genuine catholic impulse. However, the issues of assimilation verses preservation of ethnic identity, and denominational pride on both sides, were probably more significant factors than theology in preventing union.

PART D: MAGYAR REFORMED IN HUNGARY AND AMERICA

Survival and Renewal in Hungary

About one fourth of the Magyars (Hungarians) of Hungary were Reformed, and had survived two centuries of persecution. The failure of revolution in 1848 brought renewed repression. After a brief reprieve, the government issued a Patent in 1859 revoking all Protestant rights. The state would supervise all church meetings, review session minutes, approve the appointment of pastors, and authorize text books for parochial schools. Emeric Revesz (1826-81) led the Reformed people in non-violent resistance. The Reformed Church simply conducted its affairs as if the government did not exist. Some meetings were broken up; some ministers were arrested. The government propagandized and harassed the people. But they persevered. In 1860 the Emperor revoked the Patent.

The piety of the Magyar church had declined through centuries of persecution. Renewal came in two forms:

1. A synod of 1881 reorganized the church, requiring congregations and the county and district organizations to meet regularly and fulfill their responsibilities.
2. Pietism developed, inspired by Germany's *Innere-Mission* and a Scottish Mission to the Jews. Aladar Szabo, ordained in 1886, conducted evangelistic services, promoted Sunday Schools, Bible classes, and instruction in the Catechism. The Susanna Lorantfy Home Missionary Association, founded in 1892, promoted lay ministry and founded a Deaconess Home in 1905.

<u>In America</u>

Economic depression led to massive emigration from Hungary to America for fifty years beginning in 1870. Magyars approached German Reformed congregations asking for communion. In 1890 the Reformed Church in the United States (RCUS) requested the church in Hungary to send pastors. Gustáv Jurányi arrived in Cleveland in 1890, and John Kovács arrived in Pittsburgh in 1891, to organize churches among the Magyars in cooperation with the RCUS (*LTH* 6:41). By 1900 nine congregations had been organized. In that year the Presbyterian Church also began organizing Magyar congregations. In 1903 the RCUS contacted the church in Hungary to see if they could help bring an end to the separation of Magyar churches in two denominations. As a result, a delegation arrived from Hungary in 1904 and began organizing churches to form a classis within the Reformed Church of Hungary. There were now three small groups of Magyar Reformed churches.

The government of Austria-Hungary tried to use its ties to the Magyar Reformed groups for its own political purposes. During World War

I, when the United States was at war with Austria-Hungary, Magyar Reformed churches were suspected of disloyalty and several pastors were investigated by the United States government. Following the war, the churches affiliated with the Church in Hungary decided to affiliate with an American group, to end any suspicion of disloyalty. The Hungarian government believed a connection with the Presbyterians would be more beneficial, but the churches in America preferred a connection with the RCUS. A series of negotiations resulted in the Tiffin Agreement of October 7, 1921. By this agreement the Magyar churches joined the RCUS, were allowed to continue the use of their language, and to stay together in non-geographic classes. A few congregations did not go along with the agreement, and organized the Hungarian Reformed Church in America. The RCUS soon had three growing Magyar classes.

PART E: ARMENIANS IN TURKEY AND AMERICA

The small Armenian Protestant community suffered the same fate as other Armenians in Turkey. Suspected of disloyalty, the government allowed Kurds to plunder them in 1880. Perhaps 100,000 Armenians were massacred by the Turks, and many made homeless, 1894-97. Armenians in Cilicia were massacred in 1909. In the early years of World War I, 1914-15, about a half million Armenians died in massacres and were driven into deserts without provisions. All these atrocities drove survivors into exile.

The first Armenian church in America, Armenian Church of the Martyrs, was organized in Worcester, Massachusetts, in 1891. Others soon followed. Congregational and Presbyterian Armenian churches had fellowship through the Armenian Evangelical Union, and engaged in benevolent and missionary work with Armenians around the world through the Armenian Missionary Association of America.

PART F: THE JAPANESE IN JAPAN AND IN AMERICA

<u>Mission to Japan</u>

Japan was closed to the rest of the world until forced open by an American fleet in 1853. Then followed a period of restricted contacts with the West; Christianity continued to be an illegal religion until 1873.

This was a time of great social change in Japan. After a period of civil war, the Meiji Emperor ruled a strong central government that strove to learn from the West in order to make Japan more powerful. With industrialization and the establishment of a conscript army, the samurai, or warrior class, had no place. Many early Christian leaders came from the samurai class. Consequently Japanese Protestantism early acquired a unique Japanese character. The samurai marked their church with a fierce sense of loyalty to their new Lord and to each other, a strong sense of patriotism, and a commitment to independence from foreign powers.

A young samurai, Shimeta Niishima (1843-90), (in America called Joseph Hardy Neesima), desiring to learn more about the West, snuck aboard an American ship and came to America. He attended Amherst College and Andover Seminary, became a Christian, was ordained, and in 1875 went to Japan as a missionary of the ABCFM. Niishima founded Doshisha University in Kyoto in 1875, a Japanese educational institution that was also a Christian college (*LTH* 5:45). The American Board had also sent a missionary to Kobe, Japan, in 1869.

Meanwhile, in 1871 a local lord in Kumamoto had hired a West Point graduate, Capt. Leroy Lansing Janes, to conduct a school of western learning. Janes' military discipline appealed to his samurai students. His Christian faith was evident in his life, although he obeyed the law and did not preach. At dawn, one morning in 1876, thirty-five of Janes' students climbed the hill of Hanoaka and took an oath of fealty to their new Lord, Jesus Christ, and for the emancipation of their nation. When Janes had to leave, he advised the members of this "Kumamoto

Band" to go to Niishima at Doshisha, which they did. Upon graduation many were ordained and dispersed across Japan preaching Christ and organizing Congregational churches.

These Congregational Churches organized a Home Missionary Society and a national organization of "Associated Churches" (*Kami-ai*). In 1895 the Kumiai resolved that all evangelistic work be supervised by it, but the Mission did not comply. The Kumiai was a young church, but energetic, nationalistic, and self-confident. The Kumiai, under Congregational mission boards, sent missionaries to Japanese immigrants in Hawaii and the United States.

The Reformed Church in the United States (RCUS) sent its first missionaries to Japan in 1879. The RCUS work soon centered in the northern city of Sendai, where two Japanese ministers had already started evangelistic work. The RCUS united its work with several other Presbyterian and Reformed mission boards from the United States; together they initiated and supported the Church of Christ in Japan (Kyodan). The Christian denomination began its first foreign mission in 1887 in the northern city of Ishinomaki.

<u>Japanese in America</u>
In 1872 four Japanese students began meeting at Third Congregational Church, San Francisco. A woman of the church, Mrs. Wilson, offered to hold a Bible class and an English class for them, but the church was not open to "orientals." She offered her classes at a Methodist Chinese mission. In 1877 Japanese students organized a Japanese Gospel Society.

Japanese population grew; a few students were followed by larger numbers employed in farming and other occupations. William C. Pond supervised the work of organizing Congregational churches among the Japanese, beginning in 1899. By 1926, fifteen congregations had been organized.

Shanjiro Okubo, a graduate of Doshisha University in Japan, urged the formation of a strong independent Japanese church in America, no longer dependent on missionary support. Under his leadership the congregation in Oakland, California, became fully self-supporting and self-governing in 1906. Other congregations soon followed. Practicing sacrificial giving, these poor immigrant churches called pastors from Japan and Hawaii. The Reformed Church in the United States began work with Japanese on the Pacific coast in 1910.

<u>Summary</u>

Immigrant groups joined African Americans and American Indians to constitute significant subcultures in the Congregational, Reformed and Christian denominations. Some constituted ethnic classes or associations; others had less formal ties. Each immigrant group maintained ties with the mother country and with congregations of the same ethnic group in different denominations in America. Many were strongly influenced by a piety developed before coming to America, often an outgrowth of the missionary movement.

The ethnic congregation was a transitional institution, a bridge between two cultures for the first generation. Each ethnic congregation would face a crisis over the language of worship, often in the third generation. Most ethnic congregations would eventually die. Yet many persons, nurtured in these congregations, would later affiliate with more "generic" congregations of the same denomination. Each of these ethnic groups has contributed to the United Church of Christ, and their influence has been far greater than their number of surviving congregations might suggest.

******

[1] In addition to the groups described below, Congregationalists engaged in ministry to other ethnic groups, including a Norwegian-Danish Department at Chicago Theological Seminary, and a Slavic Mission directed by Henry A. Schauffler (b. 1837) in Cleveland. Surviving ethnic Congregational Churches in the UCC include Finnish congre-

gations and an Assyrian Church. The Reformed Church began Bohemian (Czech) congregations in Illinois and Iowa.

CHAPTER SIXTEEN

American Church in Global Context

In the hundred years following the ordination of the first missionaries (1812), the role of the missionary movement in the life of the church had expanded greatly. At the same time, the influence of the United States in the world had also expanded greatly.

The founders of the American Board of Commissioners for Foreign Missions (ABCFM) saw themselves as outsiders engaged in a religious war against the Unitarian establishment. Their efforts in Boston and Mumbai were parts of one struggle for God on every continent. A hundred years later the missionary movement through its piety had transformed the church at home, and had *become* the establishment. The first missionaries carried to non-Christians a faith that created a counter-culture in both lands; a century later missionaries went abroad as representatives of what they believed to be a superior Christian civilization. The early missionaries faced the opposition of the British East India Company, the skepticism of a Hawaiian king, and the restrictions of Turkish pashas. A century later, missionaries moved easily into cozy cooperation with colonial powers.

In 1812 the United States were a small outpost of Western civilization. A hundred years later they had a population greater than every European nation except Russia, had become a major industrial power, and governed an empire. American Christians entered into the national debate over whether this country's power would be used for peace or for imperialism. Finally, a "Great War" captured the passion of the nation. No group in the United States felt the burden of this war more severely than the German-Americans of the Evangelical Synod.

PART A: ADMINISTRATION OF FOREIGN MISSIONS

Dwight Moody's 1886 challenge to young people to commit themselves to missionary service created the Student Volunteer Movement for Christian Missions, and a virtual army of recruits for every existing missionary society and any new societies that might be formed. The *watchword*, the slogan "the evangelization of the world in this generation," inspired thousands of idealistic young people to devote themselves to Christian service abroad. The missionary movement flowed at high tide.

<u>Mission Controversy in the Evangelical Synod</u>

The Evangelical Synod had been created through the labors of European missionary societies. From the beginning, pastors and churches supported missions through those societies, with funds raised at annual missionfests (*LTH* 5:10) in each congregation. By 1881 Synod churches were giving over $6000 annually to the major missions.

Another missionary society also received support: the New York based German Evangelical Missionary Society of the United States. Oscar Lohr (1824-1907), a missionary to India of the Gossner Mission – a Lutheran Mission from Germany – fled to the United States at the time of the Sepoy Mutiny in 1857. While serving German Reformed congregations in New Jersey, he convinced mission supporters among German-speaking Reformed, Lutheran, Evangelical Synod and other churches to organize this new missionary society in 1865. Under its sponsorship Lohr returned to India in 1868. Evangelical Synod pastors served on the Board of this new mission alongside others, and raised funds for it.

In 1879 Conrad Bechtold (1845-1927) read a paper (*LTH* 4:48) to his district meeting urging the Evangelical Synod to establish its own foreign mission. This proposal faced strong opposition from clergy graduates of Basel whose loyalty was to the society that sent them to America. They argued that the European societies were adequate outlets for the missionary interest of the Synod. Soon the Evangelical Synod had two missionary magazines, one advocating a Synod mission, the other opposing it; the debate throughout the Synod became heated and personal. In 1882 the Bechtold group organized a voluntary missionary society and began collecting funds.

The controversy came to the 1883 Synod meeting apparently an unresolvable conflict. At that meeting the society that sent out Lohr appealed to the Synod to take over its work. Providentially the Synod received an established mission with property and experienced leadership, and both sides were satisfied.

Evolving Mission Policy in the ABCFM

As long as Rufus Anderson directed the ABCFM it pursued the one "great object" of evangelism, and the development of self-supporting, self-governing, self-propagating native churches, leading to "devolution" and the withdrawal of the missionaries. In his later years Anderson's views were considered old-fashioned by younger persons who believed missions to be a multi-faceted movement of cultural transformation. However, Anderson's power and the respect in which he was held prevented any change during his administration. Following Anderson's retirement in 1866, new views slowly began to emerge.

In 1881 the ABCFM published *The Ely Volume*. Funded by Alfred B. Ely and compiled by Thomas Laurie (1821-97), this volume's intent was, "to interest some in the great work, through its incidental results, who had not yet learned to love it for its own sake." The *Ely Volume* outlined the contributions made to Western knowledge through missionary observations and publications in the fields of geography, geology, meteorology, zoology, botany, archeology, philology, ethnography, music, religion and history. The missionaries had gone out to proclaim the Christian gospel to the world. In the process they had carefully observed that world and had made it known to the people at home. The *Ely Volume* pointed out that ABCFM missionaries had:

- given written form to over twenty languages, and published dictionaries, grammars and a wide variety of literature in these languages;
- introduced and increased literacy through common schools, and in the process firmly established the right of women to education;
- promoted commerce by promoting trustworthiness and honesty;
- provided medical care and introduced western medical practices;
- distributed relief to sufferers in famine;
- negotiated truces that ended wars and taught values that made war less harsh;
- opposed social injustice in the form of caste, polygamy, and the mistreatment of women.

The producers of the *Ely Volume* still considered evangelism to be the first objective of missions, but it was no longer the only object.

After the Andover Controversy brought pressure on the American Board to be more responsive to the increasingly liberal theological views of its constituency, the Board elected James L. Barton (1855-1936) foreign secretary in 1894.

James Levi Barton (1855-1936)

Raised in a Quaker family in Vermont, James L. Barton graduated from Hartford Seminary in 1885. He and his new wife then traveled to the Ottoman Empire as missionaries of the ABCFM. He supervised a large missionary school system, then became president of a theological seminary for Armenian ministers. The Bartons returned to America in 1894 because of his wife's declining health.

James Barton served as foreign secretary of the ABCFM from 1894 to 1927. Under Barton's leadership the American Board became the most progressive and innovative major mission board in America. In a series of articles in the *Missionary Herald*, titled "By Products of Missionary Work," and published in 1912 as *Human Progress Through Missions*, Barton outlined the "changes in methods of approach to the people" that had become commonplace through the previous twenty-five years. Instead of one "grand object" Barton described "five great departments" of missionary work: (1) evangelistic, (2) educational, (3) medical, (4) literary, and (5) industrial.

Barton promoted quality institutions of higher education in the mission field. He believed the native churches could not become fully independent of missionaries until they had a well-educated laity. A Christian intelligentsia would also provide devout leadership for native society. Believing that the mission giving of the churches should not be used for these schools, he created a Higher Educational Work Endowment Fund in 1907, and raised from American laypersons of means over a million dollars to support sixteen colleges. Four of these colleges had incorporated Boards of Trustees in America, independently raising their own funds.

In the half century following Anderson's retirement his philosophy of missions had been replaced. Under Barton's leadership the Board addressed the whole gospel to the whole person, material as well as spiritual. Neither the missionary nor the native Christian could entirely separate the gospel from its expression in Western civilization, and consequently much culture was exported with the "whole gospel." The new reliance on large institutions created a problem for devolution. Native churches were becoming self-supporting, but missionaries remained to oversee the large educational, medical and other institutions owned by agencies in America.

<u>Tainted Money</u>

In March, 1905, the ABCFM announced that they had received a gift of $100,000 from Standard Oil Company president John D. Rockefeller. Washington Gladden vigorously protested against receipt of the gift because of Rockefeller's unscrupulous and immoral business practices. Gladden used a phrase he had coined in an 1895 article, "tainted money," and argued that the acceptance of ill-gotten gain would be harmful to the spiritual character of the recipient. Gladden and the Board each had their supporters and the debate ranged across the Congregational Churches and beyond. The great majority and the most influential defended the Board. They declared they were not responsible for how money was gained, provided it was used for good. When it was learned that the Board had solicited the gift from Rockefeller, their guilt was confirmed in the eyes of their critics.

With no real chance of success, Gladden presented a resolution to the annual meeting of the American Board in Seattle in September, 1905: "that the officers of this society should neither solicit nor invite donations to its funds from persons whose gains are generally believed to have been made by methods morally reprehensible and socially injurious."

A counter resolution was presented and both referred to a committee to which Gladden was appointed. Unable to agree, the committee presented two reports. Gladden read the reports to the Board on September 15, then presented an address of his own, "Shall Ill-Gotten Gain Be Sought for Christian Purposes?" The Board members listened quietly in the center section of the church while visitors filling the sides and rear of the hall interrupted the address with frequent enthusiastic applause. A motion to table both resolutions passed easily.

At a private conference on November 1, the Prudential Committee of ABCFM assured the protestors that in the future the Board would not solicit funds from doubtful sources. Against all odds, Gladden had challenged an alliance between big missions and big money, had generated national debate, and had won a concession.

Near East Relief

In September, 1915, James Barton, ABCFM secretary, was contacted by the U. S. State Department and informed of a cable from the American ambassador in Turkey, "the destruction of the Armenian race in Turkey is rapidly progressing." On September 16, Barton gathered a committee for Armenian relief, which was later incorporated as Near East Relief. The committee included representatives of government, Protestant, Catholic and Jewish communities, and the major Protestant mission boards. The core of the committee consisted of lay trustees of Congregational and Presbyterian colleges in the Ottoman Empire. They set a goal of $100,000 to be raised for the relief of those suffering in Southwest Asia. In the next fifteen years they raised and distributed over $91,000,000 in aid plus $25,000,000 in food and supplies provided by the U. S. government and others.

In 1915 war-time censorship prevented news of Armenian massacres from reaching the West. Many American Board missionaries remained at their posts, powerless to prevent the tragedy. Mission stations provided shelter and protected orphaned and abandoned children, distributing whatever food and medical supplies they had at hand. Some missionaries accompanied refugees across the mountains to Russia. Others refused to leave without the children that had come to them for protection.

Late in 1915 the Turkish government relaxed its persecutions and allowed relief work to be done. The mission schools and hospitals became refugee centers. Food, shelter and medical care – the immediate needs – were provided. When the War ended, the U. S. government's American Relief Administration took over most of the material relief; Near East Relief concentrated on care and placement of orphans. Near East Relief cared for 132,000 orphans, placing all they could in families, and preparing the rest for independent, self-sufficient living at age sixteen. At one time they administered an "orphan city" of 30,000 children in Alexandropol (renamed Leninakan, then Gyumri).

Civil War in Russia lasted into 1922, and in Turkey until 1923. In the chaos of war, Near East Relief again provided general relief to adults, organized refugee exchanges between Greece and Turkey, and relocated orphanages when necessary.

Near East Relief was something new: a non-sectarian missionary enterprise for humanitarian relief with participation from both church and state, but independent of both. Under the direction of James Barton, and with the cooperation of the extensive ABCFM missionary force in Turkey, Near East Relief pioneered new missionary strategies, some of which set precedents for future humanitarian mission:

- appealed to the general public, without regard to religion, for aid to be given without regard to nationality or religion.
- used missionaries and other personnel already in the field to administer aid, at no expense to Near East Relief.
- made extensive use of "food for work," putting healthy refugees to work, for example sewing bedding and clothing for more refugees.
- observed absolute neutrality in politics, working with all governments. Near East Relief established its own working agreements with Soviet and Republican Turkish governments when they were not recognized by the United States government.
- followed through after the immediate crisis was over, until every child had a home or reached the age of sixteen.

In 1928 James Barton called Near East Relief "the greatest private relief organization in history," and estimated that over a million lives had been saved by its efforts.

PART B: MISSIONS AND CHURCHES

The **ABCFM** after the division of work with the Presbyterians in 1870 was no longer the largest mission board in America. The geography of the ABCFM changed with the withdrawal of Dutch Reformed (1857) and Presbyterian (1870) missions, the completion of devolution in Hawaii (1863), and transfer of American Indian missions to the American Missionary Association (1883). The ABCFM continued several missions, and entered new fields.[1] The first member of the **Christian** denomination to go as a missionary, Isaac Scott, was an African American ordained in 1852 and sent to Liberia by the Colonization Society. In 1887 Christians of the North and South united in sending out their first missionaries under the sponsorship of the denomination.[2] The General Conference of **German Congregational Churches** began sending missionaries to Argentina in 1927 in response to a request from German Russians there in 1921. In 1935 this mission expanded to German Russians in adjoining parts of Brazil. The **Reformed Church in the United States** (RCUS) began a mission to Japan in 1879 and to Hunan Province of China in 1900. The **Evangelical Synod,** supported its adopted mission in east-central India. The **American Missionary Association** began work in Puerto Rico in 1899. The **Afro-Christian Convention** extended into Guyana, Trinidad and Barbados in 1909, organizing church work begun by Joseph A. Johnson of Guyana.

Several missions and churches are of particular significance to the history of the United Church of Christ because of their inclusion by immigration or as conferences.

Haoles[3] and Hawaiians

In 1863 the Hawaiian Mission closed, leaving the Hawaiian Evangelical Association (HEA) on its own. However, many of the former missionaries and their children became Hawaiian citizens and pastors of the HEA. Although functioning in the Hawaiian language, the HEA continued to be directed by missionary descendants, who now looked upon themselves as Hawaiian.

From 1864 to 1893 conflict over its constitution disturbed the political life of Hawaii. The king arbitrarily exerted greater power, in order to preserve the Hawaiian identity of Hawaii in the face of increasing immigration. There were Hawaiians and haoles on both sides, however the HEA, both haole and Hawaiian, at first opposed the deterioration of democracy. After 1876 haoles developed large sugar plantations and imported immigrant laborers; now the haole sugar planters, some of whom were missionary descendants, opposed both royal power and democracy. In 1893 a haole revolution instigated by sugar planters and supported by other missionary descendants overthrew the monarchy, and established a "republic" which the United States annexed in 1898. Missionary descendants continued to communicate with the American Board, and influenced its opinion in opposition to Hawaiian royalty. As a result many Hawaiians felt alienated from the HEA, now dominated by haoles, and withdrew.

<u>Hawaii's Ethnic Mosaic</u>

In 1868 the Hawaiian Evangelical Association board appointed S. P. Aheong its first Chinese evangelist. An indentured laborer who married a Hawaiian and learned English, Aheong preached for two years before returning to China. The Hawaiian Board imported Chinese pastors, and in 1879 Sit Moon founded the first Chinese church in Hawaii. Some sugar planters supported churches for their workers and paid the pastor's salary.

Some Portuguese came to Hawaii on whaling ships, others came to work on the plantations. The Hawaiian Board brought a Portuguese-speaking Protestant pastor to Hawaii, Antonio V. Soars, who organized a Portuguese Evangelical Church in Honolulu in 1892.

Japanese came to Hawaii beginning in 1885 as contract laborers and by 1896 constituted one-fourth of the population of the islands. Kenjiro Aoki, a theology student from Doshisha University in Japan came with the first group of laborers. Under the leadership of the Methodists more Japanese seminary students came and churches were organized. In 1891 the Methodist Board of Missions, lacking funds, turned this Japanese work over to the Hawaiian Board, which brought more pastors from Japan and organized more churches. Christians in Japan organized a Hawaiian Missionary Association in 1903 to support this work.

Filipinos came to Hawaii beginning in 1906. From 1909 to 1935 over 122,000 Filipinos came. José Alba, who began holding services in his home in 1911, was ordained by the HEA in 1914. Simon Ygloria, ordained in the Philippines, came to Hawaii in 1913. Filipino churches were organized beginning in 1915.

The ABCFM provided aid to ethnic churches on Hawaii until 1903, after which time the American Missionary Association and Congregational Home Missionary Society provided aid. In 1904 the Hawaiian Evangelical Association, previously an ethnically Hawaiian and haole organization, extended membership to every Congregational and Presbyterian church in the territory without regard to language or race.

<u>The Church in Samoa</u>

Samoa's exposure to the corrupting influence of the West increased when a German business firm located its Pacific headquarters there in 1857. The rivalry of European powers prevented Samoa from losing its independence until 1900, when Germany took possession of the western islands and the United States occupied the East. During World War I New Zealand occupied the German possession and after the war administered it as a mandate of the League of Nations. Meanwhile the church in Samoa achieved self-support, sent out its own missionaries across the Pacific, and developed its own style of church life.

The Samoan church developed its distinctive church polity that expressed traditional Samoan respect for elders and decision-making by consensus. As Samoans had adopted Christianity as a *community*, not just as individuals, the result was more of a parish church than a gathered church. The local pastor became leader of the community, as well as the church. In 1875 the *Fono tele* ("big meeting" or "General Assembly") of the church in Samoa was initiated as an occasion for consultation with the missionaries. In 1893 lay representatives were included, and the body assumed more authority. In 1898 responsibility for ordination was transferred from the local church to the *Fono tele*.

In 1906 the church changed its constitution, transferring the placement of pastors from the congregation to the district meeting. The 1906 constitution also created the *Au Toeaina* (Council of Elders), consisting of 45 persons, ordained and lay, elected by the districts. In theory the *Au Toeaina* was only advisory, but as its members were selected for their wisdom and were respected, the *Fono tele* did not act without the approval of the *Au Toeaina*. When the London Missionary Society proposed in 1906 that Samoans fill the position of district superintendents, the Samoans opposed. Although Samoans had a strong and effective tradition of collective leadership, each local community resisted direction from a person outside the community. In 1928 the *O le Au Taitai tausi le Ekalesia* (or "Company of Church Leaders") assumed oversight of the districts.

The Samoan church took over direction of the mission's high schools, college, and press in 1916, and in 1922 achieved full self-support, including the salaries and pensions of the remaining missionaries.

Samoan missionaries preached the gospel in New Guinea, Kiribati, and other islands, accompanied Samoan chiefs exiled to Saipan in the Mariana Islands, and worked with Solomon Islanders brought to Samoa to work on plantations.

Puerto Rico

Following the annexation of the historically Spanish Catholic island of Puerto Rico by the United States in 1898, American Protestant missionary societies occupied the island. The American Missionary Association and the United Brethren in Christ arrived in 1899. The Christian denomination came in 1901. The Protestant denominations divided the island by comity agreement. Congregationalists occupied the eastern end of the island, including Humacao and Fajardo. United Brethren occupied the south-central area around Ponce. Christians came to a small area on the coast east of Ponce.

On March 5, 1930 representatives of the seven Protestant denominations in the Evangelical Union of Puerto Rico agreed to a Plan of Union, using the plan developed by the United Brethren and Presbyterians as the starting point. Together they published a religious paper, conducted a theological seminary, the Seminario Evangelico de Puerto Rico (1919), and held summer conferences. By the late 1920s missions and churches were discussing church union. The formation of a united church was linked in their minds to greater independence from the missionary societies. People were not members of a particular denomination by choice, but by geography. Denominational distinctions were irrelevant to the Puerto Ricans.

Discussions between the United Brethren and the Congregationalists collapsed in May of 1929, because of opposition of a few native Congregational pastors. By December United Brethren and Presbyterians were preparing a Plan of Union. On March 5, representatives of the seven Protestant denominations in the Evangelical Union of Puerto Rico agreed to a Plan of Union, using the plan developed by the United Brethren and Presbyterians as the starting point. The Plan was then submitted to the churches and mission boards for their approval. The Methodists held back because of pressure from their bishop, but United Brethren, Presbyterians, Congregationalists, and Christians had all voted in favor by mid-May. However, following a Presbytery meeting in September the Presbyterians withdrew. The Iglesia Evangelica Unida de Puerto Rico (IEUPR) was organized on January 28, 1931, composed of United Brethren, Congregationalists, and Christians, using the Plan of Union developed by the seven denominations, and hopeful that other denominations would join later.

The Iglesia Evangelica Unida was organized into two districts, Humacao (Congregational) and Ponce (United Brethren and Christian). Once created, the new church moved toward greater unity and independence. In 1933 the IEUPR asked the mission boards to send funds to the united church, rather than to their district. In 1935 the church entered a fifteen year plan to gradually reduce subsidies and achieve self-support.

As Puerto Rico has debated the relationship it should have with the United States – statehood, commonwealth or independence – the IEUPR has also debated its relationship to the denominations in the United States. In 1955 the Congregational Christian Churches in the United States recognized it as a constituent conference. In 1961, after each local congregation voted, the IEUPR voted to become a Conference of the United Church of Christ.

The IEUPR favored the relationship with the Congregationalists over the United Brethren, as Congregationalists treated the IEUPR as a constituent conference of the denomination, while the United Brethren treated them as a foreign mission. The IEUPR withdrew from the United Church of Christ in 2006, in opposition to General Synod's support of gay marriage. However the two ecclesial bodies continue to have a fraternal relationship.

<u>The Philippines</u>

Protestant missionaries arrived in the Philippines in the middle of a revolution. In 1896 Emilio Aguinaldo began a war of liberation against the Spanish. In 1898 the United States replaced the Spanish, but the war went on until 1902. To some nationalists the Roman Catholic Church was an agent of Spanish oppression, which they rejected. They showed an interest in Protestant missions from the beginning. With their novel doctrine of separation of church and state the American Protestants managed to maintain enough distance between themselves and their government to be credible to many Filipinos. Protestant preaching received an immediate response from Filipino intellectuals, and slowly spread to the general population.

Presbyterian missionary James B. Rodgers (1865-1944) arrived in Manila in 1899. Presbyterian missionaries moved from Manila south, establishing stations on southern Luzon and the central islands. Methodists arrived in 1901 and established stations from Manila north. The United Brethren in Christ arrived in 1901 and concentrated their work in northwest Luzon, in the southern part of the Ilokano ethnic area. The Disciples of Christ also arrived in 1901 and worked in the northern part of the Ilokano ethnic area and other scattered locations. These denominations and the Baptists joined in an Evangelical Union in 1901. They made a comity agreement, assuring each denomination an exclusive location, and agreed to all call their churches "the Evangelical Church" with the denomination's name in parentheses.

The ABCFM arrived in 1902 and was assigned the southern island of Mindanao, inhabited mostly by Muslims and traditional religionists. From the beginning the American Board mission was an extension of the larger Presbyterian mission. Presbyterian native pastors and an occasional American Presbyterian missionary were assigned to work with the American Board. Presbyterians among new settlers to Mindanao provided the first church members.

Presbyterians and Congregationalists began cooperating in educational work in 1920. A plan of union for the two groups was developed and approved by the Presbyterians. Before the American Board churches could act on the proposal they needed a regional organization. They organized as the Presbytery of Cagayan in 1922. Having adopted Presbyterian polity, the American Board churches had no problem working with the Presbyterian Synod.

The movement for unity initiated by the mission boards was at this point broadened and turned over to the Filipino churches. The United Brethren Conference and an interdenominational United Church of Manila joined the Presbyterian Synod and the Presbytery of Cagayan in forming the United Evangelical Church of the Philippines in 1929.

PART C: WAR AND PEACE

<u>The Peace Movement, 1861-1917</u>

Slavery was a state of constant warfare in the opinion of many peace advocates. When forced to choose between peace and a war to end slavery they chose war, supported the Civil War, and the peace movement yielded.

After the Civil War, the United States was saturated with a nationalistic and militaristic spirit. However, a small American Peace Society, now more conservative, continued to advocate for arbitration and a World Court.

James Browning Miles (1822-75) was secretary of the American Peace Society from 1871 to 1875. A native of Rutland Vermont, Miles studied theology at Yale and Andover and was ordained as pastor of the First Congregational Church of Charlestown, Massachusetts in 1855. He served that parish until 1871. During his brief tenure with the Peace Society Miles agitated for the codification of international law and the institution of a high court of nations. At a congress held in Brussels in 1873 the International Association for the Codification of International Laws was organized, and he was chosen its secretary.

Peace advocates in the late nineteenth century were often patriotic, believing the United States had a mission to bring peace to the world. When the Spanish-American War broke out in 1898, some peace advocates opposed it; others, like Lyman Abbott, called it a "noble war" and supported the extension of United States power.

In the period from 1898 to 1914 peace advocacy gained popularity within the cultural establishment of the country. Frederick Lynch (1867-1934), a Congregational minister and editor, cultivated the friendship of philanthropist Andrew Carnegie. In February, 1914, Carnegie gave an endowment of $2,000,000 and created the Church Peace Union to administer it, with Lynch as executive secretary. Lynch channeled most of the funds to a Commission on Peace and Arbitration of the Federal Council of Churches (FCC). Congregationalist Charles S. Macfarland (1866-1956), executive of the FCC from 1911 to 1937, cooperated closely with Lynch. Sidney L. Gulick (pronounced "Gyewlick") (1860-1945), ABCFM missionary to Japan, returned to America in 1913. With the support of Lynch and Macfarland he spoke widely and lobbied Congress to end Japanese exclusion and to improve Japanese-American relations. For a brief time peace was fashionable and appealed to the powerful.

This establishment peace movement had a fatal weaknesses. Dependant on an industrialist's benevolence, they felt obliged to honor their benefactor's wishes and not associate with more radical peace groups.

Working through the FCC, which sought to represent Protestantism in general through consensus, Lynch and associates were prevented from becoming too "controversial" in their peace advocacy. This establishment peace movement was swept into the war fever of 1917 by the appealing idealistic slogans of President Wilson, to fight a crusade, the war to end all wars. The Church Peace Union, Macfarland and Gulick, supported the National Committee on the Church and the Moral Aims of the War.

Young pastors and lay people of many denominations, critical of the weakness of the establishment peace movement, gathered in Garden City, New York, on November 11, 1915, and organized the Fellowship of Reconciliation. Members of this new organization declared themselves unwilling to fight in war, and committed to fight social injustice through nonviolent means.

War Fever

All of the churches fell in line to support the war effort in 1917. Their first concern was pastoral care of the "boys" in the service. The FCC's General War-Time Commission of the Churches coordinated the efforts of parallel commissions in each denomination with the War Department. Each denomination recruited chaplains, supplied them, aided churches in the vicinity of military camps in this country in ministering to the soldiers, and helped each local church keep in touch with their young men in the war.

Most ministers went further, promoting the "moral aims of the war," and the sale of bonds on "Liberty Bond Sunday." Some of their rhetoric generated hatred for the enemy, and suspicion of the Germans in America.

The most notorious propagandist against the Germans was Newell Dwight Hillis (1858-1929), pastor of Plymouth Congregational Church, Brooklyn. He spoke over 400 times in the second Liberty Bond drive, emotionally motivating his hearers with tales of atrocities by German soldiers. Hillis demonstrated a disregard for the fact in telling his stories. He wrote: "Society has organized itself against the rattlesnake and the yellow fever. Shepherds have entered into a conspiracy to exterminate the wolves. The Board of Health are planning to wipe out typhoid, cholera, and black plague. Not otherwise, lovers of their fellow-men have finally become perfectly hopeless with reference to the German people. They have no more relation to the civilization of 1918 than an orang-outang, a gorilla, a Judas, a hyena, a thumbscrew, or a scalping knife in the hands of society. These brutes must be cast out of society."

Hillis went on to outline a scheme for genocide: sterilization of ten million German soldiers and segregation of the women. Hillis said of many German Americans, "while their lips announce that they are Americans, in their heart they feel that their first loyalty is to the Kaiser." Suspected of being spies, they could become the targets of violence or vandalism at any time. Some "patriotic" Americans expressed their enthusiasm by making war on the German language. South Dakota banned the use of German on the telephone or in meetings of three or more persons. Montana banned the use of German in the pulpit. Iowa banned the use of any foreign language in public.

The Evangelical Synod and World War I

Federal marshals arrested Paul Krusius (b. 1879) on August 22, 1917, as he was about to board a train in Steubenville, Ohio. Pastor of Saint John's Evangelical Church near Powhatan Point, Ohio, Krusius was on his way to begin his new position, professor at Elmhurst College. As an alien enemy he was placed in an internment camp, Fort Oglethorpe, Georgia. The authorities never allowed him to confront an accuser, never charged him with a crime, and never gave him a trial. In the summer of 1919 he was deported to Germany. Other Evangelical pastors were tried for violation of the espionage act and made the targets of vigilante justice.[5]

The German Evangelical Synod was under attack from without and deeply divided within. Every immigrant church passes through a period of conflict between the older generation, attached to the language and culture of the old country, and the younger generation, eager to be "American." The War intensified that conflict in the Evangelical Synod. Other denominations took several decades to pass through the language transition; every Evangelical Synod congregation faced this issue in 1917 and 1918.

The conflict within the Evangelical Synod was not simply between the old Germans and the young Americanizers. Many young pastors opposed the war on moral grounds. This younger, English-speaking anti-war group constituted a third faction. The older generation was not a bunch of spies, "loyal to the Kaiser," but reacted to the war against the German language and culture within the United States. President John Baltzer guided the Evangelical Synod on a middle course, with a pastoral sense, expressing the patriotism of the Synod while avoiding hyper-patriotism.

The Synod's War Welfare Commission, led by Reinhold Niebuhr, received complaints from two soldiers, that the word "German" in the name of the denomination on the masthead of the *Evangelical Herald,* which they received, gave them discomfort. This renewed the movement to change the name of the denomination by taking "German" out of "German Evangelical Synod of North America." Baltzer consulted with other church leaders. The name could only be changed by the General Conference, which would not meet until 1921. However they reached a consensus that the offensive word could be dropped from unofficial documents, and the *Evangelical Herald* simply dropped the denomination's name from the masthead. At the General Conference in 1921, after two days of debate, the word "German" was dropped from the denomination's name.

Julius Horstmann (1869-1954)

Ordained into the ministry of the Evangelical Synod in 1891, Julius Horstmann served churches in Texas and Indiana. From 1906 to 1939 he edited the Synod's English-language paper, *Evangelical Herald*. Horstmann introduced the Evangelical Synod to the social gospel and chaired the Synod's Commission on Christianity and Social Problems from its creation in 1922 to 1933. He spoke eloquently for Christian unity and participated in the negotiations that created the Evangelical and Reformed Church. Throughout the war years he expressed his concern for peace, and against the war on the German language.

In the *Evangelical Herald* Julius Horstmann had editorialized against compulsory military service, against war, against hyper-patriotism, against labeling opponents of war as disloyal, against the war fever of the press, for prophetic anti-war preaching, in support of the more radical anti-war groups, in defense of conscientious objectors, against anti-German hysteria, and against the suppression of the German language. He wrote, "The world has become accustomed to war by thousands of years of cruel and bloody conflict. So called Christian nations have continually been at war with each other. War has been carried on in behalf of the Church, and the Church herself has sometimes engaged in war. But all this does not change in the least the fact that warfare is un-Christian and therefore incompatible with the principles and aims for which the Church must stand if she desires to remain true to her Founder, Head and Lord, and to herself. The Churches therefore have every right to be opposed to war on principle. . . . It follows from this that the Church as such cannot be expected to support war or war measures, or to encourage or promote anything that may be construed as an approval of war". (August 9, 1917).

Evangelical Synod congregations came under steady pressure to use English, and many made the change during the war. English was usually adopted in the Sunday School before the worship service. From 1913 to 1920 the proportion of Evangelical Synod Sunday Schools using only English rose from 25% to 59%, those using only German declined from 53% to 19%.

The Evangelical Synod had passed through the most severe crisis of its history. It emerged a more American church, strongly professing its loyalty to the nation that had persecuted it, and practicing an American freedom of expression and tolerance of divergent views.

******

[1] The ABCFM continued its missions to the Zulu of South Africa, across Turkey including the Balkans, in West India, South India, Sri Lanka, Fuzhou (Foochow) in China, and North China, and in Micronesia in cooperation with the Hawaiian Missionary Society. In 1869 they began a major missionary enterprise in Japan (See Chapter 15, Part F, Mission to Japan). In 1872 they absorbed another society with missions in "Papal Lands"–Mexico, Spain, and the Austrian Empire (now Czech Republic). Then followed new missions to West Central Africa (Angola; 1880), South China (1883), East Central Africa (Zimbabwe; 1893), and the Philippines (1902).

[2] The Christian denomination initiated missions in Japan (1887) and Puerto Rico (1901).

[3] "Foreigners," or non-Hawaiians, generally used to refer to Caucasians from North America.

[4] For more information on the trials of Evangelical pastors and the conflict in the denomination see: Charles A. Maxfield, *Germanness on Trial: The German Evangelical Synod of North America and the Espionage Act of 1917* (Santos, 2025).

CHAPTER SEVENTEEN

The Church Faces a Changing World

For about forty years after the First World War, the groups that would compose the United Church of Christ passed through a critical time in their histories: a process of church unions through which four denominations became two, then one. Significant changes in the world influenced the church, and the church, while in the process of union, participated in the events of a changing world. The process of church union will be described in Chapter Eighteen. Other events in this period are the subject of this chapter.

The United States passed over a roller coaster of prosperity, depression, war, and cold war. Life changed dramatically for Americans as they acquired electricity, indoor plumbing, hard surfaced roads, and automobiles. Values not necessarily religious influenced Americans through the cinema, radio and television. Cities grew through suburban expansion as rural communities declined.

The "Great War" of 1917-1918 shocked Christians, who reacted in several ways.

1. The Church had failed. All its pronouncements for peace and world community were for naught. The War demonstrated the impotence of the church to influence the course of nations. A desire to wield greater influence motivated church union efforts, and increased international contacts.

The Niebuhrs

Young Reinhold and Helmut Richard Niebuhr were "Americanizers" in the Evangelical Synod. Americanization to them meant (1) use of the English language, (2) patriotic support of the War, (3) support of such "English" causes as prohibition and the social gospel, (4) upgrading Elmhurst and Eden to meet American accreditation standards, and (5) greater fellowship and cooperation with "English" denominations.

Reinhold Niebuhr acquired a national reputation, writing articles and speaking on social ethical issues. Like Barth and the neo-orthodox, Reinhold Niebuhr criticized the old liberalism with its optimistic view of progress, naive confidence in human nature, and over-emphasis on God's immanence. From his Evangelical Synod background Niebuhr carried into the Twentieth Century Biblical rootedness, and a missionary concern for the less fortunate in society. Unlike the Neo-orthodox at that time, Niebuhr felt compelled to live his faith in the social and political world. Niebuhr called his ethics "Christian Realism." He continued the activism of the Social Gospel, but without the post-millennial vision of the Realm of God and without the moral absolutes. In the real world we often make decisions, not between good and evil, but between a greater and lesser evil.

A member of the Socialist Party from 1929 to 1940, Reinhold Niebuhr condemned the evils of modern industrial society in *Moral Man and Immoral Society* (1932). Advocate for the rights of labor and racial justice, and a vigorous opponent of fascism, Niebuhr served as an officer of the Fellowship of Reconciliation 1929-33. He also took an active role in organizing anti-communist liberals in the Americans for Democratic Action (1947). He explored the implications of original sin and creation in God's image in *The Nature and Destiny of Man* (1941, 1943). Niebuhr pushed American Protestantism politically to the left and theologically to the right.

Gustav Niebuhr (1863-1913) served the Evangelical Synod as a home missionary and vigorously promoted its *Innere-Mission*. He and wife *Lydia (Hosto) Niebuhr* (1869-1961) raised four children, three of whom became seminary professors. *Karl Paul Reinhold Niebuhr* (1892-1971), after graduating from Elmhurst and Eden, and ordination in 1913, attended Yale Divinity School. As the Synod schools were not accredited, he attended Yale as a special student, receiving a Master's Degree in 1915. Reinhold served Bethel Evangelical Church in Detroit from 1915 to 1928. His mother, Lydia, joined him and became unofficial assistant pastor. Reinhold directed the Synod's War Welfare Commission 1917-1920. In spite of his lack of the normal degrees, he was called to teach ethics at Union Theological Seminary in New York in 1928, and remained until his retirement in 1960. Mother Lydia moved to New York with Reinhold. When he married in 1931, Lydia moved in with Hulda, who was then in New York doing graduate study. Reinhold's brother, *Helmut Richard Niebuhr* (1894-1962) had also graduated from Elmhurst and Eden and was ordained in 1916 as pastor of Walnut Park Evangelical Church in Saint Louis. He taught at Eden, 1919-22, then attended Yale Divinity School, receiving the B.D. and Ph.D. in 1924. He then served as President of Elmhurst College, 1924-27, and dean of Eden Seminary, 1927-31. He moved both schools toward the goals of English and accreditation. From 1931 until his death in 1962 he taught ethics at Yale Divinity School. Helmut Richard expressed some of his frustration with his ethnically-defined denomination in *Social Sources of Denominationalism* (1929). He chaired the Synod's Committee on Relations with Other Churches when it initiated union discussions with the Reformed Church. Their sister *Clara Augusta Hulda Niebuhr* (1889-1959) joined Reinhold and their mother in Detroit, assisting with parish work and with secretarial work for the War Welfare Commission. Hulda and Lydia moved to Chicago in 1946, where Hulda taught at a Presbyterian College of Christian Education, then became the first female faculty member at McCormick (Presbyterian) Seminary.

Fundamentalists and Evangelicals

The Fundamentalist-Modernist conflict troubled many American denominations through this period. Fundamentalists opposed the teaching of the theory of evolution and opposed the influence of liberal theology, called "modernism," in denominational institutions. The denominations that became the United Church of Christ were not as deeply troubled by this conflict as were the Baptists and Presbyterians.

In 1940 a middle group developed between the main-line Protestants and Fundamentalists. These "Evangelicals" followed most fundamentalist doctrine, but criticized the old fundamentalism for its separatism, negativism, contentiousness, anti-intellectualism, and lack of social responsibility.

Harold John Ockenga (1905-85), pastor of Park Street Congregational Church in Boston, 1936-69, gave leadership to the new Evangelical movement. Ockenga co-founded the National Association of Evangelicals in 1942-3, served as founding President of Fuller Theological Seminary in California in absentia, 1947-54, and 1960-63. He was also founding President of Gordon-Conwell Theological Seminary in Massachusetts, 1969-79. He led Park Street Church out of the Congregational denomination into the Conservative Congregational Christian Church.

Piety and Worship

The denominations that formed the United Church of Christ experienced liturgical renewal during this period. The Constitution of the Evangelical and Reformed Church stated: "Congregations are allowed freedom of worship. The forms and order of worship that are set forth in *The Book of Worship* and in the hymnal approved by the General Synod shall be followed as accepted norms."

The apparent contradiction of these two sentences did not trouble the members of this liturgical denomination. They expected the denomination to provide worship forms, but accepted that not all would follow them. A committee began work on the hymnal and *Book of Worship* before a Constitution was adopted. *The Hymnal* became available in 1941, *The Book of Worship* in 1942.

Surveys of Evangelical and Reformed pastors indicated increasing use of liturgical forms, as follows:

	1946	1957
wear vestments	81%	98%[1]
altar centered church (as opposed to pulpit centered)	70%	85%
altar communion all or part time (as opposed to pew communion)	80%	64%
Pastor faces altar when praying	31%	49%
Cross on altar	85%	92%
Candles on altar	80%	90%

The only "low church" trend was increased pew communion, perhaps a sign of Americanization. By 1957, 88% of the pastors reported using *The Hymnal*, and 89% *The Book of Worship*.

For Congregationalists liturgical renewal was a more radical innovation. The National Council created a Commission on Evangelism and Devotional Life in 1917. In 1919 the Commission began publishing *The Fellowship of Prayer*, a daily devotional guide for Lent. This was the first acknowledgment of the Church Year by Congregationalists. The Commission introduced Congregational Christians to Advent in 1935 with *A Devotional Guide for Advent*.

Congregational Christians published *The Pilgrim Hymnal* in 1931 and *A Book of Worship for Free Churches* in 1948. The *Book of Worship* for the first time provided Congregational Christians with denominational resources for the Church Year, a lectionary, and a Confirmation service. The *Book of Worship* also contained an essay on symbolism, describing arrangement of an altar, with linens, cross, candle, flowers, and colors for the church year. Although Congregational Christians did not look upon denominational resources as "accepted norms" quite the way the Evangelical and Reformed did, these resources gradually led to changing attitudes among many Congregational Christians. Liturgical renewal was reshaping the piety of the denominations. These changes had little or no impact on numerous small, more conservative, and ethnic congregations, nor on the Afro-Christian Convention.

The Congregational Commission on Evangelism and Devotional Life, finding through a survey that their churches gave very little instruction for church membership, prepared material for a "Pastor's Class," usually conducted in Lent, leading to the reception of new members on Palm Sunday. Evangelical and Reformed churches had a long tradition of Confirmation classes lasting two or three years, in which students studied and memorized catechisms. As that educational methodology came under increased criticism, the Evangelical and Reformed Church developed a new resource for Confirmation classes, *My Confirmation*, edited by Nevin C. Harner, published in 1942.

Howard Chandler Robbins asked Reinhold Niebuhr for permission to put a prayer written by Niebuhr in a prayer book for American servicemen in World War II. Niebuhr had used the prayer in a worship service in the summer of 1934. Niebuhr gave permission, and the prayer appeared in *A Book of Prayers and Services for the Armed Forces*.

Give me the serenity to accept what cannot be changed.

Give me the courage to change what can be changed–

The wisdom to know one from the other.

Alcoholics Anonymous began using the prayer, slightly reworded, in the post-war period. Today, millions of persons recite the prayer every week at twelve-step group meetings around the world. It expressed in simple words Niebuhr's theology of "Christian Realism" and a piety of both faith and works, and of constant reliance on God.

PART B: MISSION TO THE WORLD

The missionary movement, rolling into the inter-war years with its massive inertia of motion, began to slow down as a result of the intellectual questioning of the time. The American Board of Commissioners for Foreign Missions (ABCFM) after starting a mission to the Philippines in 1902, initiated no new missions. The Evangelical Synod, relatively new to mission work, initiated its second mission in 1921, to Honduras.[2]

American mission boards had a big investment in China. The Reformed Church reported in 1909 that one third of the assessed value of its mission property was in China. The ABCFM reported in 1920 that 29% of its missionaries and 34% of its expenditures on missions went to China. As that great nation passed through Civil War and Japanese occupation, the missionaries did what they could to continue operations and to minister to human need. When the Communists came to power in 1949, and sent the missionaries home, the missionary movement received a major setback.

Pioneer missionary work appeared to be a thing of the past. Every mission field had a native church which by the Twentieth Century became an autonomous denomination. Mission and Church cooperated in negotiating with other denominations to form united churches.[3] The native churches took responsibility for most evangelistic work, and moved toward self-support, while the mission boards funded and provided leadership for medical, educational, and other humanitarian institutions.

<u>Re-Thinking Missions</u>

In the decades prior to World War I, missionaries saw themselves not simply as proclaimers of a message of grace, but as emissaries of the West's "Christian civilization." After "Christian civilization" had committed unprecedented carnage and mayhem between the trenches of northern France, critics questioned the validity of the missionary movement. Theologians, including Karl Barth and H. Richard Niebuhr, re-examined the relationship between Christ and culture. Barth tried to divorce grace from "religion." Many within and outside the church saw the missionaries as the promoters of a religion that could no longer claim superiority. Fewer young people offered themselves for missionary service, and many who did were compelled by humanitarian motives rather than by evangelistic motives. Declining contributions made it difficult for the boards to send out even these candidates.

The continuation committee of the Edinburgh Missionary Conference (1910) organized the International Missionary Council, which met in Jerusalem in 1928. The ABCFM was well represented. The Jerusalem statement on "The Christian Message" outlined new attitudes in missions. The Message:

- called on the missionary to proclaim Christ, making every effort to distinguish the person of Christ from the now discredited "Christian civilization;"
- urged the church to approach other religions as allies in a common struggle against materialism, secularism and nationalism;
- viewed every land as a mission field. Every church could both send and receive missionaries on a basis of equality;
- recognized mission activities other than evangelism as legitimate in their own right.

In 1930 philanthropist John D. Rockefeller, Jr., funded a Laymen's Commission on Foreign Missions. Congregationalist William E. Hocking (1873-1966), professor of philosophy at Harvard University, chaired this commission which investigated the work of seven major American mission boards, including the ABCFM, in India, Burma, China and Japan.

On November 18, 1932, Hocking released the commission's report, *Re-Thinking Missions*, which generated controversy from that day onward. *Re-Thinking Missions* reflected the ideas of the Jerusalem Conference. However the greatest controversy revolved around a philosophical statement of "General Principles" by Hocking which presented Christianity as an intellectual system with a contribution to make alongside other religions.

Hocking released the report at a press conference in the crowded ballroom of the Roosevelt Hotel in New York City, making *Re-Thinking Missions* a major publicity event to which all mission boards had to respond. Most mission executives welcomed the practical suggestions, but could not accept the "General Principles." The ABCFM, Evangelical Synod Board of Missions, and Reformed Church Foreign Mission Board all studied the report, used it to promote practical reforms in their missions, but rejected the Report's philosophy.

Frank Charles Laubach (1884-1970)

Remembered as the most effective literacy crusader of the Twentieth Century, Frank Laubach was a multi-faceted ABCFM missionary. Raised a Methodist in Benton, Pennsylvania, Laubach was ordained Congregational in 1913. He seriously cultivated the spiritual life, which he described in *Letters By a Modern Mystic* in 1937.

The ABCFM sent Laubach to Cagayan, on Mindanao, in the Philippines, in 1915. From 1924 to 1926 he served Union Theological Seminary in Manila as dean. In 1929 Laubach returned from advanced studies in the United States to begin a mission at Dansalan, Lanao Province, on Mindanao. Laubach was an effective evangelist and church builder. He organized the Cagayan Presbytery and actively participated in all church union discussions while he was in the Philippines. His *The People of the Philippines: Their Religious Progress and Preparation for Spiritual Leadership in the Far East* (1925) affirmed the Filipino role in the history of the church in the Philippines, and advocated independence.

Laubach called on missionaries to advocate for social justice from a Filipino perspective. He wrote in 1926, "The question in this country for missionaries is whether Christianity is chloroform poured on a feather with which missionaries tickle the chins of the Filipinos, while America, big business, persuades Congress to pour upon the Philippines the same curse of landlordism that has paralyzed Ireland for a thousand years."

He called on American missionaries to attack, "war, militarism, usury, economic imperialism, exploitation of poor by rich, abominable working conditions, etc."

Not meeting with success in Lanao in 1929, Laubach climbed nearby Signal Hill to pray. In prayer, God spoke to him, "My child, you have failed because you do not really love these Moros. You feel superior to them because you are white. If you can forget you are an American and think only how I love them, they will respond."

Laubach called this his reconversion.

Concerned that his neighbors were handicapped by illiteracy, Laubach devised a method by which he could teach a person to read in an hour. Literacy became his major ministry. When Depression in America cut missionary funding, Laubach laid off his native literacy teachers. But his new readers insisted that they could do the teaching. "Each one teach one" became the slogan of his literacy crusade. Laubach was soon traveling across Mindanao, the Philippines, and the world, promoting literacy education.

Following World War II Laubach spoke across the United States and wrote his thoughts on world peace. The real issue of the Cold War, Laubach wrote, was not between the United States and the Soviet Union. In Laubach's eyes the great divide in the world separated rich from poor, the developed from undeveloped countries. He advocated efforts by both church and state to address the problems of hunger, racism, and lack of economic opportunity around the world.

PART C: THE CHURCH AND WORLD WAR II
War, Peace, and International Reconstruction

When the First World War ended, American Christians opened their wallets to aid the people of war-torn Europe. The Evangelical Synod sent aid to Germany for six years. Although Congregationalists had special ties to Near East Relief, other denominations, including the Reformed Church, officially endorsed it and gave generously. Assistance also flowed to France and Belgium from American churches.

Christian leaders, many of whom had enthusiastically supported the War, soon became disillusioned. When Reinhold Niebuhr saw the desperation and bitterness of Germans in the French-occupied Ruhr Valley in 1923, he declared in disgust, "I am done with this war business." Many others joined the chorus of revulsion.

Evangelical Synod's General Conference declared in 1925, "international warfare and the Gospel of Love and Brotherhood which we profess are incompatible. . . . We will not as a Christian Church ever bless or sanction war."

Congregationalists declared at National Council that same year, "We record our conviction that War is contrary to the mind of Christ; that the continuance of civilization demands its entire elimination and that it is the duty of all Christians and all Churches to find a Christian way to meet international situations which threaten war."

The Reformed Church declared in 1926, "The Church of Christ as an institution should not be used as an instrument or an agency in support of war."

With an overwhelming feeling of revulsion against war, the churches supported every scheme to build peace - League of Nations, World Court, movement to Outlaw War, Kellog-Briand Pact, arms limitations talks. Congregationalist Henry A. Atkinson (1877-1955) became general secretary of the World Alliance for International Friendship Through the Churches in 1918.

Henry Avery Atkinson (1877-1960) Son of a Methodist minister, Henry A. Atkinson was ordained into the Congregational ministry in 1902. He served churches in Illinois, Ohio and Georgia. In 1911 he left the parish ministry to devote himself to the advancement of justice and peace. He promoted the social gospel, serving the Congregational denomination as secretary of its Department of Church and Labor, 1911-18. He then became general secretary of the Church Peace Union, 1918-55. This was the agency created by the benevolence of Andrew Carnegie to promote world peace. Like many advocates of peace he was seduced by President Wilson's idealism, and in 1918 was general secretary of the National Commission on the Churches and the Moral Aims of the War. In 1929 Atkinson traveled around the world, visiting religions leaders, such as Mohandas Gandhi, searching for ways the world religions could work together for peace. He participated in the global ecumenical movement, as general secretary of the Universal Christian Conference on Life and Work, 1920-32 and as a founding member of the World Council of Churches (1948). Atkinson was also an outspoken opponent of anti-Semitism and supporter of the creation of the state of Israel.

Reinhold Niebuhr joined the executive council of the Fellowship of Reconciliation (FoR) in 1929, and became its chair in 1931, although he never became a non-resister. FoR advocated for economic and racial justice as well as world peace. The organization became divided in 1933, when their executive secretary advocated violence in resisting capitalism. Niebuhr agreed with the executive and resigned from FoR leadership when the executive was fired. Niebuhr's "Christian Realism" led him to advocate violence in opposition to fascism.

When war came to the United States in 1941, the churches gave their support, but with a very different spirit from 1917. The churches did not preach hatred of the enemy as propagandists for the state. They were more respectful of minority opinions, and carefully defended the rights of their conscientious objectors. The churches did not nurture unrealistic expectations about the result of war.

Both the Evangelical and Reformed Church and the Congregational Christian Churches registered conscientious objectors and supported them in their decision while the vast majority of young men served in the armed forces.

After World War II the churches again conducted massive campaigns of relief for those suffering in the former theaters of war. The War

Emergency Relief Commission of the Evangelical and Reformed Church in 20 years beginning in 1940 raised and distributed twelve million dollars worth of aid. The Congregational Christian Committee for War Victims and Reconstruction at its peak in 1946 raised one and a quarter million dollars in one year. The committee later became the Congregational Christian Service Committee, providing humanitarian aid wherever needed.

Japanese Christians in Japan, Hawaii, and the Mainland

The Christian church in Japan continued to grow with strong indigenous leadership. Efforts to unite Japanese Christians failed until they were reinforced by governmental pressure. The government wanted to control all aspect of society through centralized organizations. The United Church of Christ in Japan (Kyodan), organized in 1941 included all legal Protestants in a centralized organization under a Director named by the government. During World War II this "official" church supported the government's war aims, while local churches and pastors concerned themselves with the abundant human needs. After the war, several denominations withdrew from the Kyodan. However Congregationalists, Disciples, Evangelical United Brethren, Methodists, and most of the Presbyterian-Reformed group remained.

The Japanese bombing of Pearl Harbor, December 7, 1941, led to the persecution of Japanese Americans on Hawaii. No effort was made to confine the entire Japanese population of 160,000 in Hawaii, but anyone suspected of sympathy with Japan was interned. Anyone fluent in Japanese or who had corresponded with Japanese officials could be removed from their homes without due process of law by the War Department. Seven Congregational ministers were detained on December 8, 1941. At Camp Livingston, Louisiana, Lordsburg, New Mexico, and Topaz, Utah, they held services and ministered with fellow internees throughout the war.

On the mainland, Japanese Americans were interned en masse. Over 120,000 persons, most American citizens, were located in ten internment camps. The church continued to function in these camps. Japanese Congregational Pastors ministered at Rohwer, Arkansas, Manzanar, California, and Paston, Arizona.

The Congregational denomination protested, as it had against acts of exclusion and discrimination in the past. The General Council pointed out in 1942, "Every time a majority deprives a minority of its civil rights it undermines its own liberties, and the unity and world-wide influence of the nation." Most Christians, Japanese and White, accepted the internment as something beyond their control and tried to ease the suffering in whatever way they could. Following the war, some Japanese Americans returned to their communities and reorganized their churches.

<u>The Church in the Philippines</u>

The United Evangelical Church in the Philippines, formed in 1929 by churches organized by the American Board, Presbyterians, and United Brethren, continued to grow. Other Protestant denominations worked each in their own area. In addition, Presbyterians and Methodists desiring churches free from foreign control had organized several independent Filipino denominations.

Japan attacked the Philippines on December 8, 1941 (December 7, USA time). Within a month the Japanese entered Manila, and by May controlled the entire archipelago. Japan favored one united Protestant church under government control, like they had in Japan. Many Filipino Protestants favored unity. They believed American missionaries - now sent home or in concentration camps - were the chief obstacles to union. Enrique C. Sobrepeña, a pastor of the United Evangelical Church and chaplain in the United States Army with the rank of Major, worked for a voluntary union, rather than one imposed by the Japanese. In April 1943 he organized the Evangelical Church of the Philippines, with the blessing of the Japanese, and was ordained its bishop. This new church, in theory, included the United Evangelical Church, the Disciples of Christ, and several independent Filipino groups.

Following the War, the Philippines began rebuilding. Major Sobrepeña faced a court martial for supporting the Japanese, but was found not guilty. Leonardo G. Dia, Moderator of the United Evangelical Church, had been in the south during the war, where the churches were not consulted and were not informed of the formation of the Evangelical Church in the Philippines. The former United Evangelical Church was now both united and divided. Dia led the southern continuing United Evangelical Church (Presbyterian and Congregational), and Sobrepeña led the northern Evangelical Church of the Philippines, a union of the United Evangelical Church (United Brethren section), Disciples of Christ, and independents. Lay people took the lead in promoting reconciliation. On May 25-27, 1948 the United Church of Christ in the Philippines came into being, uniting the United Evangelical Church, the Evangelical Church of the Philippines, and the Philippine Methodist church (an independent Filipino separation from the Methodists in 1933).

PART D: SOCIAL ISSUES

In the Afro-Christian community there was never a distinction between the spiritual and social aspects of the gospel. The people experienced and understood injustice, and found in their faith the strength to face oppression. Many others, rooted in pietism, followed the Christ they loved into a concern for the world around them.

The General Conference of the Evangelical Synod in 1921 resolved "that the Church must be the conscience of society in the social problems of our days." The social gospel had gained power in the churches in the Twentieth Century. Denominations embraced "social action" as a new mission, adopting statements, passing resolutions, and creating new agencies. Through numerous publications and addresses this controversial concern did begin to trickle down to persons in the local church.

The Federal Council of Churches (FCC), permeated by the social gospel, adopted a "social creed" at its first meeting in 1908. These fourteen short statements advocating rights for workers in industrial society, were patterned after a Methodist statement adopted six months earlier. Other denominations followed suit, adopting the FCC statement as their own or revising it. Congregationalists in 1910 adopted a Declaration of Principles based on the FCC statement. The Reformed Church in the United States in 1917 received from its Social Service Committee a Social Creed, which presented a theological justification for social action, and included the FCC social creed (as revised in 1912 with 16 points) (*LTH* 5:53). Evangelical Synod in 1925 adopted "The Social Ideals of the Churches" as revised by the FCC in 1919 (*LTH* 5:53).

Congregationalists in 1925 adopted their own Statement of Social Ideals, organized in five parts: (1) education, (2) industry and economic relationships, (3) agriculture, (4) race relations, and (5) international relations. The Evangelical and Reformed Church adopted "Objectives for Christian Social Action" in 1942. It began with a prayer of Confession, a "Declaration of Social Repentance." It outlined specific objectives under the headings of (1) the home, (2) social regulations, (3) the economic system, (4) justice for labor, (5) rural life, (6) civil liberties, (7) race relations, and (8) the political order.

The Congregational Council had created a Committee on Capital and Labor in 1892, chaired by Washington Gladden. This committee passed through a few name changes, was chaired by Henry A. Atkinson 1911-19, and in 1934 became the Council for Social Action. The 1934 action made it a church funded agency, with a status similar to a mission board. The Council for Social Action was directed to (1) conduct research, (2) educate the church, and (3) take action (*LTH* 5:55). The Evangelical Synod's Commission on Christianity and Social Problems began in the Missouri District in 1922, and gained recognition as a Synod commission in 1925. Julius Horstman gave consistent leadership. Its task was to (1) gather information regarding social conditions, (2) study it in the light of the teachings of Christ, (3) keep in touch with the FCC and other churches, and (4) keep the church informed.

The original FCC social creed focused on industrial labor issues: abolition of child labor, safe working conditions, a living wage, reasonable hours, a day of rest, the right of labor to organize, etc. Many other issues were addressed in succeeding years.

Prohibition of the sale of alcoholic beverages was advocated by every denomination in the FCC except the Evangelical Synod, which was deeply divided over the issue. An FCC study in 1925 demonstrated that Prohibition was not working - a fact the churches slowly accepted.

Congregationalists had a long history of advocacy for racial equality, but they were not alone. All of the groups that came into the United Church of Christ advocated for a federal anti-lynching law, an end to segregation, and voting rights for all. The Congregational Christian (CC) General Council in 1946 declared, "We repent of our sin of segregation as practiced both within and outside our churches and respond to the mandate of the Christian Gospel to promote with uncompromising word and purpose the integration of our Congregational Christian Churches and our democratic society of all persons of whatever race, color, or ancestry on the basis of equality and mutual respect in an inclusive fellowship."

The Evangelical and Reformed Church in 1947 quoted this CC statement and said, "We affirm as our own these words." Both denominations designated race relations to be a priority of the church for the coming two years.

In the Depression years social gospel anti-capitalist views occasionally received acceptance from church bodies. The adoption of an "anti-profit motive" resolution by the Congregational Christian Council in 1934 generated considerable criticism. The General Council in 1952 declared that it no longer held that view, but that, "no economic system embodies the perfect will of God."

The churches addressed many other issues. When Hitler persecuted Jews in Germany, the Evangelical and Reformed Church strongly condemned anti-Semitism. The churches were concerned about sexually explicit cinema, penal reform, stability of the farm economy, and rights of farm workers. The concern for world order, disarmament and an end to War, and criticism of discrimination against the Japanese have been discussed in Part B of this chapter.

<u>Summary</u>

The ship of the church passed through the storm-tossed seas of the early and mid-Twentieth Century, forced to change in response to the crisis. Old theologies of progress were furled, replaced by the more modest sails of neo-orthodoxy and Christian Realism. The direction of the missionary movement was examined, and new courses plotted. After throwing overboard its patriotic embrace of war, the church had to later scale down its pacifist reaction in the face of fascism. The failure of the great experiment called Prohibition did not deter the church from advocating other social ideals. The church emerged from World War II, an even deeper encounter with evil, with a new sense of global solidarity, and reawakened to the horror of racism. The yearning for a fuller expression of the catholicity of the church – always part of the church – was reinforced by the need to cooperate in turbulent times. Four denominations committed to Christian unity became two, then one, as they passed through the storm of the Twentieth Century.

	1946	1957
wear vestments	81%	98%[1]
altar centered church (as opposed to pulpit centered)	70%	85%
altar communion all or part time (as opposed to pew communion)	80%	64%
Pastor faces altar when praying	31%	49%
Cross on altar	85%	92%
Candles on altar	80%	90%

******

[1] Of the total, 4% wore cassock and surplice, the remainder wore some form of black robe.

[2] The Reformed Church in the United States joined other American Presbyterian and Reformed churches in initiating a small mission

to Iraq in 1924. The General Council of Congregational Christian Churches initiated "Missions of Fellowship" with European churches in 1942. In 1946 the Evangelical and Reformed Church (E&R) Board of International Missions joined with Evangelical United Brethren and northern and southern Presbyterians in initiating the United Andean Mission to Indians in Ecuador. Armenian Evangelicals, German Congregationalists and Magyar Reformed churches in America developed their own channels for sending aid to refugees of their group in other lands. The Evangelical Synod assisted German Unionists of the La Plata Synod (Argentina) but did not consider it a foreign mission. In 1947 the E&R Board responded to a request for help from Africa. The Bremen Mission had initiated a mission among the Ewe people of West Africa in 1847. When the mission was isolated from its German supporters in the war years, the Church of Scotland Mission stepped in to help. As neither society could adequately support the mission after the Second World War, they approached the E&R Church for help.

[3] Former mission churches initiated by the predecessor denominations of the United Church of Christ have entered into the following united churches: South India United Church (1908) followed by the Church of South India (1947) (includes Sri Lanka); United Church of Northern India (1924), followed by Church of North India (1970); Church of Christ in China (1927) continuing as Hong Kong Council; United Evangelical Church of the Philippines (1929) followed by United Church of Christ in the Philippines (1948); United Church of Christ in Japan (1941); United Evangelical Church of Ecuador (1964); United Congregational Church of Southern Africa (1967).

CHAPTER EIGHTEEN

The Road to Union

Four denominations entered a series of mergers in the Twentieth Century that in 1957 became the United Church of Christ.

- The National Council of Congregational Churches and the General Convention of Christian Churches united in 1931 to form the General Council of Congregational Christian Churches.
- The Reformed Church in the United States and the Evangelical Synod of North America united in 1934 to become the Evangelical and Reformed Church.
- The General Council of Congregational Christian Churches and the Evangelical and Reformed Church in 1957 became the United Church of Christ.

None of these unions were accomplished in a day – or even in a year. Each union was preceded by lengthy discussions and negotiations. Years following the union were spent writing constitutions and consolidating agencies. The process of union began for Congregational Christians in 1923, in 1928 for the Evangelical and Reformed, and continued until the last geographic conference of the United Church of Christ was organized in 1966.

A study of American denominations published in 1934, ranked the Reformed Church, Congregational Christian Churches, and Evangelical Synod, one, two, and four, respectively, in attitudes favorable to church union. Church leaders of all denominations attributed the intensified interest in Christian unity to World War I. Certainly they believed in unity and worked for unity before the war; after the war they sensed the urgency of unity. After daily encounters with matters of life and death in the trenches, issues dividing Christians appeared so trivial as to be offensive. Chaplains ministered to the needs of soldiers without thought of denomination – or religion. Church leaders viewed the divisions of the church as a cause of the church's impotence in preventing war.

Organic union was only one strategy of the ecumenical movement, which intensified in the Twentieth Century on every level from the rural neighborhood to the global community. In 1947, 239 Union Churches (Lutheran and Reformed) remained. By 1946 Congregational Christians counted at least 239 Federated Churches, 113 congregations in "yoked fields," and 82 congregations in Larger Parishes.

The denominations that became the United Church of Christ all participated in the World Missionary Conference in Edinburgh, Scotland, in 1910 (See *LTH* 6:12,52), and were inspired by their participation in the three faces of developing global catholicity: "Life and Work" meetings in Stockholm (1925) and Oxford (1937), "Faith and Order" meetings at Lausanne, Switzerland (1927) and Edinburgh (1937), and International Missionary Council meetings at Jerusalem (1928) and Madras (1938) (See *LTH* 6:15,35,58,59,86). When "Faith and Order" and "Life and Work" came together as the World Council of Churches at Amsterdam in 1948, the Evangelical and Reformed and Congregational Christian churches were again both present (*LTH* 6:87,88).

PART A: CONGREGATIONAL UNIONS
Evangelical Protestants
The UCC's road to union began with events within the Evangelical Protestant Church of North America. This liberal German-speaking denomination founded in 1912 (See *LTH* 6:16), consisted of twenty-three congregations clustered around Pittsburgh and Cincinnati, with

one congregation in Saint Louis. Too small to provide its congregations any significant services, the Evangelical Protestant Church began to search for a larger denomination with which to affiliate. On October 25, 1925, the Evangelical Protestant Church joined the National Council of Congregational Churches.

Not a union of equals, the Evangelical Protestants joined the larger Congregational Church. The smaller group continued as a separate non-geographic conference for several years, with perfect freedom to follow its own customs. The Congregational Council remained unchanged.

Christians and Congregationalists

On December 15, 1923, the Congregational Commission on Inter-Church Relations received word from Christian leaders that the Christians were ready to discuss "federation if not merger." The following March, Frank Coffin, President of the Christian Convention, wrote to the Moderator of the Congregational Council, formally requesting discussion of church union.

A courtship – as pastors and members of both denominations became better acquainted – paralleled the formal negotiations. The joint Congregational and Christian committee in April, 1928, urged their two denominations to vote to proceed on the preparation of a Plan of Union, then presented a Plan of Union (*LTH* 6:39) to the denominations on April 22, 1929. The two denominations endorsed the Plan at their national meetings in 1929. On June 27, 1931 at Seattle, Washington, each unanimously approved a Constitution for the new General Council of Congregational and Christian Churches (CC). They met together as a united church on the same day, adopted the Constitution, then spontaneously joined in singing "Blest be the tie that binds."

The Congregational Christian union did not require local congregations to change their names, organization or doctrine – neither did they vote on the union. The Plan encouraged the regional bodies to unite, but did not require it, and granted the existing Conferences and

Conventions of both denominations representation in the new General Council. The autonomous Congregational mission boards absorbed the work of the much smaller Christian non-autonomous mission boards. The greatest controversy centered around ministers' pensions (Congregationalists had them, Christians didn't). Clergy of the two denominations did not reach parity in pensions until seven years after the union.

Congregationalists and Christians united because they believed in Christian unity. The command of Christ was more compelling than any differences in tradition or culture. Both denominations practiced congregational polity; neither used creeds as tests of faith (See *LTH* 6:19,37,38). The principal opposition came from Christians who feared being "swallowed up" and Congregationalists who declared the denominations were "not homogeneous."

The two groups were not homogeneous. Congregationalists had over four times as many churches and almost nine times as many members as Christians. On average, Congregationalists were more affluent, urban, better educated, and less emotionally expressive in worship than Christians. Most Christian pastors were part-time, not seminary-educated, and did not fit well into the Congregational system. The "not homogeneous" complaint did not go away. As late as 1933 the Prudential Committee of the ABCFM defended the union, writing, "Have we not taught opposition to race discrimination, while at the same time this attitude toward the merger smacks of class discrimination?"

Fifty years after the Congregational Christian union, only 36% of the Christian Churches remained in the United Church of Christ. Many small rural congregations experienced a natural death, while others withdrew, feeling not fully accepted by the dominant group.

<u>African American Christians and Congregationalists</u>

When the Congregational and Christian communities came together, both had segregated regional bodies in the South. Denominational leaders thought these two groups should come together into one regional segregated body. They did not take into consideration the deep cultural differences between the two groups:

Black Congregationalists	Afro-Christian
105 congregations	129 congregations
6,975 members	12,640 members
subsidized by A.M.A.	Self-supporting
pastors with college or seminary education	pastors with high school and some training at Franklinton Institute
worship patterned after white worship	African-centered worship
infant baptism	believer's baptism
no revivals	revivals

The two groups continued to function separately until united in 1950 into the Convention of the South. This uneasy union lasted only sixteen years. Afro-Christians felt pressure to conform to Congregational standards; however the Afro-Christians maintained with pride their worship style, standards and organization. The Convention united with white Congregational Christians and Evangelical and Reformed into the Southern Conference of the United Church of Christ in 1966.

PART B: THE EVANGELICAL & REFORMED CHURCH

A decade after the "Great War," the Evangelical Synod and the Reformed Church both searched for partners in establishing a larger denomination and a fuller expression of Christian unity. Helmut Richard Niebuhr chaired the Evangelical Synod's Commission on Closer Relations with Other Church Bodies (See *LTH* 6:61-64); George W. Richards chaired the Reformed Church's Commission on Closer Relations and Church Union.

The Reformed Church began union negotiations in 1926 with the Evangelical Church[1] and the United Brethren in Christ. The Evangelical Church soon withdrew. The Evangelical Synod, having concluded that union with other Lutheran groups could not be attained (*LTH* 6:65,66), joined discussions in 1928. The joint commission prepared a Plan of Union and presented it to the denominations in 1929 (*LTH* 6:67). All three denominations gave initial approval and referred it to their regional bodies. The Evangelical Synod enthusiastically supported the Plan. Opposition within the United Brethren caused them to withdraw. Within the Reformed Church some classes urged one more effort to unite with the Presbyterians. As a result, when the Reformed and Evangelical commissions met in Pittsburgh in December 1930, the Reformed Church discontinued negotiations. By June 1931, Reformed discussions with the Presbyterian Church had collapsed.

On February 12, 1932, the Reformed and Evangelical commissions met again in Pittsburgh. They took the Plan of Union developed with the United Brethren, and simplified it by removing passages that had been included to address United Brethren concerns. The Reformed General Synod approved this brief Plan of Union (*LTH* 6:68) of thirteen articles in June 1932 and referred it to the classes. The Evangelical Synod districts also approved it and then the General Conference in October, 1933.

On June 26, 1934, the General Synod and General Conference met in Cleveland separately to ratify the Plan of Union (*LTH* 6:53). At 7:00 P. M. they marched two by two, Evangelical and Reformed, into Zion Evangelical Church. After the declaration that the union was in effect, delegates joined in singing "Now Thank We All Our God," in the Lord's Prayer, a doxology, and a benediction. At 8:00 P. M. the new Evangelical and Reformed Church (E&R) began its existence with the celebration of communion (*LTH* 6:69).

Church leaders often repeated the mantra, "A church may make a constitution, but a constitution does not make a church." The church entered union with only a brief Plan of Union and no constitution as an intentional act of faith. In this way they declared spiritual union in Christ took precedence over the merger of organizations. However, a church still does need a constitution. The General Synod of the new church in 1936 approved a Constitution and Bylaws, referred them to the classes and districts, received a favorable response in 1938, and the constitution went into effect in 1940. Other committees prepared a *Hymnal* and *Book of Worship*, approved by General Synod in 1938 and 1942 respectively.

The Constitution and Bylaws of the Evangelical and Reformed Church included the following:

- *Heidelberg Catechism*, *Luther's Catechism*, and *Augsburg Confession* declared the doctrinal standards of the church.
- Local church to be governed by a Consistory or Church Council composed of Elders and Deacons who may be ordained or consecrated.
- Pastors to be elected by congregation from candidates approved by the Synod Placement Committee.
- Property of churches withdrawing from the denomination to revert to the denomination.
- A full constellation of boards, commissions and auxiliary organizations.
- Election of seminary faculty to be confirmed by General Synod.

The Evangelical and Reformed union received widespread support throughout both denominations. Strongest opposition came from Reformed people of German-Russian origin, who believed that by accepting doctrinal standards other than the *Heidelberg Catechism*, the E&R Church had ceased to be a Reformed church. The Eureka Classis, in South and North Dakota, in 1938 declared itself to be the true Reformed Church in the United States, from which the rest of the denomination had withdrawn. They disturbed the new E&R Church with law suits until a judgment in 1947 brought their claims to an end.

This "first round" of church unions, creating the Congregational Christian Churches and the Evangelical and Reformed Church set precedents that would shape expectations as the two groups approached the formation of the United Church of Christ. Despite numerous similarities, differences led to mis-understanding and controversy. Similarities in the CC and E&R unions included:

- Advocates of both unions presented both spiritual and pragmatic arguments for union.
- Both identified their union as part of the global ecumenical movement.
- Both promised local congregations they would not have to change.
- Both considered a time of "courtship" – getting to know each other – as essential.

Differences included:

- The CC union was a union of the national representative bodies only – the National Council and General Convention – while the E&R union was a union of the whole church.
- The CC union was celebrated when a constitution was adopted; the E&R union was celebrated when a Plan of Union was adopted without a constitution.

PART C: THE UNITED CHURCH OF CHRIST

<u>The Rocky Road to Cleveland</u>

On January 26, 1937, Truman B. Douglass, pastor of Pilgrim Congregational Church in Saint Louis, invited Samuel Press, President of Eden Seminary, to join a group of ministers studying their faith (*LTH* 6:70). Douglass described himself as one of those "who have been wandering in a vague liberalism and have discovered the sterility of that approach." For about eight months this group of Congregational ministers, on a journey from "vague liberalism" to neo-orthodoxy, encountered Evangelical theologians, on a journey from an ethnic ghetto to the American mainstream. Sensing a strong unity of mind and heart, they were confident their recently merged denominations could unite with each other.

Press, a member of the E&R Commission on Closer Relations with Other Churches, met informally with Douglas Horton, minister and secretary of the CC General Council. Horton sent an official overture to George Richards, President of the E&R Church. Appropriate commissions of the two denominations entered discussions. In 1942 General Synod (E&R) and General Council (CC) officially endorsed union negotiations. A joint committee prepared a *Basis of Union*, received feedback from congregations and church agencies, and made revisions. Meanwhile, "getting acquainted" and mutual edification activities took place (*LTH* 6:72,73,75,76,78).

George Warren Richards (1869-1945) was ordained into the ministry of the Reformed Church in 1890. After serving a church in Allentown, Pennsylvania, he was elected professor of Church History at Lancaster Theological Seminary in 1899 and served as President of the seminary from 1920 to 1939. Richards was President of the Reformed Church in the United States from 1923 to 1933, and first President of the Evangelical and Reformed Church, from 1934 to 1944. He was an active leader of the commissions of both the Reformed Church and the Evangelical and Reformed Church as they worked through the processes of church union. An active ecumenist, Richards served on the executive committee of the Federal Council of Churches from its formation for forty years, and was at one time President of the World Alliance of Reformed Churches Throughout the World Holding the Presbyterian Order. He was active on the continuing committee of the World Conference on Faith and Order, through the process by which it became a constituent part of the new World Council of Churches. Influenced by neo-orthodoxy, he translated *Come Holy Spirit* (1933) and *God's Search for Man* (1935), both collections of sermons by Karl Barth and Eduard Thurneyson. Richards expressed his own embrace of their teachings in *Beyond Fundamentalism and Modernism* (1934). Richards said in 1946, "What we have and what we want, is not an ecumenical Church, but an ecumenical spirit among the churches. We do not want imperialistic uniformity, but democratic unity–one body in Christ.

Douglas Horton (1891-1968) was ordained into the ministry of the Congregational Church in 1915, and served churches in Connecticut, Massachusetts and Illinois. The influence of neo-orthodoxy on Horton is evident in his translation in 1928 of Barth's *The Word of God and the Word of Man*. He expressed his interest in Christian unity in his involvement in the Federal Council of Churches and the Faith and Order movement that became part of the World Council of Churches. Horton was at one time moderator of the International Congregational Council. He took leadership of the Faith and Order Commission of the World Council of Churches in 1957.

Horton served as minister and general secretary of the Congregational and Christian Churches from 1938 to 1955. He navigated that group through the difficult process of union with the Evangelical and Reformed Church. Horton served as dean of Harvard Divinity School from 1955 to 1960.

The joint committee agreed to the eighth – and they hoped last – edition of the *Basis of Union* (*LTH* 6:77) on January 22, 1947, and submitted it to the denominations. The committee asked the E&R General Synod to vote on it in 1947. If approved by two-thirds vote it would be sent to the district synods. If approved by two-thirds of them it would be declared adopted. This was E&R constitutional procedure. The CC churches did not have a definite procedure. The Congregational Christian union was a union of the national representative bodies of the two denominations, enacted by vote of those national bodies. This *Basis of Union* proposed a union of the whole church. The committee recommended the CC General Council vote approval of the *Basis of Union* if 75% of the conferences, associations, churches voting and members voting approved. They anticipated a uniting General Synod in 1948.

Opponents of union on the Congregational side soon derailed these plans. They were obsessed with a fear that the local congregations would lose their autonomy. Pro-union Congregational leaders tried to appease critics, risking alienation of the E&R community. Opposition was vigorous, vocal and vindictive. Douglas Horton, minister and secretary of the CC churches, ardent advocate of union, trying to avoid schism in Congregationalism, appeared to promise too much to too many different people. He personally became the lightning rod for criticism.

Malcolm K. Burton, pastor of Second Congregational Church in New London, Connecticut, led the opposition, publishing over 350 anti-union tracts (See *LTH* 6:80-83). In addition to consistently misrepresenting the *Basis of Union* as a threat to local church autonomy, Burton criticized the union on these grounds:

- Appeals for church union on the basis of Jesus' prayer for unity were a mere "sentimental plea."
- The union would bring together advocates of neo-orthodoxy, which was "to go back to the child's play of 'other-worldliness.'"
- The union would bring together those who wanted the church to speak more authoritatively on social issues.
- The new church would impose more consistent ministerial standards, eliminating ordination by vicinage council, such as Burton received.

Reinhold Niebuhr *had* moved the American church to the right theologically and to the left politically. Uncomfortable with both of these trends, Burton found in the merger process the opportunity to resist.

In July 1947 the E&R General Synod adopted the *Basis of Union* by a vote of 281-23 and referred it to the synods.

In November 1947, 190 CC clergy and lay people opposed to the union met at Evanston, Illinois. They called for a Constitution before churches voted, urged the churches to postpone action or vote "no," advocated a federation instead of organic union, and organized to oppose union (*LTH* 6:79). The Executive Council of the CC churches issued a brief statement of "Interpretations" (*LTH* 6:84) of the *Basis of Union*. According to the *Interpretations,* the *Basis of Union,* "will define and regulate as regards the General Synod but describe the free and voluntary relationships which the churches, associations, and conferences shall sustain with the General Synod and with each other." This satisfied many Congregational critics, but it had not been discussed with E&R leaders.

When the General Council of the CC Churches met in June, 1948, the *Basis of Union* had been approved by 94% of the Conferences, 80% of the Associations, 65.5% of the churches voting, and 63.3% of the members voting. The General Council decided to resubmit the *Basis of Union with Interpretations* to the churches voting "no" or not voting, in hopes of getting up to 75%. However they did not consider the 75% mark binding, voting, "In the event of the failure to secure the recommended 75 per cent before January 1, 1949, the General Council, at a special meeting, shall determine whether the percentage secured is sufficient to warrant the consummation of the union."

These actions created a problem. If the E&R Synods approved the *Basis of Union,* and the CC churches approved the *Basis of Union with Interpretations,* they would be entering the union on the basis of two different documents. This couldn't work. The E&R Church would have to re-vote, on the enlarged document.

The General Council of the CC church convened in Cleveland on February 4, 1949 and received a report that 72.8% of the churches voting approved of the union. The General Council voted 757-172 to accept this as satisfactory support and to proceed with union. The E&R

General Synod met in special session in Cleveland, April, 20-21, and approved the *Basis of Union with Interpretations*, 249-41. That Spring, 33 of the 34 synods gave their approval of the expanded document.

With consummation of the union only 14 months away, opponents turned to the courts. On April 19, 1949 Cadman Memorial Congregational Church in Brooklyn filed suit in the state of New York against Helen Kenyon, in her capacity as moderator of the General Council of CC churches. At issue was Congregational polity. Plaintiffs complained that the General Council had no authority to make a decision for union on behalf of local churches. On January, 26, 1950, the lower court judge, in *Cadman v. Kenyon*, ruled in favor of Cadman and placed a permanent injunction against any collaboration or joint activity between the two denominations. The General Council appealed.

Abruptly, the train was stopped just before it arrived at the station. For how long? What would be the final outcome? No one knew. The task facing Congregational proponents and opponents of union was to define Congregational polity – on this would rest the final decision of the court.

Douglas Horton conducted historical research and delivered lectures to the Congregational assembly in England, published as *Congregationalism: A Study in Church Polity*. Horton argued that each meeting of an association, conference or general council was a temporary congregation, responsible to follow Christ to the best of its ability at that time. Therefore each regional and national body and agency was autonomous and free to act.

On 5 May 1952 the appellate division of the superior court of New York reversed the decision of the lower court. The injunction against cooperation remained in effect while that decision was appealed. On December 3, 1953 New York's highest court ruled in favor of the General Council and terminated the injunction (*LTH* 6:91).

After four years of estrangement, could the CC and E&R churches pick up where they left off? Had Horton's definition of Congregationalism, and continued agitation on the CC side for a constitution before union, moved the churches further apart? The Executive Committees of the two denominations met together in October 1954. Through honest conversation and prayer participants sensed the presence of the Holy Spirit inspiring them to complete the union on the foundation of the *Basis of Union with Interpretations*. Each denomination at its 1956 national meeting voted to proceed to union on the basis of actions taken before the injunction. On June 25-27, 1957 the two denominations met in Cleveland and formally became one (*LTH* 6:92-94).

Defining the New Denomination

Now that the two had become one, the work of writing a constitution began. Two other documents, adopted before the constitution, more significantly shaped the identity of the new denomination: a statement of faith and a statement of social policy.

Many participants looked to July 8, 1959 as the formative moment of the United Church of Christ. At that time the UCC General Synod unanimously adopted a Statement of Faith, and rose spontaneously to sing a doxology and to recite the new Statement. All members of the Commission to Prepare a Statement of Faith contributed to discussions, but Roger Shinn, successor to Reinhold Niebuhr on the faculty of Union Seminary in New York, was the principal author. Designed for use in worship as a testimony to faith, the new Statement expressed the neo-orthodox emphasis on God's initiative, and German theologian Dietrich Bonhoeffer's commitment to discipleship.

That same day, July 8, 1959, before acting on the Statement of Faith, General Synod adopted a *Call to Christian Action in Society*. The social action departments of the two denominations, united immediately after the Cleveland synod meeting, prepared this document. The *Call* encouraged the rule of law in international relations, justice for labor and farmers, and an end to segregation, among other issues. Both denominations had endorsed more detailed and more controversial social creeds in the past. The *Call* was significant because it placed the church on the side of social justice from its inception.

The 1959 General Synod challenged the Commission to Prepare a Constitution to speed up its process: to prepare the draft of a constitution for study by the churches by December 1, 1959. They would then receive comments, make revisions, and present the constitution to a special session of General Synod in the summer of 1960. Next the constitution would be sent to the CC congregations and E&R synods for action, in order to be declared in force by General Synod in 1961. The content of the constitution proved less controversial than the earlier decision to not write it until after the union. Combining the mission agencies and defining their accountability to the churches were the most difficult tasks of the committee writing the constitution. The special session of Synod in 1960 endorsed the constitution unanimously. All parties interpreted the vote on the constitution in CC churches as a vote on joining the UCC. When General Synod met in 1961, it received a report that CC congregations voted for the constitution 3547-342 (91.2%) and E&R synods voted "yes" 32-1.

<u>Creating a United Church</u>

Step by step the many pieces of the two denominations needed to be brought together. *The United Church Herald* began publication on October 9, 1958. Christian educators announced a new United Church Curriculum in October 1959. The women's organizations and men's organizations each came together on a national level in 1959. The constitution brought together the mission boards in 1961. Youth Fellowship and Pilgrim Fellowship united in 1962.

General Synod in 1959 adopted a plan to integrate financial structures of the church called "Our Christian World Mission" (OCWM). Under this plan, each congregation sent its mission giving to the Conference, which retained a percentage for its work, and sent the remainder to the national church. Funds received by the national church were distributed to the various boards and agencies on a percentage basis according to a budget adopted by the General Synod.

Two small formerly German-speaking seminaries united in 1960. A special commission recommended that Mission House (E&R) of Wisconsin and Yankton (CC) of South Dakota unite and locate in the Pacific Northwest – an area of the country without a major seminary. However the schools chose to locate closer to their historic constituencies and opened United Theological Seminary of the Twin Cities in September 1962.

A Committee on Realignment, better known as the "Committee of Nine," began in 1958 the process of uniting synods and conferences. The committee proposed guidelines for the formation of new conferences:

1. Conferences should be large enough to support adequate staff (at least 150 congregations or 30,000 members).
2. State borders were logical for realignment of conference borders.
3. Boundaries should be drawn to make conferences inclusive of racial, ethnic and national groups.
4. Wherever possible there should be minimum of discontinuity to existing structures, programs and services.

The committee encountered resistance to some of these norms. Many churches had strong emotional ties to church sponsored institutions, and did not want to be separated from them. For example, Christians in Eastern Virginia wanted to keep their strong ties to Elon Home in North Carolina. Smaller states, like Rhode Island, did not want to be absorbed into larger entities to meet minimum size requirements. Southern whites asked for more time to work out racial integration. The principle of a "minimum of discontinuity" often led to smaller groups in each area being absorbed into the dominant group's organization – not exactly a union of equals. Sometimes powerful personalities got in the way.

Consolidation of regional bodies began in 1962; most UCC Conferences were organized in 1963, and on January 1, 1966, with the formation of Southern Conference, the process was completed.

<u>Calvin Synod</u>

Believing in "integration," the new united church called for abolition of all racial and ethnic regional bodies. As a result, Magyar Synod in 1961 voted against the UCC Constitution, and began negotiating with the Presbyterians. The Americanization of Magyar churches had been postponed by the arrival of two new waves of immigrants from Hungary – displaced persons after World War II, and refugees after the failed Hungarian Revolution of 1956. Magyar Synod continued to work for union with other Magyar Reformed groups in America, and sustained ties with the church in Hungary, and refugee groups in Latin America and Australia. Magyar Synod leaders appealed to the denomination to honor the Tiffin Agreement. In 1963 General Synod reversed denominational policy, allowing Magyar churches to continue as a non-geographic synod. Magyar Synod reorganized as Calvin Synod in 1964, and began calling its executive officer "bishop" in 1971.

CHAPTER NINETEEN

Addressing Social Issues as a United Church

The United Church of Christ came into being at a time of great social change. The Civil Rights Movement, the War in Vietnam, the Feminist Movement, and the movement for Gay Rights all shaped the new denomination. General Synod in 1963 adopted one resolution on a social issue – racial justice – as did the following synod. In 1967 Synod adopted five resolutions on social issues, in 1969 twenty. From 1973 through 1991, each General Synod adopted an average of 33 social action resolutions, peaking in 1983, at 54.

Did this barrage of resolutions have any impact on the local church? In a survey of persons attending Illinois Conference congregations in 1981, only 7.5% of the people rated "participation in racial justice, civil liberties, etc." as a "very important" work of the church. A similar survey in Indiana-Kentucky Conference in 1989 revealed that 60% of the membership knew little or nothing about the national church. In spite of this ignorance, 45% were pleased with the idea of the national church making pronouncements on social issues, and only 24% opposed.

Whether or not they knew about Synod resolutions, UCC people and congregations did apply the gospel to the world around them. In the 1981 survey, 46% of the respondents participated in community organizations, two-thirds of whom saw this as an expression of their Christian faith. A random survey of UCC church members in 1990 reported that 50% had given an hour or more over the past month to help the poor or sick, 17% had given an hour or more to promote social justice, and 27% had participated in a meeting or march in the past year to promote social change. A survey of UCC churches in 2000 reported that 96% of the congregations responding provided some sort of food assistance to the needy in their community. General Synod, local churches, and members were all moving in the direction of increased social action, although in different ways.

The UCC responded to oppressed and under-represented groups in three ways.

1. <u>Advocacy</u>–The church addressed political entities and society at large to make specific changes to grant rights and power to the marginalized.
2. <u>Inclusion</u>–The church made changes in its own methods of functioning to assure that the marginalized participated fully in all aspects of church life.
3. <u>Theological reflection</u>–The church listened, and lifted up theological insights originating from groups that had been marginalized.

PART A: CIVIL RIGHTS

Churches forming the United Church of Christ had a long history of advocacy for racial equality, principally through the American Missionary Association (AMA), although they did not always practice what they preached.

<u>Institute at Fisk</u>

The AMA in 1944 began an Institute of Race Relations at Fisk University. For at least twenty summers, the Institute brought religious, labor and community leaders from across the country to Fisk to study race relations with experts. The Institute created a national network of leaders who would support the Civil Rights Movement when it finally came.

Civil Rights Movement

Martin Luther King, Jr., a Baptist minister, and the Southern Christian Leadership Conference (SCLC) led the civil rights movement in opposing racial segregation in schools, public accommodations, and wherever else it appeared. They supported full legal equality of persons of all races. From the Supreme Court ruling for desegregation in 1954, to the assassination of Martin Luther King in1968, the UCC participated in this movement alongside persons of all churches and religions. Andrew Young, a United Church of Christ minister, was active in the leadership of the SCLC.

Andrew Young (b. 1932) grew up in New Orleans, where he was active in the Congregational Church. Educated at Howard University and Hartford Theological Seminary, Andrew Young was ordained into the ministry in the CC church in 1955, then served Evergreen Congregational Church, Beachton, Georgia, and Bethany Congregational Church, Thomasville, Georgia. Two years later he accepted a position with the National Council of Churches (NCC) Department of Youth Work. In 1960 he joined the Southern Christian Leadership Conference (SCLC), led by Martin Luther King, Jr. Working closely with King and the SCLC, Young was often the "negotiator" of the Civil Rights Movement, calmly and directly addressing adversaries and finding allies in the White business community. He was named executive director of SCLC in 1964. Young served in Congress from 1972 to 1977; Ambassador to the United Nations, 1977-79; mayor of Atlanta, 1981-89; co-chair of the Summer Olympics, 1996; President of the National Council of Churches, 2000-01.

When the state of Tennessee closed Highland Folk School, near Knoxville, in 1961, Young persuaded BHM to allow its Citizen Education Project to locate on BHM property near Savannah, Georgia, and to put Young on the BHM staff to direct the project. Conducted in cooperation with the SCLC, the project trained over a thousand leaders from across the South in the next four years to teach their neighbors to read and help them register to vote.

Robert Spike (1923-66), a socially concerned Baptist pastor, affiliated with the CC Church in 1955, and worked for BHM (1955-63) as secretary for Evangelism. When the NCC created a Commission on Religion and Race in 1963, they called on Spike to lead it. Spike's work included mobilizing participation in the Civil Rights Movement, political lobbying for the SCLC agenda, and supporting programs for self-development in the South. Spike was murdered in Columbus, Ohio, on October 17, 1966.[1]

At General Synod in 1963 President Ben Herbster called for the creation of a "Racial Justice Now" committee, to address the problem of racial injustice in both church and society. Appointed by the President to serve until the next General Synod, the committee was reconstituted in 1965 and 1967, and made a permanent Commission for Racial Justice (CRJ) in 1969. Charles E. Cobb (1916-98) directed CRJ from 1966 to 1985.

CRJ organized United Church Ministers for Racial and Social Justice (MRSJ) to be a "Black Caucus" within the denomination. At MRSJ's insistence, African Americans filled a majority of the seats on CRJ beginning in 1969. CRJ pursued a three-fold strategy of empowering African Americans through (1) access to education, (2) economic justice, and (3) political power. Under Cobb's leadership, CRJ found scholarships for 4,000 African Americans to attend college, initiated a ministry to women in prison, and drew attention to the practice of locating toxic waste dumps in minority communities. Through the work of CRJ, African Americans gained more leadership positions in the UCC.

Black Power

On Easter Sunday, 1967, Central UCC in Detroit dedicated an eighteen foot mural of Mary and the baby Jesus, both black. Albert Cleage (1911-2000), pastor of the church, soon renamed "Shrine of the Black Madonna," had received CC ordination in 1943, and had served churches in Lexington, Kentucky, San Francisco and Springfield, Massachusetts, before organizing Central Church in 1953. Cleage advocated "Black Pride" and "Black Power." Cleage helped found a community organizing group that promoted a "Black Manifesto." In the Black Manifesto, issued in April, 1969, spokesperson James Foreman called on all White institutions to pay reparations for the exploitation of African Americans in slavery. He delivered to the White churches and synagogues of America a bill for 500 million dollars.

General Synod in 1969 was a turning point. Before this, African Americans and their white allies had called for integration and civil rights. Beginning in 1969 the Black constituency of the church demanded a larger role in church decision-making, and placed on the agenda the economic oppression of African Americans.

Cleage[2] inspired others to develop his thoughts on Black Theology, an endeavor to interpret the Christian faith from the perspective of the Black experience. Cleage argued that Jesus was a Black fighting White oppression. Black Theology emphasized experience, affirmation of self-worth, community, and concrete application. The distinction White Theology made between a "spiritual gospel" and a "social gospel" was irrelevant to Black Theology.

Wilmington Ten

Racial tensions were high in Wilmington, North Carolina, in February, 1971, when CRJ field worker Benjamin Chavis (b. 1948) and nine others were arrested for allegedly bombing a grocery store. The UCC provided bail, lobbied, petitioned and demonstrated on behalf of the

"Wilmington Ten," throughout their trial, appeals, and incarceration. A federal court overturned their convictions on 4 December 1980.

Chavis was ordained in 1980 and directed CRJ 1985-93. On February 23, 1997, Chavis announced he had joined the Nation of Islam[3] and changed his name to Benjamin Chavis Muhammad. The Eastern North Carolina Association of the UCC rejected Chavis Muhammad's claim he could belong to the Nation of Islam and the UCC at the same time, recommending termination of his ministerial standing on April 24, 1997.

African Americans in the UCC in 2000

Change has come gradually as African Americans have been slowly accepted to staff positions, committees and boards on the national and Conference levels. African Americans have held leadership positions in the UCC, as denominational officers, beginning with Joseph H. Evans as Secretary in 1967, and President, 1976-77, as instrumentality executives, beginning with Charles Cobb at CRJ and Reuben Sheares at the Office of Church Life and Leadership in 1973, and as Conference Minister, beginning with W. Sterling Cary in Illinois Conference in 1974. White leaders have been slow to embrace Afro Christian worship styles, viewing their worship patterns of European origin as superior. From 1957 to 1999 fifty-five new African American churches joined the UCC. From 1979 to 1999 the African American presence in the UCC increased from 3.9% to 4.5% of the congregations, and from 2.8% to 4.2% of the membership. A significant part of the membership increase came from one congregation, Trinity UCC in Chicago. With only 87 adult members when Trinity in 1972 called Jeremiah Wright (b. 1941) to be its pastor, the congregation by end of century had become the largest congregation in the denomination, with over 8,000 members.

PART B: JUST PEACE

The United Church of Christ picked up where its predecessor denominations left off, defending the right of its members to be conscientious objectors and advocating support for the United Nations, human rights, arms reduction talks, and test ban treaties.

United States involvement in Vietnam grew gradually through the early 60s and became intense after the Gulf of Tonkin Resolution in 1964. Through General Synod the church supported its conscientious objectors (1961), endorsed the principle of selective conscientious objection against a specific war (1967) and by 1969 was vigorously protesting against the war.

In spite of the strong positions taken by General Synod, the membership of the denomination, like the nation, was deeply divided over the war. General Synod in 1969 tried to address this problem, calling on its agencies to "develop programs of peace education."

In the UCC the debate over Vietnam evolved into theological reflection on the nature of peace. Walter Brueggemann, a Bible scholar at Eden Seminary, in 1976 published a collection of sermons, *Living Toward a Vision: Biblical Reflections on Shalom*. Brueggemann examined the concept of peace (shalom) in the Bible and found it to mean much more than the absence of war. Shalom meant the health and well-being of society.

From 1981 to 1985 a Peace Theology Development Team, authorized by General Synod and led by Susan Thistlethwaite, examined the concept of shalom, which it translated "just peace." The Team prepared a statement adopted by General Synod in 1985, declaring the UCC to be a "Just Peace Church." It defined just peace as "the presence and inter-relation of friendship, justice, and common security from violence." The pronouncement repeated the proposition of peace advocates and peace societies of the previous century, "War can and must be eliminated."

The UCC and its predecessor denominations had been passing peace resolutions for 150 years. But never had it made such a comprehensive and theologically perceptive statement. Christian educators soon prepared curriculum materials centered around shalom, and the Team's findings were published as *A Just Peace Church* for adult study.

The just peace theology has undergirded other General Synod stands on social and economic justice, boycott of South Africa, responsible investment policies, the environment, and peace in Central America, Southwest Asia and elsewhere.

PART C: FEMINISM

The feminist movement of the late 1960s grew through the 70s and affected the churches, including the United Church of Christ. At first concerned about equal treatment under the law and equal employment opportunities, the movement grew to include inclusive language, and concern over sexual harassment and domestic violence.

Women's Organization in the UCC

In its desire to be fully integrated, the new United Church of Christ did not provide for separate national women's and men's organizations. It created a Council for Lay Life and Work as a department of the national church, to relate to both groups. In 1974 this council united with the Council for Church and Ministry to form the Office of Church Life and Leadership (OCLL). However, Women's Fellowships persisted in local churches and conferences.

General Synod in 1971 advocated equal rights, equal employment opportunities for women in church and society, and created a Task Force on Women. This evolved into an Advisory Commission (1975), then a Coordinating Center for Women in Church and Society (CCWCS) in 1979. The Center promoted the advancement of women in the denomination, published study materials, organized regional and national meetings of UCC women, produced creative worship resources and promoted an annual "Women's Sunday" in the church. In 1987 Synod constituted the CCWCS a permanent instrumentality of the church.

The Women's Missionary Societies, organized in the Nineteenth Century to advance the cause of missions, also became centers of feminist activity in the church. The new CCWCS, established to promote the feminist agenda, also supported the traditional missionary interest of women's groups. Together, the CCWCS and the conference and local women's organizations unleashed significant creative energy into the church.

Female Clergy

In 1970 only 2.5% of UCC clergy were female. The proportion of clergy who were female rose steadily from 1970 until in 2001 it was 26%. In the 1981-2 academic year women outnumbered men for the first time in the Master of Divinity programs at UCC related seminaries. Before 1970, women in ministry often served as assistants to male pastors. The situation slowly changed, and in 2001, 25% of the senior or sole pastors were women. In 2023 53.4% of ordained United Church of Christ ministers were female. Of sole or senior pastors, 43% were female. The salary discrepancy has also been narrowed slightly, from the 75% of what men were paid that women received in 1985, to 85% in 2002. Women have also served as conference ministers, beginning with Murdale Leysath in Minnesota in 1980, and as denominational officers, beginning with Carol Joyce Brun as Secretary in 1983.

Inclusive Language

The church joined the movement of secular feminists in using inclusive language, that is, not using male terms for people in general. General Synod in 1973 revised the UCC Constitution, making it inclusive, and directed that all newly printed materials use inclusive language. Soon conferences and associations were busy revising constitution and by-laws.

In the church the concern for inclusive language extended to God. The use of exclusively masculine language for God had contributed to alienation from God and low self-esteem among women. Calling God "Father" is difficult for those whose earthly fathers have been far from God-like. Some urged more frequent use of feminine images of God, along with the traditional male images. Others advocated the elimination of all gender-specific pronouns and metaphors for God. Resistance developed to the latter. Critics believed feminists were taking too many liberties with the text of the Bible, changing its meaning. General Synod in 1979 called on all who used Scripture to indicate the version or paraphrase from which they had quoted. General Synod in 1993 directed the committee preparing a new hymnal to not exclude the title "Lord" with reference to Jesus Christ.

The language of worship and study in the UCC became more inclusive, promoted by new worship resources. Resistance was strongest when changes in language appeared to alter theological meaning. Controversy centered around language for the Trinity, and the baptismal formula, "Father, Son and Holy Spirit." UCC worship resources retained the traditional trinitarian language for baptism to assure that its baptisms would be recognized by other Christian denominations.

At what point does changing language become changing theology? For some advocates of inclusive language, the changes in words were shaped by new understandings of the sacred, derived from feminist theology. Feminist Theology entailed looking at the Bible and at religion through the experience of women. Generally, feminist theology lifted up intuitive ways of knowing, sought cooperative rather than authoritarian forms of community, and criticized hierarchical understandings of God.

Although the most widely known authors of feminist theology came from other denominations, the United Church of Christ led the way in applying the movement's language and ideas in worship. Ruth Duck (1947–2024), who served UCC congregations in Illinois, Wisconsin and Massachusetts before becoming instructor in worship at Garrett Evangelical (United Methodist) Theological Seminary, compiled *Bread for the Journey* in 1981. She followed up this collection of worship resources – inclusive in language and thought – with other collections of prayers and hymns. Using a collaborative style characteristic of feminism, she gave other feminist writers of liturgical material opportunity to circulate their work. Two UCC theologians, Sharon H. Ringe and Susan B. Thistlethwaite, participated actively in a National Council of Churches project begun in 1980 to put the lectionary scriptures into inclusive language, and continued as editors of an inclusive New Testament.

PART D: SEXUAL ORIENTATION

Over the first half of the Twentieth Century psychologists advanced the concept that homosexuality was not a sin, but a mental disorder. Alfred Kinsey in a 1948 report, *Sexual Behavior in the Human Male*, brought both views into question, as he described homosexuals functioning well in all classes and occupations of society. Gradually views changed. In 1974 the American Psychiatric Association removed homosexuality from its list of mental disorders. By then the church had begun to re-examine its attitude toward homosexuality.

<u>Ordination of Homosexuals</u>

William R. Johnson (b. 1951)

On June 25, 1972, Golden Gate Association of the United Church of Christ, in northern California, ordained William Johnson, a professed homosexual, to the Christian ministry. No one doubted that many secretly homosexual persons had been ordained to the ministry in the past. Johnson believed he should be honest about his identity. After thorough examination and scrutiny by conference and association, an ecclesiastical council on April 30, authorized the action, and Johnson became the first openly homosexual person ordained by a major denomination in America. Johnson continued to be an active advocate and organizer for LGBT people throughout his ministry. The ordination of William Johnson forced the denomination to face the question of ordination of homosexuals. The debate over homosexual ordination continued the debate over whether homosexuality was a sin, mental disorder, or a natural healthy condition of a portion of humanity. In UCC polity the decision to ordain was left to each association when examining specific candidates. The Executive Council on 30 October 1973, recommended that, "homosexuality, per se, not be a bar to ordination but that associations consider a candidate's total view of human sexuality and its moral expression."

The Church Takes a Stand

The UCC's Council for Christian Social Action in 1969 supported the civil rights of homosexuals, called for decriminalization of private acts by consenting adults, and an end to discrimination in employment. General Synod in 1975 affirmed this concern for civil rights.

Advocating for someone's civil rights is not the same as accepting them as persons of worth in the church. Recognizing the need first of all to study human sexuality in the light of the Bible, Christian ethics, and the most recent social scientific research, General Synod in 1975 called for "a study concerning the dynamics of human sexuality and the theological basis for a Christian ethic concerning human sexuality." Although the ordination of a homosexual was the immediate cause for this study, the synod, and the Working Group doing the study, defined its subject as "human sexuality" in general. The church needed to respond in some way to the many-faceted sexual revolution taking place. An ethical approach to homosexuality was expected to develop, as one aspect of that broader study. A working group of Bible scholars, ethicists, social scientists and denominational agency representatives conducted a thorough study and submitted their findings to General Synod in 1977. The *Study* addressed a broad range of sexuality subjects, with thorough Biblical, theological and social analysis, only incidentally making reference to homosexuality. The Executive Council attached 18 recommendations to the *Study*.

Sexuality emerged at General Synod in 1977 as the most divisive and explosive issue in the short history of the United Church of Christ. Opponents argued that (1) the church had not enough time to study the *Study*, and (2) the *Study* was not inclusive of more traditional Biblical interpretations and ethical positions. Although the recommendations did not use the word "homosexual," both sides perceived that as the basic issue. General Synod approved the Recommendations by a vote of 409-210. Barbara Weller, leader of the opposition, presented a minority report.

The opponents of the *Study* organized a group that later became Biblical Witness Fellowship (BWF). The opposition prepared a collection of essays, *Issues in Sexual Ethics*, about half of which specifically addressed the issue of homosexuality. The *Study* and *Issues* both circulated across the UCC before the 1979 General Synod. That Synod called for a National Task Force to further study the subject of sexuality for the next four years. Unlike the earlier Working Group that was composed of academics, the Task Force was political, with representatives of various interest groups, and could not develop a consensus. General Synod in 1983 adopted the resolutions of the pro-homosexual majority.

James Nelson, ethics professor at United Seminary, expanded and published his report to the Working Group as *Embodiment* in 1979. Through the *Study*, *Embodiment*, and later works by Nelson, the UCC has led the way in the study of sexual ethics.

Biblical Witness became a voluntary society within the denomination, calling the denomination to traditional Biblical faith, and developing a multi-faceted program of church renewal.

<u>Open and Affirming</u>

General Synod in 1985 invited congregations of the UCC to declare themselves "Open and Affirming." Such a declaration would publicly assure anyone that the congregation accepted LGBT individuals nonjudgmentally as persons of worth. Slowly and deliberately congregations have studied the issue, and many have made the commitment. In 2003 the denomination reported 443 congregations had declared themselves Open and Affirming. By 2022 over 1800 congregations had declared themselves Open and Affirming.

General Synod has addressed hundreds of social issues, almost always taking a socially liberal position. The UCC has consistently striven to bring its behavior into congruence with what it understood to be the gospel. A few issues became persistent and generated discussion throughout the church. With these persistent issues, the denomination engaged in serious Bible study and theological reflection, and in the cases of Peace and Sexuality produced pioneering theological statements.

******

[1] The crime scene was arranged to make it appear that the murder was related to his sexual orientation (Spike was bisexual). The crime remains unsolved; suspicions that it was a political assassination have been neither proven nor disproved.

[2] Cleage moved further in the direction of Black Nationalism, organizing the Pan African Orthodox Christian Church in 1970, and later changing his name to Jaramogi Abebe Agyeman. The Shrine of the Black Madonna at century's end had dual standing in the UCC and in Agyeman's new denomination.

[3] The "Black Muslims" of the Nation of Islam should not be confused with orthodox (Sunni) Muslims, who consider the Nation heretical because of the messianic claims they make for their founder.

CHAPTER TWENTY

Piety, Theology and Ecumenism

How did people in the new United Church of Christ encounter God? What disciplines did they follow to cultivate that relationship? The various traditions of the UCC intermingled and new trends developed. Theology, the foundation of piety, was also in transition.

PART A: THEOLOGY IN THE NEW UNITED CHURCH

The United Church of Christ was birthed in an ethos of neo-orthodoxy and Christian Realism. The chief executive officers of the two denominations were the first translators into English of Karl Barth. The most influential theologian of the new UCC was Reinhold Niebuhr. The Statement of Faith was written by Niebuhr's disciple and successor. New currents in theology soon made themselves felt. Liberation theology, developed by Roman Catholics in Latin America, read the Bible through the eyes of the poor. Black, Feminist, American Indian and several Asian theologies read the Bible and interpreted the divine-human encounter through the experiences of those communities. All these theologies served to broaden the church's perspective from its middle-class-White-intellectual-male-North Atlantic base, and to challenge some of its assumptions. The moral collapse of Western civilization, demonstrated by two world wars, led to doubts about the superiority of Western civilization's religion. Most Christians were more open to learning from the wisdom of other religions.

In times of uncertainty, those who offer certainty have a strong appeal. Fundamentalism continued to have its supporters. The milder "Evangelicalism," grew to much greater significance than exclusive Fundamentalism. The Pentecostal/Charismatic movement, born in 1900, grew rapidly, until by century's end this movement affirming personal reception of the gifts of the Spirit claimed one of every four Christians worldwide.

The United Church of Christ moved into the future, pulled from its original ethos in multiple directions.

Sound Teaching

In 1976 the Office of Church Life and Leadership convened a seminar on theology. The seminar report identified two dangers faced by the denomination. On the one hand, the social concern of the denomination had led it to act in response to issues before it had time for theological reflection. On the other hand, concern for institutional maintenance led some to such a close identification with the cultural values of harmony, growth, and efficiency, that the church's teaching became indistinguishable from American civil religion. The seminar report expressed the conviction that, "The ministry of the church must become more intentional and disciplined in teaching the faith of the church, in valuing its theological tradition and in responding to the present place of the church in culture."

The seminar report, *Sound Teaching*, made theological statements on (1) confessions of faith, (2) polity, and (3) collegiality for accountability. It then made a strong affirmation of liberation theology: "In Jesus Christ, God takes sides with the poor." This Christocentric liberation affirmation called on the church to be in "constant conflict" with the powers that legitimate injustice, to oppose the "death dealings" of the culture, and to work for a culture obedient to God's will without being co-opted by the culture. It affirmed the corporate nature of worship and the importance of disciplines of piety.

Gradually, *Sound Teaching* influenced the life of the church. The denomination created working groups for theological reflection on issues such as peace and sexuality. Other denominations looking for a UCC doctrinal statement found in *Sound Teaching* a basis for discussion.

<u>Theological Ferment</u>

Theological discussion increased, until nine years after *Sound Teaching*, denominational publications recognized "theological ferment" in the church. The Board for Homeland Ministries devoted the Spring, 1985 issue of *New Conversations* to this theological ferment, presenting and discussing four theological statements:

1. *The Dubuque Declaration*, adopted by Biblical Witness Fellowship in November, 1983, written by Donald Bloesch.
2. *Craigville Colloquy Letter*, prepared by a consultation of UCC clergy and laity, May 16, 1984.
3. *A Most Difficult and Urgent Time*, an appeal from 39 UCC seminary faculty in October, 1983, addressed to denominational leaders.
4. *The Prophet Speaks to Our Times*, a commentary of *Isaiah 58* prepared by UCC social activists specifically for the *New Conversations* issue.

The first three statements were motivated by a concern over "a tendency for theological thought to be utilitarian, in the service of programmatic ends, without sustained, disciplined reflection," and "the caucus mentality of our churches." All four statements began with the Bible and ended with action in the world. The first two made strong appeals to past creeds and faith statements of the church, and the central doctrines of Christianity.

The *Dubuque Declaration* expressed the doctrinal stand of BWF, using much traditional creedal language. It affirmed the trinity, Christ's divine-human nature, sacrificial atonement, and the infallibility of the Bible.

The first Craigville Colloquy was organized by the "Biblical, Theological, Liturgical Group," an ad hoc movement for theological reflection begun in 1978. Craigville Colloquy became an annual event leading to the organizing of "Confessing Christ" in 1993. Seminary professor Gabe Fackre and Wisconsin Conference Minister Fred Trost were among the leaders of this movement, which blended Barthian neo-orthodoxy, Mercersburg Theology concern for worship and doctrinal continuity with the past, and a liberation theology solidarity with the oppressed. The *Colloquy Letter* condemned the "idolatries of our time": racism and sexism, materialism and consumerism, secularism, militarism, identity with any ideology of the right or left, cultural captivity and accommodation. Confessing Christ soon included over a thousand clergy and lay people, following a daily lectionary and gathering periodically for theological reflection.

"Theological ferment" did not lead to immediate direct results, but gradually influenced the church in a multitude of ways. The "ferment" influenced worship and educational resources prepared by the denomination. New publications included a theological journal, *Prism*, and a seven volume collection of primary documents from the church's past, *Living Theological Heritage*. Confessing Christ came into being, and BWF broadened its theological agenda.

Theologians

UCC theologians participated actively in denominational life, as well as in academia. Douglas Horton and George Richards led their denominations into union. Roger Shinn, who wrote the first draft of the Statement of Faith, continued to provide resources for educational ministries. Others came forward.

Frederick Herzog (1925-1995) was born in Ashley, North Dakota, in a Midwestern German Reformed environment. He studied with Karl Barth in Switzerland, and from 1960 until his death taught at Duke University in North Carolina. Herzog, in his life and thought, formed a unique link between the church of the past – neo-orthodox Germany – and the church of the future – liberation theology Latin America. In *Liberation Theology* and *Justice Church* Herzog applied liberation theology to the North American situation. He made a sharp distinction between liberation theology and liberal theology. He blended neo-orthodoxy's condemnation of culture-religion with liberation theology's commitment to struggle for justice. Herzog participated in the discussions between the UCC and the Evangelical Church of the Union in Germany, was on the committee that produced *Sound Teaching*, and wrote the first draft of "A Most Difficult and Urgent Time."

Donald Bloesch (1928-2010), son of an Evangelical Synod pastor, and grandson of two Evangelical Synod pastors, studied at Elmhurst College, Chicago Theological Seminary and University of Chicago Divinity School. Uncomfortable with the liberal theologies of the latter two schools, Bloesch found spiritual nourishment in Evangelical[1] groups. Ordained into the Evangelical and Reformed Church in 1953, Bloesch taught theology at the University of Dubuque Theological Seminary 1957-1993.

Although not well known in his own denomination, the UCC, Bloesch's many works were widely read throughout the world Evangelical community. Bloesch called his theology "progressive evangelical," a synthesis of neo-orthodoxy and evangelicalism, rooted in Evangelical Synod piety. Interested in intentional Christian community, the church and the sacraments, Bloesch also took strong stands on social issues (anti-war, pro-labor, anti-abortion). Firmly committed to the authority of Scripture, yet opposed to a rigidly literal interpretation, he challenged both Evangelicals and mainline liberals to intellectual responsibility. Described as "a catholic evangelical ordained in a mainline denomination," Bloesch remained a loyal – and often critical – member of the UCC. He wrote the *Dubuque Declaration* and was active in BWF. Piety and church renewal were constant themes in his writing, integral to his theology.

Walter Brueggemann (1933-2025) rooted in the Evangelical Synod tradition, graduated from Elmhurst and Eden and taught Old Testament at Eden before going to Columbia Theological Seminary in Georgia. This "contemporary prophet" applied the scriptures to modern issues in his writing. In addition to his interpretation of peace in *Visions of Shalom*, he addressed environmental and economic issues in *The Land* (1977). Brueggemann chaired the committee that produced the *Sound Teaching* statement, and contributed to the "Most Difficult and Urgent Time" statement.

Susan Thistlethwaite (1948-) graduated from Duke University and Divinity School, was ordained in 1973, and later joined the faculty, then became President, of Chicago Theological Seminary. A constant advocate of non-violence and justice, Thistlethwaite has promoted feminist theology and addressed the racial divide in the nation and world. In addition to giving leadership to the Peace Theology Development team, 1981-1985, and contributing to the development of inclusive language scriptures, she also participated in the development of "A Most Difficult and Urgent Time."

As the Twenty-first Century began, the theological leadership of the United Church of Christ was still shaped by the neo-orthodoxy of Barth and Christian Realism of Niebuhr. Theology was profoundly practical and ethical. American Civil Religion was seen as the greatest threat to the integrity of the church; the Bible and sound teaching its strongest defense.

PART B: MOVEMENTS FOR DEEPENING SPIRITUALITY

Traditional forms of piety persisted in the United Church of Christ. In a 1990 random sampling of UCC members, 71% reported that they prayed or meditated, 30% read the Bible, and 24% read other religious literature at least once a week. In a 1989 survey of worshipers in the Indiana-Kentucky Conference, one-third claimed to practice proportionate giving; 12% tithed. Adult Bible Study groups met in 56% of the churches in 1978, 42% in 2000.

Other findings indicated changes in piety. In 1997, 79% of UCC congregations used the lectionary, a sign of the increasing role of liturgy. In 2000, 34% of UCC congregations held occasional spiritual retreats.

Afro-Christian Convention Spirituality

The spirituality of Afro-Christian congregations continued to be shaped by its roots in Africa and the Great Awakenings in America. Vivian M. Lucas recalled, "In my church, baptism occurred the first Sunday after revival, a week-long program of evening preaching, singing, and reaffirmation to Christ held in the early fall when the weather was still warm. When it was time to baptize new believers, Afro-Christian Church folks of Saints' Delight would sing powerful and compelling songs like, 'Wade in the Water' and 'Take Me to the Water to Be Baptized' while processing down to the banks of the majestic Clifton Pond. . ."

Yvonne Delk recalled: "Worship at Macedonia was the celebration of the power to survive and to affirm life with all its complex, contradictory realities. When we worshiped God in song, in prayer, and through the preached word, we were encouraged to make a joyful noise before our God. There was movement, there was the freedom to respond. There were no spectators, all were participants. The Word was experienced, the Word was felt . . ."

Revivals continue to be held in Christian background churches, both black and white, in the South. In the Afro-Christian tradition, this aspect of spirituality is not a retreat from the world, but a continuing call to engagement with the world. As the United Church of Christ has evolved, Afro-Christian spirituality has been a significant counterpoint to the intellectualism and liturgicalism often found in the rest of the UCC.

Confirmation

How were youth prepared for church membership? The E&R pattern of a systematic course of study soon spread to CC background churches. A 1976 survey calculated that the average confirmation class consisted of ten students, ages 13 and 14, meeting 34 times for an hour and twenty minutes. Pastors or Associate Pastors were the sole instructors in 53% of the programs. In 99% of the programs the principle teaching method was discussion. Although the UCC produced several series of confirmation materials, *My Confirmation* was still used by 60% of the programs in 1976, and continued to be published by the denomination into the 21st Century.

Children and Communion

Should communion be offered to children, or only to confirmed church members? Generally, churches of the Reformed tradition restricted communion, believing it to be harmful to a person who had not made a profession of faith (*1 Corinthians* 11:27-29). Intermittently through the years, a few churches opened communion to all as a "converting ordinance." In the UCC, Christian Educators who highly valued both children and communion, believing it was "a gift of grace from God," advocated inclusion of children in communion. BHM in 1981 held a consultation on Children and Communion, and in 1984-85 produced teaching materials interpreting communion to children. Several Conferences passed resolutions in 1991-92 supporting the inclusion of children, and carried their concern to General Synod, which in 1993 endorsed the concept.

In UCC polity, this kind of policy decision was made by each congregation separately. Gradually, the policy of serving communion to children spread. Resistance was strongest in congregations with a long tradition of a first communion service after Confirmation.

Liturgical Renewal

The Twentieth Century liturgical renewal movement lifted up: (1) active participation by the laity, (2) continuity with the church of all times and places, and (3) the importance of symbolic actions, such as the sacraments, of equal value with the spoken word. The UCC inherited a strong interest in liturgy from the Mercersburg movement. Congregational Christians, historically suspicious of set forms of worship, were by mid-century moved by ecumenical interest to be open to liturgical innovation.

The UCC published new worship resources in pamphlet and loose-leaf formats. General Synod in 1977 called for a book of worship using inclusive language. The UCC published *Book of Worship: United Church of Christ* in 1986.

Worship shapes the faith of the church. The *Book of Worship* offered several options for Sunday morning worship, all rooted in the Western Christian tradition. Innovations, besides inclusive language, included greater use of the Church Year (Advent, Ash Wednesday, Easter Eve) and services for healing. Within a decade the *Book* was being used frequently by 28% of UCC congregations, occasionally by 38%.

The UCC produced *The United Church of Christ Hymnal* in 1974. Criticized for its lack of inclusive language and relatively small hymn selection, it did not gain wide acceptance. A 1989 survey showed that only 21% of UCC congregations used the *UCC Hymnal*, 38% used the *Pilgrim Hymnal* (1958), and 20% used *The* (E&R) *Hymnal*. General Synod in 1977 called for a new inclusive language hymnal. BHM began work on the project in 1989, and in 1995 published *The New Century Hymnal*, which soon exceeded the *UCC Hymnal* in sales and usage. Like the *Book of Worship* it provided more resources for the church year

and for healing services. The *New Century Hymnal* included a larger selection of new hymns, as well as older gospel songs, and music from the
racial/ethnic communities of the denomination. In spite of controversy
over the theological implications of some of the inclusive language, and
new wording for old familiar hymns, the *New Century Hymnal* received
wide usage in the UCC.

Charismatic Movement in the UCC

The Pentecostal movement began in 1900, claiming the gift of
speaking in tongues as a sign of reception of the Holy Spirit. Pente-
costals organized their own denominations and generally held Fundamentalist theology. In the 1960s the "charismatic movement" affected
many in non-Pentecostal denominations with celebration of all gifts of
the Spirit (*1 Corinthians* 12:27-30), not just speaking in tongues. In
1976, seventy-one UCC people attended a major charismatic gathering
in Kansas City, decided to promote the work of the Spirit in the UCC,
and organized Focus Renewal Ministries (FRM). FRM developed lay
witness programs, training events, and retreats, which it offered to congregations.

"Spirituality"

In the 1980s many Americans searched for meaning through "spirituality." Some turned to the Roman Catholic monastic tradition, others to Eastern religions, or psychologies of self-fulfillment. Within the
United Church of Christ, some persons believed the emphasis on social
action led to a neglect of "spiritual life." In March, 1984, seventy persons gathered in Cleveland and organized a "Spiritual Development
Network." The Network enabled persons interested in spiritual development to share ideas and resources and to work together on regional
and national events. The Network promoted spirituality grounded in
the historic piety of the UCC, and affirming its social justice concern
and its diversity. General Synod in 1985 designated "Spiritual Renewal"
a priority of the church for four years. The Office of Church Life and

Leadership developed resources and designed *The Pilgrimage: A Retreat Movement.*

<u>What is UCC Piety?</u>

Through the Spiritual Development Network and Spiritual Renewal Priority, the United Church of Christ began to recover its own authentic piety. UCC piety was intellectually responsible, nurturing the knowledge of God through Confirmation classes, adult study, and retreats. UCC piety was not individualistic, but communal, growing toward God through fellowship in the church. UCC piety valued both Word and Sacrament, developing rich liturgy, rooted in the ancient traditions and relating to contemporary issues in plain language. Word and Sacrament helped worshipers to focus on the central events of salvation history, the Cross and the resurrection. UCC piety ideally encouraged living a Christian life in gratitude to God, had a passion for justice in society, and was ecumenical. Communion in Christ led to a desire for communion with all in Christ. UCC understandings of piety were broad, including social action and charismatic renewal. The church of Jonathan Edwards, John Nevin and Charles Sheldon had rich resources for cultivating a walk with God.

PART C: THE NEW UNITED CHURCH AND THE ECUMENICAL MOVEMENT

"United" was the first name of the United Church of Christ, the center of its denominational identity. This new denomination entered union discussions with other denominations before its own union was complete. The UCC soon had to divert its attention from more plans of union to concentrate on its own internal ongoing process of becoming one people of God, (1) creating a common identity from different denominational traditions; (2) uniting by inclusion into the leadership of the church, racial, ethnic and other groups that had been on the margins; and (3) uniting with Christ's compassion for the poor. A third round of organic union did not materialize.

Those who believed the UCC's ecumenical ardor was fading, proposed in 1986 that the President have a full time staff assistant for ecumenical affairs. Because of financial restraints the position was not created until 1991, when John Thomas entered this new office.

Marjorie H. Royle of BHM Research Department reported in 1990: "Has the ecumenical movement stalled? If ecumenism is understood as the union of denominations into one new denomination, that seems to be true. . . . Ecumenists, themselves, see the lack of progress toward denominational union, not as a failure, but as a sign that the ecumenical movement has moved forward toward a new understanding of unity."

Its commitment to catholicity severely tested by the long process of union, the UCC was unwilling to immediately enter another organic union.

The UCC continued involvement in ecumenical activities, from the local to the global level. A World Council of Churches consensus document *Baptism, Eucharist and Ministry* (*BEM*), released in 1982, was thoroughly studied on all levels of the UCC, and General Synod adopted a response in 1985. As a consensus statement, BEM described a theology and policies of faith and order that no one denomination followed; it represented a direction toward which all denominations could move, and facilitated ecumenical activities.

The UCC continued to search for ways to grow in spiritual unity with other Christians. Four significant efforts, leading to new relationships short of organic union, were (1) partnership with the Christian Church (Disciples of Christ), (2) Consultation on Church Union, (3) full communion with the Evangelical Church of the Union in Germany, and (4) a formula of agreement among Lutheran and Reformed churches.

Ecumenical Partnership

The Christian Church (Disciples of Christ) expressed interest in participating in the Congregational Christian-Evangelical and Reformed union discussions in 1946. The latter two denominations believed their negotiations had progressed too far to introduce a third party at that point, but promised to consider union with the Disciples as soon as the UCC union was accomplished. Accordingly, Disciples observer-consultants participated in the UCC commissions on the constitution and the Statement of Faith.

The Disciples of Christ had discussed union with Christians and Congregationalists several times in the past. Disciples shared with the UCC a commitment to Christian unity, congregational polity, and one founder–Barton Stone.

The UCC and Disciples began talks on union in 1962, and in 1965 General Synod authorized the UCC Commission on Christian Unity to develop a Plan of Union when it believed the time was right. In 1966 the two denominations suspended union conversations in deference to the Consultation on Church Union (see next section).

The UCC and Disciples resumed talks in 1977, and in 1979 agreed to a six year "covenant for study" across the denominations. This study revealed a "widespread apathy towards union." In 1985 the two denominations declared an "ecumenical partnership," which was to be more than cooperation but less than organic union.

The United Church of Christ and the Christian Church (Disciples of Christ) recognized "full communion" in 1989, established procedures for mutual recognition of ministers in 1994, and united their foreign mission work in a "Common Global Mission Board" in January 1, 1996.

Consultation on Church Union

I am moved by the conviction that Jesus Christ, whom all of us confess as our divine Lord and Savior, wills that His church be one.

Eugene Carson Blake, stated Clerk of the Presbyterian Church, elaborated on this conviction in a sermon at Grace Episcopal Cathedral,

San Francisco, on December 4, 1960, by calling on the Presbyterian and Episcopal churches to invite the Methodist Church and the new United Church of Christ "to form with us a plan of union both catholic and reformed." Such a union would bring most American main line Protestants into one denomination.

On April 9, 1962, representatives of the four denominations met and gave birth to the Consultation on Church Union (COCU). The number of participating denominations grew through inclusion of groups with whom the four charter members had close relations, and through most of its history COCU had from six to ten members. The Consultation soon reached theological consensus and prepared a *Plan of Union* which it commended to the churches in 1970. Over 1300 study groups across the country examined the *Plan*. Responses, reported to the Consultation in 1973, were overwhelmingly negative. The *Plan* created too much bureaucracy and a "Parish" system that left congregations with less control over their own lives than they had in any of the existing denominations. The office and powers of "bishop" were too authoritarian for the UCC. The Consultation could never resolve the issue of apostolic succession through bishops in a way fully satisfactory to both Episcopalians and the other denominations.

The Consultation did not prepare a new plan, neither did it dissolve. COCU was the only major church union discussion to include both predominantly White and predominantly African American denominations. It had the potential of addressing not just the theological and ecclesial divisions in the church, but also the racial divide. So it continued, looking for ways to promote unity short of union.

In 1984 the Consultation sent a theological statement, the *COCU Consensus*, to the churches, which the UCC General Synod accepted in 1989 as a "sufficient theological basis" for a covenant with the other denominations. COCU followed up this theological document in 1988 with *Churches in Covenant Communion*. This proposal called for intercommunion, mutual recognition of ministers, cooperation in missions, and "covenanting councils" with oversight of the covenant. UCC

General Synod approved *Churches in Covenant Communion*, as did all the other denominations except the Episcopalians. This proposal was revised, not requiring covenanting councils, and postponing action on mutual recognition of ministers to a future date. In this form the proposal, now called "Churches Uniting in Christ" (CUIC) was approved by the denominations,   including the UCC, in 2001, and went into effect in January, 2002. Member denominations of CUIC were: African Methodist Episcopal Church, African Methodist Episcopal Zion Church, Christian Church (Disciples of Christ), Christian Methodist Episcopal Church, Episcopal Church, International Council of Community Churches, Presbyterian Church (U. S. A.), United Church of Christ, and United Methodist Church.

Kirchengemeinschaft

Soon after the uniting General Synod in 1957, two representatives of the Evangelical Church of the Union (EKU) of Germany approached the co-presidents of the new United Church of Christ to discuss closer ties between the EKU and the UCC.

The Evangelical Church of the Union was a federation of *landeskirchen* (state churches) in Germany that united Lutheran and Reformed churches. The Evangelical Synod had looked to the EKU as its parent, providing it with most of its members through immigration, although they never had formal ties. Both the Evangelical and Reformed Church and the Congregational Christians had assisted the German church in reconstruction after World War II and had participated in pastoral exchanges. The EKU, as the largest united church in the world, followed with interest the development of the UCC. Following the formation of the UCC, the two denominations continued to cultivate their relationship with pastoral exchanges and visits of delegations.

Germany was divided by the Cold War into two states, communist East Germany and democratic West Germany. In 1972 the EKU was forced to divide into two synods, reflecting the political boundary. Through common contacts with the UCC, the East and West Synods of the EKU could keep in touch with each other. Also, having to justify its existence in an atheist and socialist state, the Eastern Synod found the UCC position on peace and social justice, expressed in *Sound Teaching*, to be helpful. From the UCC perspective, closer ties with a church in another country was an antidote for American provincialism.

At the invitation of the EKU-East, contact with the UCC increased and the relationship deepened. After further discussions of theology and ministry, the two German synods in 1980 voted to enter *kirchenge-meinschaft* (full communion) with the United Church of Christ, which reciprocated in 1981. Kirchengemeinschaft included mutual recognition of ministers and full fellowship of pulpit and altar.

Kirchengemeinschaft led to more exchanges of pastors, lectures of scholars, discussion of social issues, and partnership agreements between regional bodies of the two denominations. Following Kirchengemeinschaft the UCC entered into numerous partnerships with denominations in other countries. Each agreement was different, pertaining to issues in that unique relationship. The EKU-UCC was the most intimate of these relationships, as the churches explored together issues of theology, ministry and society.

<u>Formula of Agreement</u>

In 1973 the Lutheran and Reformed churches of Europe, and union churches derived from them, adopted a plan, called the Leuenberg Agreement, by which they could have full communion and recognition of each other's ministers. The World Alliance of Reformed Churches (WARC) and Lutheran World Federation began similar discussions in 1982. In the United States, Lutheran-Reformed dialogue began in 1962.

Lutheran-Reformed dialogue directed itself to resolving the theological disagreements of the Sixteenth Century, in particular the understanding of communion. The potential benefits would include the possibility of shared ministry in union churches and local cooperation in many small communities.

Although the United Church of Christ had roots in both traditions, it was looked upon as a member of the Reformed side because of its membership in the WARC. The UCC did not enter the dialogue until the second round of discussions in 1972. A proposal for reconciliation and mutual recognition, *Invitation to Action*, was sent to the churches in 1984. As the two major Lutheran churches in the United States could not agree on their position toward the dialogue, action was delayed until the new Evangelical Lutheran Church of America could organize and re-examine the proposal as one body. Some Lutherans had problems with the UCC because its polity did not bind ministers to particular confessions. After further discussion, the Formula of Agreement was presented to the churches and approved by all four bodies in 1997.

******

[1] To avoid confusion between "Evangelical" as a reference to Evangelical Synod, and "Evangelical" as a reference to the theological position of churches related to the National Association of Evangelicals, I will *in this section* use "Evangelical Synod" for the former and "Evangelical" for the latter.

CHAPTER TWENTY ONE

Mission and Structure of the United Church

Mission, as traditionally understood, decreased in importance in the United Church of Christ. Congregations reduced the proportion of receipts sent to Conferences from 9.6% in 1965 to 4.2% in 2000. By 2022, this had fallen to 2.3%. Conferences reduced the proportion they forwarded to the national church from 61% in 1965 to 38% in 2000. By 2022, this had fallen to 22%. The denomination reduced the proportion of the national budget given to the historic mission boards. In 1973, the United Church Board for World Ministries (BWM) and the United Church Board for Homeland Ministries (BHM) received allocations of 35% and 32% of the national church budget, respectively. By 1999, the proportions were 21% and 20%. Overall, out of every ten dollars given in the local church, over twenty cents went to World Missions in the early days of the UCC; by 2000, it was down to three cents.

Two factors contributed to this decline: (1) competition for limited resources in a church of declining membership, and (2) new understandings of mission, emphasizing the mission of each local congregation in its community. Congregations and members engaged directly in mission. Habitat for Humanity, a housing enterprise founded by a UCC layman, became a major local mission of many congregations. Various racial and ethnic minorities moved from being objects of mission to being organized groups within the denomination. The UCC struggled to redefine and practice "evangelism," once considered the "grand object" of missions. Declining financial support led to restructuring.

PART A: RACIAL/ETHNIC PLURALISM

The United Church of Christ continued the ministry of its predecessor denominations to immigrants, many of whom in the old country had church relations similar to the UCC. Several racial and ethnic groups – American Indians, Hispanics, and Pacific Asian Americans – followed the example of African Americans in organizing to claim a larger role as a constituent part of the UCC.

By 2000, the UCC had, in addition to its predominantly English, German, and African American congregations, the following number of congregations with ethnic identities.

With the exception of the Magyars, all new work with European immigrants had ceased, and those ethnic churches were in decline. The principal growth was among Pacific Islanders, Asians, and Hispanics.

Samoan Congregationalists in America

By the century's end, over 60,000 Samoans had immigrated to the United States. The overwhelming majority of Samoans were Congregational. Samoan Congregationalists organized their own congregations in the United States, without outside help. Three groups of Samoan Congregational churches co-existed in the United States, with some movement between them, and some dual affiliations: (1) congregations affiliated with the parent denominations in Samoa; (2) independent congregations; (3) congregations affiliated with the UCC. A General Synod resolution in 1997, "Declaration of the Intention to Work Toward Partnership Between the Congregational Christian Church in American Samoa and the United Church of Christ," helped to improve relations and to facilitate the exchange of pastors.

Most Samoan congregations were extended kinship groups with fewer than fifty members. Following the kinship pattern, the Samoan constituency of the UCC grew through the multiplication of small congregations, rather than growth into larger congregations.

<u>Filipino Churches</u>

By 2000 over 1.8 million Filipinos had settled in the United States. Although the United Church of Christ in the Philippines (UCCP) was the largest Protestant church in the Philippines, it constituted less than 1% of the population. The UCCP chose to work with the UCC because it was another united church, and the two denominations established a partnership agreement in 1987. BHM cooperated with UCCP in organizing churches and placing ministers from the Philippines. Before 1980 the Filipino presence in the UCC was confined to Hawaii; from 1980 to 1993 thirteen Filipino congregations were opened across the US mainland.

<u>American Indian Ministry</u>

In the wake of African American efforts for greater self-determination within the denomination, American Indians took similar action. The Three American Indian groups in the UCC, Dakota Association, Fort Berthold Council, and Ho Cak church, came together as the Council for American Indian Ministries (CAIM) in 1970. BHM authorized this council of representatives of the Indian churches to set policy and allocate funds (a portion of the Neighbors in Need offering) for the denomination's Indian ministry. In 1971 General Synod recognized CAIM as an agency of the church. In 1982, the UCC opened its first urban Indian congregation, All Nations Church in Minneapolis.

<u>Hispanic Ministry</u>

Hispanic UCC related communities in Puerto Rico, Mexico, and the mainland of the USA developed closer relationships in this period. ABCFM missionaries arrived in Guadalajara, Mexico in 1872, and in 1879 organized a Mexican Congregational church. In 1896 one of these missionaries to Mexico was transferred to California to work with Mexicans there. Congregational work with Mexican-Americans, an extension of the mission to Mexico, led to the organization of churches in Chino, California (1920), El Paso, Texas (1924), Albuquerque, New Mexico (1926), and other locations in California. Hispanic Congregational churches also developed in Chicago and a few other urban centers. The ABCFM transferred its Mexico Mission to the care of Southern California Conference in 1927. In 1972 the Christian Congregational Church of Mexico became fully autonomous.

In the summer of 1972 several UCC Hispanic pastors from different areas began the process of getting to know each other. They identified and contacted other Hispanics in the UCC and in 1977 organized the Hispanic Council. Through the Council, Hispanics became more visible in the life of the UCC and gave each other support.

Hispanic delegates walked out of the General Synod in 1987, when they believed their concerns were not being heard, then, after negotiations, walked back in. General Synod created a Hispanic Ministries Implementation Team. Concerns of the Hispanic Council were:

1. *Pastors*–They called for seminary training designed with Hispanic input, to be appropriate for Hispanic students; and for scholarships.
2. *Churches*–They asked for financial assistance in organizing new congregations without having to use the expensive and culturally inappropriate methods of BHM.
3. *Resources*–They requested Spanish language and culturally appropriate resources for congregations and Church Schools.

After 1987 slow progress came on these concerns. Hispanic new church starts multiplied on the mainland, and Hispanic representation in denominational life increased. In 1983 the Hispanic Council held its annual meeting in Mexico. Beginning in 1981 Youth Encuentros were held alternately in Mexico and the United States, occasionally on Puerto Rico. The Hispanic Council also established the Centro Alberto Rembar Lectureship, which took place alternately in the United States and Mexico. In 1990 the Iglesia Evangelica Unida de Puerto Rico conducted a plebiscite of its membership and decided overwhelmingly to remain affiliated with the UCC. In these various ways the UCC

Hispanic communities of Puerto Rico, Mexico and the USA mainland grew together into one community. In 2006 the Iglesia Evangelica Unida de Puerto Rico withdrew from the United Church of Christ in reaction to General Synod's endorsement of gay marriage. However friendly relations and some cooperation continue.

<u>Pacific Asian American Ministries</u>

In 1972 the Japanese American Council of the UCC decided to organize an Asian American caucus. They contacted representatives of other ethnic groups, together organized Pacific and Asian American Ministries (PAAM) in 1974, and received recognition from General Synod in 1975. This collection of nine ethnic groups with diverse languages and cultures included recent immigrants, second to fourth generation Americans, and one indigenous group (Hawaiians). Leadership development and youth ministry have been central PAAM concerns.

Theological reflection of Pacific and Asian Americans began with the gospel and ethics of the missionaries, and included a respect for other religions, and the need to deal with shame. Theology and polity were both shaped by the high value given to family.

African Americans, American Indians, Hispanics, and Pacific and Asian Americans organized caucuses within the United Church of Christ to assert their concerns. This strategy moved these groups from being objects of mission to being colleagues in mission with the rest of the UCC. They gained greater control over their own community's life and a larger role in the life of the denomination. These groups joined forces in 1983 to form the Council for Racial and Ethnic Ministries (COREM).

PART B: EVANGELISM AND CHURCH GROWTH

From 1960 to 2000 United Church of Christ membership declined by 39% and Sunday School enrollment declined by 74%. From 1960 to 2022 membership declined by 68% and Sunday School enrollment declined by 91%. The UCC was not unique; all "mainline" predominantly white American denominations had declined.

"Evangelism," formerly a central activity of the church, was out of favor because of association with the practices of more conservative Christians, from whom most UCC people distanced themselves. A theology that de-emphasized the urgency of conversion, combined with the societal trend toward secularization, create a crisis. The new United Church of Christ had to define "evangelism" before it could develop a strategy. General Synod in 1973 declared: "Evangelism is the costly and joyous response of the people to God's acts in Christ and through His disciples in every age. It is not an activity separate unto itself, but it is related to the total life of the church. For the United Church of Christ evangelism must be a way of telling the story and living it, of being God's people and of celebrating God's grace."

BHM soon began creating resources, training leaders and conducting research, and the following Synod affirmed a more lengthy Statement on Evangelism.

BHM began New Initiatives in Church Development (NICD) in 1979, fully supporting organizing pastors and sending them into demographically promising communities, where they gathered congregations that gradually became self-supporting. General Synod in 1983 called for a southern strategy, organizing churches in the South, where population growth was great and UCC presence small. Because of the cost, relatively few new projects could be undertaken each year.

The racial and Hispanic groups, who had different methods of church development, criticized the money-intensive and clergy-intensive methods of NICD; in time multiple strategies were used. In the decade of the 1980s, of the approximately 125 new church starts, approximately 48% were by non-white ethnic groups; about 21% were predominantly white congregations in the five southern conferences.

Millard Fuller (1935-2009) was a self-made millionaire before he reached 30. He found that the pursuit of wealth was destroying his marriage, health, and faith. In 1966, he gave it all away and looked for ways to serve God.

Fuller had been active in the church all his life, serving as President of the Pilgrim Fellowship for the CC Southeast Conference, and later as president of the conference's laymen's organization. After giving his money away, Fuller joined a UCC-Disciples of Christ tour of mission work in Africa and was impressed with the widespread need for decent housing. After fundraising for African American UCC colleges and directing a "partnership housing" project building homes for low-income people in Georgia, Fuller returned to Africa in 1973. As a BWM missionary working with the Disciples of Christ in Zaire [Democratic Republic of the Congo], Fuller directed a self-help housing project in Mbandaka, Equator Province. Millard Fuller had a passion for decent housing. He believed this depressing aspect of poverty could be overcome by constructing sound, low-cost houses and selling them to the working poor with no-interest mortgages. In 1976, he organized Habitat for Humanity, a non-denominational mission society constructing decent houses around the world. By 2001, Habitat had built 100,000 houses, over 40,000 in the United States. UCC congregations and volunteers participated in this work alongside Christians of all denominations.[1] Fuller directed Habitat until his resignation in 2003.

PART C: THE NATURE OF MINISTRY

The new United Church published a *Manual on the Ministry* in 1963, to guide association ministry committees. The *Manual* provided for (1) students in care of association, (2) licenture, and (3) ordination. A licentiate was a seminary student serving a church, licensed to perform ministerial duties. The *Manual* also mentioned (4) commissioned workers, in full-time non-ministerial church work, and (5) lay ministers, doing supply preaching, assisting a minister, or occasionally serving a church part-time. The UCC revised its constitution and by-laws in 1983 (ratified by the Conferences in 1984), defining three forms of authorized ministry: ordained, licensed and commissioned. The licensed minister category combined the former licentiate and lay minister, as both were ministers of Word and Sacrament limited to a specific place for a specific period of time. Steadily the UCC and its association ministry committees asserted ministerial standards and disciplined offending ministers. The shock of the Jim Jones incident, in which a minister recognized by the Disciples of Christ led his followers in mass suicide in 1978, combined with incidents of sexual misconduct over the succeeding decades, reduced resistance to the imposition of strong ministerial standards.

Marie Fortune, a UCC minister, founded the Center for the Prevention of Sexual and Domestic Violence in 1977 in Seattle. In 1983 this Center received its first call from a woman who had experienced sexual abuse from her pastor. The Center studied clergy sexual misconduct, provided support for victims, and developed education for churches. Fortune published *Is Nothing Sacred* in 1989, challenging the churches to address this issue. She has continued to work with faith communities to prevent sexual and domestic violence.

PART D: STRUCTURAL ISSUES

Douglas Horton's definition of Congregationalism – that every unit of the church was autonomous – gave the Congregational Christian General Council the freedom to unite with the Evangelical and Reformed Church. However, it forced on the new United Church of Christ a polity in which every congregation, association, conference, instrumentality, college, seminary and benevolent institution was autonomous. The lack of cohesion in the new church was aggravated by the development of caucuses. One pastor believed a misprint to be descriptive, which read "Untied Church of Christ." Slowly, the new church developed an identity and evolved into a new polity.

<u>Institutions</u>

Colleges, seminaries and "Health and Welfare Service Institutions" tended toward the Congregational pattern of autonomy in the early years of the United Church of Christ. Of the 66 colleges in the United States organized by the antecedent groups of the UCC, most no longer maintained ties to the denomination or identified with it in any more than a historical sense. General Synod in 1979 called on the UCC Council for Higher Education to develop a clearer understanding of the relationship between the denomination and its colleges. A consultation with the colleges at Defiance, Ohio, November 14, 1980, developed a covenant of mutual recognition and cooperation. In 2003, twenty colleges were full members of the UCC Council for Higher Education.

The Evangelical Synod's inner mission had created most of the health and human service institutions that came into the UCC. In the next four decades, conferences established many more institutions, mostly for the elderly. Close ties between the institutions and the national denomination slowly declined through neglect. General Synod in 1983 created a Special Advisory Commission Related to Health and Human Services to determine the relationship between the UCC and the Council for Health and Human Services Ministries (CHHSM). This new group, organized in 1985, replaced the Council for Health and Welfare Services. The institutions soon established covenants with the conferences in which they were located.

The E&R denomination subsidized its seminaries, the CC churches did not. The new United Church of Christ gave the E&R seminaries a diminishing subsidy for a decade. General Synod in 1973 recognized six (later seven) "closely related seminaries," and called on local churches and conferences to support them. General Synod in 1993 adopted criteria by which the seven seminaries were designated "seminaries of the United Church of Christ." The Presidents of the seven seminaries began meeting in 1977; the Executive Council recognized the existence of this council of seminary presidents in 1985. The seven seminaries began publishing *Prism: A Theological Forum for the United Church of Christ* in 1985.

The seminaries and the denomination depended on each other. In the 1995-96 school year, 59% of all UCC Master of Divinity students were enrolled in one of the seven closely related seminaries. The seminary's search for closer ties was realized in the restructuring, accomplished in 2000, with the formation of a Council for Theological Education.

Conferences

To Evangelical and Reformed leaders, whose synods had only one staff person, a full-time or part-time President, the multiple-staffed Congregational Christian Conferences looked like a taste of heaven. The E&R influence showed itself in the new UCC Conferences in an increasingly pastoral role for Conference leadership. Many Conferences recognized this new emphasis by changing their leaders' titles from "Conference Superintendent" to "Conference Minister." The UCC Conference was (1) the basic link between the national and local levels of the UCC, (2) developer of mission within its borders, (3) aid and advisor to local churches seeking pastors, and (4) provider of resources of both staff and material for supporting local church ministries. Gradually, specialized staff in education, stewardship and mission were replaced by regionally deployed "pastors to pastors and churches." BHM transferred responsibility for several mission activities to the conferences in which they were located. Faced with declining financial support, the Conferences sometimes did not maintain them. Ministers of Metropolitan Mission and Campus Ministers faded away; church camping also declined.

A few numerically small but geographically large Conferences could not support adequate staff; temporary subsidies from BHM became more frequent, and the denomination realized not all Conferences were financially viable.

Conference Ministers met together as the Council of Conference Ministers, an extra-constitutional body with much influence.

A "caucus mentality" pervaded the UCC. Not only racial/ethnic groups, but Conference Ministers, Health and Human Service Institutions, Seminary Presidents, and groups with various theological and spiritual concerns organized themselves, were perceived by the denomination, and often perceived themselves, as caucuses.

<u>Restructuring</u>

In its quest for internal unity, and a need to "downsize" because of declining funds, the United Church of Christ General Synod in 1989 appointed a Committee on Structure. In 1995 General Synod received the committee's report and created another committee to prepare the needed amendments to the constitution and bylaws. General Synod approved constitutional amendments in 1997, the conferences ratified them in 1998, and General Synod adopted bylaw changes in 1999. The new structure went into effect July 1, 2000.

Restructuring marked the maturing of a new church polity. In place of the autonomy-of-everybody polity of the 1960 Constitution, the 1997 amendments defined a covenant polity: "Within the United Church of Christ, the various expressions of the church relate to each other in a covenantal manner. Each expression of the church has responsibilities and rights in relation to the others, to the end that the whole church will seek God's will and be faithful to God's mission. Decisions are made in consultation and collaboration among the various parts of the structure. As members of the Body of Christ, each expression of the church is called to honor and respect the work and ministry of each other's parts. Each expression of the church listens, hears, and carefully considers the advice, counsel, and requests of others. In this covenant, the various expressions of the United Church of Christ seek to walk together in all God's ways.–*Article 3.*"

The goal of the founders of the United Church of Christ to create a new polity, neither congregational nor presbyterian, appeared to have been achieved. Restructuring created non-hierarchical mutual accountability. Restructuring replaced eight instrumentalities with three "covenanted ministries": Justice and Witness Ministries, Local Church Ministries, and Wider Church Ministries. The executives of these ministries, with the "General Minister and President" and "Associate General Minister," composed the "collegium," which met together and coordinated the work of the denomination. The General Synod elected all of the new executives. Conferences were directly represented on the Executive Council and the three Covenanted Ministry Directorates.

Restructuring marked the "coming of age" of the United Church of Christ. The denomination had finally left behind the version of congregational polity it was forced to adopt as a result of the legal attacks of Congregational opponents of union. Its diversity and freedom still intact, members of the United Church of Christ had now bound themselves together with the bonds of love to share in the work of the mission of God. Whether or not this will bring about renewal in a "united and uniting" church, only time will tell.

Epilogue

At General Synod, in Baltimore in 2017, we were celebrating the 500th anniversary of the Reformation. At General Synod, many smaller meetings occur around the edges of the actual general synod sessions. I attended the Ecumenical meeting, where a bishop from Germany spoke about Martin Luther. For Luther, she said, "It's not about us, it's about God." Our hope depends not on what we do, but on what God has done in Jesus Christ. Then I attended the History meeting, where one of our seminary professors spoke about Luther, and gave the same message, "It's not about us, It's about God." Then I attended the big worship service on Sunday afternoon. It was all about *us*. We praised ourselves for all the wonderful things we had done throughout history and in the present. I was shocked!

As a historian, I know we are not perfect. I have told the story of the United Church of Christ with love and honesty. We did have our witch trials. We did let the color line creep into our churches. The relationship between missions and colonialism has been complicated. Yet we have done marvelous things for God.

Suppose you walk into one of our congregations on a Sunday morning. In that case, you are likely to find a dedicated and underpaid pastor preaching the Word—for God, visiting the sick—for God, and involved in the community—for God. You will find a congregation of people who genuinely care about each other, sing their hearts out for God, and try to live their lives to the glory of God.

The United Church of Christ has experienced steady numerical decline since its inception. Some of this is for good reason: We stood up for civil rights, women's rights, peace, and gay rights. I believe we have done these things for God. In spite of numerical decline, the United Church of Christ is still spiritually alive and listening for God's direction.

In his many volumes of church history, Kenneth Scott Latourette liked to recall the scripture, "we have this treasure in earthen vessels" (*2 Corinthians 4:7*). We, the church, are common clay pots, people made from the dust of the earth. We are prone to all sorts of foolishness. Yet we are entrusted with a message of infinite value. Somehow, sometimes, that treasure shines through us common clay pots. Praise God!

As we look at our history, we can see much of which we can be proud. But I do not tell the story of the United Church of Christ to install another idol. Our history is filled with common clay pots that have shared with us some of the precious treasure that gives life. Ultimately church history is not about us - it is about God. It is about how God has inspired and empowered some of God's servants to somehow imperfectly do the will of God. Whatever the future may hold for the United Church of Christ, it cannot be about us - it must be about God.

Further Reading

The following is not meant to be an exhaustive bibliography, but suggestions for further reading for persons interested in the subject. Also included are sources used in the text. Many of the items that are not in print may be on line or can be borrowed through Inter-Library Loan from an academic library. Some primary sources may be available in many editions. The books and articles listed below are each listed only once, although they may contain material that would be helpful further reading for several different chapters.

General - References containing a review of the entire scope of the history of the United Church of Christ and its antecedents.

Ahlstrom, Sydney E. *A Religious History of the American People.* New Haven: Yale, 1972.

González, Justo L. *The Story of Christianity.* Vol. 2: *The Reformation to the Present Day.* San Francisco: Harper, 1983.

Von Rohr, John. *The Shaping of American Congregationalism, 1620-1957.* Cleveland: Pilgrim, 1992.

Walker, Williston. *The Creeds and Platforms of Congregationalism.* New York: Pilgrim, 1991.

Walker, Williston, Norris, Richard A., Lotz, David W., and Handy, Robert T. *A History of the Christian Church.* 4th ed., New York: Charles Scribner's Sons, 1985.

Chapter 2: Part A: Reformation on the Continent

Bromeley, G. W., ed. *Zwingli and Bullinger. The Library of Christian Classics,* vo. 24. Philadelphia: Westminster, 1953.

Calvin, John. *Calvin: Institutes of the Christian Religion. The Library of Christian Classics.*, vols. 20 and 21. Philadelphia: Westminster, 1960.

Good, James Isaac. *History of the Reformed Church in Germany, 1620-1890.* Reading, Pa.: Daniel Miller, 1894.

Luther, Martin. *Three Treatises.* Fortress, 1970.

Ozment, Steven. *The Age of Reform, 1250-1550: An Intellectual and Religious History of Late Medieval and Reformation Europe.* New Haven: Yale University, 1980.

Revesz, Imre. *History of the Hungarian Reformed Church.* Translated by Knight, A. F. Washington, D.C.: Hungarian Reformed Federation of America, 1956.

Toth, William. "European Background–Reformed." In *A History of the Evangelical and Reformed Church*, David Dunn, ed., 3-22. Philadelphia: Christian Education, 1961.

Chapter 2: Part B: Reformation in England

Dickens, Arthur Geoffrey. *The English Reformation.* 2d ed., University Park, pa.: Pennsylvania State University, 1991.

White, B. R. *The English Separatist Tradition from the Marian Martyrs to the Pilgrim Fathers.* London: Oxford, 1971.

Chapter 3: Part A: The Pilgrims

Bartlett, Robert. *The Faith of the Pilgrims: An American Heritage.* New York: United Church, 1978.

Chapter 3: Part B: The Puritan Migration

Hall, David. *The Faithful Shepherd: A History of the New England Ministry in the Seventeenth Century.* Chapel Hill, N.C.: University of North Carolina, 1972.

Hambrick-Stowe, Charles E. *The Practice of Piety: Puritan Devotional Disciplines in Seventeenth-Century New England.* Chapel Hill, N.C.: University of North Carolina, 1982.

Miller, Perry. *Errand Into the Wilderness.* Cambridge, Mass.: Harvard, 1956.

Miller, Perry, ed. *The American Puritans: Their Prose and Poetry.* Garden City, NY: Doubleday & Company, Inc., 1956.

Morgan, Edmund S. *The Puritan Dilemma: The Story of John Winthrop.* Boston: Little, Brown, 1958.

__________. *The Puritan Family: Religion and Domestic Relations in Seventeenth-Century New England.* New York: Harper and Row, 1944, 1966.

__________. *Visible Saints: The History of a Puritan Idea.* New York: NYU Press, 1963.

Chapter 3: Part C: Puritan Controversies

McLoughlin, William Gerald. *New England Dissent, 1630-1833.* Cambridge, Ma.: Harvard University, 1971. 2 vol.

Miller, Perry. *Orthodoxy in Massachusetts.* Cambridge, Mass.: Harvard, 1933.

Chapter 3: Part E: Steps Toward Inclusiveness

Miller, Perry. *The New England Mind: From Colony to Province.* Cambridge, Mass.: Harvard, 1953.

Pope, Robert G. *The Half-Way Covenant: Church Membership in Puritan New England.* Princeton: Princeton, 1969.

Chapter 4: Part A: Beginning of the Reformed Church in America

Frantz, John B. "How Firm a Foundation: The Founding of the Co-etus of the German Reformed Congregation in Pennsylvania." *United Church of Christ Historical Council: Annual Historical Lectures* 7 (1997).

Glatfelter, Charles H. *Pastors and People: German Lutheran and Reformed Churches in the Pennsylvania Field, 1717-1793.* Vol. 2: *The History. Publications of the Pennsylvania German Society*, Vol. 15. Breinigsville, Pa.: Pennsylvania German Society, 1982.

Good, James Isaac. *History of the German Reformed Church, 1729-1792*. Reading, Pa.: Daniel Miller, 1899.

"On the Frontiers of a New Land." In *A History of the Evangelical and Reformed Church*, David Dunn, ed., 23-52. Philadelphia: Christian Education, 1961.

Wentz, Abdel Ross. "Relations Between the Lutheran and Reformed Churches in the Eighteenth and Nineteenth Centuries." *Bulletin of the Theological Seminary of the Reformed Church in the United States* 4:3 (Jul 1933): 46-72.

Chapter 4: Part B: Evolution of Congregationalism in New England

Boyer, Paul, and Nissenbaum, Stephen. *Salem Possessed: The Social Origins of Witchcraft*. Cambridge: Harvard University, 1974.

Miller, Perry. *The New England Mind: From Colony to Province*. Cambridge, Mass.: Harvard, 1953, 1961.

Starkey, Marion L. *The Devil in Massachusetts: A Modern Inquiry into the Salem Witch Trials*. New York: Alfred A. Knopf, 1950.

Chapter 4: Part D: The Revolution and the Churches

Baldwin, Alice R. *The New England Clergy and the American Revolution*. Durham, N.C.: Duke University, 1928.

Frantz, John B. "'Prepare Thyself... to Meet the Lord Thy God!': Religion in Pennsylvania During the Revolution." *Pennsylvania Heritage* 2:3 (Jun 1976):28-32.

Chapter 5: Part A: Pietism in Europe

Menzel, Theophil W. "European Background–Evangelical." In *A History of the Evangelical and Reformed Church*, David Dunn, ed., 147-57. Philadelphia: Christian Education, 1961.

Spener, Philip Jacob. *Pia Desideria*. Philadelphia: Fortress, 1964.

Chapter 5: Part B: The Moravians and the Reformed in Pennsylvania

Schwarze, W. N. "Some Features of the Relation Between the Reformed Church and the Moravian Church During the Colonial Period." *Bulletin of the Theological Seminary of the Reformed Church in the United States* 7:4 (Oct 1936): 48-60

Stoudt, John Joseph. "Pennsylvania and the Oecumenical Ideal." *Bulletin of the Theological Seminary of the Evangelical and Reformed Church* 12:4 (Oct 1941):171-97.

Chapter 5: Part C: Jonathan Edwards and the Great Awakening

Blake, S. L. *Separate or Strict Congregationalists in New England.* Boston: Pilgrim, 1902.

Goen, C. C. *Revivalism and Separatism in New England, 1740-1800: Strict Congregationalists and Separate Baptists in the Great Awakening.* New Haven: Yale University, 1962.

Edwards, Jonathan. *A Faithful Narrative of the Surprising Work of God in the Conversion of Many Hundred Souls in Northampton, and the Neighboring Towns and Villages of the County of Hampshire, in the Province of Massachusetts Bay in New England.* In *The Works of President Edwards*, ed. Sereno E. Dwight, 4: xi-74. New York: S. Converse, 1829.

__________. *An Humble Attempt to Promote Explicit Agreement and Visible Union of God's People in Extraordinary Prayer for the Revival of Religion and the Advancement of Christ's Kingdom on Earth, Pursuant to Scripture Promises and Prophecies Concerning the Last Time,* In *The Works of President Edwards*, ed. Sereno E. Dwight, 4:429-503. New York: S. Converse, 1829.

__________. *The Nature of True Virtue,* In *The Works of President Edwards*, ed. Sereno E. Dwight, 3:93-157. New York: S. Converse, 1829.

________. *Personal Narrative.* In *Jonathan Edwards: Representative Selections*, eds. Clarence H. Faust and Thomas H. Johnson, 57-72. American Century Series. New York: Hill and Wang, 1935, 1962.

________. *A Treatise Concerning Religious Affections*, In *The Works of President Edwards*, ed. Sereno E. Dwight, 5:1-344. New York: S. Converse, 1829.

________, ed. *An Account of the Life of the Late Reverend Mr. David Brainerd, Minister of the Gospel, Missionary to the Indians from the Honourable Society in Scotland, for the Propagation of Christian Knowledge, and Pastor of a Church of Christian Indians in New-Jersey.* Boston: D. Henchman, 1749.

Miller, Perry. *Jonathan Edwards.* Amherst, Mass.: University of Massachusetts, 1949, 1981.

MacCormac, Earl R. "Jonathan Edwards and Missions." *Journal of the Presbyterian Historical Society* 39 (1961):219-29.

Chapter 5: Part D: Otterbein and the German Reformed Church

Dipko, Thomas E. "Philip William Otterbein and the United Brethren." In *Hidden Histories of the United Church of Christ 2*, Barbara Brown Zikmund, ed., 115-29. New York: United Church, 1987.

Drury, A. W. *The Life of the Rev. Philip William Otterbein, Founder of the Churches of the United Brethren in Christ.* Dayton: U. B. Publishing House, 1884.

Chapter 5: Part E: The Second Great Awakening

Cott, Nancy F. *The Bonds of Womanhood: 'Woman's Sphere' in New England, 1780-1835.* New Haven: Yale University, 1977.

________. "Young Women in the Second Great Awakening in New England." *Feminist Studies* 3 (1975):15-29.

Foster, Charles I. *An Errand of Mercy: The Evangelical United Front, 1790-1837.* Chapel Hill, N. C.: University of North Carolina, 1960.

Frantz, John Bortzfield. *An Example of Revivalism and Renewal in American Church History: The Reformed Church in the United States, 1820-1861.* Paper delivered to the Historical Society of the Evangelical and Reformed Church, 31 May, 1966. Evangelical and Reformed Historical Society, Lancaster, Pa.

Keller, Charles Roy. *The Second Great Awakening in Connecticut.* New Haven: Yale University, 1942; reprint, Archon, 1968.

Matthews, Donald G. "The Second Great Awakening as an Organizing Process, 1780-1830: An Hypothesis." *American Quarterly* 21 (1969): 23-43; reprint, in *Religion in American History: Interpretive Essays,* eds. John M. Mulder and John F. Wilson, 199-217. Englewood Cliffs, N.J.: Prentice Hall, 1978.

McLoughlin, William Gerald. *Revivals, Awakenings, and Reform.* Chicago: University of Chicago, 1978.

Melder, Keith. "Ladies Bountiful: Organized Women's Benevolence in Early 19th-Century America." *New York History* 28 (1967):231-54.

Miller, Perry. *The Life of the Mind in America: From the Revolution to the Civil War.* New York: Harcourt, Brace & World, n.d.

Shiels, Richard D. "The Feminization of American Congregationalism, 1730-1835." *American Quarterly* 33 (1981):46-62.

__________. "The Second Great Awakening in Connecticut: Critique of the Traditional Interpretation." *Church History* 49 (1980):401-15.

Tyler, Bennet. *Memoir of the Life and Character of Rev. Asahel Nettleton, D.D.* Hartford: Robins and Smith, 1845.

Chapter 5: Part F: Revival Theology

Finney, Charles Grandison. *Autobiography.* Ed. By Helen Wessel. Minneapolis: Bethany Fellowship, 1977.

Hambrick-Stowe, Charles E. *Charles G. Finney and the Spirit of American Evangelicalism.* Grand Rapids: William B. Eerdmans Publishing Co., 1996.

Hardman, Keith J. *Charles Grandison Finney, 1792-1875: Revivalist and Reformer.* Syracuse, NY: Syracuse University, 1987.

Mead, Sidney L. *Nathaniel William Taylor, 1786-1858: A Connecticut Liberal*. Chicago: University of Chicago, 1942.

Chapter 5: Part G: Winebrenner and the Reformed Church

Gossard, J. Harvey. "John Winebrenner: From German Reformed Roots to the Church of God." In *Hidden Histories of the United Church of Christ 2*, Barbara Brown Zikmund, ed., 130-48. New York: United Church, 1987.

Kern, Richard. *John Winebrenner, Nineteenth Century Reformer*. Harrisburg: Central Publishing, 1974.

Chapter 6: Part A: No Name But Christian

Bennet, Simon Addison. *The Christian Denomination and Christian Doctrine*. Dayton, Oh.: Christian Publishing Association, 1926; reprint, Old Union United Church of Christ, Edinburg, In., 1966.

Kilgore, Charles Franklin. *The James O'Kelly Schism in the Methodist Episcopal Church*. Mexico City: Casa Unida de Publicaciones, 1963.

Morrill, Milo True. *A History of the Christian Denomination in America*. Dayton: Christian Publishing Association, 1912.

Nordbeck, Elizabeth C. "Origins of the Christian Denomination in New England." In *Hidden Histories of the United Church of Christ 2*, Barbara Brown Zikmund, ed., 46-65. New York: United Church, 1987.

Stokes, Durwood T., and Scott, William T. *A History off the Christian Church in the South*. Elon College, N.C., 1977.

Stone, Barton. *An Address to the Christian Churches in Kentucky: On Several Important Doctrines of Religion*. Lexington, Ky.: I. T. Cavens & Co., 1821

__________. *Atonement: The Substance of Two Letters Written to a Friend*. Lexington, Ky.: Joseph Charles, 1805.

Williams, D. Newell. *Barton Stone: A Spiritual Biography*. Saint Louis: Chalice, 2000.

Chapter 6: Part B: The Unitarian Schism

Channing, William E. *Unitarian Christianity*. Boston: American Unitarian Association, 1919.

Clark, Joseph Sylvester. *A Historical Sketch of the Congregational Churches of Massachusetts from 1620 to 1858*. Boston: Congregational Board of Publication, 1858.

Sprague, William Buell. *The Life of Jedidiah Morse*. New York: Anson D. F. Randolph, 1874.

Stuart, Moses. *Letter to the Rev. Wm. E. Channing*. Andover, Mass.: Flagg nd Gould, 1819.

Ware, Henry. *Letter to the Reverend Dr. Woods*. Boston: Monroe & Franco, 1820.

Woods, Leonard. *History of the Andover Theological Seminary*. Boston: James R. Osgood, 1885.

________. *Letters to Unitarians*. Andover, Mass.: Flagg & Gould, 1820.

Worcester, Samuel. *Letter to the Rev. William E. Channing*. Boston: Samuel T. Armstrong, 1915.

________. *A Second Letter to the Rev. William E. Channing on the Subject of Unitarianism*. Boston: Samuel T. Armstrong, 1915.

________. *A Third Letter to the Rev. William E. Channing on the Subject of Unitarianism*. Boston: Samuel T. Armstrong, 1915.

Worcester, Samuel M. *The Life and Labors of Rev. Samuel Worcester, D.D., Former Pastor of the Tabernacle Church, Salem, Mass.* Boston: Crocker and Brewster, 1852. 2 vol.

Wright, Conrad. *The Unitarian Controversy: Essays on American Unitarian History*. Boston: Skinner House Books, 1994.

Chapter 7: Mission to the World: Part A: The Societies

Andrew, John A., III. *Rebuilding the Christian Commonwealth: New England Congregationalists and Foreign Missions, 1800-1830*. Lexington, Ky.: University of Kentucky, 1976.

Clark, Calvin Montague. "The Brethren: A Chapter in he History of American Missions." Society of Brethren Papers. Andover Newton Theological School, Newton Center, Mass.

Griffin, Edward D. *A Sermon Preached September 2, 1828, at the Dedication of the New Chapel Connected with Williams College, Massachusetts.* Williamstown: Ridley Bannister, 1828.

Hewett, John N. *Williams College and Foreign Missions.* Boston: Pilgrim, 1914.

Hopkins, Mark. "Historical Discourse." In *Memorial Volume of the First Fifty Years of the American Board of Commissioners for Foreign Missions,* by Rufus Anderson. Boston: ABCFM, 1861.

Hutchison, William R. *Errand to the World: American Protestant Thought and Foreign Missions.* Chicago: University of Chicago, 1987.

London Missionary Society. *Reports of the Missionary Society from Its Formation in the Year 179 to 1814, Inclusive.* London: J. Dennett, [1815].

Lovett, Richard. *The History of the London Missionary Society, 1795-1895.* London: Henry Frowle, 1899. 2 vol.

Naylor, Natalie Ann. "Raising a Learned Ministry: The American Education Association, 1815-1860." D.Ed. diss., Teachers College, Columbia University, 1971.

Perry, Alan Frederick. "The American Board of Commissioners for Foreign Missions and the London Missionary Society in the Nineteenth Century: A Study of Ideas." Ph.D. diss., Washington University, 1974.

Phillips, Clifton Jackson. *Protestant Americans and the Pagan World: The First Half Century of the American Board of Commissioners for Foreign Missions, 1810-1860.* Cambridge, Mass.: Harvard University, 1969.

Pierce, Richard Donald. "A History of the Society of Inquiry at Andover Seminary, 1811-1820." B.D. Thesis, Andover Theological Seminary, 1938.

Spring, G. *Memoirs of Mills.*

Strong, William Ellsworth. *The Story of the American Board: An Account of the First Hundred Years of the American Board of Commissioners for Foreign Missions.* Boston: Pilgrim, 1970.

Tracy, Joseph. *History of the American Board of Commissioners for Foreign Missions.* New York: M. W. Dodd, 1842.

Chapter 7: Mission to the World: Part B: The Missions

Andrew, John A., III. *From Revivals to Removal: Jeremiah Evarts, the Cherokee Nation, and the Search for the Soul of America.* Athens, Ga. and London: University of Georgia, 1992.

Arpee, Leon. *A Century of Armenian Protestantism, 1846-1946.* New York: Armenian Missionary Association of America, 1946.

[Evarts, Jeremiah]. (William Penn, pseud.). *Cherokee Removal: The 'William Penn' Essays and Other Writings*, ed. Francis Paul Prucha. Knoxville: University of Tennessee, 1981.

Hinman, George Warren. *The American Indian and Christian Missions.* New York: Fleming H. Revell, 1933.

Maxfield, Charles A., III. "The Legacy of Jeremiah Evarts," *International Bulletin of Missionary Research* 22:4 (Oct 1998):172-75.

________. "The Presbyterian and Congregational Churches Among the Dakota." Th.M. thesis, Union Theological Seminary, Richmond, Va., 1991.

McLoughlin, William Gerald. *Cherokees and Missionaries, 1789-1839.* Norman, Ok.: University of Oklahoma Press, 1984, reprint 1995.

________. "Civil Disobedience and Evangelism Among the Missionaries to the Cherokees, 1800-1830." *Journal of Presbyterian History* 51 (1973):116-39.

Meyer, Roy W. *History of the Santee Sioux: United States Indian Policy on Trial.* University of Nebraska Press, 1967..

Wagner, Sandra E. "Mission and Motivation: The Theology of the Early American Mission in Hawai'i." *Hawaiian Journal of History* 19 (1985):62-70.

Chapter 7: Mission to the World: Part C: Mission Theory

American Board of Commissioners for Foreign Missions. *Annual Report, 1846.*

Anderson, Rufus. *Foreign Missions: Their Relations and Claims.* New York: Charles Scribner, 1869.

__________. *Memorial Volume of the First Fifty Years of the American Board of Commissioners for Foreign Missions.* Boston: ABCFM, 1861.

__________. "On Raising Up a Native Ministry Among the Heathen." ABCFM Annual Report, 1841.

Beaver, R. Pierce. "Eschatology in American Missions." In *Basileia: Walter Freytag zum 60 Geburtstag,* eds. Jan Hermelink and Jochen Margull, 60-75. Stuttgart: Evang. Missionsverlag G. M. B. H., 1959.

__________. "The Legacy of Rufus Anderson." *Occasional Bulletin of Missionary Research* 3 (1979):94-97.

Greene, David. "Extracts from the Instructions of the Prudential Committee to the Rev. Sherman Hall and Rev. William T. Boutwell, Missionaries to the Ojibeways of the North West Territory of the United States." ABCFM Annual Report, 1832.

Schneider, Robert A. "'A Bewildering Passion': Rufus Anderson, Foreign Missions, and American Denominational Identity, 1850-1870." *Historical Intelligencer* 2:2 (1983):7-13.

__________. "The Senior Secretary: Rufus Anderson and the American Board of Commissioners for Foreign Missions, 1810-1880." Ph.D. diss., Harvard, 1980.

Chapter 8: The Multiple Fruit of Mission

Maxfield, Charles A. "The Reflex Influence of Missions: The Domestic Operations of the American Board of Commissioners for Foreign Missions, 1810-1850. Ph.D. dissertation, Union Theological Seminary, Richmond, Virginia,

Newell, Harriet, and Leonard Woods. *Memoirs of Mrs. Harriet Newell, also, a Sermon on the Occasion of Her Death by L. Woods.* London, John Mason, 1833.

Nott, Samuel, Jr. *Sermons foe Children: Designed to Promote Their Immediate Piety.* Reviewed in *Christian Advocate*, vol. 1 (1823).

Chapter 8: Part A: The Sunday School

A Brief History of the Mass. Sabbath School Society, and the Rise and Progress of Sabbath Schools in the Orthodox Congregational Denomination in Massachusetts. Boston: MSSS, 1850.

Bullard, Asa. *Incidents in a Busy Life: An Autobiography.* Boston: Congregational Sunday-School and Publishing Society, 1888.

Cope, Henry Frederick. *The Evolution of the Sunday School.* Boston: Pilgrim Press, 1911.

Ewing, William. *The Sunday School Century: Containing a History of the Congregational Sunday-School and Publishing Society.* Boston: Pilgrim, 1918.

Chapter 8: Part B: Gallaudet and the Deaf and Dumb

Gallaudet, Edward Miner. *Life of Thomas Hopkins Gallaudet.* New York: Henry Holt & Co., 1888

Humphrey, Heman. *The Life and Labors of the Rev. T. H. Gallaudet, LL.D.* New York: Robert Carter & Brothers, 1857.

Chapter 8: Part C: Peace

Brock, Peter. *Pacifism in the United States: From the Colonial Era to the First World War.* Princeton, N.J.: Princeton University Press, 1968.

Curti, Merle Eugene. *Peace or War: The American Struggle, 1636-1936.* New York, 1936; reprint, Boston: J. S. Canner & Co., 1959.

Galpin, William Freeman. *Pioneering for Peace: A Study of American Peace Efforts to 1846.* Syracuse: Bardeen, 1933.

Hemmenway, John. *Memoir of William Ladd: The Apostle of Peace.* Boston: American Peace Society, 1872.

Macfarland, Charles S. *Pioneers for Peace Through Religion.* New York: Fleming H. Revell, 1946.

Steece, Arvel M. *Congregationalism and Pacifism.* pamphlet, reprint of article in *Glad Tidings*, Spr. 1983.

[Tuttle, Sarah]. *The Little Soldier; A Plea for Peace*. Boston: MSSS, 1837.

Worcester, Noah. *Solemn Review of the Custom of War*. Dec. 1814, reprint, Boston: S. G. Simpkins, 1833.

Ziegler, Valarie H. *The Advocates of Peace in Antebellum America*. Bloomington, In.: Indiana University Press, 1992.

Chapter 8: Part D: Women in Mission and in the Church

Beaver, R. Pierce. *All Loves Excelling: American Protestant Women in World Missions*. Grand Rapids: Eerdmans, 1968; rev. ed., *American Protestant Women in World Mission: A History of the First Feminist Movement in North America*, Grand Rapids: Eerdmans, 1980.

Burnett, John Franklin. *Early Women in the Christian Church: Heroines All*. Booklet Six. Dayton, Oh.: Christian Publishing Association, n.d.

Cazden, Elizabeth. *Antoinette Brown Blackwell: A Biography*. Old Westbury, NY: Feminist Press, 1983.

Grimshaw, Patricia. "'Christian Woman, Pious Wife, Faithful Mother, Devoted Missionary.' Conflicts in Roles of American Missionary Women in Nineteenth Century Hawaii." *Feminist Studies* 9 (1983):489-521.

________. *Paths of Duty: American Missionary Wives in Nineteenth-Century Hawaii*. Honolulu: University of Hawaii, 1989.

Nobles, Gregory. *The Education of Betsey Stockton: An Odyssey of Slavery and Freedom*. Chicago, University of Chicago Press, 2022.

Welter, Barbara. *Dimity Convictions: The American Woman in the Nineteenth Century*. Athens, Oh.: Ohio University, 1976.

Zikmund, Barbara Brown. "Abigail Roberts: 'Female Laborer' in Christian Churches." *Historical Intelligencer* 2:1 (1982): 3-9.

Zwiep, Mary. *Pilgrim Path: The First Company of Women Missionaries to Hawaii*. Madison, Wisc.: University of Wisconsin, 1991.

Chapter 9: Part A: Congregational/Presbyterian Expansion

Clark, Joseph B. *Leavening the Nation: The Story of American Home Missions.* New York: Baker & Taylor, 1903, reprint 1913.

Goodykoontz, Colin B. *Home Missions on the American Frontier, with Particular Reference to the American Home Missionary Society.* Caldwell, Id.: Caxton, 1939; reprint, New York: Octagon Books, 1971.

Hartman, Edward George. *Americans from Wales.* Boston: Christopher Publishing House, 1967.

Loetscher, Lefferts A. "The Problem of Christian Unity in Early 19th Century America." *Church History* 32 (1963):3-16.

Nichols, Robert Hastings. *Presbyterianism in New York State: A History of the Synod and Its Predecessors.* Philadelphia: Westminster, 1963.

Norich, Ronald H. "'Jealousies and Contentions': The Plan of Union and the Western Reserve, 1801-1837." *Journal of Presbyterian History* 60 (Sum 1982): 130-41.

Punchard, George. *History of Congregationalism* Vol. 5. Boston: Congregational Publishing Society, 1881.

Rohrer, James R. *Keepers of the Covenant: Frontier Missions and the Decline of Congregationalism, 1774-1818.* New York: Oxford University, 1995.

Sweet, William Warren. *Religion on the American Frontier: 1783-1850.* Vol. 3: *The Congregationalists.* Chicago: University of Chicago, 1939.

Williston, Seth. "Diaries of the Rev. Seth Williston, D.D., 1796r-1800. *Journal of the Presbyterian Historical Society* 7:4 (Dec 1919): 175-208.

Zorbaugh, Charles L. "The Plan of Union in Ohio." *Church History* 6 (1937): 145-74.

Chapter 9: Part B: Reformed Church Expansion

Bollinger, Theodore P. *The Westward Expansion of the Reformed Church.* Reprinted from *Bulletin: Theological Seminary of the Reformed Church in the United States* 2 (Jan 1931):63-103.

Crusius, Paul N. "Growth and Outreach." In *A History of the Evangelical and Reformed Church*, David Dunn, ed., 222-51. Philadelphia: Christian Education, 1961.

Friedli, Josias. "The Winning of the West." In *A History of the Evangelical and Reformed Church*, David Dunn, ed., 115-43. Philadelphia: Christian Education, 1961.

Jubilee Addresses on Home Missions: Delivered on the Occasion of the Fiftieth Anniversary of the Board of Home Missions of the Reformed Church in the United States. Philadelphia: Publication and Sunday School Board of the Reformed Church in the United States, 1914.

Schaeffer, Charles Edmund. *Our Home Mission Work: An Outline of the Home Mission Work of the Reformed Church in the United States.* Philadelphia: Publication and Sunday School Board of the Reformed Church in the United States, 1914.

Weaver, Glenn. "The German Reformed Church and the Home Mission Movement Before 1863: A Study in Cultural and Religious Isolation." *Church History* 22 (1953): 298-313.

Chapter 9: Part C: Evangelical Unionists

Beach, Curtis. "The German Evangelical Protestants." In *Hidden Histories of the United Church of Christ 2*, Barbara Brown Zikmund, ed., 32-45. New York: United Church, 1987.

Gelzer, David Georg. "Mission to America: Being a History of the Work of the Basel Foreign Mission Society in America." Ph.D. diss., Yale University, New Haven, Conn., 1952.

Hanko, Charles William. *The Evangelical Protestant Movement.* Brooklyn, N.Y.: Educators Publishing Co., 1955.

Menzel, Theophil W. "Frontier Beginnings." In *A History of the Evangelical and Reformed Church*, David Dunn, ed., 158-89. Philadelphia: Christian Education, 1961.

Rauch, Frederick A. "German Characteristics." *Home Missionary* v. 8 (1836).

Schneider, Carl E. *The German Church on the American Frontier: A Study of the Rise of Religion Among the Germans of the West.* Saint Louis: Eden Publishing House, 1939.

Chapter 10: Part B: The American Anti-Slavery Movement

Bannan, Phyllis Mary. "Arthur and Lewis Tappan: a Study in New York Religious and Reform Movements." Ph.D. diss., Columbia, 1950.

Beard, Augustus Field. *A Crusade of Brotherhood: A History of the American Missionary Association.* Boston: Pilgrim, 1909.

DeBoer, Clara Merritt. "Blacks and the American Missionary Association." New York: United Church, 1984.

__________. "Congregationalism and Racism: The 19th Century Challenge." *Bulletin of the Congregational Library* 48:3; 49:1,2 (Spr/Sum/Fall 1997, Win 1998).

Kromer, Helen. *Amistad: The Slave Uprising Aboard the Spanish Schooner.* Cleveland: Pilgrim, 1997.

Maxfield, Charles A. "The 1845 Organic Sin Debate: Slavery, Sin, and the American Board of Commissioners for Foreign Missions." In *North American Missions, 1810-1914: Theology, Theory and Policy*, ed. Wilbert R. Shenk, 86-115. Grand Rapids: Eerdmans, 2004.

McKivigan, John R. *The War Against Proslavery Religion: Abolitionism and the Northern Churches, 1830-1865.* Ithaca, N. Y.: Cornell University, 1984.

Ray, Stephen G. "The Remembrance of Integrity: African-American Congregationalists of New England and the Politics of History." *Prism* 14:1 (Spr 1999): 30-42.

Sewall, Samuel. *The Selling of Joseph.* Boston: Bartholomew Green & John Allen, 1700.

Stowe, Harriet Beecher. *Uncle Tom's Cabin.* New York: D. Appleton & Co., 1898.

Tappan, Lewis. *The Life of Arthur Tappan.* New York: Hurd & Houghton, 1970.

Thomas, Herman E.. *James W. C. Pennington: African American Churchman and Abolitionist.* New York: Garland Publishing, 1995.

Wheatley, Phillis. *Poems on Various Subjects, Religious and Moral.* London: A. Bell, 1773.

Wyatt-Brown, Bertram. *Lewis Tappan and the Evangelical War Against Slavery.* Cleveland: Case Western Reserve University, 1969.

Chapter 10: Part C: Reconstruction

Carpenter, John A. *Sword and Olive Branch: Oliver Otis Howard.* Pittsburgh: University of Pittsburgh, 1964.

DeBoer, Clara Merritt. *His Truth is Marching On: African Americans Who Taught the Freedmen for the American Missionary Association, 1861-1877.* New York: Garland Publishing, 1995.

Delk, Yvonne V., ed., *Afro-Christian Convention: The Fifth Stream of the United Church of Christ.* Cleveland, United Church Press, 2023.

Drake, Richard Bryant. "The American Missionary Association and the Southern Negro, 1861-1888." Ph.D. diss., Emory University, 1957.

McMillan, Joseph T., Jr. "From Hope to Hope–The First Fifty Years of the American Missionary Association: A Metaphor for Race Relations in Twenty-first Century America." *United Church of Christ Historical Council: Annual Historical Lectures* 5 (1996).

McPherson, James. "White Liberals and Black Power in Negro Education, 1865-1915." *American Historical Review* 75 (Jun 1970): 1357-86.

Richardson, Joe M. *Christian Reconstruction: The American Missionary Association and Southern Blacks, 1861-1890.* Athens, Ga.: University of Georgia, 1986.

Story of Music at Fisk University. Nashville: Fisk, 1936. [portions quoted in: Garcia, William Burres. "The Life and Choral Music of John Wesley Work (1901-1967)." Ph. D. Diss.. University of Iowa, 1973.]

Ward, Andrew. *Dark Midnight When I Rise: The Story of the Jubilee Singers Who Introduced the World to the Music of Black America.* New York: Farrar, Straus and Giroux, 2000.

Chapter 11: Part A: Mercersburg Movement

Binkley, Luther G. "The German Theological Antecedents of the Mercersburg Theology." *Bulletin of the Theological Seminary of the Evangelical and Reformed Church* 21:3 (Jul 1950):120-48

Bricker, George F. *A Brief History of the Mercersburg Movement.* Occasional Paper of Lancaster Theological Seminary. 1982.

Dunn, David. "The Synod of the East." In *A History of the Evangelical and Reformed Church*, David Dunn, ed., 53-81. Philadelphia: Christian Education, 1961.

Good, James Isaac. *History of the Reformed Church in the U. S. in the Nineteenth Century.* New York: Board of Publication of the Reformed Church in America, 1911.

Nichols, James Hastings. *Romanticism in America: Nevin and Schaff at Mercersburg.* Chicago, 1961.

Nevin, John W. *The Anxious Bench; Antichrist; and the Sermon on Catholic Unity.* Eugene, Or.: Wipf and Stock Publishers, [1999].

Payne, John B. "Philip Schaff: Christian Scholar and Prophet of Ecumenism." *United Church of Christ Historical Council: Annual Historical Lectures* 2 (1993).

Richards, George W. *History of the Theological Seminary of the Evangelical and Reformed Church in the United States, 1825-1934; Evangelical and Reformed Church, 1934-1952.* Lancaster, Pa.: The Seminary, 1952.

Schaff, David. *The Life of Philip Schaff.* New York: Charles Scribner's Sons, 1897.

Schaff, Philip. *America: A Sketch of the Political, Social, and Religious Character of the United States of North America.* New York: C. Scribner, 1855.

__________. *The Principle of Protestantism.* Philadelphia: United Church Press, [1964].

Shetler, John C. "The Ursinus School." In *Hidden Histories of the United Church of Christ*, Barbara Brown Zikmund, ed., 37-49. New York: United Church, 1984.

Chapter 11: Part B: Horace Bushnell

Bushnell, Horace. *Christian Nurture*. New York: Scribner, Armstrong & Co., 1876.

Edwards, Robert L. *Of Singular Genius; Of Singular Grace: A Biography of Horace Bushnell*. Cleveland: Pilgrim, 1992.

Chapter 12: Part A: New Theology for a New Day

Averill, Lloyd J. *American Theology in the Liberal Tradition*. Philadelphia: Westminster, 1967.

Brown, Ira V. *Lyman Abbott, Christian Evolutionist: A Study in Religious Liberalism*. Cambridge, Mass.: Harvard University, 1953.

Buckham, John Wright. *Progressive Religious Thought in America: A Survey of the Enlarging Pilgrim Faith*. Boston: Houghton Mifflin, 1919.

Craig, Austin. *Writings and Addresses of Austin Craig*. Ed. Martyn Summerbell. Dayton: Christian Publishing Association, 1911.

Dorn, Jacob Henry. *Washington Gladden: Prophet of the Social Gospel*. Columbus: Ohio State University, 1967.

Elliott, Willis, "Forgotten Legacy: The Historical Theology of the 'Christian' Component of the United Church of Christ." *Historical Intelligencer* 3:1 (1984): 9-14.

Fry, C. George, and Jon Paul Fry. *Congregationalists and Evolution: Asa Gray and Louis Agassiz*. Lanham, Md.: University Press of America, 1989.

Harwood, W. S. *Life and Letters of Austin Craig*. New York: Fleming H. Revell, 1908.

Hopkins, Charles Howard. *The Rise of the Social Gospel in American Protestantism, 1865-1915*. New Haven: Yale University, 1940.

Horstmann, Julius H. "The Rise of the Social Viewpoint in the Evangelical Synod of North America." *Theological Magazine of the Evangelical Synod of North America* 62 (Sep 1934): 32-33.

Hutchison, William R. *The Modernist Impulse in American Protestantism*. Cambridge, Mass.: Harvard University, 1976.

Luchs, Fred E. "The Social Consciousness of Reformed Church Ministers from 1850 to 1900." *Bulletin of the Theological Seminary of the Reformed Church in the United States* 9:3 (Jul 1938): 115-26

McLoughlin, William Gerald. *The Meaning of Henry Ward Beecher: An Essay on the Shifting Values of Mid-Victorian America, 1840-1870.* New York: Knopf, 1976.

Muelder, Hermann R. "Congregational Social Pioneers." *Social Action* 14:6 (Jun 1948): 4-35.

Stockwell, Clinton E. "Graham Taylor: Urban Pioneer." *Chicago Theological Seminary Register* 86:1 (Win 1996): 1-23.

Strong, Josiah. *Our Country.* New York: AHMS, 1891; reprint with introduction by Jurgen Herbst, Cambridge, Mass.: Belknap Press, 1963.

Walker, Williston. "Changes in Theology Among American Congregationalists." *American Journal of Theology* 10 (1906): 204-18; reprint, *Congregationalist* 94:30 (24 Jul 1909): 108-10.

Williams, Daniel Day. *The Andover Liberals: A Study in American Theology.* Morningside Heights, N. Y.: Kings Crown, 1941.

Chapter 12: Part B: The Churches Express Their Faith

Fackre, Gabriel. "The Kansas City Statement as a Confession of Faith." *Bulletin of the Congregational Library* 39:3 (Spr/Sum 1988).

Guptill, Nathanael M. "Councils and Synods: With Special Reference to Kansas City, 1913." *Bulletin of the Congregational Library* 40:1 (Fall 1988).

Irion, Daniel. *Evangelical Belief and Doctrine: The Evangelical Catechism Explained. Evangelical Fundamentals Part Two.* Saint Louis: Eden Publishing House, 1916.

Chapter 12: Part C: Changing Piety

Gladden, Washington. *Being a Christian: What It Means and How to Begin.* Boston: Pilgrim, 1910 [originally 1876].

Sheldon, Charles M. *In His Steps: What Would Jesus Do?* Chicago: Moody, 1956.

Walker, Williston. *Congregational Idea of Worship*. Hartford: Hartford Seminary, 1895. Reprinted from *Hartford Seminary Record*, Dec. 1894.

Chapter 12: Part D: Liberal Protestantism is Challenged

Bell, Enoch Frye. "The Andover Controversy." The Hyde Lecture. Andover Theological Seminary, 1943.

Zuck, Lowell H. "Evangelical Pietism and Biblical Criticism: The Story of Karl Emil Otto." In *Hidden Histories of the United Church of Christ 2*, Barbara Brown Zikmund, ed., 66-79. New York: United Church, 1987.

Chapter 12: Part E: Fundamentalism

Trumbull, Charles Gallaudet. *The Life of C. I. Scofield*. New York: Oxford University, 1920.

Chapter 13: Part A: National Organization

Atkins, Gaius Glenn, and Fagley, Frederick L. *History of American Congregationalism*. Boston: Pilgrim, 1942.

Bailey, J. Martin. "Religious Journalism: A Legacy of the Christian Church." In *Hidden Histories of the United Church of Christ 2*, Barbara Brown Zikmund, ed., 101-14. New York: United Church, 1987.

Brüning, David, Kockritz, Ewald, and Horstmann, Julius H. *Evangelical Fundamentals: Part 1*. Saint Louis: Eden Publishing House, 1916.

Crusius, Paul N. "Western Consolidation." In *A History of the Evangelical and Reformed Church*, David Dunn, ed., 190-221. Philadelphia: Christian Education, 1961.

Dexter, Henry Martyn, *A Handbook of Congregationalism*. Boston: Congregational Society, 1880.

Dunn, David. "The Era of the General Synod." In *A History of the Evangelical and Reformed Church*, David Dunn, ed., 82-114. Philadelphia: Christian Education, 1961.

Kamphausen, H. *The Story of the Religious Life in the Evangelical Synod of North America.* Saint Louis: Eden Publishing House, 1924.

Laaser, Robert O. *Our Beloved Eden.* Saint Louis: Eden Theological Seminary, 1993.

McGiffert, Arthur Cushman, Jr. *No Ivory Tower: The Story of Chicago Theological Seminary.* Chicago: CTS, 1965.

Reformed Church in the United States, Laymen's Missionary Movement. *A Survey of the Reformed Church in the United States.* Laymen's Missionary Movement of the Reformed Church in the United States, 1914.

Chapter 13: Part B: Reaching Out for Christian Unity

Frantz, John Bortzfield. "The Unionistic and Separatistic Movements in the Evangelical and Reformed Church with Particular Reference to These Movements in the Former Reformed Churches in the United States." S.T.M. diss., Temple University, Philadelphia, Pa., 1957.

McDaniel, S. C. *The Origin and Early History of the Congregational Methodist Church.* Atlanta: Jas. P. Harrison & Co., 1881.

Sills, Horace S. "The Union Church: A Case of Lutheran and Reformed Cooperation." In *Hidden Histories of the United Church of Christ 2*, Barbara Brown Zikmund, ed., 13-31. New York: United Church, 1987.

Taylor, Richard H. *Southern Congregational Churches.* Benton Harbor, Mi.: Richard H. Taylor, 1994.

Yoder, Donald Herbert. "Lutheran-Reformed Union Proposals, 1800-1850: An American Experiment in Ecumenics." *Bulletin of the Theological Seminary of the Evangelical and Reformed Church* 17:1 (Jan 1946):39-77

Chapter 13: Part C: Women in the Churches

Bass, Dorothy C. "The Congregational Training School for Women." In *Hidden Histories of the United Church of Christ 2*, Barbara Brown Zikmund, ed., 149-67. New York: United Church, 1987.

Hedges-Hiller, Marilyn. "A Trickle of Ordained Women." *Bulletin of the Congregational Library* [pending].

Mosier, Debra Duke. "Gaining Voice and Vote: The Congregational Women's Movement Toward Full Participation in the American Board." *Prism* 14:1 (Spr 1999): 58-71.

Staats-Westover, Hazel. "The Beginnings of Feminism at CTS." *Chicago Theological Seminary Register* 86:2 (Spr 1996): 7-9.

Stuckey-Kauffman, Priscilla. "Women's Mission Structures and the American Board." In *Hidden Histories of the United Church of Christ 2*, Barbara Brown Zikmund, ed., 80-100. New York: United Church, 1987.

Walker, Randi Jones. *Emma Newman: A Frontier Woman Minister.* Syracuse, N.Y.: Syracuse University Press, 2000.

Yockey, E. S. *Historical Sketch of the Origin and Growth of the Women's Missionary Societies of the Reformed Church.* Alliance, Oh.: The Woman's Journal, 1898.

Zikmund, Barbara Brown, and Sally A. Dries. "Women's Work and Women's Boards." In *Hidden Histories of the United Church of Christ*, Barbara Brown Zikmund, ed., 140-53. New York: United Church, 1984.

Chapter 14: Part A: Inner Mission

Ohl, J. F. *The Inner Mission: A Handbook for Christian Workers.* Philadelphia: General Council Publication House, 1913.

Rasche, Ruth W. *The Deaconess Heritage: One Hundred Years of Caring, Healing and Teaching.* Saint Louis: Deaconess Foundation, 1994.

__________. "The Deaconess Sisters: Pioneer Professional Women." In *Hidden Histories of the United Church of Christ*, Barbara Brown Zikmund, ed., 95-109. New York: United Church, 1984.

Chapter 14: Part B: Ministry to Children and Youth

Bower, William Clayton, and Hayward, Percy Roy. *Protestantism Faces Its Educational Task Together.* Appleton, Wi.: C. C. Nelson, 1949.

Brown, Arlo Ayres. *A History of Religious Education in Recent Times.* New York: Abingdon, 1923.

Clark, Francis Edward. *Memories of Many Men in Many Lands.* Boston: United Societies of Christian Endeavor, 1922.

Koenig, Robert E. "Our Educational Heritage Through the Evangelical Tradition." *Church School Worker* 17:4 (Dec 1966): 19-23.

Scott, William T., Sr. "Our Educational Heritage Through the Christian Tradition." *Church School Worker* 17:3 (Nov 1966): 9-12.

Spotts, Charles D. "Our Educational Heritage Through the Reformed Tradition." *Church School Worker* 17:2 (Oct 1966): 15-17.

Weigle, Luther A. "Our Educational Heritage Through the Congregational Tradition." *Church School Worker* 17:1 (Sep 1966): 12-14.

Chapter 14: Part C: African Americans in the South After Reconstruction

Alston, Percel O. "The Afro-Christian Connection." In *Hidden Histories of the United Church of Christ*, Barbara Brown Zikmund, ed., 21-36. New York: United Church, 1984.

Stanley, Alfred Knighton. *The Children Is Crying: Congregationalism Among Black People.* New York: Pilgrim, 1979.

Stanley, J. Taylor. *A History of Black Congregational Christian Churches of the South.* New York: United Church, 1978.

Chapter 14: Part D: American Indian Missions

Beaver, R. Pierce. *Church, State, and the American Indians.* St. Louis: Concordia, 1966.

Bollinger, Theodore P. *The Wisconsin Winnebago Indians and the Mission of the Reformed Church.* Cleveland: Central Publishing House, 1922.

Eastman, Charles A. "Ohiyesa." *Indian Boyhood.* New York: Dover Publications, 1971 (Originally published by McClure, Phillips & Co., 1902).

Hummon, Serge F. "American Indians, Missions, and the United Church of Christ." In *Hidden Histories of the United Church of Christ*, Barbara Brown Zikmund, ed., 3-20. New York: United Church, 1984.

Kerber, Linda K. "The Abolitionist Perception of the Indian." *Journal of American History* 62 (1975-76):271-295.

Chapter 15: Part A: Germans from Russia

Chrystal, "German Congregationalism." In *Hidden Histories of the United Church of Christ*, Barbara Brown Zikmund, ed., 64-80. New York: United Church, 1984.

Eisenach, George J. *A History of the German Congregational Churches in the United States.* Yankton, S.D.: Pioneer Press, 1938.

__________. *Pietism and the Russian Germans in the United States.* Berne, Ind.: Berne Publishers, 1946.

Chapter 15: Part B: The Chinese in America

Zikmund, Barbara Brown (with assistance from Dorothy Wong, Rose Lee, and Matthew Fong.) "Chinese Congregationalism." In *Hidden Histories of the United Church of Christ 2*, Barbara Brown Zikmund, ed., 168-88. New York: United Church, 1987.

Chapter 15: Part C: Congregationalists and Mission Covenant

Hale, Frederick. "The Swedish Department of Chicago Theological Seminary." *Bulletin of the Congregational Library* 32:2 (Win 1981): 4-14.

Chapter 15: Part D: Magyar Reformed in Hungary and America

Benkart, Paula K. "The Hungarian Government, the American Magyar Churches, and Immigrant Ties to the Homeland, 1903-1917." *Church History* 52 (1983): 312-21.

Butosi, John. "The Calvin Synod: Hungarians in the United Church of Christ." In *Hidden Histories of the United Church of Christ,*

Barbara Brown Zikmund, ed., 124-39. New York: United Church, 1984.

Revesz, Imre. *History of the Hungarian Reformed Church.* Translated by Knight, A. F. Washington, D.C.: Hungarian Reformed Federation of America, 1956.

Szilagyi, Anthony. "Years of Transition: A Brief History of the Hungarian Reformed Church in the United States from 1918 to the Tiffin Agreement." *United Church of Christ Historical Council: Annual Historical Lectures* 3 (1994).

Chapter 15: Part E: Armenians in Turkey and America

Tootikian, Vahan H. "Armenian Congregationalism: From Mission to Membership." In *Hidden Histories of the United Church of Christ,* Barbara Brown Zikmund, ed., 50-63. New York: United Church, 1984.

Chapter 15: Part F: The Japanese in Japan and in America

Alika, Clifford, and Miya Okawara. "Sho-Chiku-Bai: Japanese American Congregationalists." In *Hidden Histories of the United Church of Christ,* Barbara Brown Zikmund, ed., 154-71. New York: United Church, 1984.

Iglehart, Charles W. *A Century of Protestant Christianity in Japan.* Rutland, Vt: Charles E. Tuttle Co., 1959.

Chapter 16: Part A: Administration of Foreign Missions

Barton, James L. *Human Progress Through Missions.* New York: Revell, 1912.

__________. *The Story of Near East Relief (1915-1930): An Interpretation.* New York: Macmillan, 1930.

__________. "Twelve Years of Humanitarian Service: The Near East Relief Makes Its Final Appeal." *Congregationalist* 113 (9 Feb 1928): 130.

Gladden, Washington. *The New Idolatry and Other Discussions.* New York: McClure, Phillips & Co., 1905.

Goodsell, Fred Field. *You Shall Be My Witnesses.* Boston: ABCFM, 1959.

Laurie, Thomas. *The Ely Volume, or, The Contribution of Our Foreign Missions to Science and Human Well-Being.* Boston: ABCFM, 1881; 2d ed., 1885.

Chapter 16: Part B: Missions and Churches

Faletoese, Kenape. "Congregationalism in Samoa." *Pacific Journal of Theology* n.s. 10 (1993): 89-95.

Goodall, Norman. *A History of the London Missionary Society, 1895-1945.* London: Oxford University Press, 1954.

Loomis, Albertus. *To All People: A History of the Hawaii Conference United*

Church of Christ. Kingsport, Tenn.: Kingsport Press, 1970.

Melick, Edith Moulton. *The Evangelical Synod in India.* Saint Louis: Eden Publishing House, 1930.

Sitoy, T. Valentino, Jr. *Several Springs, One Stream: The United Church of Christ in the Philippines.* Volume 1: *Heritage and Origins (1898-1948).* Quezon City: UCC in the Philippines, 1992.

Chapter 16: Part C: War and Peace

Abrams, Ray Hamilton. *Preachers Present Arms.* New York: Round Table, 1933.

Chrystal, William G. "Reinhold Niebuhr and the First World War." *Journal of Presbyterian History* 55 (1977): 285-98.

Cooper, Sandi E. *Patriotic Pacifism: War on War in Europe, 1815-1914.* New York: Oxford University Press, 1991.

Derr, Nancy. "Lowden: A Study of Intolerance in an Iowa Community During the Era of the First World War." *The Annals of Iowa* 3d series, 50:1 (Summer 1989): 5-22.

Luebke, Frederick C. *Bonds of Loyalty: German Americans and World War I.* DeKalb, Ill.: Northern Illinois University, 1974.

Marchand, C. Roland. *The American Peace Movement and Social Reform, 1898-1918.* Princeton, N.J.: Princeton University Press, 1972.

Putney, Clifford. "The Legacy of the Gulicks, 1827-1964." *International Bulletin of Missionary Research* 25:1 (Jan 2001): 28-35.

Renton, Margaret, ed. *War-Time Agencies of the Churches.* New York: General War-Time Commission of the Churches, [1919].

Wittke, Carl F. *German Americans and the World War.* Columbus, 1936.

Chapter 17: Part A: The Christian Faith in a Changing World

Bingham, June. *Courage to Change: an Introduction to the Life and Thought of Reinhold Niebuhr.* New York: Charles Scribner and sons, 1961.

Chrystal, William G. "'An Intolerable Extreme': Karl Barth and the Evangelical Synod." *Historical Intelligencer* 1:2 (1981):12-19.

__________. "'A Man of the Hour and the Time': Legacy of Gustav Niebuhr." *Church History* 49 (1980): 416-32.

__________. "Samuel D. Press: Teacher of the Niebuhrs." *Church History* 53 (Dec 1984): 504-21.

Diefenthaler, Jon. "H. Richard Niebuhr: A Fresh Look at His Early Years." *Church History* 52 (1983): 172-85.

Fackre, Gabriel. *The Promise of Reinhold Niebuhr."* Philadelphia: J. B. Lippencott Co., 1970.

Federal Council of Churches in America, Commission on Worship. *A Book of Prayers and Services for the Armed Forces.* New York: Christian Commission for Camp and Defense Communities, 1944.

Fox, Richard Wightman. *Reinhold Niebuhr: A Biography.* New York: Pantheon Books, 1985.

Helt, John C. "Lydia Hosto Niebuhr, 1869-1961: 'The Queen Bee of American Theologians.'" *On the Way* 10:1 (1993).

Niebuhr, Helmut Reinhold. *The Social Sources of Denominationalism.* Cleveland: World Publishing Co., 1964.

Niebuhr, Reinhold. "Intellectual Autobiography of Reinhold Niebuhr." In *Reinhold Niebuhr: His Religious, Social and Political*

Thought, eds. Charles W. Kegley and Robert W. Bretall. New York: Macmillan, 1956, 1-23.

__________. *Moral Man and Immoral Society*. New York: Charles Scribner's Sons, 1932.

__________. *The Nature and Destiny of Man*. London: Nisbet & Co., 1943.

Richards, George W. *Beyond Fundamentalism and Modernism: The Gospel of God*. New York: Scribners, 1934.

__________. "Movements in Religious Thought the Last Fifty Years." *Reformed Church Review* 5:2 (Apr 1926): 113-31.

Shinn, Roger L. "The Pilgrimage of H. Richard Niebuhr: 1894-1962." *Prism* 12:1 (Spr 1997): 27-41.

Chapter 17: Part B: Mission to the World

American Board of Commissioners for Foreign Missions. *The American Board and the Laymen's Report*. Boston: ABCFM, 1933.

The Christian Life and Message in Relation to Non-Christian Systems. Report of the Jerusalem Meeting of the International Missionary Council, March 24th - April 8th, 1928, Vol. 1. London: Oxford University Press, 1928.

Hocking, William Ernest, chair, Committee of Appraisal. *Rethinking Missions: A Laymen's Inquiry After One Hundred Years*. New York: Harper & Brothers, 1932.

Lauback, Frank. *Letters by a Modern Mystic*. Syracuse, N.Y.: New Readers Press, 1955; first published 1937.

__________. *The Silent Billion Speak*. New York: Friendship Press, 1945.

Mason, David E. *Apostle to the Illiterates: Chapters in the Life of Frank C. Laubach*. Grand Rapids, Mi.: Zondervan, 1966.

Wagner, James E. "The New Witness." In *A History of the Evangelical and Reformed Church*, David Dunn, ed., 296-337. Philadelphia: Christian Education, 1961.

Chapter 17: Part C: The Church and World War II

Apilado, Mariano C. "UCC in the Philippines: Historical and Theological Essay." *Asia Journal of Theology* 10:1 (Apr 1996):154-67.

Crusius, Paul N. "The Postwar Era." In *A History of the Evangelical and Reformed Church*, David Dunn, ed., 252-75. Philadelphia: Christian Education, 1961.

DeBenedetti, Charles. *Origins of the Modern American Peace Movement, 1915-1929*. Millwood, NY: KTO Press, 1978.

Doi, Masatoshi. "How the Japanese Church Survived the War." *Chicago Theological Seminary Register* 41:2 (Mar 1951):24-26.

Hafer, Harold F. *The Evangelical and Reformed Churches and World War II*. Boyertown, Pa.: Boyertown Times Publishing Co., 1947.

Harner, Nevin C. "The Church of Christ in the First and Second World Wars." *Bulletin of the Theological Seminary of the Reformed Church in the United States* 13:3 (Jul 1942):174-83.

Robert, Dana. "The First Globalization: The Internationalization of the Protestant Missionary Movement Between the Wars." *International Bulletin of Missionary Research* 26:2 (Apr 2002):50-66.

Chapter 18: The Road to Union

Douglass, Harlan Paul. *United Local Churches: An Interpretation Illustrated by Case Studies*. Federal Council of Churches, ca. 1930.

Chapter 18: Part A: Congregationalists, Evangelical Protestants and Christians

Humphrey, Seldon B. "The Union of the Congregational and the Christian Churches." Ph.D. diss., Yale University, New Haven, Conn., 1933.

Taylor, Richard H. " The Congregational Christian Union at Fifty Years: An Assessment." *Bulletin of the Congregational Library* 32:3 (Spr/Sum 1981): 4-13.

Chapter 18: Part B: The Evangelical and Reformed Church

Horstman, Julius H. "A Study of the Relationship in Lutheranism and Calvinism." *Theological Magazine of the Evangelical Synod of North America* 47:4 (Jul 1919): 258-65.

Schneider, Carl E. "Journey Into Union." In *A History of the Evangelical and Reformed Church*, David Dunn, ed., 279-95. Philadelphia: Christian Education, 1961.

Chapter 18: Part C: The United Church of Christ

Burton, Malcolm K. *Disorders in the Kingdom.* Part 1: *A History of the Merger of the Congregational Christian Churches and the Evangelical and Reformed Church.* ca. 1978; revised, New York: Vantage, 1980.

Colwell, David G. "The Ecumenical Vision of the Church as Mission." In *Crisis in the Church: Essays in Honor of Truman B. Douglas,* ed. by Everett C. Parker, 108-23. Philadelphia: Pilgrim, 1968.

Fukuyama, Yoshio. "Non-Theological Aspects of Church Union: The Institutional Formation of the United Church of Christ." *Chicago Theological Seminary Register*   30-39.

Gunnemann, Louis H. *The Shaping of the United Church of Christ.* New York, 1977.

_________. "Unity and Church Union in the Antecedent Communions of the United Church of Christ," *Historical Intelligencer* 1:1 (1980): 4-11.

Horton, Douglas. *Congregationalism: A Study in Church Polity.* London: Independent, 1952.

_________. *The United Church of Christ: Its Origins, Organization, and Role in the World Today.* New York, 1962.

_________, et al. *Exploring the United Church of Christ: Reform & Renewal.* Philadelphia: United Church Press, 1966.

Kriebel, Martha B. "Schwenkfelders and the United Church of Christ." In *Hidden Histories of the United Church of Christ*, Barbara Brown Zikmund, ed., 110-23. New York: United Church, 1984.

Szabó, Stephen. "History of the Magyar 'Calvin' Synod." In *The 50th Anniversary Album of the Calvin Synod of the United Church of Christ*, Király, Zoltan., ed. 1990.

Trost, Theodore Louis. "The Ecumenical Impulse in Twentieth Century American Protestantism: A Study of Douglas Horton's Illustrative Career (circa 1912-1968)." Ph.D. diss., Harvard University, Cambridge, Mass., 1998.

Chapter 19: Introductory Material

Obenhaus, Victor, and Ross Blount. *And See the People: A Study of the United Church of Christ.* Chicago: CTS, 1968.

Royle, Marjorie H. Royle. "Effective Christian Education–1990." UCC Papers. UCBHM Research–Findings. Reports, 1972-2000.

__________. Indiana-Kentucky Conference Survey, 1989. UCC Papers. UCBHM Research–Findings. Reports, 1972-2000.

Chapter 19: Part A: Civil Rights

Jones, Lawrence N. "Black Theology in the United Church of Christ." *Prism* 1:1 (Spr 1986): 59-67.

Roberts, J. Deotis, Sr. "The Ben Chavis Case." *Journal of Religious Thought* 33 (Fall-Winter 1976):5-10.

Spike, Paul. *Photographs of My Father.* New York: Alfred A. Knopf, 1973.

Spike, Robert W. *The Freedom Revolution and the Churches.* New York: Association, 1965.

"Write the Vision, Make It Plain: African Americans in the United Church of Christ." *New Conversations* 19:3 (Fall/Win 1999).

Young, Andrew. *A Way Out of No Way.* Nashville: Thomas Nelson Publishers, 1994.

Chapter 19: Part B: Just Peace

Brueggemann, Walter. *Living Toward a Vision: Biblical Reflections of Shalom.* Philadelphia: United Church Press, 1976. Republished as *Peace.* Saint Louis: Chalice, 2001.

Thistlethwaite, Susan, ed., for the Peace Theology Development Team. *A Just Peace Church*. New York: United Church Press, 1986.

Chapter 19: Part C: Feminism

Fackre, Gabriel. "Ways of Inclusivity–The Language Debate." *Prism* 9:1 (Spr 1994): 52-62.

National Council of Churches of Christ. *An Inclusive Language Lectionary*. Pilgrim Press, 1983-85.

__________. *The New Testament and Psalms: An Inclusive Version*. New York: Oxford, 1995.

Zikmund, Barbara Brown. "The Feminist Movement as a Source of Vitality in American Christianity." *Chicago Theological Seminary Register* 68:1 (win 1978):16-24.

Chapter 19: Part D: Homosexuality

Duffy, Martin, ed. *Issues in Sexual Ethics*. Souderton, Pa.: United Church People for Biblical Witness, 1979.

Fukuyama, Yoshio. "The United Church of Christ and Human Sexuality: The Life Cycle of a Social Concern." *Chicago Theological Seminary Register* 76:3 (Fall 1986): 1-10.

Golder, W. Evan. "Ordaining a Homosexual Minister." *Christian Century* 89 (28 Jun 1972): 713-16.

Nelson, James B. *Embodiment: An Approach to Sexuality and Christian Theology*. Minneapolis: Augsburg, 1978.

United Church of Christ, Working Group on Human Sexuality.. *Human Sexuality: A Preliminary Study*. New York: Pilgrim, 1977.

Chapter 2O: Part A: Theology in the New United Church

Brueggemann, Walter. *The Land: Place as Gift, Promise, and Challenge in Biblical Faith*. Minneapolis: Fortress Press, 1977

Colyer, Elmer M. "Donald G. Bloesch & His Career." In *Evangelical Theology in Transition*, ed. Colyer, Elmer M., 11-17. Downers Grove, Ill.: Intervarsity, 1999.

Herzog, Frederick. *Justice Church: The New Function of the Church in North American Christianity.* Maryknoll, N. Y.: Orbis, 1980.

________. "Liberation and Process Theologies in the Church." *Prism* 5:2 (Fall 1990): 57-68.

________. *Liberation Theology: Liberation in the Light of the Fourth Gospel.* New York: Seabury, 1972.

Johnson, Daniel L., and Hambrick-Stowe, Charles E., eds. *Theology and Identity: Traditions, Movements, and Polity in the United Church of Christ.* New York: Pilgrim, 1990.

Thistlethwaite, Susan Brooks. "Theological Ferment in the United Church of Christ." *Chicago Theological Seminary Register* 40-46.

Trost, Frederick R. "Confessing Christ and the Future of the Church: A Call for Continuing Theological Work." *Prism* 10:1 (Spr 1995): 3-11.

Chapter 20: Part B: Movements for Deepening Spirituality

Christensen, Richard L. "What Language Shall We Recognize: A Critique of *the New Century Hymnal.*" *Prism* 10:2 (Fall 1995): 42-52.

Dipko, Thomas E. :The *Book of Worship* After Ten Years: Reflections on Its Development, Reception and Future." *Prism* 10:2 (Fall 1995): 106-13.

Hambrick-Stowe, Charles E. "A Spiritual Vision for the United Church of Christ."

Historical Intelligencer 3:2 (1985):12-17.

Kessler, Vicki. "'Let Them In': Children and the Lord's Supper." *Prism* 8:1 (Spr 1993): 100-09.

New Conversations 8:1 (Spr 1985).

Thistlethwaite, Susan Brooks. "Spiritual Renewal as a Priority." *Chicago Theological Seminary Register* 76:3 (Fall 1986):11-15.

Thomas, John H. "The Ecumenical Nurture of Piety." *Prism* 3:2 (Fall 1988): 76-84.

United Church of Christ. *Practices of Faith in the United Church of Christ.* Cleveland, UCC, ca. 2001.

Walker, Randi Jones. "The Roots of UCC Spirituality." *Impact* no. 23 (1989): 23-36.

Wuellner, Flora. "Spiritual Renewal Within the United Church of Christ: What Are Its Foundations?" *Prism* 1:2 (Fall 1986): 77-85.

Zikmund, Barbara Brown. "Historical Sources of Spiritual Vitality in the UCC." *Historical Intelligencer* 3:2 (1985):8-12.

Chapter 20: Part C: The New United Church and the Ecumenical Movement

Crow, Paul A., Jr. "The Lure and Languishing of Disciples-United Church of Christ Unity." *Midstream* 32 (Jul 1993):1-8.

__________. "The Quest for Unity Between the Disciples of Christ and the United Church of Christ: History's Lessons for Tomorrow's Church." *Prism* 9:1 (Spr 1994): 66-84.

Dickinson, Richard D. N. "UCC-Disciples Saga Continues–Slowly." *Prism* 8:2 (Fall 1993): 26-33.

Gilliom, James O. "The UCC-Disciples Ecumenical Partnership: Issues and Prospects." *Prism* 2:2 (Fall 1987): 43-51.

Gunnemann, Louis H. *United and Uniting: The Meaning of an Ecclesial Journey.* New York, 1987.

Johnson, Daniel L. "The Ecumenical Calling of the United Church of Christ." *Prism* 15:1 (Spr 2000): 14-20.

Kessler, Diane Cooksey. "The Consultation on Church Union: Where We Are and Where We Are Going." *Prism* 11:2 (Fall 1996): 95-106.

__________. "Ripples in a Pond: UCC Involvement in the American Lutheran-Reformed Dialogue." *Prism* 3:2 (Fall 1988): 47-59.

Royle, Marjorie H. "The Meaning of an Ecumenical Partnership." UCC Papers. UCBHM Research–Findings. Reports, 1972-2000.

Chapter 21: Part A: Racial/Ethnic Pluralism

Acosta, Samuel. "The Hispanic Council of the United Church of Christ: Its History, Impact, and Ability to Motivate Policy." *Chicago Theological Seminary Register* 80:3 (Sum 1989): 28-41.

"American Indians in the United Church of Christ: Nurturing Our Spirituality Across Many Cultures." *New Conversations* 20:1 (Spr 2000).

"A Church Inclusive of All People." *New Conversations* 18:2 (Sum 1997).

Hirano, David. "Theology Among Asian Americans in the United Church of Christ." *Prism* 1:2 (Fall 1986): 69-75.

Jackson, Norman W. "Native American Theology and the United Church of Christ." *Prism* 5:1 (Spr 1990): 67-80.

"A Light to the Nations: Sharing the Gifts of Pacific Islanders and Asian Americans in the United Church of Christ." *New Conversations* (Win 1998/9).

Machin, Vilma M. *The United Church of Christ: Council for Hispanic Ministries, Past, Present, and Future.* Cleveland: The Council for Hispanic Ministries of the United Church of Christ, 1998.

"The UCC Hispanic Community." *New Conversations* 18:3 (Win 1997/8).

"Voices of Indigenous People." *New Conversations* 17:3 (Fall-Win 1995).

Chapter 21: Part C: Millard Fuller

Fuller, Millard. *Bokotola*. New York: Association Press, 1977.

Chapter 21: Part D: Nature of Ministry

Bass, Dorothy C. "By What Authority? Historical Reflections on Ministry in the United Church of Christ." *Chicago Theological Seminary Register* 77:3 (Fall 1987): 26-33.

Fortune, Marie. *Is Nothing Sacred?* Eugene, Or.: Wipf and Stock, 1989.

Gerhardy-Keim, Carole. "In Praise of Wrenching Our Guts: Theological Reflections on Sexual Misconduct by Persons Authorized to Ministry, and the Adjudication of Such Events by Committees on Ministry." *Prism* 10:1 (Spr 1995): 55-63.

Steckel, Clyde J. "Authorizing Ministry in the United Church of Christ: Slouching Toward Order." *Prism* 11:2 (Fall 1996): 26-36.

Chapter 21: Part E: Structural Issues

Black, Geoffrey. "Decision Making and the Multiracial, Multicultural Church: A Case for Discernment." *Prism* 14:2 (Fall 1999): 49-58.

Bracke, John M. "Restructuring and Seminaries in the United Church of Christ." *Prism* 11:2 (Fall 1996):54-67.

Copenhaver, Martin B. "United or Untied? Searching for Sources of Unity in the United Church of Christ." *Prism* 11:1 (Spr 1996): 16-23.

Frantz, Charlotte L. "The New Structure of the United Church of Christ." *Prism* 15:2 (Fall 2000): 3-7.

Lynes, John W. "Nurturing the Flock: The Role of Conferences in the Restructured United Church of Christ." *Prism* 15:2 (Fall 2000): 40-49.

Paul, Robert S. *Freedom with Order: The Doctrine of the Church in the United Church of Christ.* New York, 1987.

Sevetson, Donald J. "The Idea of a Conference." *Prism* 9:2 (Fall 1994): 50-58.

Index of Persons